Engineering Your Start-Up

ENGINEERING YOUR YOUR START-UP

A Guide for the High-Tech Entrepreneur

Second Edition

JAMES A. SWANSON
MICHAEL L. BAIRD

Professional Publications, Inc. • Belmont, CA

How to Locate Errata and Other Updates for This Book

At Professional Publications, we do our best to bring you error-free books. But when errors do occur, we want to make sure that you know about them so they cause as little confusion as possible.

A current list of known errata and other updates for this book is available on the PPI website at **www.ppi2pass.com**. From the website home page, click on "Errata." We update the errata page as often as necessary, so check in regularly. You will also find instructions for submitting suspected errata. We are grateful to every reader who takes the time to help us improve the quality of our books by pointing out an error.

ENGINEERING YOUR START-UP
Second Edition

Current printing of this edition: 1

Printing History

edition number	printing number	update
1	4	Minor corrections. Copyright update.
1	5	Minor corrections.
2	1	New edition. Copyright update.

Printed in the United States of America

Professional Publications, Inc.
1250 Fifth Avenue, Belmont, CA 94002
(650) 593-9119
www.ppi2pass.com

Swanson, James A., 1945–
    Engineering your start-up : a guide for the high-tech entrepreneur / James A. Swanson, Michael L. Baird.– 2nd ed.
        p . cm.
    Rev. ed. of: Engineering your start-up / Michael L. Baird. 1st ed. 1992.
    Includes bibliographical references and index.
    ISBN 1-888577-91-6
    1. High technology industries–United States–Management. 2. New business enterprises–United States–Management. 3. Entrepreneurship–United States. I. Baird, Michael L. II. Baird, Michael L. Engineering your start-up. III. Title.

HD62.37.S93 2003
658.1'1--dc21

2003050440

For my wife, Sharlotte Althausen Swanson, and
my parents, Adolph and Beatrice Swanson.
–J.A.S.

For my wife, Heidi Baird.
–M.L.B

Table of Contents

List of Figures

List of Tables

List of Sidebars

Foreword

Over the years, I've fielded hundreds of questions about start-ups, so I'm always on the lookout for a comprehensive guide for entrepreneurs. Frankly, I don't have all the answers, but I know that the answers are out there.

Thus, it was great for me to find out about *Engineering Your Start-Up*. It is a very good source for the information that every entrepreneur needs (and is sometimes too embarrassed to ask others about).

You should read this book voraciously and keep it around for when you hit "speed bumps" in the night. Jim Swanson and Mike Baird espouse a philosophy and prescribe a code of ethics that capture my feelings:

- Trust your own judgment. But, as you set out on your journey, learn as much as you can from those who went before you.

- Protect your integrity. There absolutely is absolute right and wrong, and as a founder, you inject either ethical or unethical DNA into the company.

- Do things you're passionate about. If you're not passionate, find something else to do, because starting a company is a process—it's not an event.

The opportunities are there. In spite of the dot-com madness, entrepreneurs will continue to lead the transformation of the world. Start-ups will create a large share of the new high-tech jobs in the next decade and beyond.

Good fortune and best of luck as you turn your dream into reality.

Guy Kawasaki
CEO, Garage Technology Ventures
www.garage.com

Preface

Plus ça change, plus c'est la même chose.

—Alphonse Karr

"Everything has changed, and nothing has changed" since the first edition of *Engineering Your Start-Up* was published in 1992.

On one hand, we have seen an entrepreneurial explosion, reflected in the great variety and number of new ideas and ventures that have emerged, and in the dramatic growth of new venture financing—much of this due to the catalyst of the Internet and related technologies. We have seen a long period of prosperity, characterized by globalization, improved communications, rapid technological innovation, increased productivity, and fabulous wealth creation. We have seen organizations and entire industries transform the way they do business, much of this under the umbrella of "new economy versus old economy." Yes, the world of today is much different from the world of 1992, and entrepreneurs have been at the center of this drama.

On the other hand, we've experienced the breathtaking ascents and descents, twists and turns, of the roller coaster ride. After rising rapidly for several years, the NASDAQ peaked at about 5000 in the year 2000 (when many experts were predicting it would continue to rise) and then dropped rapidly to 1600 in a period of several months, with further decline after that. Human nature typically causes the highs to be too high and the lows to be too low, but such trends are not obvious when they're happening, and they're not predictable.

During the last several years we have reviewed hundreds of business plans, talked with countless entrepreneurs, and observed the ebb and flow of ideas, trends, fads, and get-rich schemes. We have seen many crazy ideas and lived through periods when the old rules were set aside. You've heard the sirens' song: "Don't worry about valuation models." "Don't even think about ever making a profit … just attract eyeballs and spend a fortune on marketing." "Everyone else is doing it, and lots of smart people have invested millions, so it must make sense." "Youthful passion is better than years of experience—just do your dot-com and you'll be able to retire by age 30."

Even pigs can appear to fly if they are catapulted into the sky with enough force—not unlike a horrible business plan. Perhaps wise men should have been able to predict the fall.

Long after we've forgotten about the highly publicized Y2K "problem," the year 2000 will still be remembered as the year the Internet IPO bubble burst. In the words of J. William Gurley, author, general partner of Benchmark Capital, a venture capital firm in Menlo Park, CA, and columnist of *Fortune* magazine's "Above the Crowd," "The year 2000 will be remembered as the year that everyone caught a disease known as sanity."

We've witnessed, and sometimes participated in, the Internet IPO madness and other forms of collective insanity. Fabulous fortunes have been gained and sometimes lost. What a ride!

At the same time, based on our own experience and the feedback we've received from numerous entrepreneurs and readers, we believe that all the core principles in the first edition of this book still apply, and will continue to apply in this 21st century. As you, the entrepreneur, go about creating and managing your venture in a rapidly changing world, you still need to do the basic blocking and tackling known as strategy, marketing, selling, team-building, raising money, partnering, and so forth. And you must do it with an intense passion. *"Plus ça change, plus c'est la même chose."*

We frequently hear questions from entrepreneurs along the following lines.

- "Is it too late to start my company?"
- "Is it harder now to start my company and make it successful?"

At the heart of these important questions is a concern about *timing*. We believe the questions spring from a view of time that is too short term. Creating a successful new venture is a marathon, not a sprint. Over the long haul of your venture, you can count on experiencing ups and downs, unexpected events, and other externalities that are beyond your control. There will always be large general cycles in funding, the economy, and the broad environment for entrepreneurship. There will also be gyrations in particular market segments, including (undoubtedly) the one you are targeting.

"But really," you might ask, "is it harder now to start my company and make it successful?" If you need venture funding and the funding environment has tightened up, the short answer is yes. However, when times are tough, it can be a great time to

- plan your venture thoroughly, with a view to raising money later in a better climate

- bootstrap your venture, aggressively and creatively pushing ahead on a shoestring

- forge ahead, thankful for the factors that are improved by a downturn (looser labor markets, reduced facility costs, fewer competitors, etc.), and planning and hoping to dazzle investors with your tenacity

We understand where the mentality of a short time frame comes from. This is the age of immediacy and time compression—largely due to technological advances, perhaps best epitomized by the Internet. As you strategize and develop your business plan, try to distinguish between what you can control and what you can't, and plan accordingly. Expect an environment of rapid change, at an ever-increasing rate of change. Plan for the long term, but act in the short term (each day) with a sense of urgency.

"Well, I'm still not sure," you might say. "Is it too late to start my company?" We can't address your particular opportunity, of course, but we do believe that more great companies will be created in the next decade than in any decade in the past, and that this trend will continue. At any point in time there will always be many successful companies with household names that didn't even exist one decade earlier.

We believe time will show that this "truth" also applies to the period of the heavily criticized Internet gold rush. As many great companies started during this period as ever—it's just that they were swamped in number by the multitude of companies that should never have been funded.

We encourage "back to basics" thinking—or really, "sticking with the basics" thinking. Everything in the world changes, but the basic elements (think hydrogen, nitrogen, etc.) remain the same.

So, as you pursue your entrepreneurial passion, be aware of the basic elements you need to create something valuable and wonderful. Do the chemistry right, and the possibilities are really endless. One certainty is that new opportunities abound.

Definitely work hard as you pursue your passion, but remember that life is short—so do have some fun along the way, and don't take yourself too seriously. Good luck!

What's New in This "All New" Edition

Although we definitely wanted to keep, and did keep, the general structure of the very popular first edition of *Engineering Your Start-Up*, virtually every section has been significantly revised, updated, and improved, and we added a lot of new material. A few of the changes and additions are highlighted here.

- three new chapters:
  - *The Term Sheet—A Practical Overview* (Ch. 12)—demystifies the structure and terms of venture financing, an all-important event in the life of most successful start-ups that is familiar ground to professional investors but unfamiliar and threatening to many entrepreneurs
  - *Protecting Your Intellectual Property* (Ch. 19)—covers the major types of intellectual property protection (copyrights, patents, trade secrets, and trademarks)
  - *The Legal Form of Your Start-Up* (Ch. 20)—discusses the various choices for your start-up (corporation, partnership, limited liability corporation, and so forth) and how to decide which is best for you
- the latest advice on researching and writing your business plan
- reasons why many entrepreneurs have difficulty writing their business plan—and practical tips to avoid the problem
- tips on creating a compelling "elevator pitch"
- much more on where and how to find money, including advice on corporate investors and strategic partners
- tips from investors on how to raise money
- the latest views on company valuation and exit strategies
- an appendix of colorful and helpful definitions (see App. A.1), many relating to venture investing
- a "back to basics" theme throughout
- updates on stock options and other forms of compensation
- an expansion of the already strong focus on the customer
- increased emphasis on partnering
- common mistakes made by entrepreneurs—and tips for avoiding them
- updates on legal and accounting matters
- recent trends in venture funding
- a greatly expanded Resources section (see App. A.2) and lots of links (URLs) to useful information

Jim Swanson
Mike Baird

Acknowledgments

Writing books is the closest men ever come to childbearing.

—Norman Mailer

Writing this book was a wonderful, rewarding experience, and it is not practical to thank individually everyone who helped and inspired us. However, we do acknowledge, with gratitude, the following individuals who served as reviewers or provided resource materials and advice: Kent Stormer, Esq., partner in Heller, Erhman, White & McAuliffe in Menlo Park, CA; Richard T. Watson, Director of the Center for Information Systems Leadership (CISL), University of Georgia, Athens, GA; Michael Moritz, partner in Sequoia Capital, Menlo Park, CA; Edward J. Radlo, Esq., Gordon (Gordy) K. Davidson, Esq., and Daniel Dorosin, Esq., all partners in Fenwick & West LLP in Palo Alto, CA; Richard S. Gostyla of Spencer Stuart, San Mateo, CA; James Pooley, Esq. of Milbank, Tweed, Hadley & McCloy LLP in Palo Alto, CA; George Von Gehr, Managing Partner of Alliant Partners, Palo Alto, CA; Dave Witherow, CEO of VentureOne Corporation; Fred Storek, partner in the accounting firm of Storek, Carlson & Strutz, Mountain View, CA; Brian J. Grossi, general partner of AVI Capital Management, Los Altos, CA; Gary Kremen, serial entrepreneur and founder of several successful start-ups, of San Francisco, CA; Sheeraz Haji, founder and CEO of

GetActive Software, Inc., in Berkeley, CA; Kenneth R. Allen, Esq., with Townsend and Townsend and Crew in Palo Alto, CA; Janet G. Effland, general partner of the venture capital firm, Apax Partners, in Palo Alto, CA; Anthony C. Bonora, executive vice president and CTO at Asyst Technologies, Inc., in Fremont, CA ; the late David H. Bowen, publisher of Software Success in San Jose, CA; William J. Wall, formerly vice president of finance and administration and CFO of Resumix, Inc., in Santa Clara, CA, now a division of HotJobs.com; Dr. David K. Lam, founder of Lam Research Corporation in Fremont, CA and chairman of David Lam Group; Janet Brewer, Esq., in Palo Alto, CA; Ed Zschau, former U.S. congressman, Silicon Valley entrepreneur, and teacher (Princeton, Stanford Business School, and Harvard Business School); Dr. James Plummer, president of QED Research and venture capital consultant in Palo Alto, CA; C. Gordon Bell of Los Altos, CA, formerly with Digital Equipment Corporation and several start-ups, and author of *High-Tech Ventures: The Guide for Entrepreneurial Success*; and Kathy Janoff of CTC Engineering Consultants (owned by the Carlyle Group) in Santa Clara, CA.

We give our most special thanks to Trinh Phan and Matthew Swanson, the two best young mechanical engineers we know, who spent countless hours formatting the manuscript text, preparing figures and tables, and helping get the job done in countless ways. They frequently worked into the wee hours of the night, always with a cheerful and positive attitude.

Last but certainly not least, we thank all the pros at Professional Publications who helped give birth to this new edition: Heather Kinser, for inspired copyediting and proofreading; Miriam Hanes, typesetting; Yvonne Sartain, artwork; Aline Magee, acquisitions; Cathy Schrott, production manager; and Sarah Hubbard, editorial manager.

THE GENESIS

Part One of *Engineering Your Start-Up* discusses opportunities for the technical entrepreneur, clarifies the key positions within your new start-up (founder, CEO, and so forth), and describes life in your new business adventure. If you have not given much thought to how starting your own business might impact your life, then these chapters should be especially beneficial.

1

Start-Up Opportunities for High-Tech Entrepreneurs

Everything that can be invented has been invented.
—Charles H. Duell, Commissioner of the U.S. Patent Office, 1899

Opportunities for start-ups always abound. At the same time, it is essential for you, the entrepreneur, in formulating your plans and executing them, to keep an eye on timing and cycles and to carefully consider the rapidly changing business environment in which your new venture will compete.

There was a huge explosion in the amount of venture funding and the number of start-ups during the period of several years ending in the spring of 2000. Although it always takes a lot of hard, smart work to obtain funding, the task was much more possible during this boom period, as a rapidly growing number of venture capitalists and other investors eagerly searched for promising start-ups and the next big thing.

In the spring of 2000, the dot-com euphoria started a quick downward spiral. The road to gold became cluttered with dot-com carnage. The market for IPOs (initial public offerings) went ice cold, and venture capital for new proposals, especially first-round financing, almost dried up. Many newcomers to the dot-com gold mines threw down their picks and shovels and scurried back home. The "B-to-C" (business-to-consumer) dot-com business model became "back to consulting" for many entrepreneurs. Many pessimists said that entrepreneurship died. It didn't.

There are always great opportunities for true entrepreneurs—those with passion and with business plans that make sense. But if you're smart, you must realistically and carefully plan how and when to act. During a funding "down period," for example, and assuming you need outside funding beyond your own resources, you would be extremely foolhardy to quit your day job and launch your new venture with an expectation of easy funding. A more logical strategy would be to plan your new venture during this down period and wait for the funding environment to improve. Also, in a tough period, it becomes that much more important for you to adhere to the basic elements of success, which is what this book is about.

There is a class of "born entrepreneurs" who cannot and should not work for others, and who must start their own businesses. The practical alternative for them is to work as consultants as they plan their ventures and wait until the storm blows over, which is never that far off.

Each decade in the future will be a better decade for entrepreneurship than *any* decade in the past. One decade from now, there will countless people, now unknown, who will have pursued their dreams and created wildly successful companies. These are passionate people who have a long-term view and see tough times as a temporary phenomenon. While the number of start-ups at any point in time may have declined from its highest historical level, the number that will succeed in the long run will remain fairly stable. And although it is true that less venture capital is available in slow economic periods, those companies that are good enough to get it are more likely to do well.

Over the last few decades, venture capitalists have seen great variations in the average rates of return for their portfolios of companies. Of course, when you consider the rates of return on an individual company basis (which should matter most to you!), there is an even greater range of outcomes—from the many ventures that are total failures to the ventures that are huge successes. This wide range of outcomes is the message of Fig. 1.1, which shows the results of one older study of 200 companies during what could perhaps be considered normal times (if any period can be considered normal). During the dot-com craze around the turn of the century, the range of outcomes for companies would probably have been rosier than that reflected in this figure, and after the bubble burst, the results would have been much bleaker. Therefore, don't get too focused on the sizes of the particular pie slices in this one figure (since the future cannot be predicted). Rather, consider the broader message.

As Fig. 1.1 suggests, venture capital-backed companies have made money for some, but not all, start-up entrepreneurs. A venture fund's investors have the safety of diversification, but your shot must be on target. Your gain will roughly mirror that of your investors' return in your start-up. So, if Fig. 1.1 turns out to roughly reflect the period in which you operate your start-up (and there's no reason to assume it will), and assuming you have successfully obtained funding from a professional venture capitalist (a task that is not easy), you have roughly a one-third chance of losing money, a one-third chance of breaking even, and a one-third chance of becoming substantially wealthy.

Note that your return will most closely mirror that of the venture capitalist when your company is wildly successful, since you will roughly share in proportion to your respective capital interests. However, because of the liquidation preferences that are typical in venture capital deals (which provide that the venture capitalist must first receive his money back, or even two or more times his money back, before you receive anything), you are likely to get nothing in cases of partial losses or even minor gains.

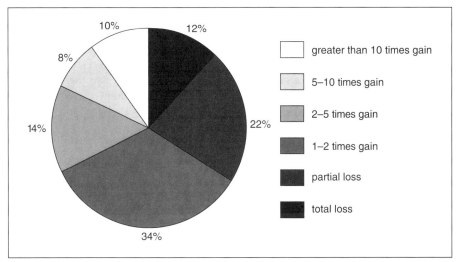

Source: TTG Research and J. Trudel, *High Tech with Low Risk: Venturing Safely into the 90s*

Figure 1.1   Typical Rates of Return for Venture Capital-Backed Ventures

This book shows you how to launch and finance your start-up successfully. There remain numerous areas of opportunity for technology-related start-up companies, some of which involve markets far larger than those of the 1980s and 1990s, and countless new opportunities will emerge. For example, consider the tremendous impact of the Internet and biotechnology revolutions upon the human species and the world—and we are just in the infancy of these profound revolutions.

New technologies will continue to drive out the old. Just consider the world and business of "computers." The word itself will continue to take on new meanings as the uses, shapes, numbers, power, connectivity, intelligence, and so on, of computers rapidly grow and mutate without apparent limits. These changes will require new hardware and software tools that you could develop. Just consider how all businesses—large and small, old and new—are affected by the rapid changes occurring at the collision of the "old economy bricks" and "new economy clicks." The opportunities are endless and simply boggle the mind.

However, as you will come to appreciate, your business success will depend on much more than simply developing an exciting new technology. But that is what you are best at—developing new technologies. While other entrepreneurs may be expert at marketing, finance, and other aspects of business, they will lack your knowledge of key enabling technologies. So who will be the winner? You are betting that you can learn how to plan and build a successful technology-based business faster and better than a nontechnical businessperson can learn how to exploit technological know-how. To discover whether that is a good bet, read on. The winner is usually the person who is most determined to win.

The Lure of Freedom

The desire for autonomy clearly ranks first on the list of reasons why individuals start their own companies, followed by the desire for income and wealth. Figure 1.2 illustrates some of the major reasons entrepreneurs cite for wanting to start their own businesses. While the specific percentages may vary by time and by specific region of the world, this figure is intended to provide you with food for thought, and the main point here is that you should consider what really motivates you.

The Professional Engineer

There are several million professional engineers and scientists in the United States, and several times more throughout the world. These well-educated, hardworking men and women represent some of the best and brightest talent in their respective countries. Their contributions to the profits of business and industry represent hundreds of billions of dollars each year. Yet many of these individuals will work extremely long hours, often for minimal satisfaction, security, and financial reward.

One MIT study indicates that about half of these professionals in the U.S. have seriously considered starting their own businesses. Another study by Execunet determined that 60% of corporate executives would start their own business if they could. Sixty percent also would prefer working for a smaller company if they changed jobs. You are not alone. Your dream is attainable. This book will teach you how to launch your dream—your own successful business—and accumulate significant wealth in the process.

This book uses "engineers" as a generic term that applies to many other technology-oriented professionals. For example, if you are a research scientist wanting to start a business, you will need to become more applied and less theoretical. To be successful, entrepreneurial engineers must become business planners and marketers as well.

This book will be very useful to all key members of a start-up's team, whether or not they have a technical background. Although this book is written primarily for technical CEOs and founders, nontechnical readers will also find it invaluable.

The Recent College Graduate

Several hundred thousand college students graduate each year with engineering and science degrees. Many of them dream of starting their own businesses but are especially

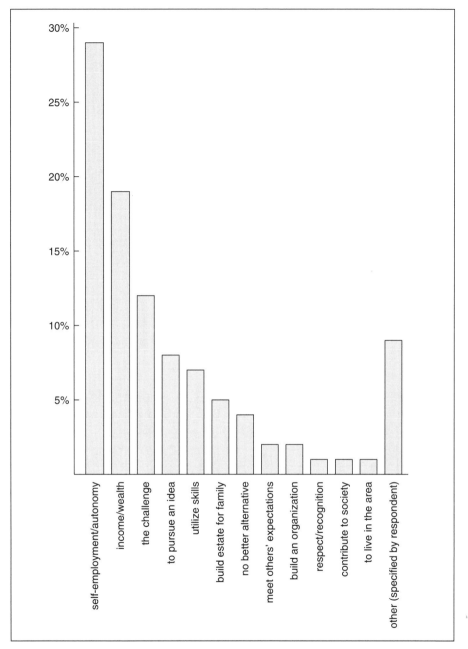

Adapted from studies of new firms in Minnesota conducted by Paul D. Reynolds, professor of business administration at Marquette University, and published in the *Wall Street Journal*, November 22, 1991.

Figure 1.2 Reasons Cited for Starting One's Own Business

frustrated by lack of experience. Nevertheless, even if you are young, this may be the best time to start your own business. Think about it—you have unequaled energy, enthusiasm, fresh knowledge, and university contacts, all of which will diminish over time. Many people at this point in life think that they can do anything, and often they are right! Yes, investors want to see practical experience on a start-up's team, but you can recruit seasoned talent to your new venture. Also, family burden is frequently less of a problem for a fresh graduate. What do you have to lose by taking the plunge?

From Technology to Product to Marketing

Whether you are a practicing engineer or a recent college graduate, if you have an interest in starting your own business, there are many opportunities for you to explore. Dreaming about starting a venture is not enough. You need to plan a course of action to launch your successful technology-based business.

- Identify appropriate products to develop, based on your technological skills. (As will be discussed in this book, although your products will be technology-based, your business must be market- and customer-driven and technology-fueled.)
- Determine how to develop and produce those products.
- Take your products to market rapidly and successfully.

Note that "product" as used in this book refers to both products and services.

Is It Time to Create Your Own Job?

There really is no such thing as job security, even in a Fortune 500 company. It has been many years since articles were written about which companies had a "no layoff" policy. IBM and Hewlett-Packard were among the last companies to abandon such policies, and they did this out of necessity many years ago. Also, IBM, along with many other companies, implemented a new policy requiring that a substantial percentage of employees be rated "unsatisfactory" in performance reviews. This forced out many workers seeking lifetime employment. Even in good times, Cisco's policy has been to fire up to 5% of its poorest performing workers each year.

Since the 1980s, as corporations have responded to global competition and technological change by merging and consolidating, restructuring, downsizing at times, and de-layering, millions of middle-management positions have been permanently eliminated. American corporations have unilaterally repealed the unwritten law that once bound them to their managers and have been jettisoning managers in large numbers.

Even in the best of times, the risk of unemployment never disappears. Although the U.S. enjoyed unparalleled economic prosperity during a period of about eight years extending into the early 2000s, with the seasonally adjusted unemployment rate dropping dramatically to about 4%, not all business sectors and not all companies enjoyed the same prosperity. Even during a strong economy, you may lose your job due to a change in management, a reorganization, the elimination of a business unit or product line, your company downsizing or going out of business, or any number of other factors beyond your control. And, as noted previously, the best companies, even during the best of times, might routinely terminate employees for performance-related reasons.

The risk of unemployment, of course, is higher during a downturn or when the economy is in recession, and it takes longer to find a new position during these times.

Even the most successful high-growth companies may be forced to retrench if they stumble or their markets soften. Wildly successful Cisco, for example, grew to 44,000 employees in 2001 from only 4000 employees six years earlier, but then announced plans to eliminate up to 5000 of these jobs (11%) and up to 3000 temporary or contract workers due to changes in their markets. At about the same time, dominant Intel announced plans to cut their workforce by up to 6% (5000 positions).

Issues to Consider

Quitting your job and starting a company is stressful and full of uncertainty. If you are a typical reader, you have been employed for several years in a large, stable company. Many other readers have switched jobs a few times, and may even have some start-up experience with a dot-com. In any case, if you are now seriously considering leaving a position that has the appearance of security and a good salary (although with a limited financial upside) for the excitement of the fast lane in a start-up, step back first to assess what this means to you and your family. There are many important issues to consider, and you need facts to satisfy your concerns. Here are some major questions you should ponder as you read the remainder of this book.

- What are your life goals?
- What is your quality of life now, and how would it change?
- What are you getting into, and is this really what you want to do? Are you prepared for very hard work, or are you more of a "quality-of-life" person?
- Have you talked frankly and in some detail with friends or colleagues who have significant start-up experience?
- Will your business have a chance to succeed financially? Are you willing to bet on yourself and one or two key employees to come out on top?
- Can you separate the excitement and glamour of a start-up from its reality?
- Are you prepared to be consumed by your business? Are you aware that it will never let up and that you will never escape it during its formative years?
- What can a start-up do to you physically and mentally? Are you strong and healthy enough to pull off a start-up?
- What are the time demands of a start-up? Do you like to recreate on weekends, or will you work? How much time do you want or need with your family?
- Are you ready for extensive travel and "give it all you have" performances for customers and investors?

- Does establishing and maintaining a reputation in, for example, the research community mean a lot to your personal development? Is going to technical conferences important? Will a start-up afford such luxuries?

- Will you still have that Fortune 500 feeling of being a wage slave, even if you launch a start-up?

- Realistically, what your the chance of becoming independently wealthy through your start-up?

- Can you survive without a paycheck for three to nine months, or longer, either while your start-up is getting funded or after your start-up falters?

- Are there better alternatives to either launching a start-up or staying with your current employer?

- Have you considered the possibility of a start-up damaging a stable marriage?

- Do you thrive on continuous change (not always improvement) or despise it?

- How old are you? When is the best time to act?

- Last, and perhaps most important: Will your spouse and family be enthusiastic about your venture? (If not, the additional stress makes your odds much worse.) Will you have their support? (Their support is critical, since they will share with you the inevitable financial and time sacrifices.)

Small Business: Not Synonymous with Start-Up

The terms "small business" and "start-up" at first may seem synonymous. Clearly, not all small businesses are start-ups (consider your favorite restaurant), but most start-ups do begin small. Your start-up is the result of setting in motion a new company, and to what size and at what rate your company grows is critical to your financial success. Though there is some debate concerning what constitutes a small business, for the purposes of this book, a small business is defined as an independently owned and operated company with fewer than 20 employees.

Successful start-ups are by definition fast growing. In the early years, coming off a revenue base of near zero, you should experience triple-digit growth. After your start-up matures and goes public, its valuation will continue to be based on expected growth rate and increased profitability. Typically, a public company having a price-to-earnings ratio of 50 will have to have an expected revenue growth rate of 50% to justify that valuation. The day you cease to grow is the day your valuation drops dramatically.

Your start-up business, if it survives, is destined to become either an income substitution business or a wealth-building business, as illustrated in Fig. 1.3, depending mostly on how fast and large it grows.

People who simply do not want to work for someone else can easily start up a small income substitution business, such as a one-man computer repair service. Small businessman Joe, for example, may earn as much repairing computers as he did working for Company X, and this may make Joe happy. This kind of small business is called an *income substitution business*.

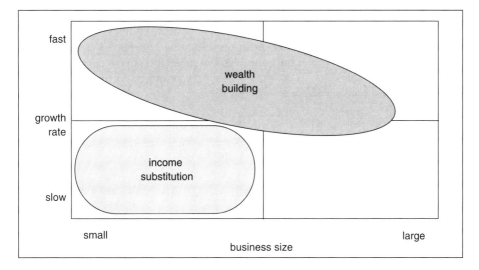

Figure 1.3   The Income-Substitution / Wealth-Building Matrix

A *consultancy* is a business formed by an individual to provide services and is generally limited to creating an income stream. You will often find unemployed engineers holding themselves out as consultants or independent contractors.

A *proprietorship* is an unincorporated business formed by an individual or related family members and also is generally limited to income substitution.

If your small business does not have high growth as an objective and is not team-driven, it most likely will not become the wealth-building vehicle you need for financial success and independence. The successful wealth-building technology start-up, which is the focus of this book, is characterized by the charter of the bygone Silicon Valley Entrepreneurs Club, which assisted entrepreneurs in "creating and managing team-driven and high-growth companies. Such companies commonly have annual sales goals of from $10–$100 million or more over a period of three to five years."

This charter goal still makes sense today, except that the sales goals have generally risen.

If Joe has the makings of a true entrepreneur, there is nothing to prevent him from growing a very profitable computer repair organization that could create great wealth for him. There may be a need for a nationally recognized quality computer repair franchise, for example.

In the late 1980s Robert Ronstadt (developer of the software package Ronstadt's Financials) categorized ventures as follows.

type of venture	sales range	employees
lifestyle	$0 to $1 million	0 to 4
smaller high-profit	$1 million to $20 million	5 to 50
high-growth	over $20 million	over 50

Although the sales figures in this chart have increased over time, the message remains the same. Individuals who want independence and autonomy start lifestyle ventures. These people do not want the aggravation that growing a business entails, and they prefer to conduct their business lives much like their personal lives. There is nothing wrong with wanting to conduct a lifestyle venture, but if that is really your objective, do not try to act like a venture-backed start-up.

One benefit of a smaller high-profit venture is that the entrepreneur need not relinquish equity or ownership control. But this potential benefit can pose a challenge to an engineer who may not have access to the financing that a high-growth business requires. This book will also be useful for smaller high-profit business venture planning.

Successful high-growth ventures usually lead to nationally and internationally known businesses. Significant outside funding is required to grow this kind of venture. The engineer aspiring to create a high-growth business will be seeking to maximize the market value of the company and, in the process, to create significant wealth for himself or herself, the venture's investors, and many of the company's employees.

The Definition of a Start-Up

In the previous section, various types of small businesses were explored, and it was pointed out that "small business" and "start-up" are not synonymous. So, is there a widely accepted definition of a start-up? No, not really. However, here's one possible definition (from the Career Action Center, formerly based in Cupertino, CA) that comes pretty close to the mark.

> You won't find a single definitive explanation, but generally a start-up is a small company, most often with a high-tech focus, that is in the early stages of development, creating a product or service, or having a product or service needing manufacturing and/or marketing. They are looking to grow through possible venture capital funding, initial public offerings (IPOs) or acquisition by larger companies.

There are several possible sources for the needed "venture capital funding,"—including angel investors, venture capital firms, and corporations—and it's also possible that the entrepreneur could draw upon wealth earned through a previous entrepreneurial success.

The central focus of this book is on start-ups, a relatively small subset of all small businesses. This focus is reflected in the book's title. If you are planning to start a restaurant, for example, this book is not really for you, but you already knew that. If you were starting a restaurant, you would say you were "starting a business," but you wouldn't say you were "doing a start-up."

Taking Risks

One study from UCLA suggested that

> ... in kindergarten, 25 percent of students show a natural need for high achievement and a willingness to take risks. By the time they get to high school, only three percent do.

If you really do have that entrepreneurial craving, don't hang onto a job you don't love. Take some calculated risks, launch your start-up, and enjoy the rest of your life knowing that you took your future into your own hands.

It would be great to retire at 40, if that is what you want to do, but there are only five ways to financial independence, and only the last one is truly satisfying and under your control.

- You might marry into it.
- You might inherit it.
- You might win the lottery.
- You could steal it.
- You could earn it—in your start-up.

If risk-taking is not part of your personality, however, you may want to seriously consider keeping your Fortune 500 job for as long as possible. There are many "big company" employees who want to be entrepreneurs and think they want to take risks, but they don't have a clue what risk really is. Look inside yourself and try to see what is right for you.

2

The Technology-Oriented Professional as Company Founder

At a start-up, life suddenly seems unfair. A deadline is a deadline. Employees don't have several layers of management to buffer them from the outside world.

—T. J. Rodgers, Cypress Semiconductor founder

As you envision your start-up's success, don't lose sight of your role as the business' founder and chief executive officer. You can create a position for yourself that's full of excitement, opportunity, and challenge. Let's look more closely at the role of the company founder.

Founder's Roles and Responsibilities

As founder of your own company, your business role initially spans the entire spectrum. Until you have the financial resources to add a competent staff in which you have great confidence, you are responsible for everything from managing the business and developing your ideas to selling the final product. Your duties will include everything from signing checks to emptying trashcans, and you must attend to all the administrative details of starting and maintaining a business. There are also legal issues related to incorporating and licensing the business. Insurance, taxes, rents, computers, Internet connections, utilities, bank accounts, and business cards will all need to be taken care of early on. These things, however, can be fun to work on and might even be delegated to others.

Some much tougher problems represent your first real challenges—managing the five elements of a successful start-up.

- creating your management team and board of directors
- evaluating markets and targeting customers
- defining and developing your product
- writing your business plan
- raising funds

Unless you start your company with a seasoned management team, you are the boss, and the burden of each of these elements falls on you. That is why you probably will give yourself the titles of *chief executive officer* and *president*.

Officers

You need to be familiar with the key *officers* of a corporation and with the roles and responsibilities of those holding such positions. Also, you must comply with certain legal filing requirements in connection with these matters. For example, if you incorporate your start-up in California, you must file with the California secretary of state a Statement by Domestic Stock Corporation form, within 90 days after filing your start-up's initial articles of incorporation. In this statement, you must identify the three officers required by the California Corporations Code, namely

- Chief Executive Officer (CEO)
- Secretary
- Chief Financial Officer (CFO)

The same person may hold any or all of the offices unless the Articles of Incorporation or Bylaws provide otherwise. You are also required to include in the statement the names of all directors of your corporation, who may or may not be officers.

The goal here is to familiarize you with the general concepts, not to make you a legal expert. A qualified attorney can and should handle the incorporation of your start-up and the various routine legal tasks associated with getting your company up and running. Chapter 20 includes a discussion of how to select your attorney.

In addition to the three legally required officers, your corporation will undoubtedly have other officers. Let's take a deeper look.

Chairman of the Board

The *chairman of the board* is the member of the corporation's board of directors who presides over its meetings and who is the highest-ranking officer in the corporation. The chairman may or may not have the most actual executive authority in a firm. In some corporations, historically at least, the position of chairman has been either a prestigious reward for a past president or an honorary position for a prominent person, a major stockholder, or a family member, and was typically not occupied by a full-time employee of the company. It may have carried little or no real decision-making power in terms of policy or operations. Of course, the numerous high-visibility corporate scandals in the early 2000s (Enron, etc.) have done much to change this. The chairman of the board, as well as the other board members, can now be expected to be more active, more competent, and more concerned about their responsibilities—not just a rubber stamp for management. In a start-up, the position of chairman of the board is usually initially held by the founder, at least until a sophisticated investor helps fund the company and requests to occupy that position.

Chief Executive Officer

The title of *chief executive officer* (CEO) is reserved for the principal executive. The CEO has ultimate management responsibility for the company and reports directly to the board of directors (who are accountable to the shareholders or owners of the company). The CEO may also hold other titles such as chairman of the board and/or president. In most seed-stage and start-up companies, the founder is both the president and the CEO, and this is frequently the case for large companies too. (Chapter 6 covers the distinctions between seed, start-up, and the various other stages of new companies.)

Secretary

The corporation's *secretary* maintains the corporate records (such as minutes of board meetings). Since this role does not take much time, this person usually also serves in some other positions in the company. Typically, the company's outside legal counsel helps ensure that things are done right, since the failure to keep adequate records and follow corporate formalities can jeopardize the company's limited liability status.

Chief Financial Officer

The *chief financial officer*, also sometimes called the *treasurer*, is responsible for managing the corporation's financial affairs. Duties include preparing financial statements and tax returns.

President

After the chairman of the board, the *president* is the highest-ranking officer in a corporation (unless the president also holds the CEO title, in which case the president and CEO can have more actual executive authority than the chairman). The president is appointed by the board of directors and usually reports directly to the board. In smaller companies, the president is usually the CEO and exercises authority over all other officers in matters of day-to-day management and policy decision making.

Chief Operating Officer

In larger corporations, the CEO title is frequently held by the chairman of the board. This leaves the president or an executive vice president as the *chief operating officer* (COO), responsible for personnel and administration on a daily basis. The COO reports to the CEO and may or may not be on the board of directors. (COOs who are presidents typically serve as board members, while COOs who are executive vice presidents usually do not.) The COO title is also often given to an operations person in recognition for taking on increased responsibility from the president or CEO.

Chief Technical Officer

The title of *chief technical officer*, also sometimes called *chief technology officer* (CTO), is a curious one. It is widely used in Silicon Valley to recognize key individuals upon whom a company is clearly dependent for technical contributions. If you are an engineer with an idea for a product and want to exploit that product in a business start-up, you do not necessarily have to be the CEO and president. Do you really want to manage? If not, maybe you would rather be the CTO. The remainder of this book explores the ramifications of taking on operations management responsibility; your preference should be clearly established by the time you get to the last chapter.

Vice President of Engineering/Research and Development

The position of *vice president of engineering* is not one to be underestimated. It involves a substantial challenge, and your company's success will depend upon this person's ability to deliver your product on specification, on budget, and on time.

For the *vice president of research and development*, schedule pressures are not as severe. This person is responsible for developing the technology needed for future generations of your company's products. Most start-ups cannot afford both a vice president of engineering and a vice president of research and development, in which case one person must serve in both roles. The company's long-term future rests on this person, and whoever holds this position should be confident in his or her ability to produce future products.

Would you be happy starting your own company but not holding the top slot? This is a very important question for you to consider. If you want to be successful but have little management experience, it makes a lot of sense to start up with other experienced management. Together, you may all make a lot more money than any one person could alone. Management teams will be discussed further in Ch. 7, but for now, plant this option in your mind. Who do you want working in your new company? What role do you want to play? What will make you happy, while allowing you to meet your financial objectives?

Title Inflation

Pay special attention to how you handle titles in your start-up. During the dot-com boom, many companies handed out Vice President titles too freely. Individuals with little or no relevant experience became vice president of sales, vice president of business development, or vice president of something else. Perhaps this was justified based on the false assumption that the rules of the game in the "new economy" had fundamentally changed and, if so, then experience wasn't very relevant.

It's best to leave a title open and available if your plan is to later, as your company grows, bring in a more qualified person to fill that position. For example, the person initially handling sales (perhaps even a cofounder) could be called director of sales, leaving the vice president of sales position open for the world-class sales professional you'll successfully recruit later. This approach actually aids the recruiting process by defusing potential ego issues and making company management look more professional.

If, however, you do give the vice president title to the person now on board, you must make certain it's with the clear understanding that this is temporary, since your plans to recruit a more senior person to fill the position will eventually result in a title reduction for the person who has been filling in. You'll want to handle this gracefully, since egos are likely to be involved, and there's no substitute for excellent personal communication. Address this face-to-face in two-way conversation. In addition, your employment letters and agreements must clearly set forth the details.

Frivolous Titles

Avoid the use of "cute" titles and official nicknames. Yes, names like "Chief Yahoo" probably helped the viral marketing of that popular name and website, but this was a rare exception rather than the rule. In addition, times have changed, and you must project to customers, partners, and investors that you and your company are serious about business. So avoid names like Vice President of Ideas, or Chief Wizard.

Founder Career Paths

The fact that you are reading this book implies that starting your own business is an idea at the top of your list. However, while you might be determined to start your own business and hold the positions of president and CEO, you might also plan a career path that eventually puts you back into a technical position where you would be most comfortable and happy. This could also make other key employees and your investors quite happy. Investors might even insist that you make such a transition as a condition of continuing to fund the business, especially if they become unhappy with your performance at a later stage.

A typical scenario for an engineer founding a high-growth, technology-based company involves first launching that company by holding the president and CEO titles. Later, bringing in professional management and funding may provide the opportunity to move into the vice president of engineering or vice president of research and development role, where one might be most productive and comfortable. The title of chief technical officer would be appropriate in such a situation. Many founding engineers get forced back into those roles either as a condition for obtaining initial or additional venture capital funding, or as a result of poor operating performance. If you want to be the CEO and president and are up to the task, by all means go for it. However, if you lack the experience or disposition, why not plan to hold a position you would really enjoy?

It is not uncommon for venture capitalists to back away from an investment opportunity because the CEO has, or appears to have, the primary goal of being the CEO forever, no matter what happens. It can be a deal killer when the CEO's ego gets ahead of what is best for the company. The investors' central goal is to maximize the value of the enterprise, and this must be your goal too. Changes in management, perhaps including the CEO stepping down to a key technical position or even leaving the company, may be necessary to accomplish this. Prospective investors should clearly hear your views on this.

In a study of management changes at 173 high-tech companies in California's Silicon Valley, professors Manju Puri and Thomas Hellmann at the Stanford Graduate School of Business determined that the majority of founders were replaced within an average of six years, and that about 60% of these founders later left their companies. Some CEOs handle a CEO transition gracefully, and even with a sense of relief because they're now able to do important work in the company—work that they're better at and didn't have the time to do as CEO, such as creating new products. In situations where the founder stays on board, it is essential that the new CEO's authority be made clear to everyone in the company. It can be disastrous for morale and company direction if the founder gives verbal support for the new CEO, but then obstructs the new CEO and effectively retains control. This is more likely to occur in situations where a major change in the company's strategy is needed, but the founder's ego gets in the way. You must prevent this from happening.

Michael S. Malone's book, *Going Public: MIPS Computer and the Entrepreneurial Dream*, which describes the successful Initial Public Offering (IPO) of MIPS Computer Systems, Inc., quotes the founders as saying,

> One of the things we did right was to recognize that we weren't going to be management. We could help in technology or any place else we were needed, but we were not businessmen. We had seen the stories of big egos that invent something wonderful and then think they can be CEO—and they can't, and it crashes the company. None of us aspired to run the company and that's why we've got this marvelous management team in place.

Learn from others' successes!

Entrepreneur's Profile

Edward B. Roberts' book *Entrepreneurs in High Technology: Lessons from MIT and Beyond* contains a comprehensive study of personality traits of the engineer creating a start-up. Many of the characteristics listed are loosely based on Roberts' scientific observations. If you can identify with many of these statements, then you know this book was written for you, since these are the characteristic influences upon the technical entrepreneur.

- I have a long-felt, strong desire to start my own business.
- I had a self-employed parent.
- I have a minimum of a four-year undergraduate degree, or a master of science degree in some technical field.
- I think I can do a better job than others in delivering a service or in producing a product. I am willing to work hard for something that is important to me.
- I am very independent and have a continuing need to meet and overcome challenges.

- I have only moderate needs for group achievement and power, and a low need for affiliation. (There is a psychological theory that looks at three human needs—achievement, power, and affiliation—and says that everyone holds two of these three needs more closely than the third. For example, if you value affiliation with associates and achievement of group results, it is unlikely that you can lead from a position of real power. As an analogy, you cannot maximize both revenue and profits—something has to give.)
- I have at least a decade of work experience.
- I have published more papers and obtained more patents than my associates. I am highly productive.
- In my work, I carry out applied development work, not research.
- In my career, I have been promoted to managerial levels.
- I have only modest concern for financial rewards (at the time of start-up).
- I am more extroverted than my technical associates at work, but relative to the rest of the world, I still look more like an introverted inventor than a business-person.
- In my current place of work, I feel challenged and find satisfaction.
- Although I am an engineer, I tend to buy more books on business than on technology.
- I read the business section of the newspaper nearly every day.

Having these characteristics does not necessarily mean you will be a successful entrepreneur. A strong orientation toward marketing and partnering is necessary and is emphasized throughout this book. One helpful book to read is *Good to Great: Why Some Companies Make the Leap... and Others Don't*, by Jim Collins.

See Sidebar 2.1 at the end of this chapter for a description of several types of founders.

The Nonengineer Founder

Although this book is written primarily for the professional technical individual who wants to do a high-tech start-up, not all founders of successful high-tech companies are engineers, scientists, or technically trained individuals. A good example is Michael Dell, a marketer at heart, who started Dell Computers in 1983 out of his University of Texas dorm room. There are countless other successful founders who come from other disciplines and backgrounds but, in general, they do have an affinity for technology, and they like to be around technology and talk about it. In many cases they have a good intuitive understanding of the possible uses and benefits of technology, and they enjoy talking with prospective customers about what the customer really needs and is willing to pay for. Many are simply good marketers. Whatever the background of the founder, a focus on the customer is critical.

Sidebar 2.1 Types of Founders

Over the years, we've seen many types of people who yearned to be successful entrepreneurs. Here, with a touch of humor, are some caricatures of founders, which are intended to enlighten. We hope that the first type is the one you are, or strive to be. As for the others, perhaps you, like us, will recognize some of the traits in yourself, your cofounders, or others—and learn to see them as warning signs.

Smart, Passionate Executioners

These are the entrepreneurs who make it, or at least have the best probability of success. They are very customer focused, and they approach planning and execution with discipline and passion.

The Paranoid

These people are reluctant to disclose much about what they're doing. They want a nondisclosure agreement (NDA) signed first, and even then their instincts are driven by suspicion and hesitancy. They believe their idea to sell toys over the Internet is a "killer application," and they're afraid someone will rip them off if they reveal it. Getting straight answers is like pulling teeth—so stay away from them unless you're a dentist. Venture capitalists do.

Entitled Youngsters

These people have seen other entrepreneurs get rich quickly, and they instinctively know they are entitled to the same rewards. "That's the way the system works," they believe. For most of their short lives, the system has been generous, without any bumps or hard knocks. They spend time admiring the pot of gold that will be theirs at the end of the entrepreneurial stroll, and they make plans to spend it. Having never learned how to swim, they watch the deceptive ease with which Olympic divers perform, and thus underestimate the degree of difficulty in the entrepreneurial jump.

Dreamers

These people excitedly crank out new ideas like an exploding piñata, but they don't know how to separate the good ideas from the bad or, more important, how to execute any one of their ideas. They don't listen well to feedback, since they simply don't want to hear the views of people who "don't get it" ... plus they're already busy thinking about the next big idea.

The "Funding Is the Only Problem" Founders

These people see venture funding as an end in itself, rather than a milestone on a long journey. How's your company doing? "Everything is wonderful—the only thing we need is $2 million in funding, and we'll have it made." When you probe deeper, you find that they lack a solid business plan. Professional investors are quick to see the shallowness.

The "One Pizza Slice" Founders

These people have a good idea or product, but it's simply too narrow and begs to be a feature in a larger pizza ... ah, we mean product. Perhaps it really belongs in Microsoft's Windows operating system, or perhaps it should be incorporated into a personal computer or browser. Even if the product could stand alone, its market is simply too small to attract any investor interest. "Get out of Dodge" is the best strategy: sell the idea if you can, or partner with a company that offers some synergy.

The "Never Met a Customer" Founders

These people understand technology and love it. However, technology is an end in itself. They speak enthusiastically about product features, but have difficulty seeing the customer's perspective. Because they love the "coolness" of the product, they know customers will too. All they need is a sales and marketing person to get the word out and gather the orders as they come in. If you take that job, remember that "S&M" doesn't always stand for "Sales and Marketing."

3

Life in Your Start-Up

... few people do business well, who do nothing else.

—Philip Dormer Stanhope, 4th Earl of Chesterfield

What are your chances of being successful and happy in a start-up? This chapter includes some statistics and observations that candidly lay the facts on the line. Some individuals thrive in the excitement of the fast lane. Others encounter an inability to cope with the overload, stress, and constant change of a start-up.

Success and Failure: Statistics

How will your life change if you launch a start-up? First, do not assume you will even be able to get started. Optimistically, perhaps only 10–30% of start-ups that seriously look for capital actually get funded. Realistically, the number is likely to be much lower, since the data on start-ups that don't obtain venture capital, private funding, or corporate funding is sketchy. Any one venture capital firm will typically fund much less than 1% of the hundreds or thousands of business plans it receives in any given year. For example, Draper Fisher Jurvetson, a top-tier venture capital firm, received about 12,000 business plans in one year and funded only about one-tenth of 1% of them.

Obtaining funding, of course, is only one milestone on a long road. Therefore, even if you get the business started and receive funding, do not take personal success for granted.

- It has been estimated that fewer than half of the entrepreneurs who start companies surviving five years or more actually remain with their start-up.
- If your company is funded, becomes successful, and goes public, your founders' stock (the CEO's stock) could be worth $5–$7 million. Of course, the actual value can vary considerably from this average range. Other founding officers' stock would typically be valued at half of your figure, or less.
- A study conducted several years ago concluded that only 10% of venture capital-funded start-ups go public. Later research by VentureOne indicates a much higher percentage. (Details follow.)
- An early study concluded that 60% of venture capital-funded high-tech companies go bankrupt. More recent research by VentureOne indicates a much lower percentage. (Details follow.)
- CEO founders of typical high-tech companies own less than 4% of the company after the initial public offering. However, many CEOs do substantially better than this, especially during bull markets, and the range of actual results is really quite broad.

VentureOne regularly tracks the "ownership status" (or "outcomes") of companies backed by venture capitalists. Since it typically takes five or more years for the outcomes of such new ventures to be determined, the data are obviously skewed depending on how long the ventures have been in business. This point is shown dramatically in Figs. 3.1 and 3.2. For venture capital-funded companies more than 10 years old, 33% had IPOs and another 33% went out of business. For such companies only 2 to 4 years old, only 7% had IPOs and only 4% had gone out of business.

According to Drew Field's book *Take Your Company Public!: The Entrepreneur's Guide to Alternative Capital Sources*, for the approximately 700,000 new incorporations in a typical year, there are fewer than 300 initial public offerings—that translates to only a 0.04% success rate for going public. Keep in mind, however, that this is a distorted figure, since it includes all sorts of small businesses.

Michael S. Malone's book *Going Public: MIPS Computer and the Entrepreneurial Dream* states that in Silicon Valley, "of the ten thousand or more companies that have been founded in the last three decades, no more than a hundred have gone public." That translates into about a 1% rate for engineering-related start-ups that also successfully complete an IPO.

Edward B. Roberts' *Entrepreneurs in High Technology: Lessons from MIT and Beyond* also provides a great deal of valuable data.

- The actual failure rate of high-technology companies founded by MIT associates is only 15–30% over the first five years.
- Entrepreneurs with PhD degrees experience more failures than those with master's degrees, except in certain fields such as biotechnology.

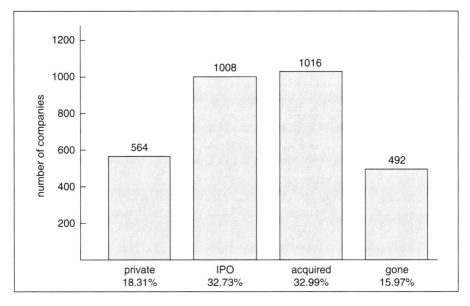

Figure 3.1   Status of Start-Ups: Private, IPO, Acquired, Gone—for 3080
Venture-Backed Companies 10+ Years Old

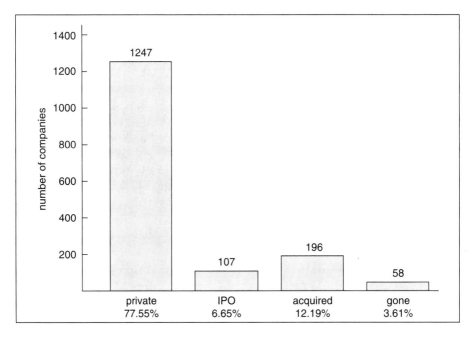

Figure 3.2   Status of Start-Ups: Private, IPO, Acquired, Gone—for 1608
Venture-Backed Companies 2–4 Years Old

- It may be harder to completely fail than imagined. Only about 20% of the large number of MIT spin-off firms are ever liquidated or go bankrupt. When the press mentions that about 80% of all businesses fail, remember that many of these are small businesses, such as small independent restaurants and used car lots.

The so-called "living dead" make up a large share of the surviving start-up endeavors. These companies do not fail in that they go bankrupt or go out of business, but they do not really succeed either. While some may provide an interesting and stable living for their employees, many others provide low salaries, no capital gains on the company's stock, no retirement funds, and no vacations. These employees might have been better off staying with their former companies. It is important to know when to bail out of a living dead situation.

As an entrepreneur, you probably have more backbone and tenacity than the average businessman. These positive qualities can make the difference between success and failure, especially when times get tough. On the other hand, these same qualities can cause you not to recognize that your company is among the "living dead" and that it's time to kill it. From your close perspective, you may not be able to "see the forest for the trees," especially if you are working incredibly long, hard hours and cannot tolerate the thought of failure. The perspective of a valued mentor or experienced entrepreneur can help you get a clearer picture. Is the company's business plan fatally flawed? Is your company just treading water without growth? Have too many of the major milestones been missed? If after cold analysis and reflection you still can't decide, you must at least set a deadline for deciding...with clear milestones attached to the deadline. It makes no sense to make heroic but futile efforts forever. Sell the company if you can, or liquidate it gracefully and go do something else. Life is too short to see how many years you can survive in the land of the living dead.

Vacation and Time Off

More than likely, you will be totally consumed by your start-up business for the first few years. It will be with you every hour of every day. It will seem at times that there is no end to it. Yogi Berra's wisdom "it ain't over 'til it's over" aptly applies. Any scheduled break, weekly recreation time, or short vacation will provide only a brief respite from the pressures of your business. Bill Gates, founder of Microsoft Corporation, took only two three-day vacations during the first few years of his start-up. Even later, he took only one week of vacation a year. Do not plan on taking two- or three-week vacations during your first few start-up years.

A MasterCard BusinessCard Small Business Survey study of small businesses showed that 22% of small-business owners took no vacation, as detailed in Fig. 3.3. A *small business* was defined here as a firm with at least one employee but fewer than 100 employees. There are several million such firms in the U.S. and, of course, only a fraction would be considered high-tech.

It is well known that small-business owners find vacations hard to take. They fear customers will evaporate. They are reluctant to trust someone else to fill in, and they will convince themselves that they are indispensable. Also, unless they prioritize

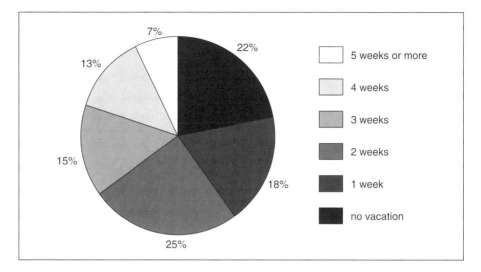

Figure 3.3   Annual Time Off for Small-Business Owners

extremely well, small-business owners believe that there is never enough time in any day to do all the important work that has to be done.

As a start-up entrepreneur you will feel many of these same pressures. You have only so much money and time to complete your product, produce sales, and generate revenues. Will you take two weeks off to recharge during your concept development, seed, or start-up phases? Probably not. You may very well go 3 to 10 years without taking a real vacation. Even if you do get a few days off now and then, you will likely find that you need or want to be in constant communication with those in the office.

It is difficult to imagine the CEO today who does not have a laptop computer, a cellular phone, and other wireless devices, and who is not in constant touch with the organization, its customers, and its investors. Modern, networked technology truly makes getting away from work impossible. The fact that you will probably take your computer with you on a family vacation could also have an impact on your family. Your loved ones may wonder why you even came along if you have to work so hard.

However, it is possible to remain very calm and relaxed as you start a venture, acting on the notion that it is good for the business if you get away and recharge yourself at regular intervals. With this attitude you may do well enough, but you most likely will not maximize the growth and valuation of your business. Putting recreation ahead of business is a quality-of-life issue, a priority only you can establish. Just be aware that there will be many pressures, internal and external, that you cannot always ignore.

For example, are you really going to skip that next board meeting where you need to ask for more funding? Is it a good idea to turn down the invitation to attend your lead VC's annual CEO meeting? Should you send someone else to talk to that critical customer who is considering taking his business elsewhere? As a start-up entrepreneur, you are an integral part of your new company, and you will find that you need to be available to handle such situations.

Perhaps if you have one or two million dollars in the bank, are still on plan, and have no exceptional problems in the business, you might be able to go skiing over a long weekend or head off to Club Med for a week. More likely, though, you will be coming up with yet another new business plan and looking for more money, cultivating customers, finding employees, lining up distributors and other partners, setting up manufacturing or service operations, conducting a press tour, or preparing for a trade show. It will seem that there is never enough time. But for a dedicated, intelligent, enthusiastic person, the stressful period in a start-up is greatly outweighed by the sense of accomplishment and fulfillment generated by creating your own successful business.

Working Hours

An *Inc.* magazine article showed that 66% of the founder CEOs of the fastest growing Inc. 500 companies worked at least 70 hours a week while the company was getting started. Only 13% were still doing so five years later. Figure 3.4 details the results of the Inc. 500 study. The only founders who managed 40-hour-or-less workweeks were presumed to have been involved in other businesses at the time of start-up.

As one drives past the many high-technology business parks housing start-up companies in Silicon Valley, it is not unusual to see cars in the parking lots in the evenings and on Saturdays and Sundays. Workweeks of six or seven days are more common than the standard five-day workweek. In addition, constantly improving technology has expanded the definition of the office by making it easier to work remotely and in multiple locations. As a result, both work hours and the location of work have expanded and become more flexible, with most executives also working at home, while travelling, and while on vacation.

Evidence suggests that start-up entrepreneurs typically work well over 10 to 12 hours a day, 6 to 7 days per week. That is almost double the number of hours put in by the typical Fortune 500 employee. In fact, in your start-up, you might work even more than this, considering that every night you will bring something home. If nothing else, you will have problems to ponder or work-related reading. Gates of Microsoft, for example, found himself regularly working 65 hours a week, even after his company went public. More than once, start-up entrepreneurs in the hard-driving, high-technology Silicon Valley may find themselves working around the clock to meet an important deadline. It is not unusual to find sleeping bags tucked away in a cabinet for those nights when it is too late and people are too tired to make it home safely, especially when they have to be up and at it in a few hours anyway.

If you already work long hours like this for someone else, then you will be in good shape for starting your own company. Working hard can be rewarding, especially if it

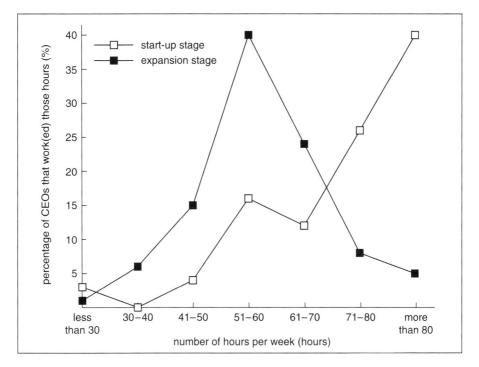

Figure 3.4   Anticipated Weekly Time Commitments of CEOs

is for your own business. Running your own business can also be very stressful. See Sidebar 3.1, Coping with Stress, for a discussion of this important issue.

Divorce

Start-up entrepreneurs have a high divorce rate. They may prefer spending more time with their businesses than with their spouses. The pressure and stress of a start-up can tarnish any relationship with time. This is not to say, however, that start-ups cause divorces. It is more likely that start-up entrepreneurs typically have more reasons for divorce. Roberts' observations reinforce this notion, but he also found empirical data hard to come by. You should, however, think seriously about what impact starting your business will have on those around you.

It is essential to have the support and encouragement of your spouse during a start-up venture. Sharing your vision and mission with a supportive loved one is going to be very important to you.

Holding Your Business Together

William H. Davidow, a noted Silicon Valley venture capitalist and author, states, "There has to be something that holds a company together beyond making money ...

the glue is that your people better love what they're doing, better be committed to the mission, [and] better believe in winning." While Davidow was addressing the problem of managing MIPS Computer Systems, Inc., after going public, his words apply to every phase of your start-up. This is your leadership challenge: to impart this same love, commitment, and belief to your team! Chapter 7 will discuss further the importance of building such a team and how to make it happen.

Personal Planning Process

When considering whether (and if so, how) to continue with your venture, you will want to examine the personal side of starting your own business. You need satisfying answers to questions that might not come out during the traditional business plan writing process, described in Ch. 10.

First, you should clearly establish an alignment of your compelling interests with those of your founding team. What are the personal driving forces behind your wanting to start this venture? Do you each share a common vision of the company's mission? What will be the respective roles of each team member, and are the levels of effort and contribution of each member agreed upon? What product will be built? Who will be the customers? How fast and how large will the business grow? Apple Computer, for example, set out to create an insanely great product. All the founders believed in it, and their initial success followed. However, you need to do more than simply recognize the need for establishing this common vision and alignment of interests. The remainder of this book should guide you toward achieving that goal.

Second, you need to objectively assess the motivation and expectations of the founding team.

Do not jump into the business plan writing mode until you have thought out the preceding questions.

Leadership and Business Basics

Success is derived from the disciplined administration of a plan (written or unwritten) for coordinating the energies and resources of a variety of players toward a common vision. The founding entrepreneur must provide this broad vision, with a sense of mission, and demonstrate the leadership needed to grow the company. While each CEO will have a particular area of interest or expertise, such as selling or developing a product, he or she must be able to operate across the broad spectrum.

For the start-up entrepreneur, Steven C. Brandt's *Entrepreneuring: The Ten Commandments for Building a Growth Company* lists 10 important operational leadership style-related activities that must be executed consistently and well. His 10 "commandments" are shown in the left-hand column of Table 3.1. The center column lists associated classical management functions, and the right-hand column lists related points that are emphasized in this book. Understanding the relationships among these business basics will help you develop your own effective leadership style.

Allocation of Effort

Roberts measured the allocation of effort in technology start-ups by engineer founders during their first six months of business. He found that less than one-third of their time at work was spent on engineering, as shown in Fig. 3.5.

The lesson here is that, although you may be successful, you may not always spend your time doing what you thought you would be doing. The following chapters discuss how you can make your business successful, rewarding, and fun.

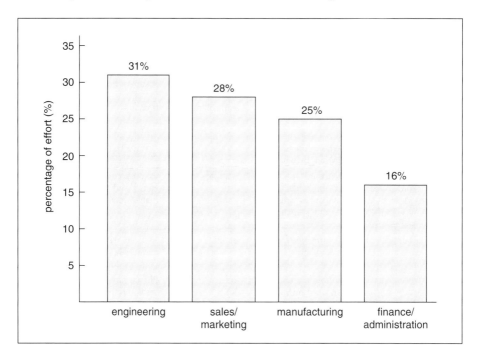

Figure 3.5   Effort Allocated by Founders During First Six Months

Table 3.1 Entrepreneurial Success Through Classical Management Functions

Brandt's commandments	classical management function	emphasis for the entrepreneur
1. Limit the number of primary participants to people who can consciously agree upon and directly contribute to that which the enterprise is to accomplish, for whom, and by when.	staffing	Launch your start-up with a complete, experienced, and compatible management team.
2. Define the business of the enterprise in terms of what is to be bought, precisely by whom (i.e., the customers), and why.	planning	Use a market- and customer-driven strategy to define your product.
3. Concentrate all available resources on accomplishing two or three specific operational objectives within a given period of time.	organizing directing controlling	A superb business plan calls for superb, focused execution.
4. Prepare and work from a written plan that delineates who in the total organization is to do what, by when.	planning	Write a solid business plan that the team believes in.
5. Employ key people with proven records of success at doing what needs to be done in a manner consistent with the desired value system of the enterprise.	staffing	Create a complete, experienced, and compatible management team.
6. Reward individual performance that exceeds agreed-upon standards.	staffing	Motivate with a fair remuneration plan, including equity participation.
7. Expand methodically from a profitable base toward a balanced business.	controlling	Pursue rapid profitability leading to high growth.
8. Project, monitor, and conserve cash and credit capability.	controlling	Never run out of money!
9. Maintain a detached point of view.	planning	Develop a market-driven strategy. Do not concentrate on your technology to the exclusion of other success factors.
10. Anticipate incessant change by periodically testing adopted business plans for their consistency with the realities of the world marketplace.	planning controlling	Develop and maintain an operational business plan after funding is obtained.

Adapted from Steven C. Brandt, *Entrepreneuring: The Ten Commandments for Building a Growth Company*, 3rd edition, 1997, with permission of the author.

Sidebar 3.1 Coping with Stress

Life is stressful, and so is work. The risk and severity of stress are typically much greater in a start-up than in a large company.

According to the National Institute for Occupational Safety and Health, stress-related disorders have become a leading cause of worker disability in the U.S. Stress on the job costs American businesses hundreds of billions of dollars annually in reduced productivity, turnover, absenteeism, medical expenses, and so forth. In severe cases, stress can lead to depression and other psychological and physical problems.

Stress has both positive and negative aspects, although you should not use this fact as a rationalization for ignoring the issue.

On the positive side, many people need some pressure to really motivate them, and many do their best, most heroic work during periods of high stress. According to the Talmud, an olive doesn't release its oil until it has been crushed—the metaphorical point being that many people achieve their greatest successes under the worst stress.

On the negative side, a steady diet of unmanaged, excessive stress can be a killer—and especially so in a start-up environment. Entrepreneurs should not close their eyes to signs of stress in themselves or in their fellow founders and employees. Males are more likely to have a macho approach toward stress, viewing recognition and discussion of it as a sign of weakness. However, an entrepreneur who is stressed out all the time becomes part of the problem, not the solution.

Numerous resources regarding stress management are readily available on the Internet. Also, you may have access to a variety of professional stress reduction programs in your area—for both you and your coworkers. Here are some ideas from just one article, which appeared in *InfoWorld* at the start of the dot-com decline (Brad Shewmake, "Start-Up Stress Hinders Entrants," June 9, 2000).

- *Problem:* Unrealistic expectations of job commitment
  Solution: Establish roles and expectations up front with everyone. Consistently guard and uphold free time.

- *Problem:* Long work hours
  Solution: Maintain perspective and take breaks.

- *Problem:* Difficulty hiring people
  Solution: Take the time necessary to get the right person. Finding qualified candidates is the best way to get help quickly and lighten everyone's load.

- *Problem:* Unrealistic expectations of job performance, unreasonable deadlines
  Solution: Don't be afraid to fail. Communicate with supervisors as problems arise, and suggest solutions.

- *Problem:* No escape from pressure or stress
  Solution: Take a personal day to recharge. Minimize the work you do from home, and make time for a social life.

Keep your eyes open for signs of excessive stress in yourself and others. You can't solve an important problem if you don't spot it, or if you refuse to acknowledge it. Coping successfully with stress is a valuable executive skill to develop.

GETTING DOWN TO BUSINESS

Part Two of this book deals with some important concepts that can make or break your start-up endeavors. As a technical entrepreneur, you must develop a keen appreciation for the essential role of marketing as a focus for growing your business. You must realize that growth will be essential for your success, and you should learn the basic finance-related terminology you will encounter as you launch your start-up.

4

Market- vs. Technology-Focused Approach to Growing a Business

Marketing is essentially viewing the enterprise from the viewpoint of the customer, and there is very little difference between it and the management of the enterprise as a whole.

—Peter F. Drucker

Delivering Benefits to Customers

If your technology enables you to quickly develop a unique product or service that customers will purchase, satisfying a vital market need and leading to rapid profitability, then you are on the right track. However, engineers are especially apt to neglect the essence of a successful business, which is delivering benefits to customers. Delivering benefits is not the same as selling technology.

As Fig. 4.1 depicts, the elements of a successful business include, among other concerns, technology and markets.

Technology and Markets

Technology is certainly an essential element of an engineering-related start-up. However, to focus your business on your technology alone is foolhardy. Understanding and exploiting markets is also an essential element of any start-up.

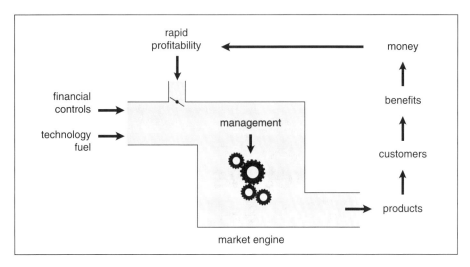

Figure 4.1   Market- and Customer-Driven Technology-Fueled Business Machine

Market Positioning

Where does your proposed product fall in Table 4.1?

Table 4.1   Market Positioning

new market	II marketing driven (new use for an existing product)	I missionary sales, technology push	
existing market	III face entrenched competition	IV market-driven, technology-fueled, market-pull	
	existing product	new product	

If your product falls in any quadrant other than quadrant IV, you need to be careful. An examination of each quadrant follows.

Quadrant III

In quadrant III, the *existing product/existing market* quadrant, you would be a new entrant in the marketplace. Although perhaps acceptable for an income substitution business, this is probably not a lucrative market position for a technology-oriented engineering start-up. Opening a new restaurant would fit into this category.

Quadrant II

Quadrant II, the *existing product/new market* quadrant, represents an opportunity for a business with superior marketing and selling skills to create new demand for an existing product or technology. Typically, engineering-related firms will not play in this position. An example is 3M, which found lucrative markets for tape-based products. 3M's Post-it™ brand self-stick removable notepad is an excellent example of marketing an existing technology (glue and paper) to a new market (almost everyone who works in an office). In order to apply an existing product or technology to a new market, one generally needs to make adjustments to the product—3M already had removable tape, and they made tape that was less sticky.

Quadrant I

Quadrant I, the *new product/new market* territory, is the classic yet very difficult path taken by pioneering, technology-driven entrepreneurs. These individuals, sometimes referred to as "missionaries," take all the arrows in their backs, often only to have new market entrants quickly exploit their expensive groundbreaking efforts—assuming, of course, that a big market actually develops. If no market develops, this is just another way for the missionary to lose. Of course, there have been some big successes in this area, but there have also been some very big failures. If you want to fish in this quadrant, be aware that you are running significant product risks and significant market risks at the same time, and it only takes one hole to sink your boat.

The first video games and home computers are examples of new products that played in new markets. The markets in these cases absorbed almost everything offered. However, early participants often had a rough beginning. Texas Instruments, for instance, offered a home computer that was wonderful for playing games. But TI had to be patient and dig deep into its pockets because it took a couple of years to get the FCC approval that finally made the new products attractive to the market. Even with some early successes, they are no longer a competitor in that market. Other ventures (such as Trilogy's attempt to create wafer-scale integration electronics for computers) consumed hundreds of millions of investor dollars before ultimately failing.

Webvan is a very visible Internet example of trying to enter (establish, really) a new market (online-based grocery delivery services) with new technology (the Internet—the granddaddy of new technology). Webvan is also an example of entrepreneurs and investors reaching boldly for "the next big thing," where both the risks and the potential rewards are simply huge. George Shaheen became CEO of Webvan, leaving behind his comfortable position as the top executive of Andersen Consulting (the world's largest consulting firm, with tens of thousands of employees), and investors poured hundreds of millions of dollars into the company before it went public. Shortly thereafter, it died. In big gambles like this, it typically takes an enormous amount of resources and smart effort, including many tweaks and twists of the strategy, to establish a viable business model. In the case of Webvan, there obviously was no guaranty that delivering groceries this way would ever become an industry. Also, the fact that none of Webvan's senior management had experience in the grocery business was a major contributor to its failure. The Internet has been, and remains, a unique catalyst for many huge "new product/new market" gambles (Netscape, Priceline, etc.)

Quadrant IV

Quadrant IV, the *new product/existing market* quadrant, is the safest category. Here, you can leverage your engineering technology to produce an advanced new product, delivering more benefits at lower cost to customers in a market that is not only receptive to your new development, but is demanding it. Here you let the market pull you into deciding which product to develop. Do not push your technology onto a resisting market. The Internet has provided countless opportunities in this quadrant, as new Internet technology has been applied to countless existing "bricks and mortar" markets.

Technology Push

A business focus based on technology is often called a *technology push* because you are relying on your new technology to push customers into a new market. Especially in the early days, the force of the Internet operated this way. For example, new online stock trading technology pushed many customers into new markets.

Engineers are especially likely to have ideas for products never before imagined. The discussion throughout this book of the importance of identifying customers and markets for your products emphasizes your need to have a commanding position in a protected market niche. You do not need a new product to do that. Instead, you can simply "do the common thing uncommonly well," as Paul Oreffice, former chairman of Dow Chemical, has said. A new concept is usually evident to the market, and it is difficult to develop any fresh idea in total secrecy. Also, unless you have an enforceable patent, you would not have a significant advantage over rivals entering into competition with you. A really new idea will place you in technology-push territory where you will be forced to do missionary sales, which require educating the market. This either delays your success or makes it impossible.

A good example of the difficulty of pushing brand-new technology into new markets to achieve business success is reflected in the experiences of Xerox Corporation. In many of Xerox's failed attempts to exploit new markets using the most advanced technology, other companies ultimately reaped the rewards when the markets were ready and entrepreneurs were willing and able. The first prototype of the personal computer (including a graphical user interface, windows, icons, and a mouse) was created at Xerox' Palo Alto Research Center (PARC), but it was an inspired Steve Jobs and others at Apple who really recognized the possibilities and created the first commercially successful personal computer.

Another example of difficulty caused by technology push appears in Sidebar 4.1, Symantec Corporation: Responding to a Changing Market Need. In this case, company management recognized the problem and changed direction, resulting in a very successful company.

Market Pull

Many high-technology start-ups are finding that instead of pushing breakthrough technology onto the market, they are better off participating at the commodity level and distinguishing themselves through exceptional service and cost. In the Internet arena, many companies in web hosting, telephony, search, ad serving, and so on are competing mainly on a "better and cheaper" basis, and sometimes their exceptional service allows them to charge premium prices. Niche-oriented markets with ever-shortening product life cycles characterized the 1990s, and this phenomenon continues to apply in this millennium. Products must increasingly be designed for world markets. From inception, growth businesses will need to compete globally.

A viable business model is to recognize unique market opportunities that slightly stretch state-of-the-art technology, and then to develop products based upon these identified market needs and your technological capability. Ask Jeeves' user-friendly natural language search is one example.

A business focus based on market need is often called *market pull* because you are relying on the market's desire for a specific benefit to be satisfied through an expansion of state-of-the-art technology. In market pull, the customers are ready and you must deliver the technology. In *technology push*, on the other hand, the presence of customers is questionable—even if you can deliver the technology.

Distilling your business' focus to two words—"customers" and "markets"—will help you think about your goals with intense clarity. This theme will be explored in greater depth later. *Every* venture capitalist has been turned off countless times by plans and presentations filled with a blizzard of charts and data, where it was clear the entrepreneur was clueless about the customer's identity, how the customer would benefit from the entrepreneur's product, and why the customer would pay for that product. So don't make the mistake of thinking of "market pull" as an abstraction. A "market" is very real and specific, and it does not exist at all without customers.

Market- and Customer-Driven Technology-Fueled Strategy

The key to launching a successful technical start-up is to make maximum use of any proprietary technology you can develop while at the same time focusing on market opportunities. This is called a *market- and customer-driven technology-fueled* strategy. The term *market-driven technology-fueled* was first embraced and popularized by Measurex Corporation in the 1980s to guide its business.

New Markets

If, instead, you have a new technology focus, you may be forced to create new markets to sell your products. Creating a new market for a new product is a very difficult and expensive task. It will take extra money and extra time to reach a break-even point if you are creating both a new product and a new market. Recent examples are interaction television and application service providers (ASPs). You must strive for rapid profitability.

Risk and Reward

Of course, the less market risk you entertain, the fewer rewards you might expect. In the early 1990s, the example given in Fig. 4.2 was used to illustrate the point. At that time, if you competed in the personal computer mass storage arena, you had several choices of products to develop. As depicted in Fig. 4.2, a low-risk, very low-reward strategy would have pointed you toward an existing "me too" stable product such as the 3.5-inch hard disk drive market. Clearly, this market lags behind technology capability. A more moderate avenue would have you developing 2.5-inch hard disk drives for notebook computers, but you would have lots of competition and the rewards would be tempered. A higher-risk path with higher potential rewards would have you producing the smaller sub-two-inch drives, already in development, and clearly desired (pulled) by the market for even more portable and compact computers. Slightly more risky would be a pure market pull memory card substitute for rotating media storage devices. On the other hand, a technology push product approach would have you developing exotic memory substitutes like holographic memory modules.

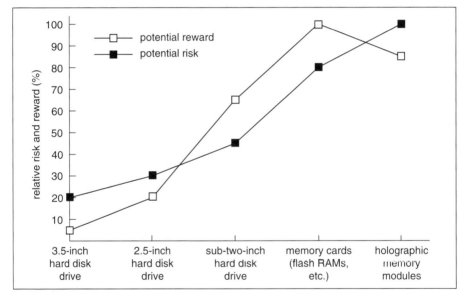

Figure 4.2   Subjective Plot of Potential Risk and Reward

Looking back at that old example (Fig. 4.2) from the perspective of this new millennium, one sees that holographic memory modules never happened, which exactly illustrates the point. A very advanced technology may become reality some day, but entrepreneurs who chase it too early will not survive. Also, the number of competitors able to survive in the commodity disk drive market has been greatly reduced. This general phenomenon of consolidation will be discussed in Ch. 5, in the section entitled "Rule of X" Competitors.

After you have itemized your alternatives, make sure

- your potential rewards greatly exceed your risks
- you maximize the spread between potential risk and reward
- the market does not lag your technology capability
- your technology is pulled by the market
- you do not push your technology on the market

In this example, the technology-focused holographic memory module approach might have been most attractive to you as an engineer in the early 1990s, but the market clearly desired more down-to-earth products such as memory cards and smaller disk drives. The point is that you must deal with your technology-related product ambitions in manageable risk stages. If you take on a risky project, make certain that you have the financial backing to complete it. The greatest mistake you can make is to start a business you cannot finance. If you need to raise money to move on to the next stage of risk, make sure you secure adequate financing. If you run out of money, you will lose all control of your business. If you have the chance, take more money than you think you'll need.

Also, be aware that the vast majority of surprises and unexpected events tend to lengthen, not shorten, your time frames. This has profound implications for your cash needs and cash management. To repeat—never run out of cash. If you don't manage your cash, it will manage you.

Rapid Time to Market

Rapid time to market and rapid profitability are commonly recognized as keys to start-up success. Time consumption, like cost, is quantifiable and therefore manageable. Many of today's most successful companies recognize time as the fourth dimension of competitiveness and, as a result, develop new products rapidly, operate with flexible manufacturing and rapid-response systems, and place extraordinary emphasis on development and innovation. Organizations are structured to produce quick responses rather than low costs and control.

All other things being equal, if you lengthen the time it takes to get to profitability, two bad things happen. First, you greatly increase the amount of invested capital you need. Second, in the eyes of your prospective investor, the current value of your company (based on the discounted present value of your future income stream) drops significantly, since a typical venture capitalist desires returns of 30%+ compounded annually.

By becoming a time-based competitor, your start-up can get there first and develop a distinct competitive advantage over more technically sophisticated companies that attempt to push the market.

The average time to market varies by industry, of course. For a discussion of an industry at the long end of the spectrum, see Sidebar 4.2, Time to Market in Life Sciences Industry.

Sidebar 4.1 Symantec Corporation: Responding to a Changing Market Need

In the early 1980s, a large number of high-technology companies were launched in the area of artificial intelligence (AI). AI included robotics, computer vision, and natural language understanding. Each of these areas drew substantial investments but almost none returned any rewards. It was a classic case of technology push. The market in the 1980s for products derived from AI technologies was virtually nonexistent despite the millions of dollars poured into it.

Symantec Corporation originally intended to develop AI products that enabled a computer to understand natural language. Potential applications ranged from natural language translators for the military and tourists to typewriters to which one could speak. Unlike most AI start-ups, Symantec's new management finally realized that the market was not responding to its technology, so they shifted focus before it was too late.

Today, Symantec is a leading public company in the personal computer utility software market. Its market has proven to be one of the highest margin niches venture capitalists could have invested in during the early 1990s.

Symantec was successful because it responded to market need. This is an interesting case because Symantec seemingly abandoned its technology base. On closer examination, however, it was obvious that its marketable technology consisted of exceptional state-of-the-art computer science and programming skills that could be applied to pressing market needs. Added to Symantec's technology fuel was its savvy market-driven strategy, which resulted in admirable success.

The Rest of the Story—an Update

The above perspective was written many years ago, in the last millennium, in 1992. Is there any lesson we can now learn from our current perspective? Yes.

Symantec deserves credit for recognizing the "push technology" problems it faced in AI and speech recognition systems. The potential new markets simply were not ready for the technology being pushed at them by dozens of "hot" companies. Symantec proactively chose to leave the land of the "living dead" and seek markets in which it could succeed. In the intervening years it has evolved, changed direction several times, and grown, and it is now focused on security solutions for businesses and individuals.

Eventually, after several years, the speech recognition market began to mature, and other companies like Nuance Communications and IBM are now benefiting. This is as it should be. If Symantec had stuck with what wasn't working, it would have joined a long list of stubborn companies (whose names are now forgotten) from the early 1990s that died pursuing AI and speech recognition.

Although Symantec's name is not the brightest star in the sky, it survived and now has a multi-billion-dollar capitalization. In 2003, Symantec was added to Standard and Poor's index of the 500 largest U.S. companies. Recognize reality—if your plan isn't working, get another plan.

Sidebar 4.2 Time to Market in Life Sciences Industry

The characteristics of a particular industry can greatly affect the length of time it takes to develop a product and bring it to market. The life sciences industry on average probably takes the longest, and we offer it here as an example. The following perspective is provided by Kent Stormer, a partner in the Silicon Valley office of the law firm of Heller Ehrman White & McAuliffe.

Pharmaceuticals, Medical Devices, and Other Biotech Products

The estimated time to bring pharmaceuticals, medical devices, and other biotech products to market is much longer than for almost all other products.

Human Trials

An extended time period is typically required for human trials, particularly for pharmaceuticals and in-vivo devices. The average novel prescription drug approval includes 70 clinical trials involving 4000 patients over a period of 5 years, according to the "Industry Profile 2001" prepared by the Pharmaceutical Research and Manufacturers of America (sometimes referred to as PhRMA).

FDA Approval

Added time and uncertainty result if approval by the U.S. Food and Drug Administration (FDA) is required.

- It typically takes 15 months for marketing approval of pharmaceuticals after completion of required trials and submission of the application to the FDA (13 months for biologicals and 11 months for devices).
- Federal legislation under which industry agreed to pay fees, commencing in 1993, has had a favorable impact by shortening FDA approval times.
- However, requests for additional data or studies often result, requiring resubmission of the application and restarting of the clock.

Total Time

The estimate of total time from product inception to market for drugs and many medical devices is measured in years rather than months. New drugs usually take 10 to 15 years.

Cost Impact

Protracted development time, along with the need to conduct expensive clinical trials, can profoundly increase the costs of development for these types of products.

Risk

A significant number of potential drugs that proceed to clinical trials never make it to the market. For each drug that reaches the market, PhRMA estimates that 5 enter clinical testing and 250 enter preclinical testing. Only one of every 5000–10,000 molecules screened in the laboratory makes it to market as a drug (according to the PhRMA "Industry Profile 2001"). Of course, the winnowing process is essential to pare off drugs that do not warrant further investment. Culling is fundamental to the natural selection process that results in the survival of the "fittest" drugs. However, it is difficult, particularly for a small company, to see its pipeline decimated, and the risk of project termination and attrition only exacerbates the problem of the high cost of drug development.

Strategy Impact

This different timing, cost, and risk calculus dictates a modified and augmented development strategy, potentially involving partnering with other companies and multiple funding rounds. This strategy is discussed further in Sidebar 11.1, Partnering in the Life Sciences Industry.

5

When High-Growth Business Is Desirable and Necessary

A growing company in a growing market can survive a lot more management blunders and bad luck than a company in a stable market and still succeed.

—Gordon B. Baty, partner in Zero Stage Capital

Why Grow?

Understanding the importance of growth in business is something one learns. Few engineers have had the required training in finance and economics to internalize the need for growth, and the need is not obvious through introspection. Thus, one of the most difficult concepts for entrepreneurs to understand is why their new businesses must grow. It follows that one of the most difficult conclusions for an engineer to accept is that growing a successful business involves much more than engineering and technology. Often, the CEO of an engineering-related start-up will be engaged in almost everything except engineering and product development.

The primary purpose of this chapter is to explain why growth is not only desirable, but necessary, if you are to achieve even modest financial objectives.

The Self-Employed

If you are a self-employed engineer and want to create wealth, you must focus on growth. Many engineers become motivated, self-employed consultants when they lose their jobs. If you find yourself in this position, you need to understand the limits of your success as a one-person business.

The 1990s revealed an increasing number of self-employed entrepreneurial individuals. About 8.97 million people (7.7% of all workers in the United States) were self-employed. This was the highest level of self-employment in 25 years. During the last three years of that decade, the percentage of workers who were self-employed rose to 11%, according to the Population Reference Bureau. The National Association for the Self-Employed (NASE) reports even higher figures. Many of these people left their jobs involuntarily. You will want to do better than these individuals; the median annual income for self-employed individuals (excluding those working in farming) was about the same as that for wage-and-salary workers ($23,754 vs. $22,287 in 1996), and would be even lower if doctors and lawyers were excluded. As you launch your technology-based start-up, whether motivated by choice or by losing a job, you will need to look to growth for financial success. Since one-person businesses (which, by definition, cannot grow) neither yield significant incomes nor create vast wealth, the successful entrepreneur must look for growth opportunities.

Investors Expect Rapid Growth

All venture capitalists and sophisticated angel investors look for high growth. You will not find a single exception. In contrast, although this point should be obvious, many entrepreneurs are small businesspeople at heart. They are really more comfortable with a small company environment and, consciously or subconsciously, bias their actions (or lack of action) to restrict growth. Venture capitalists seek companies that can attain commanding positions in huge markets, and they are looking for entrepreneurs who want the same thing. This is at the core of the venture capitalist's business model, and nothing else works for them. They seek companies that can go public in three to six years. If a small *lifestyle* company is what you want, that's fine, but don't expect any professional investor to finance it.

Grow a Commanding Position in a Defensible Market Segment

According to William H. Davidow's *Marketing High Technology: An Insider's View*, "Marketing must invent complete products and drive them to commanding positions in defensible market segments."

What this means in terms of growth is that your business must expand at least to the point where it can survive. A classic General Electric study showed that companies with a market share greater than 30% were almost always profitable, whereas companies with a market share of less than 15% almost always lost money. Since mathematically no more than six companies can each have a 15%+ market share, you must grow your business to one of a few commanding a 15–30% minimum market share. This does not mean you have to be a giant company to play in a giant market. Rather, you must identify significant segments of your market that you can dominate, and you must grow rapidly to achieve this goal. Before you try to compete with General Motors, IBM, or Microsoft, make sure you can garner a 15% minimum market share in a small, related, and well-protected market segment.

Whether you are trying to exploit an existing market or establish a new market, you may find yourself competing with dozens of companies. To have any chance in this situation, you must grow at a rate both substantially faster than the market and substantially faster than your competition. Treading water by simply keeping even with the competition almost certainly puts you on the road to failure.

"Rule of *X*" Competitors

Entrepreneurs should carefully consider how many competitors can really survive in the market segment they are targeting. Of these competitors, how many will simply struggle to stay alive? How many will truly prosper, grow rapidly, and make above-average returns?

The *rule of X* simply states that in any particular market, at any point in time, there is room for only *X* viable competitors.

X is not a fixed number, but will vary depending upon the characteristics of your particular market, which include

- the maturity of the targeted market
- barriers to entry
- patent and other intellectual property protection
- economies of scale
- switching costs for customers
- the distribution channels
- the relative importance of brand
- the size of the market
- the rate at which the market is expected to evolve and change

If the market is accounting services in Los Angeles, then *X* is large—in the hundreds. If the market is operating systems for the desktop computer, then *X* is only 1 (spelled "M-i-c-r-o-s-o-f-t"). Whatever the number is, it can change over time and, in the case of desktop operating systems, it will become 2 if the world is lucky.

If you are the typical high-tech reader of this book, the *X* for your contemplated market is a small number, not greater than 7. However, if you are simply planning to start your own consulting company and provide technical services, then *X* is a very high number, and this book is not really intended for you.

Many markets, whether high-tech or not, are dominated by two competitors. Consider Coke and Pepsi, or Kodak and Fuji, or Boeing and Airbus. In cases like this, it's very difficult for a new competitor, even a large competitor, to attain success.

Because of the tremendous impact of the Internet and related technologies, X has shrunk for many markets. The "rule of 7" for some markets has become the "rule of 3" or occasionally even the "rule of 1." This trend has also been fueled by global competition and massive consolidation in many industries through both mergers and business failures.

Is there room in online investing for dozens and dozens of brokerage firms to succeed? Not really. Yet numerous companies jumped into this market during the Internet frenzy. In many markets like this, the top two or three competitors will harvest the lion's share of the profits, a couple more may squeak by, and the rest in total will either be acquired or lose money and wither.

An excellent book on this topic is *The Rule of Three: Surviving and Thriving in Competitive Markets*, by Jagdish Sheth and Rajendra Sisodia. This book also discusses how and why a market dominated by a few large competitors may have room for a few successful *specialist* companies, which in many cases have substantially higher profit margins than do their larger competitors. Numerous specific cases are analyzed, including cases in which profitable specialty companies have made the mistake of chasing market share, only to experience a rapid decline in profitability before failing as a business. If your plan is to become a specialist company, you need to understand especially well your market positioning and value added, and to be especially focused in your strategy and execution. This book may help you, as a nimble competitor, determine a way to use the dynamics of your industry, plus the size of your competitors, to your advantage—and offer a new business model that benefits customers in ways other than lowered costs. David can slay Goliath, and dinosaurs die if their environment changes and they don't adapt.

Companies, including very large successful corporations, increasingly have tried to focus on what they do best. This raises the competitive standard for markets and tends to drive down the number of competitors. Consider the case of Ericsson, the Swedish telecom giant and world leader in cell phones. It decided early in this millennium to stop competing in the manufacturing of cell phones, and it outsourced this function to a contract manufacturer. Even though Ericsson sold, at that time, more than 40 million cell phones per year and was number three in worldwide sales (behind Nokia and Motorola), it was losing ground to competitors and finding it difficult to compete on price as cell phones rapidly became a consumer commodity product.

The central point here is not that you must determine the exact number, X, for your contemplated market, but rather that you must carefully analyze your particular market structure, with a view to understanding its dynamics, and with the expectation that this analysis will profoundly impact your chosen strategy for success. Many large, successful companies have a strategic policy of exiting a business (or never entering it) if they cannot be number one or number two in that business.

Attract Customers in Expanding Markets

Although it is understood that customers want to be sure their vendors will still be around in a few years to provide them with parts, service, software upgrades, and so on, it is frustrating for the start-up engineer to make a sales presentation and then hear the customer say, "The product is just right, but will you be there next year to service it?" After all, how are you supposed to launch your new business if customers want to purchase only from proven sources? This is one reason you need to identify an unfilled market need, and to provide a product with several times the performance-price advantages over competitive products.

Don't ignore or underestimate the risk that buyers (both the buying company and the individuals in the company who make purchasing decisions) are running when they go with you. This will be discussed more in Ch. 8, in the section entitled Your Customers as Risk Takers.

Many start-up businesses find good customers in Fortune 500 companies. Individual customers in these companies can often relate to a struggling entrepreneur, and will help you over many hurdles. In return you need to help these individuals do their jobs well by providing a product that delivers on its promises. Empathize with your customer, and always try to understand the customer's point of view. For example, distinguish between situations where it really won't matter much to the customer if you go out of business and situations where the customer is very dependent on your survival.

Develop a Product Family

A single product does not constitute a business. Therefore, you must strive to provide a family of products to meet market needs. You should grow to provide solutions to different customers with varying needs. For example, a successful software company (say, a company that offers virus protection) may need to make its software available on a variety of hardware platforms and operating systems.

Venture capitalists express this point in different ways, and you may have seen it on a checklist of what venture capitalists look for, but here's the essential question: Is there really a business here? Simply having a wonderful feature or a cool product is typically not enough to constitute a business.

In planning your products and determining your *value added*, you should recognize the important balancing act that's part of the process. How much should you try to do, and when? If you think too small, you won't have a viable company. If you bite off more than you can chew, you'll encounter schedule slippages, morale problems, and a host of other adverse consequences. Typically, entrepreneurs are much more likely to try to do too much too quickly, usually because they have not taken the time and effort to realistically size the work involved. Here's how Accel Partners (a venture capital firm headquartered in Palo Alto, CA) looks at this balance.

Ideally, a company should initially serve highly specific customer needs that lie within a broader generic category of needs of the same customers or industry. The company can then execute profitably in the short-term as well as grow smoothly through a coherent product line and market expansion. To grow continuously, a company must constantly and more broadly redefine its contribution to the market. Last year's contribution must become next year's "feature" within a broader definition.

Because customers are most often drawn to brand names, your product's trade name will only gain national or international recognition with volume sales and extensive publicity. Marketing communications and public relations efforts need to be amortized over a large, growing product base.

Since your first product serves a finite part of the market, you must grow to reach new markets with new needs. If you have only that first product, once your market is saturated your business ceases to grow.

Achieve Critical Mass and Economy of Scale

All the supporting infrastructure of your business, including your plant and equipment, management salaries, inventory control systems, accounting systems, and all other fixed costs, need to be spread out over your product base. Without a growing product base, the single-product enterprise may soon be overburdened with fixed costs. Until your company revenues exceed some critical mass, your fixed costs will restrain profitability.

Growth also permits you to add staff with specialized experience to your business. Without a sufficient volume of activity, you and your managers will be forced to become jacks-of-all-trades; you may be doing many things, but not particularly well or efficiently. Since your business must be efficient to be competitive and profitable, it follows that you will need an expanded staff including various divisions of expertise. To attract top employees to your business you must provide both opportunity and financial reward. These, too, come from growth.

Economy of scale applies to every successful business. Henry Ford was perhaps the most famous entrepreneur to understand and apply the concepts of economy of scale to achieve critical mass, since he introduced mass production and the moving production line, transforming the early twentieth century handcrafted automobile business into a modern industry.

The Boston Consulting Group's 1968 book *Perspectives on Experience* argued that the cost of doing business decreased 20–30% every time business (sales) doubled. The thrust of this argument is still true. Although BCG recommended that "if market dominance cannot be achieved, then an orderly withdrawal from the business is best," you will not always have to completely dominate a market. Many markets can support a number of successful companies, particularly if the markets themselves are growing. However, you need to carefully assess your particular market and your chances. Even if you conclude that multiple competitors could do pretty well in your targeted market, your goal should always be complete domination. High growth is the main road to that goal.

Speed Is Not a Substitute for Strategy

Especially during the Internet craze, speed was commonly viewed as the number-one business objective for start-ups. Many venture capitalists encouraged this perspective, and one entertaining result was the creation of many expensive Superbowl ads by dot-com companies. The conventional rules of business were suspended, and speed to market and speed in building the company were believed to be essential to achieving success in the "new economy." However, speed is simply not a substitute for strategy. If you don't know what direction your boat should be going, simply rowing faster is foolish and sometimes fatal. Speed has its place, but only in the context of a broader, market-driven strategy.

In a study reported in the McKinsey Quarterly (www.mckinseyquarterly.com), 2001, Number 3, "How Fast Is Too Fast," three researchers studied 80 Internet companies and concluded,

> The benefits of speed outweigh the costs only for companies that are first movers in markets with huge potential and that face no clear obstacle to success. For the rest, speed provides no competitive advantage and often results in wasted resources, missed opportunities, and flawed strategies.

Speed was an advantage for only about 10% of the companies studied.

One problem with worshiping speed is that you may take leaps before you're ready—such as launching a new product before it has been adequately tested. In this case, disappointed customers and other adverse consequences may cause "faster" to really mean slower, and perhaps even fatal.

Getting to market as fast as possible does have a certain forceful and positive ring to it. It sounds right. However, speed has its costs, risks, and rewards, and intelligent management will do some intelligent balancing. Higher speed typically means higher costs, and where to set the accelerator depends upon the perceived risks and rewards. On the risk side, are you acting without adequate time for gathering information and validating your plans and products with customers? Customers are not hungry pigs that will eat anything tossed their way. If you take the time to validate your plans, you will feel much more confident in spending your limited resources to implement those plans.

Diversify to Diminish Business Risks

Though it has been said that you can always win the game of business as long as you do not place all your bets on one product, one customer, one supplier, or one investor, some attempts are going to fail. However, diversifying your business by producing a family of products and selling to customers in different industries can increase your chances for success. It is wise, though, to make sure you're on solid ground (i.e., with an established 30% market share) before you start diversifying.

Your company must grow in order to diversify. This is not to say you should not stick to what you know best. As your business grows and reaches customers with different economic buying cycles and different problems to be solved, you will decrease the risk that a single catastrophic event could end your business.

Start-ups are exciting and risky, and you can thrive on that precariousness to make the most of your personal, financial, and emotional investment, but you do not want to persist in that state of uncertainty forever. It may be an oversimplification, but most start-ups are destined to either die, join the living dead (i.e., barely subsist), or grow to success. For example, if you stay small and maintain a one-customer, one-product kind of business, you will someday have a cash-flow crisis that will bankrupt your venture. If you grow just to the size where your business breaks even, you have created an income substitution business. Finally, if you grow and never stop, you can achieve great wealth and security.

If you have to be in a start-up to get your kicks, don't make it the same start-up for a decade! Grow to success, and then restart if you have to.

Create Career Opportunities

Great companies are run by great people. Great people are attracted to great companies. Getting, and then keeping, key employees is essential. Exceptional people need to grow, learn, and take on increasing responsibility. Only a growing company can provide such an attraction for the people you need. Almost everyone wants to be promoted to a better position, and those positions can only be created through growth.

Create Future Start-Up Opportunities

One of the best sources of a start-up idea is one's current or previous employer. If the company you work for grows, it will create an abundance of new ideas. Not all of these ideas can or should be exploited by the core business, and many employees will someday leave to create new start-ups based, in part, on exploiting these untouched opportunities. These start-up opportunities can be yours if you choose. Or, your company can beneficially invest in those ideas that need a start-up environment to flourish by providing initial funding in exchange for equity ownership in the new start-ups.

Create Market Value, Attract Investments, and Cash Out

You and your investors will someday want to exchange your stock certificates for cash. To do this, your company must be of sufficient size and profitability to either go public or be acquired by another (usually public) company. In either case the result is that you and your investors would then hold marketable securities. This is normal and desirable—and it requires that your company grow.

6

Start-Up Financing
Terminology and Stages

Money is the seed of money, and the first guinea is sometimes more difficult to acquire than the second million.

—Jean Jacques Rousseau, A Discourse on Political Economy

This book is concerned with the formation of your new company, which falls into the category of early-stage financing—what is loosely called a *start-up*. Starting and developing your own successful high-growth company will typically take you through three major financing stages, known in investment circles as

- early-stage financing
- expansion financing
- IPO/acquisition/buyout financing (also called later-stage financing)

Each of these stages consists of key financing events. For example, in early-stage financing, there is a *seed* financing event that occurs when you first obtain funding to launch the business (or even just to explore a product idea or for research and development, long before there is a business); *start-up* financing, which is used for product development and initial marketing; and *first-stage* or *early-development* financing, which allows you to initiate manufacturing and sales. Many venture capitalists speak of seed financing events as comprising a separate investment stage because of the diversity and range of scope in these incubation deals.

The best way to characterize the stages of your company's growth is to speak the language of investors. Stanley E. Pratt's *Pratt's Guide to Venture Capital Sources* and James L. Plummer's *QED Report on Venture Capital Financial Analysis* converge on the investment community's various definitions. You must understand what these investment and company growth terms mean if you are to properly represent your situation to prospective investors, team members, and employees. Figure 6.1 is derived from Pratt's and Plummer's prose.

From Fig. 6.1, it is evident that a start-up is a private company in a very early stage of maturation. It is thus interesting to note that the term "start-up" is often inappropriately used in reference to young, public high-technology companies (i.e., companies that have successfully progressed through all the stages reflected in Fig. 6.1 and whose stock is now publicly traded). Someone once said start-up is a state of mind. Perhaps some of these small public companies are able to retain the flair of start-ups, but most likely they do not have the risk, financial leverage, and reward opportunity, or the lack of infrastructure, instability, and uncertainty associated with a true start-up. Nor do they meet the start-up financing level description of "not having sold product" yet.

The term start-up as misused by the layperson is often similarly misused by first-time entrepreneurs in their representations and presentations to investors. Be certain not to expose naïveté in these circumstances. Likewise, the term *early development* (or *first-stage*) is often erroneously used by entrepreneurs to refer to a pre-start-up or pre-seed-level company. If you incorrectly represent your recently incorporated but as yet uncapitalized company to investors as one in early development when it is actually in pre-seed stage, you may have just lowered your valuation by about 50% in their eyes! Study Fig. 6.1 closely before approaching investors for funds. You must speak the language to play the start-up game. There is not that much to learn here, but it is essential that you learn a few key terms. It really isn't that difficult. This chapter has been kept short so that you can study and master this vernacular.

Figure 6.1 is an overview of the stages a very successful start-up might progress through—from birth to a successful IPO or buyout. However, the variations from this overview are numerous and significant, and each start-up will have its own particular journey. Many will never get beyond early-stage financing, and some will be very successful with fewer rounds of financing, perhaps even without any external financing. In general, professional investors anticipate, for planning purposes at least, that their companies will more or less progress through the stages in Fig. 6.1. Accordingly, assuming you intend to seek professional funding, your goal here should be to understand the general process, the terminology, and how your prospective professional investors think.

Where to draw the line between the financing stages necessarily involves some degree of arbitrariness, and companies that track the venture financing industry

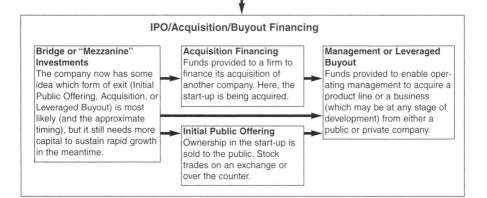

Early-Stage Financing

Seed Financing
A relatively small amount of capital provided to an inventor or entrepreneur to prove a concept. It may involve product development but rarely involves initial marketing.

Start-Up Financing
Financing provided to companies for use in product development and initial marketing. Companies may be in the process of being organized or they may have been in business for one year or less, but they have not sold their product commercially. Usually, such firms would have already assembled most of the key management team, prepared a business plan, made market studies, and generally prepared themselves to do business.

First-Stage Financing
Financing provided to companies that have expended their initial capital (often in developing a prototype) and that require funds to initiate manufacturing and sales. Investment only proceeds through this stage if the prototypes look good enough so that further technical risk is minimal. Likewise, the market studies must look promising enough to set up a manufacturing process to ship in quantity. The company is unlikely to be profitable at this stage and will have negative cash flow.

Expansion Financing

Second-Stage Financing
Working capital for the initial expansion of a company that is producing and shipping and that has growing accounts receivable and inventories. Although the company has clearly made progress, it may not yet be showing a profit, and cash flow may still be negative.

Third-Stage Financing
Funds provided for major expansion of a company with an increasing sales volume and that is breaking even or profitable. Cash flow remains a concern. These funds are used for further plant expansion, marketing, working capital, or development of an improved product.

Fourth-Stage Financing
Financing for a company that still needs outside cash to sustain rapid growth, but is successful and stable enough that risk to investors is much reduced. The cash-out point for venture capital investors is thought to be within a couple of years.

IPO/Acquisition/Buyout Financing

Bridge or "Mezzanine" Investments
The company now has some idea which form of exit (Initial Public Offering, Acquisition, or Leveraged Buyout) is most likely (and the approximate timing), but it still needs more capital to sustain rapid growth in the meantime.

Acquisition Financing
Funds provided to a firm to finance its acquisition of another company. Here, the start-up is being acquired.

Initial Public Offering
Ownership in the start-up is sold to the public. Stock trades on an exchange or over the counter.

Management or Leveraged Buyout
Funds provided to enable operating management to acquire a product line or a business (which may be at any stage of development) from either a public or private company.

Figure 6.1   Stages of a Company's Growth

categorize things in different ways. For example, you might see venture capital data broken down into the following four categories.

- seed/start-up
- early stage
- expansion
- later stage

VentureOne, a leading venture capital research firm, breaks down the data somewhat differently, as seen in Figs. 6.2 and 6.3.

Since the world of venture investing is full of jargon, different investors and analysts may use different terms to describe roughly the same thing. Thus, you are likely to hear terms that don't even appear on Fig. 6.1. Again, your goal is to understand the general process. Think in terms of stages and focus on the big picture. Here are a few comments about the stages and some of the terminology.

- *Series A round*—This financing round is very clearly defined by the *type of stock* that is sold to investors—preferred stock. It is called Series A because the company issues preferred stock for the first time and calls it Series A. Typically, this is the first professional investor round and involves a venture capital firm or another type of organized investment fund. Thus, it is sometimes called the *first venture round* or the *first professional round*. Angels sometimes receive preferred stock (say Series A) and sometimes receive common stock.

- *Series B, Series C*, and so on—Additional professional investor rounds may follow, all involving preferred stock. The common practice is to label these financing rounds with letters of the alphabet, but a few companies number them. (It makes no difference which you do, of course.)

- As for the common stock—The earlier financing that precedes the professional (series A, B, and C) rounds typically involves common stock, and it may occur in one or more rounds. Here is some additional terminology.

  - *Founders' round*—This is the first money used by the new venture and is provided by the founders. The founders put in some cash, and sometimes they even use their credit cards. Most have to scrape together what they can, although some fortunate founders are in the position of being able to use some of the money they made in a prior start-up.

  - *Family and friends round*—People who are close to the founders put in some money. This may be part of the founders' round, or it may follow it.

  - *Angel round*—Rich individuals invest.

- The websites of prospective venture investors typically profile the types of investments they seek (stage of company, industries considered, size of investment, etc.). You may even find some special terminology they use to describe what they are interested in.

Your central goal is not to achieve one round of financing after another, but rather to create a valuable company that grows rapidly, achieves profitability, and creates a

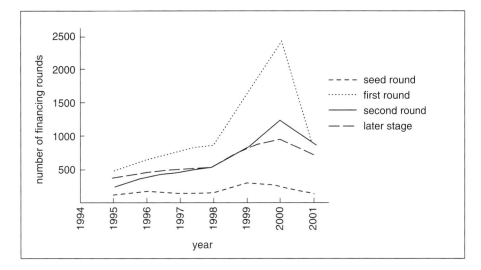

Figure 6.2   Venture Capital Investment—Number of Financing Rounds, by Round Class

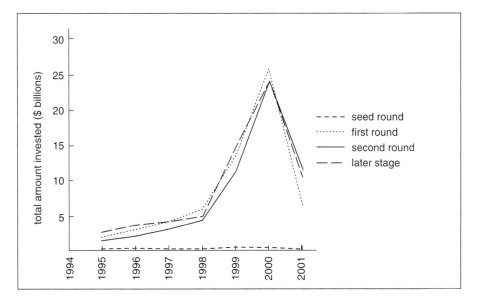

Figure 6.3   Venture Capital Investment—Total Amount Invested, by Round Class

lot of shareholder value. Outside venture financing may or may not be necessary to achieve this goal. Some entrepreneurs who led high-flying dot-coms during the Internet frenzy noted that each cash infusion from their venture capitalists felt like a cocaine high, causing an immediate sense of exhilaration and success, but before long the entrepreneurs were back on the road seeking more financing.

Financing and running your business will require, of course, a certain understanding of accounting. See Sidebar 6.1, Financials for Engineers—a Crash Course.

Although you naturally may be most interested in understanding early-stage financing, you should also be conversant with expansion financing terms and business growth milestones. Postexpansion financing terminology helps you recognize the need for and understand the alternatives to cashing out when you are finished with your start-up. You will hear your investors discussing their postexpansion financing exit strategies. They will need to return to themselves, their limited partners, or other funding sources their invested capital and gains at some point in time, usually within three to seven years. During weak IPO markets (e.g., from the late 1980s into 1990, during several brief periods in the 1990's, and again starting in mid-2000 when the IPO market became extremely weak), investors found themselves taking a longer ride with their private start-up investments than they did in strong IPO markets (e.g., during the mid-1980s, and especially in the late 1990s). During a strong IPO market, such as that experienced in 1991 and early 1992, and especially from the late 1990s into early 2000, things turn around rapidly. However, no one can predict how long the latest hot IPO market window will last, or how long the window will remain shut when the IPO market is cold.

Human memory tends to be short when it comes to remembering the big swings in the IPO market. Although the recent Internet frenzy is without parallel in terms of scale, one can go back less than a decade before that—to 1991 and early 1992—to see another remarkable event: in the midst of an extended recession, the IPO market unexpectedly opened up. Many start-ups on the verge of bankruptcy, with nil sales and millions of dollars in accumulated losses, suddenly found themselves on the IPO bandwagon. The tone of the press at the time could have applied to the later Internet frenzy. For example, on March 19, 1992, the *Wall Street Journal* reported

> IPOs continue to explode with sales headed for a record first quarter. More than 120 companies have raised $7.4 billion from initial stock sales since January 1. At this rate, first quarter IPO sales are expected to be a record. If the pace continues, this year could well shatter the record $18.3 billion raised by IPOs in 1986, as well as last year's near-record $16.4 billion.

All this was happening in the midst of one of the longest and hardest recessions in years. If you simply increased the numbers in the above quote, it could have described accurately the later Internet bubble.

Figure 6.4 illustrates the volume (in total dollars and number of issues) of IPOs over a more recent period of six years. Although, in general, the most lucrative successful exit is an IPO, the most common one is typically an acquisition of the venture

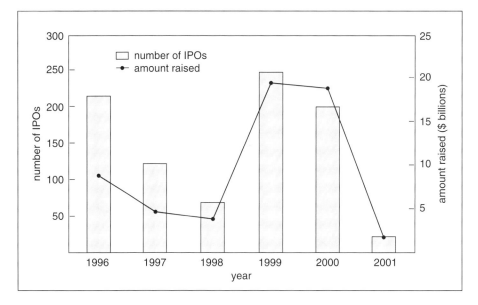

Figure 6.4   Several Years of Venture-Backed IPOs

by a larger corporation. One reason for this is the volatility of the IPO market. Also, many factors beyond a private company's control help determine whether it can go public.

Investment bankers, in effect, are the gatekeepers that determine whether or not a company can go public. In doing their due diligence and making their judgments, they traditionally (e.g., from the 1970s and well into the 1990s) used certain rules of thumb and, of course, checked the temperature of the market for new IPO stock issues. One rule of thumb frequently heard by entrepreneurs was that a growing company with good momentum could go public if it had at least two consecutive quarters (*trailing* quarters) of profitability with annual revenues of perhaps $20 million or more.

Such general rules, along with common sense, were thrown out the window during the Internet madness from the late 1990s into 2000. The result was the hottest IPO market ever, as many bogus companies went public with only a slim promise or hope of future profitability. Before 1996, the start-ups that went public took an average of six to seven years to go from birth to IPO. This period dropped to less than two years at the peak of the Internet frenzy. What had traditionally been a long-distance race to build company value became a sprint to grab the IPO pot of gold.

What does this mean for you, the entrepreneur? Well, there are things you can control and things you can't, and the public market for new IPO issues is simply one of the things you can't control. Entrepreneurs are very likely to fail when they consistently run their businesses at the edge, always counting on several factors beyond their control to come out just right. Learn from the mistakes of others. Manage your business with a view to surviving and prospering no matter what the financial times are like. Create value for the long haul, but don't be afraid to "cash out" when things seems too good to be true.

For a case study involving one of the authors, see Sidebar 6.2, Trials and Tribulations in the Financing of One Start-Up Company.

Sidebar 6.1 Financials for Engineers—a Crash Course

An Overview

The following three financial statements are at the core of accounting.

- balance sheet
- income statement
- cash flow statement

These are discussed in Ch. 10, which is where you should begin your investigation into accounting. If you pick up the annual report for any company, you will find these key financial statements. If you already have, or you develop, a good understanding of these three, you will know most of what you really need to know about accounting. What follows in this sidebar are some other tools and some additional information, which you should view as frosting on the cake. If your accounting knowledge is weak, you should focus on the core three (the cake), and perhaps only make a cursory review of the rest of this sidebar (the frosting). Taking an accounting course is also a good idea.

Of all the discussion that follows in this sidebar, *burn rate* is the term you are most likely to hear when you talk with other entrepreneurs or prospective investors. The burn rate discussion appears at the end of this sidebar.

Measures of Financial Stability

A topic related to raising funds is that of maintaining the financial stability of your company once it is launched. As you build your business, you will want to institute financial controls to make sure that your business stays healthy and does not get into trouble, and you'll need to know when additional funds will be required. Because it is important that you be conversant and comfortable with financial concepts when selling your business plan, this sidebar will explain some relevant indicators of financial health, insolvency, and bankruptcy.

Ratio Analysis

There are numerous key ratios that analysts use in evaluating a company's financial position. These ratios relate to

- *balance sheet conditions:* asset evaluation, cash accounts, receivables risk, inventory risk, prepaid expenses, company investments, fixed asset analysis, intangibles such as goodwill, deferred charges, and estimated liabilities for future costs and losses

- *liquidity analysis:* cash adequacy, trend in current liabilities to total liabilities, current liabilities to stockholders' equity, current liabilities to revenue, financial flexibility, funds flow evaluation, and availability and cost of financing

- *solvency analysis:* long-term funds flow, financial solvency, unrecorded assets, unrecorded liabilities, and noncurrent liabilities
- *probability of business failure:* bankruptcy prediction

Others break ratios down into liquidity, profitability, and efficiency ratios.

Since your start-up will likely have almost no sales, no profits, few assets, little inventory, no retained earnings, and so on, most of these traditional ratios are meaningless. The use of a few key ratios, however, might suffice for a quick "sanity check" of the possibility of going bankrupt, which is your main concern over the near term.

GLOSSARY OF TERMS FOR RATIO ANALYSIS

Here are some very brief and informal definitions of the basic terms needed to compute and understand the few key ratios discussed in this sidebar. These terms are used in the ratio equations that follow.

- *accounts payable:* outstanding obligations to pay for goods or services that have been acquired on open account from suppliers
- *accounts receivable:* amounts due to the company on account from customers who have bought merchandise or received services
- *current assets:* total cash, securities, inventory, accounts receivable, and other assets that are likely to be converted into cash within one year
- *current liabilities:* total of all debts incurred by the company in its normal operations that are due within one year, including such things as accounts payable, salaries payable, short-term loans, and that portion of long-term loans that is due within one year
- *net sales:* equals gross sales less returns and allowances, cash discounts, and so on
- *total assets:* equals current assets plus fixed assets
- *working capital:* net working capital (which is what most people mean when they refer to working capital) is a liquidity measure equal to current assets minus current liabilities. It is called working capital because it is the amount available to operate your business on a daily basis. (Gross working capital is the amount of current assets.)

KEY LIQUIDITY RATIOS

The current ratio, quick ratio, and turnover of cash ratio are the three key liquidity ratios you should know.

The *current ratio* measures your ability to meet short-term obligations.

$$\text{current ratio} = \frac{\text{current assets}}{\text{current liabilities}}$$

A good general rule is that your current ratio should be greater than or equal to 2.0 (i.e., current assets should be at least twice current liabilities). If your current ratio is too low, you may not be able to pay your bills. In his book *Entrepreneurs in High Technology: Lessons from MIT and Beyond*, Edward B. Roberts reports that, of the high-technology companies he studied, a typical current ratio was 2.5. Companies in the electronics industry averaged 3.17.

The *quick ratio* is a variation of the current ratio; it is more of an acid test of your ability to meet short-term obligations. The quick ratio eliminates inventory (which is less liquid), and some people further discount accounts receivable by 25% to better reflect liquidity.

$$\text{quick ratio} = \frac{\text{cash} + \text{accounts receivable}}{\text{current liabilities}}$$

A safe quick ratio would be at least 1.0.

The *turnover of cash ratio* measures the turnover of working capital to finance your sales. The ratio should be below 5 or 6. Make sure you have sufficient working capital to finance your level of sales.

$$\text{turnover of cash ratio} = \frac{\text{sales}}{\text{working capital}}$$

KEY EFFICIENCY RATIO

The investment turnover ratio is the one key efficiency ratio you should know.

The *investment turnover ratio* measures your ability to generate sales in relation to your assets, which is especially important if your business requires a large investment in fixed assets.

$$\text{investment turnover ratio} = \frac{\text{net sales}}{\text{total assets}}$$

Altman's *Z*-Score for Predicting Bankruptcy

One interesting computation you can try is Edward Altman's *Z*-Score, which is intended to predict the probability of bankruptcy within two years. (Altman developed a few different models of the *Z*-Score using data from large companies, and his models, therefore, are not really intended for small businesses.) Auditors are required to recognize and report on possible business failure. If a business does fail and the auditor has not mentioned problems concerning the continuity of the business, the auditor could be exposed to a lawsuit. Do not be surprised if Altman's formula shows your start-up to have a high probability of failure—many of the numerators in the equation will be zero. At least you'll know where you stand; start-ups are a risky business!

$$Z \text{ score} = \frac{(\text{working capital})(1.2)}{\text{total assets}} + \frac{(\text{retained earnings})(1.4)}{\text{total assets}} + \frac{(\text{operating income})(3.3)}{\text{total assets}}$$

$$+ \frac{(\text{market value of common and preferred stock})(0.6)}{\text{total liabilities}} + \frac{(\text{sales})(1.0)}{\text{total assets}}$$

Z score	probability of failure
1.8 or less	very high
1.81 to 2.7	high
2.8 to 2.9	possible
3.0 or higher	very low

Insolvency and Bankruptcy

Many start-up founders will someday find their ventures to be "insolvent" or (technically) "bankrupt." You need to know what these terms mean.

INSOLVENCY

Insolvency may refer to either equity insolvency or bankruptcy insolvency.

Equity insolvency means that the business is unable to pay its debts as they mature. It is common for a start-up business to be equity insolvent (unable to meet its daily debts), yet have assets that exceed its liabilities in value. Such a business would be said to be *illiquid*.

Bankruptcy insolvency means that the aggregate liabilities of the business exceed its assets.

Similarly, it is common for a business to be bankruptcy insolvent yet be able to survive and meet its current daily debts.

Insolvency, while not in itself proof that your business will fail, should be treated as a serious warning signal—one that can lead to bankruptcy.

BANKRUPTCY

Bankruptcy is a serious condition that can lead to the liquidation or reorganization of your company in order to satisfy creditor or stockholder claims.

Technical bankruptcy is the term used when a company has already committed an *act of bankruptcy* while insolvent, which would allow a creditor to file a court petition forcing the company into formal bankruptcy. There are six acts of bankruptcy (which are specified in federal bankruptcy law), one of which is giving preference to a creditor during insolvency.

Burn Rate and Runway

You also will want to get a quick intuitive handle on your cash needs. To do this, examine how much you are spending each month, factor in any cash from sales that you will generate, and then compute how long you can last until you secure a new round of financing or achieve cash flow breakeven.

The *burn rate* (which is slang) is the net amount of cash a start-up spends ("burns") per month. *Runway* (also slang) is the number of months you have before you run out of cash. If you have $100,000 in cash and your burn rate is $25,000, then you have four months of life left, assuming nothing changes.

$$\text{runway} = \frac{\text{total cash}}{\text{burn rate}}$$

Always keep your eye on that point where you could run out of money, and do your best never to let it happen.

Sidebar 6.2 Trials and Tribulations in the Financing of One Start-Up Company

This is both a happy and a sad story. It tells of one of the more interesting small start-ups in the high-technology field. PPT (originally incorporated as Pattern Processing Corporation), based on exciting technology in an exciting field, got a great start and was supported financially for a long time despite six years of continuous losses. Two of the three founders left the company before it became profitable. New management took over to turn the company around, and the original exotic technology was set aside for a more practical variety. Included in this case study are many numbers, valuations, and percentages to give a realistic example of what you might expect in your start-up. Of course, there has been a lot of inflation over the years.

Background

In the early 1980s, Larry Werth, 34, decided to quit his job at Medtronic, Inc. (a high-tech medical products company in Minneapolis) in order to launch his start-up. A few years earlier, Werth had done some graduate work on an interesting technical idea for robotic machine vision—giving eyes to computers to inspect industrial parts. This was exciting technology that was being eyed by venture capitalists across the country. Control Data Corporation provided a popular low-cost incubator facility for many Minneapolis start-ups in its modern downtown building. Werth rented 500 square feet in the Control Data incubator with the aid of a business assistance grant from the Small Business Administration, which subsidized two-thirds of the first $10,000 of costs for business services provided to PPT by an affiliate of the Control Data Business Advisors Program.

High Technology

In the mid 1970s, Werth was a research assistant in the electrical engineering department at the University of Minnesota. There he invented a statistical pattern classification machine vision algorithm that was motivated by neurophysiology studies. His business idea was to cast this algorithm into hardware, creating a unique, high-speed device to offer to the emerging machine vision market. An interesting twist was that he would not disclose the function of the algorithm to his potential customers or investors, promoting instead only its benefits when applied to solving certain problems. Werth gave little thought to the potential market for his invention. However, members of the investment community were soon stumbling over each other looking for deals in the new and exotic machine vision and robotics industry.

Seed Financing

Werth wrote a partial business plan while employed at Medtronic and told several investors the story of his invention and of his passion to build a business around it. The business was incorporated December 9, 1981. For the next three months, while employed at Medtronic, Werth and company searched for capital and researched the availability of patent protection.

A few months later, two venture capital firms seeded the business with a total of $60,000 (enough to carry Werth's team for about six months) in exchange for 15.6% of the company. This valued PPT at $385,000 on a post-money basis. As soon as this seed capital was ensured, Werth and his two cofounders quit their jobs at Medtronic.

Werth's start-up team consisted of himself, Mike Haider (a financial specialist who also led marketing), and Larry Paulson, a sharp hardware design engineer. Werth's lean team, representing the bare necessities, was quite attractive, containing leadership, marketing, and quality engineering. Commencing April 1, 1982, Werth, Paulson, and Haider began receiving $35,000 annual salaries.

Start-Up and IPO at the Same Time

Because a new securities law permitted the creation of quick, small intrastate public stock offerings, in early 1983, less than one year after start-up, Werth and his team were members of a publicly traded corporation. Pattern Processing Technologies' IPO raised $300,000 in exchange for 44% of the stock, for a post-offering valuation of about $650,000.

Early Development Financing

PPT soon thereafter raised its total equity financing to $1.7 million.

Just before the IPO, Werth owned 129,600 shares (33.8%) at a cost of $800, Haider and Paulson each owned 97,200 shares (25.3%) at a cost of $600, and the two small venture firms owned 30,000 shares each (7.8%) with warrants to purchase an additional 40,000 shares each, for a total cost of $60,000. The founders' shares cost them about six-tenths of a cent per share (adjusted for splits and stock dividends).

Expansion Financing

PPT had raised over $10.5 million in private and public equity financing through 1991. Its stock price was published in the paper daily, and it did quite well from 1983 to 1987, rising from $1.00 to about $10.00. After six years of continued non-profitability, from 1983 to 1989, however, the stock was reverse split in 1989 into one share for every 20.

Shares sold for well over $2.00 in 1992, which is equivalent to about $0.10 adjusted for splits. PPT was not profitable until fiscal year 1990, and the founders' shares were substantially diluted in the meantime. Stockholders made money in late 1989 to 1991, as the stock rose from $0.50 to over $3.00 when the company finally made the transition to profitability on a quarterly annualized sales rate of $2.6 million.

With just under 2 million shares outstanding on a fully diluted basis, this small company of 25 employees had a market capitalization of about $5 million on sales of about $1.8 million. It is worth noting that the company had net operating loss (NOL) carryforwards for tax purposes of about $8 million. The value of this company for its NOL tax write-off potential alone would be worth about $4 million to an acquiring business in the 50% tax bracket.

Postscript—2003

PPT no longer utilizes the original technology upon which the company was based, and is one of the last surviving companies in the machine vision business. In 1989, Werth moved on to pursue his pattern-recognition idea at Electro-Sensors, Inc., with the backing of a related investor group. Werth notes,

> There is still value in the idea of casting algorithms into hardware to realize high speed. My technology was important then and it contributed to helping PPT survive while most others in that business failed.

Werth is right, and you'll want to make sure that you have technology fuel for your business. Werth came out of the experience whole—not rich, not impoverished. Werth suggests,

> Don't underestimate the slow pace at which industry makes purchases [of high-technology products]. Promotion alone won't change that fact.

In conclusion, if you too have a good idea, a little luck in finding funds, a willingness to leave your present job, and the passion and conviction to start your own business, the preceding story could be about you. Becoming more successful in your business than the PPT founding team, however, requires a more focused market- and customer-driven technology-fueled strategy.

You cannot go public as a start-up today unless you find yourself in an exceptional situation. You might, however, be able to go public in an irrational IPO market after your investors have put in several million dollars and if you have a new product with prospects for sales, even if you are toying with insolvency and have nil sales to date.

Finally, be cautious of inventing on company time and with company resources. If Werth's invention had been of any interest to Medtronic, he could have had a nasty intellectual property rights challenge on his hands.

Werth remains interested in start-ups and is planning to do another. This time he is doing his research and development first and focusing on a specific application (market need): computerized reading of paper forms filled out by hand. Along the way he has acquired years of valuable experience in running and growing a small company. He offers this advice to entrepreneurs in high-tech start-ups.

A true technological breakthrough can provide the vision and opportunity to drive a startup. The biggest challenge, however, is the market research required to identify the specific niche for which the breakthrough offers the most value and then to direct the start-up to a market-driven, solutions-oriented effort.

ELEMENTS OF A SUCCESSFUL START-UP

Part Three of this book really gets into the meat of things. Before you launch your business, you'll need to thoroughly understand the basic ingredients of a successful start-up. You will need a very clear map of where you must travel if you expect to get to a satisfactory destination.

The process of investigating your start-up's success factors is called *due diligence*. Before investors put cash into a start-up, they exercise due diligence to try to discover everything that could impact their business investment. You must do likewise. Investigate and master all the success-contribution elements that will make or break your business: (1) management team, including board of directors, (2) markets and customers, (3) products or services, (4) business plan, and (5) funding. These form the base upon which you will build your business.

These critical elements, being tightly connected, cannot be thoroughly examined out of context. The following chart illustrates the relative importance of each element for a typical start-up situation. As for other ingredients of success, such as luck and persistence, you are on your own.

Because it is so important for the entrepreneur to understand what makes a business successful, in this Part Three a separate chapter is devoted to each of these five principal start-up elements. In addition, for clarity, there's a sixth chapter devoted to the important topic of term sheets, which relates directly to the chapter on funding.

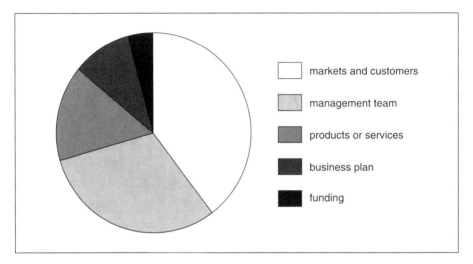

Five Controllable Ingredients for Start-Up Success

7

Create Your Management Team and Board of Directors

A great idea in the hands of a second-rate management team isn't going anywhere.

—Brad Silverberg, chairman and CEO of Ignition

Management

An old maxim of real estate is that the three most important factors in selling a house are location, location, and location. Arthur Rock, a venture capitalist, was quoted as saying that, in starting a new company, the three most important factors are "people, people, people." As is discussed throughout this book, there are several dimensions for success in selling your business, including people (management), markets and customers, products and technology, planning, and funding. This chapter focuses on the people (namely the management team), as well as your board of directors and your board of advisors.

You will start your business somewhere in the management completeness-experience grid depicted in Fig. 7.1. Will you start your business with a full or a partial management team? Will that team be experienced or inexperienced?

The value of your management team in the eyes of investors will be directly related to the experience and completeness of your team. One simple metric is obtained by assigning zero, one, or two points each for completeness and experience. The sum

	inexperienced (0)	experienced (1)	very experienced (2)
complete team (2)	2	3	4
partial team (1)	1	2	3
no team (0)	0	1	2

Figure 7.1   Management Completeness-Experience Grid

then indicates the overall perceived capability of your start-up's management to investors and customers. Which companies in the grid would you want to invest in or buy a product from—the 1s, 2s, 3s, or 4s?

It has been established that in order to achieve high growth and be successful in the long run, you will want to grow your business with a top-notch management team. There are many examples of successful start-ups founded by inexperienced management (Apple Computer, Inc., Sun Microsystems, Yahoo!, Google, etc.). In the specific case of Google, it was founded in 1998 by Larry Page and Sergey Brin, two Stanford University PhD candidates who developed a technologically advanced method for finding information on the Internet. Inexperienced founders sometimes turn out to be top-notch managers, and sometimes they have to be replaced. Frequently, the founders of successful companies stay on board but take different, "lower" positions on a greatly strengthened management team, and everyone benefits. The key is to identify when and if one needs to bring in more experience. In particular, you will have to decide for yourself how important and practical it is for you to be or remain the CEO. As an example, Yahoo! was cofounded in 1995 by Jerry Yang and David Filo, who were graduate students at Stanford, and the following year they added several seasoned executives to their team, including CEO Tim Koogle. The result was the creation of billions of dollars in shareholder value. Sometimes, a company later encounters rougher seas, and another change of management results. This was also the case for Yahoo! In 2001, former Hollywood movie mogul Terry Semel replaced Koogle as Yahoo!'s CEO.

Another prominent example is eBay, Inc., the largest person-to-person trading site on the Internet. This highly valued public company was founded as a pet project in 1995 by Pierre Omidyar, a software developer. In 1996 he quit his regular job to focus on turning eBay into a real business. Benchmark Capital made an investment, and the management team was expanded to include, among others, Meg Whitman as CEO and president. The Harvard Business School prepared an excellent case study of this success story, *Meg Whitman at eBay, Inc.* (which is listed in the Recommended Reading section at the end of this book). Under her leadership, a prosperous company prospered even more.

A weak management team is a deal-killer for many venture capitalists, even if the idea is outstanding. A wonderful business idea is a necessary, but not sufficient, condition. The investors must believe that the management team will be able to execute. Yes, the investors can help the company fill holes in the management team, but to satisfy the execution requirement, a strong enough team must already exist. Wonderful ideas don't last forever—they have a half-life. Venture capitalists don't want to run the company—especially when they are very busy, which is all of the time. A weak team is the number one reason investors pass on a deal.

Though a good market is also critical, without an exceptional management team even the most ideal market cannot be fully exploited. This is evidenced by the fact that many business plans with no product and no technical team have attracted financing when they were written by a proven management team and targeted toward a growing market that obviously had customers.

For a list of the questions most frequently asked by venture capitalists about the management team, see Sidebar 7.1, What Venture Capitalists Look for in a Management Team.

Some venture capital firms and other organizations have expressed their confidence in outstanding talent by establishing Entrepreneurs In Residence (EIR) programs, in which a few individuals "between opportunities" are given space at the firm and time to explore new market opportunities and new technologies. These individuals are often paid a stipend by the host firm. It's a form of incubation and focuses on the "next big idea," and the benefit to the host firm is that it has an inside track on investing in the opportunities that emerge. Typically, the entrepreneur in an EIR program has a specific idea or group of ideas to explore and pursue, with the goal of having a solid business plan in several months.

A more recent variation, largely unproven as a concept, is one in which a talented and experienced entrepreneur arrives with no specific idea in mind but with the intention of finding or creating something wonderful. Benchmark Capital, a top-tier firm in Silicon Valley, helped pioneer this concept and has hosted more than 20 entrepreneurs, leading to numerous liquidity events and the creation of over $15 billion in market value. Alumni of the Benchmark EIR program include successful Silicon Valley entrepreneurs Keith Krach, cofounder of Ariba, and Eric Greenberg, founder of Scient. Based on its EIR success in the '90s, Accel Partners, another top-tier venture capital firm, expanded its EIR program to inhabit the entire second floor of its Palo Alto headquarters. The point here is that venture capitalists know, in the final analysis, that people create shareholder value, and their best bet is to bet on the best and those with a good track record.

Numerous start-ups have achieved great success with a business strategy that turned out to be very different from the strategy set forth in their initial business plan. The fact is that strong executive teams have a significantly better chance of eventually getting it right. Looking at the other side of this coin, weak management teams are unlikely to be successful, even with a great business plan.

The size and commitment of your management team will have a lot to do with the reception of your business plan by the investment community. Stanley R. Rich and David E. Gumpert's *Business Plans That Win $$$: Lessons from the MIT Enterprise Forum* contains an evaluation system that captures the fact that the quality and completeness of the management team and product are important to investors. Figure 7.2, adapted from Rich and Gumpert, makes it obvious that investors prefer strong, complete management teams.

Venture capital investors would like to build their start-up portfolios based on 6s, 7s, and 8s. Less likely to attract venture capital are the companies that evaluate to less than 6s.

MIPS Computer, the subject of Michael S. Malone's book, *Going Public: MIPS Computer and the Entrepreneurial Dream*, was known as the $100 million company with the $1 billion over-the-hill-gang management team. Largely because of its solid management

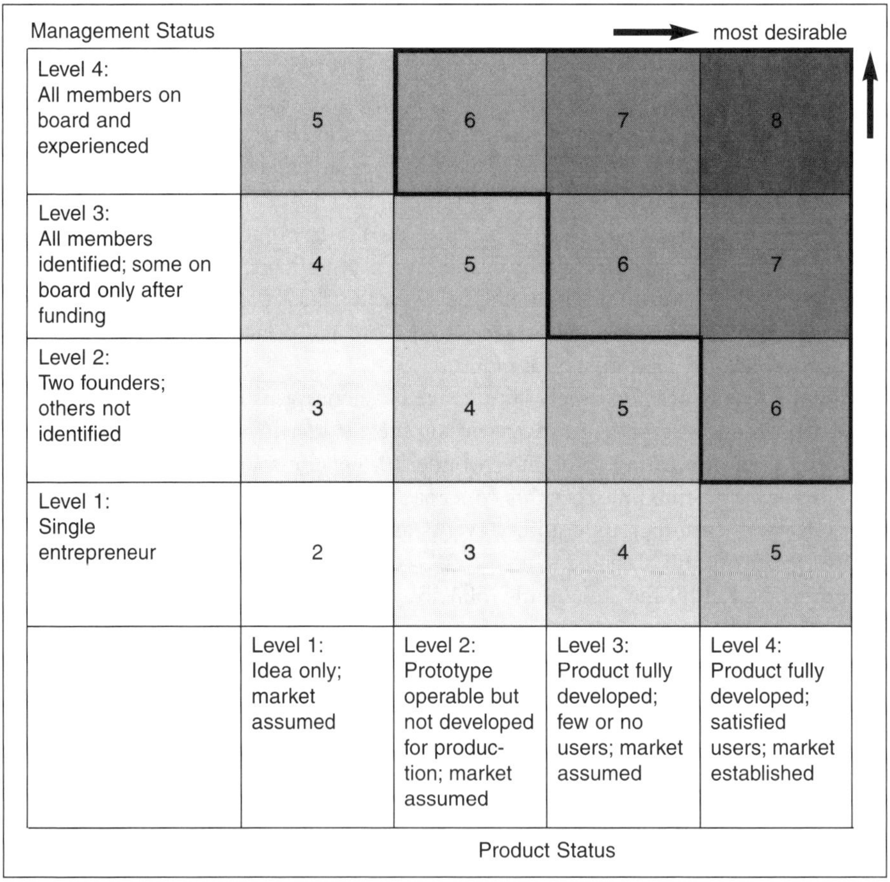

Management Status				most desirable
Level 4: All members on board and experienced	5	6	7	8
Level 3: All members identified; some on board only after funding	4	5	6	7
Level 2: Two founders; others not identified	3	4	5	6
Level 1: Single entrepreneur	2	3	4	5
	Level 1: Idea only; market assumed	Level 2: Prototype operable but not developed for production; market assumed	Level 3: Product fully developed; few or no users; market assumed	Level 4: Product fully developed; satisfied users; market established
			Product Status	

Figure 7.2 Team Size and Product Status in Business Plan Reception

team, MIPS was one of the first high-technology companies able to go public after the 1987 stock market crash.

Most start-ups are founded by people much like you. These founders have ambition, persistence, good ideas, and an ability to work with and motivate people. They may also have financial savvy. Founders are often persistent to a point of obsession. Unfortunately though, some founders may retain all control, give poor direction, make business decisions for nonbusiness reasons, hire ineffective relatives or friends, and be slow to correct operational problems. Worst of all, they may not be capable of learning from the past, thus tending to repeat mistakes. Will your start-up team have perfect, proven management? Probably not initially. In an imperfect world, how do you go about selecting quality team members?

A Kind of Marriage

The management team of a start-up will likely share more time and experiences, solve more problems, and ride rougher waters together than any other association of individuals. It really is a kind of marriage. Few secrets will or can be kept, and common interests and visions drive the survival of the relationship. Deep feelings, from respect to hatred, are likely to develop. Like marriages, many relationships will dissolve. It is vitally important that you choose the right team members at the beginning. Do not launch your start-up with any less due diligence than you would exercise before entering into a marriage.

If possible, consult or work part time with candidates before making any decisions. Get to know the people. Make sure they pass the chemistry test. If you like a good laugh now and then, but a candidate never cracks a smile, you two might not make a very happy team.

Integrity

Integrity, in the broadest sense, is the one personal characteristic you must not compromise when considering individuals for your management team. Yes, you want the smartest software developer in the world to write your software code, and, yes, you want the best sales professional to run your sales department, but in the real world you make some compromises on professional skill sets. However, integrity is different—it's the one ingredient you cannot afford to compromise. Life is simply too short. Do you really want to employ someone who brags about various little ways he cheated his last employer? Can you afford to rely upon someone who is just not trustworthy? So do your due diligence on a candidate's integrity, and don't ignore any little red flags that might pop up regarding integrity. Just because you can't prove something in a court of law doesn't mean you should ignore it. Professional investors also rate integrity as a "must-have" attribute—any question about your ethics or integrity can sink your ship like a torpedo.

For one venture capitalist's perspective on the most important personal characteristics of leaders, see Sidebar 7.2, Truly Great CEOs and Mentors.

Team Members

Your core start-up team will probably consist of three members.

- team leader (presumably you, holding the CEO and president titles)
- vice president of marketing and sales
- vice president of engineering (perhaps also holding the chief technical officer (CTO) title)

Together, this team will drive the business and determine what product to develop and how to build and sell it.

Reasonably soon you will need to add, at least part time, a chief financial officer (CFO) for financial controls and a vice president of manufacturing if your product has significant manufacturing content (unlike software). You should consider using a part-time bookkeeper before your CFO comes on board. From the start, you will want to keep accurate accounts and records. In the long run, you'll be miles ahead if you do things right the first time. An experienced part-time bookkeeper can do the job for you at a very low cost.

As CEO, you will have far too many duties to manage the entire business while also managing the engineering development activity. Many start-up entrepreneurs cannot let go of the engineering roles with which they have been associated and in which they find their primary strengths. You will have to make the decision to

- be the CEO and leave the engineering to someone else
- let one of your team members take the CEO position
- risk compromising the initial growth of your business by acting as both the CEO and the engineer

Some entrepreneurs might argue for the last option, pointing to the many success stories. However, in almost all of these cases, initial growth was limited, impacting the rapid creation of wealth. When the businesses were eventually successful, it was usually because the entrepreneur was able to grow to assume the CEO role full time, successfully replacing his or her part-time engineering position with a full-time engineering manager, or because the entrepreneur eventually relinquished the role of CEO, taking on the engineering management position full time.

Know Yourself

Before jumping ahead to build your winning team, you first need to get to know yourself. Dr. Philip B. Nelson of the Institute for Exceptional Performance is frequently called upon by top executive recruiting firms to measure the characteristics and competencies of candidates, compare that data with the desired position characteristics and competencies, and recommend individuals who would be compatible and synergistic in top-performing management teams. He utilizes a proprietary Position Suitability Profile System™ worksheet to plot the following characteristics and competencies.

- *Problem solving*—thoroughness, practicality, analytical ability, creativity, broad perspective

- *Motivation*—drive, determination, persistence, initiative, goal orientation
- *Work habits*—self-discipline, responsibility, decisiveness, integrity, dependability
- *Organization/planning*—planning, organization, setting priorities, punctuality, flexibility
- *Interpersonal characteristics*—self-confidence, amiability, persuasiveness, stability, perceptiveness
- *Leadership characteristics*—delegation, firmness, participation, recognition, example

Not every reader will have access to Dr. Nelson, but you can achieve similar self-analysis results with a little work.

- Get candid feedback from your peers on how you appear to them.
- Decide on the types of team members you will need to complement your skills, challenge you to do your best, and supplement your weaknesses.
- If you bring together team members with whom you are most comfortable, you may not end up with a well-balanced team. For example, if you are not a thorough person, but you feel most comfortable with similar people, who on your team will be thorough enough when you need it?
- Use a matrix to plot some of Nelson's characteristics, styles, and competencies of potential team members. Look for dangerous similarities or extreme incompatibilities with your personality.

A Winning Team

Now that you have a clearer view of your own strengths and weaknesses, you can visualize what characteristics and competencies in others will round out and complement your team. High-performing management teams must be compatible and synergistic. Each member must

- challenge the others
- provide mutual inspiration
- get along and work well with the others
- be able to perform in contained chaos
- maintain control despite the extreme pressure

One profile of successful winning start-up presidents (recounted by Charles A. Skorina, an executive search consultant with Charles A. Skorina & Co., in the *San Jose Mercury News*, July 8, 1991) provides a three-point checklist, useful not only for yourself but for your potential team members as well.

1. Winners thrive on risk.
2. Winners are incurable optimists.
3. Winners have dogged persistence.

Make sure both you and your team will thrive on the chaos often associated with a start-up. In all likelihood, at some point in time, key employees will leave, prototypes will fail, money will run out, or key customers will vanish. You must be able to stay the course, pursue the goal, and enjoy the game.

Successful Matches

Do more than just hope for smooth teamwork. If prolonged disputes or shouting matches occur in the frenzy of your start-up, it will be destructive to morale and performance. Look for good matches. Avoid the following incompatible differences in work habits and ethics, too many of which may signal danger in your proposed relationship.

- small company orientation versus big company orientation
- open and generous versus protective
- sense of humor versus humorless
- high energy versus low energy
- team player versus individual player
- honest and direct versus cagey and indirect
- sees glass as half-full versus sees glass as half-empty
- treats others with respect versus treats others as objects

If your values, goals, and objectives don't mesh with those of a proposed partner, it would be wise not to join together in a start-up. Assuming you have identified no serious conflicts, teaming with otherwise qualified old friends may work well if you can establish a decision-making process that works smoothly.

Signing on Management Team Members

You do not simply interview people to select them for inclusion in your team. You need to develop trust and respect in a relationship, and you must share a common vision of what the business can and should be. It takes time to find and meet the right people, and this step in growing your business is critical.

If you select even one poor team member, your venture is highly likely to fail. A start-up generally does not have the luxury of making such a costly mistake. Besides, beyond creating wealth, you will want more than anything else to make this an enjoyable adventure.

It's frequently said that "A" players actively recruit "A" players, and that "B" players hire "C" players. The best people, the "A" players, are likely to be actively involved in another opportunity, and it may take some patient recruiting over time to convince them to join your venture. You simply need the best people in your company, and the smart manager will welcome people at each position who are more capable than the manager at their respective jobs.

Make sure you understand your candidates' backgrounds: where they have succeeded and failed, what they have learned, how they intend to help run this business differently, and so on. Ask for references of past employers and coworkers, and speak with those individuals regarding the personalities and work habits of the candidates.

If you think an unproven management candidate has potential, consider whether that person be willing to step down to replace himself or herself with more professional management if need be as the business grows. Will your potential team members agree to move aside if they prove to be less than effective? You must create a team with a balance between doing and managing that will result in action. As technically oriented and creative managers, you and your team members must, if you discover an inability to manage among yourselves, be the first to suggest hiring your own replacements. Ask people such questions directly, though, and you may be surprised at the variety of answers you will hear. Ask, and then listen carefully to the answers. Do not rely on the assumption that your management candidates must be good to have gotten where they are.

The Entrepreneurial Team

Bob Hansens, past president of the Silicon Valley Entrepreneurs Club, artfully described the entrepreneurial team members and their related roles. It may be useful for you to think of your start-up team in terms of his structure, which is slightly modified and transcribed in Table 7.1.

Table 7.1   The Entrepreneurial Team

team leaders	achievement-oriented managers	technology team leaders	advisory board (part time)
chairman of the board	chief operating officer (COO)	chief technical officer (CTO)	entrepreneurial team members
chief executive officer (CEO)	chief financial officer (CFO)	vice president of engineering	providers of professional services (legal, accounting, etc.)
president	vice president of marketing	director of technology	providers of capital
	vice president of sales	chief scientist	industry experts and consultants
	vice president of manufacturing		university professors

As described in Ch. 2, one individual can hold multiple titles and positions. The CEO is the most important and, consequently, potentially the weakest link in a start-up. As the CEO, you must be able to manage teams of people who are difficult to manage.

As you begin adding key technical employees to your payroll, you will be looking primarily for technical competence. However, do not overlook that team-player quality that you sought in your management team. You will want the entire enterprise to share the vision and live the mission of the business.

Two qualities you should require are energy and enthusiasm. Employees with these attributes know no limits, think they can do anything, and often come pretty close to doing so in practice. Especially amazing is the extreme productivity of some of the younger and less-experienced employees who often exhibit this pure energy and enthusiasm. These individuals, usually hired at relatively low entry-level salaries, often rapidly become key employees in a business, and they deserve to be treated and financially rewarded as such. Do not hire solely on the basis of age, however. Age discrimination is illegal, and clearly not all young people are energetic and enthusiastic. Many older individuals still have the energy and enthusiasm you are looking for, in addition to their valuable experience, and they are likely to have a higher degree of loyalty. Also, while many young free spirits may produce terrific results for you in the short term, their long-term interests may reside elsewhere. The turnover of new college graduates (those holding their first jobs) can be quite high.

In building your dynamic team, learn from the experiences of other entrepreneurs. See Sidebar 7.3, Gary Kremen on the Entrepreneurial Spirit.

Board of Directors

Power of the Board

The board of directors determines how much you will be paid and has the power to replace you as the CEO, so it is natural that you would want control over who holds a seat on your board. When your company is first incorporated and before it is capitalized, you are the only significant shareholder and can appoint whomever you want. In California, you can be the entire board of directors by yourself if you so desire.

A board of directors is elected by the shareholders of the company and is empowered to carry out certain tasks as spelled out in the corporation's charter. Among such powers are appointing senior management, naming members of executive and finance committees (if any), issuing additional shares, and declaring any dividends. Boards normally include the top corporate executives (the inside directors), as well as outside directors chosen from both the business community and the community at large to advise on matters of broad policy. You should discuss with your advisors whether only you as the CEO, or other members of your management team as well, should be on the board. See Sidebar 7.4, Powers and Duties of the Board of Directors.

Evolution of Your Board of Directors

As your company moves forward and grows, the size, role, and importance of your board of directors should also grow. Therefore, consider and plan for the "evolution" of your board. As noted earlier, when you found your company you'll probably have a small, limited board and, in the early days, virtually no significant activity (such as setting strategy) will occur at the board meetings. At this stage, the board meetings are typically just rubber-stamp formalities to approve and document what has already been decided by you and your core group of founders and advisors. Any action that requires board approval (such as selecting officers and adopting a stock option plan) may be done by unanimous written consent without a board meeting.

However, as you get established and raise some seed money, you'll need the advice and help of an active board, and you may add an experienced businessman or two to your board. After the first venture round, assuming you contemplate raising money from venture capitalists, you will probably have a five-person board, so plan accordingly. It can be awkward to ask a board member or two to step down to make room for a venture capitalist or two. Either leave board vacancies to accommodate growth, or make sure your early board members understand that they may be asked to step aside later. In particular, if you initially place any of your cofounders on the board, make sure they understand that they will most likely be asked to resign later when other directors are added.

What a Board Should Do

The best-utilized boards will provide objectivity and sound judgment. Directors will question your assumptions, contribute to the resolution of specific problems, and bring new ideas to the table. Expect the board to review financial performance, marketing plans, key hiring decisions, and any other major development affecting the business.

How Often Does a Board Meet?

Venture-backed start-up boards usually try to meet every four, six, or eight weeks, or quarterly, but this varies significantly. An active, hands-on board is likely to meet monthly.

How Long Does a Board Meet?

Board meetings should last from 90 minutes to three hours, but many run the better part of a day in start-up situations when many issues, including operational matters, are to be discussed.

Selection of Directors

Because they generally want to retain some control over their investments, you will probably end up having investors on your board. It is generally wise to attract concerned board directors, and your investors will certainly fall into that category. Whether or not they will have too much vested interest in looking out for their finances is pertinent. Sometimes the board of a Silicon Valley start-up comprises only the funding venture capitalists and the CEO.

Investors regularly demand seats on the board as a condition for investing, even if they do not have sufficient shares to ensure their election. For example, it is not at all unusual for investors holding preferred shares to have expanded voting rights over the common shareholders, to facilitate their own board membership, and to perhaps control the board. Also, these investors frequently sit on and control two important committees of the board—the compensation committee and the audit committee.

If you have investors on your board, try to attract individuals who are experienced in your industry and can genuinely help. These people will have run companies themselves. You will want someone on your board who understands financial affairs and the problems of running a business profitably. You should find individuals with sound judgment and who hold positions of leadership in your field. All directors should be relatively free from conflicts of interest and be able and willing to devote the time required.

It is also recommended that you strive for diversity on your board. Areas of expertise that are most valued are legal, finance, management, marketing, and human resources. An ideal board for a high-technology firm might consist of a venture capital firm partner, a university president, a Fortune 500 company financial strategist, an operations manager from your industry, and a retired CEO of a related company.

The board of directors is important in the long run, and having a supportive and knowledgeable board is crucial to the success of a company and the well-being of its founders.

Edward B. Roberts, chairman of the MIT Entrepreneurship Center, in examining high-technology companies, found that boards typically comprise six to seven members (both outside and inside) with a variety of backgrounds. Representative professions prevalent on boards were, in order of frequency,

1. finance (venture capital, banking, private investing)
2. in-house
3. business (company-related, general)
4. consulting
5. academia
6. law

In addition, you should consider how each director candidate treats other people, especially CEOs and founders of start-ups. For example, in a situation where the CEO has to be replaced, some investor board members will err on the side of fairness and generosity (e.g., offering several months of severance pay, and continued vesting of stock and stock options during the severance period). In doing so, they may have the objective of making the involuntary termination reasonably amicable, with the expectation that the outgoing CEO will sincerely speak well of the company and its backers. Other board members, especially during tough times, will take a hard line on the termination and refuse to offer anything beyond the minimum required by an employment contract or applicable law.

A board of directors can be a very powerful source of ideas, guidance, and leadership. The wrong board can be a nightmare. Most boards prefer to let the CEO run the business, and only step in on a more frequent basis when they see problems. As CEO, you should be on the board, and you might very well occupy the position of chairman of the board. Practically speaking, however, the chairman position carries little additional power, especially if you are already the CEO.

It's helpful to have board members who understand that ups and downs are part of a typical start-up, and who are experienced in managing companies in tough times. A positive, stabilizing influence is invaluable when the seas get rough, which they will. So is experience in company exit strategies. In some cases the board may have to replace the CEO, and you want directors who will be able to do this in a professional and fair manner, with their eyes always on what is in the best interest of the company.

How Many Members Should Be on Your Board?

A start-up company can do well with a small board. A good recommendation would be to have between four and six directors. Janet G. Effland of the venture capital firm Apax Partners prefers to see five or seven, since with an odd number there is always resolution of a controversial subject. One workable combination for your initial board would be

- you
- an outside financial advisor (perhaps your part-time CFO)
- your first-round investor
- a highly respected business advisor (a potential second-round investor would be ideal, but be aware that most active investors do not have time for noninvestor boards)

Five is the most common number of directors for a venture capitalist-backed company after the first round of financing. At that time, the board composition most likely will be the CEO (you), one or two outside investors, and other outside directors who are not investors (except for the stock options you grant them) but who understand your business environment and are able to add a lot of value to your venture. Sometimes an additional non-CEO founder also sits on the board.

Compensating the Board

If a board member is a significant shareholder in the company, no compensation is required. Specifically, representatives of large investors (such as venture capital funds), as well as insider directors (founders and officers) usually receive no stock options or other compensation (other than reimbursement for out-of-pocket expenses) for their director services. They already have the motivation to be active, be attentive to the business, carefully review documentation, attend meetings, and perform committee work. The inside directors already own a lot of stock, and the investor representatives usually participate in their venture fund's investment via (1) their *management fee* (which is an annual fee equal to a percentage, typically 2%, of the fund's assets), and (2) their *carried interest* (also called the *carry*), which is a percentage, frequently 20%, of the fund's total appreciation.

If a director is not already a shareholder or a representative of a venture fund, you will want to offer stock or stock options (and possibly some cash, although you may only be able to afford stock or stock options in your start-up phase). With some exceptions, directors of private companies don't receive cash fees for their services as directors. (This is in sharp contrast to directors of public companies, whose compensation typically includes a cash component, partly because the public company can likely afford it, and partly because directors of public companies face a greater risk of legal liability). The amount of stock options granted to directors varies widely depending upon the stage of the company, as well as other factors such as the experience and status of the directors. You should think in terms of percentages of fully diluted capitalization. The earlier the stage of the company, the greater should be the percentage of stock for the outside director. A typical stock grant to an outside director is about 0.50–0.75% of the fully diluted capitalization after the first outside financing round, although many arrangements fall outside this rough estimate. This equity compensation usually vests over the same schedule that applies to employees of the company, although more rapid vesting is sometimes appropriate. If outside directors wish greater equity participation in the company, you should allow them to buy preferred stock in the company's financing round.

The vesting is intended to help ensure that those who stick with you get their rewards. Also, you may want to grant a smaller additional stock option each year to each of your outside directors. While people will sometimes serve on boards of large, prestigious companies for little or no compensation, more than likely you will need to compensate your nonstockholder directors. A survey by the American Electronics Association (AeA) (www.aeanet.org) found that of its 423 reporting private companies, 379 (90%) provided no compensation for inside directors. Slightly more than half provided no compensation for outside directors. Twenty-seven percent provided stock benefits. However, AeA private companies include some pretty large businesses, along with some smaller start-ups. Also, since the time of the AeA survey, equity participation for outside directors has become much more common. You should provide stock or stock options to your outside directors.

Management of the Board

Primarily, your management of the board will consist of making sure that it is composed of competent people who will put time and energy into helping your enterprise. Do not let directors run the business on a day-to-day basis unless a problem arises and you have no choice.

You should also set the tone for board meetings and try to organize the agenda to focus on crucial issues. It helps to give directors assignments to complete prior to the next board meeting. Do not turn the directors' meeting strictly into a show-and-tell by you for your investors.

Prepare for Meetings

By properly preparing for board meetings, you will help to manage the board more efficiently. Providing current financial statements and updates on major developments and carefully selecting the issues to bring to the board's attention will assist you in thinking through your business.

Before a board meeting, consider each issue and the options involved. Know what actions you want from your board, and let them know their part up front. Be proactive.

It helps to give premeeting information to your directors a minimum of two days before the meeting so they can be prepared. Also keep in mind that your company's attorney (often a difficult person to schedule) might act as secretary of the board.

Be aware that your board members will judge you, in part, by how well you plan and run the board meetings. How you perform and communicate with them will give them some idea as to how you work with customers and strategic partners. For some practical tips, see Sidebar 7.5, Five Things a CEO Should Not Say at a Board Meeting.

Responsibilities of the Board

The directors owe a *duty of loyalty* and a *duty of care* to the corporation and its shareholders, and a breach of either duty can result in legal liability. Although private companies face far fewer lawsuits alleging breach of these duties than do public companies, they are not immune. When these lawsuits do occur, they frequently involve allegations by minority shareholders that their rights have been violated by the majority shareholders. Your attorneys can provide you with a standard document on director responsibilities that you can distribute to the board.

Legal Liability for Directors

Since boards are legally responsible for the actions of the corporation, many people will not formally serve due to legitimate concerns about liability. Even though your legal counsel, in helping you incorporate and set up your business, will structure things under applicable law to reduce exposure for board members, members will remain somewhat exposed. Purchasing director's liability insurance, while it sounds like a good idea, will most likely be beyond your initial financial capability. The expense of liability insurance is reflected in AeA statistics that show that fewer than 10% of private AeA members provide director's liability insurance. Consult your legal counsel to determine how you should best address this issue in your start-up.

Advisory Board

Most start-ups establish a board of advisors that can provide independent business advice and contacts. Some companies also establish a scientific board of advisors. Advisory boards have become increasingly common, and they come in different sizes and with different roles. In addition to offering good advice, these advisors frequently are willing to invest some cash in your venture. If you want a board of advisors, you need to decide on what type of advice and services you need, the number of members, the experience and skills you seek, and the expected time commitment from your advisors.

These advisory boards sometimes have just two to four members, but frequently they are much larger, with a dozen members or more. When determining how many advisors you will have, first consider how you intend to use them.

Your board of advisors can help you get in the front door at venture capital firms, but be aware that venture capitalists will not invest just because you have an impressive list of advisors. The point here is that you should not waste time building a board of advisors solely for the purpose of having a marquee of names to wave in front of prospective investors. Also, investors will tend to value more highly the active advisor who is more a part of the start-up. The key is for you to decide what you want and manage it appropriately. Prospective advisors will want to know what you expect from them. For example, if you have a large advisory board, you'll probably have regular quarterly or bimonthly meetings, with some additional email communication between meetings. Don't make the common mistake of setting up an advisory board and then not using it.

Because these advisory boards have no real legal purpose, they invoke very limited legal liability exposure, and many individuals would be honored to be included as advisors. In addition to giving them the opportunity to invest in your company, you should grant your advisors stock or stock options, with the number of shares at about half or less what you offer to members of your board of directors.

Mentors

If you have managed to form a mentor relationship during your career, be sure to include your mentor in your start-up business activities, perhaps as chairperson of an advisory board. This is the time to reward such a valuable individual with some stock options and to keep him or her interested and involved in what you are doing.

Personnel Policies

As a practical matter, your start-up is not going to put in place all of the many written personnel policies that a large company has. Your attorney can help you put together a minimum starter set that meets legal requirements, and as your company grows, you can add policies and guidelines as appropriate. As always, common sense goes a long way toward anticipating and handling people issues that arise.

Since any best-selling book has to have a little sex and romance, following are a few comments on one area of concern for companies. Also see Sidebar 7.6, Interoffice Relationships. Although large companies spend more time thinking about this, small companies also run the risk of becoming defocused by silly (or perhaps deadly serious) office romances.

Sexual harassment has become a significant issue in antidiscrimination law. Garry G. Mathiason, senior partner in the San Francisco law firm of Littler Mendelson, one the nation's largest employment law firms, notes a major trend and risk: "In recent years I've been involved in more CEO terminations because of sexual harassment claims than any other type of claim." You and your team, of course, need to take sexual harassment laws and all other types of antidiscrimination laws seriously.

In general, there are two main types of sexual harassment: (1) *quid pro quo harassment* and (2) *hostile environment harassment.* Courts have ruled that an adverse job-related action against an employee (such as a termination of employment or a failure to promote) because of that person's refusal to respond to the sexual advances of a supervisor is a violation of Title VII of the Civil Rights Act of 1964. This is called quid pro quo harassment. As for hostile environment harassment, it can be caused by requests for sexual favors, unwelcome sexual advances, and other conduct (verbal or physical) of a sexual nature when certain conditions are present—and it can exist even if the complaining employee has not suffered psychological injury.

Title VII of the Civil Rights Act of 1964 also protects employees from discrimination based on race, color, religion, sex, or national origin. It applies to all businesses with 15 or more employees, although some states have passed comparable laws that apply to all businesses regardless of size. Although Title VII does not apply to independent contractors, in litigation there frequently is an issue as to whether or not the plaintiff is actually an employee. In addition to injunctive relief (such as reinstatement of employment), both compensatory damages and punitive damages are available under Title VII claims. These cases can also be costly and distracting to litigate.

The discussion in this section is intended to highlight just one significant area of employment law and, of course, is not intended to be complete. You should rely on your attorney in these matters, and remember that an ounce of prevention is worth a pound of cure.

Signed Agreements

It's important that you enter into signed written agreements with your management team, directors, and advisors, as well as other employees and consultants. This protects both the company and the individuals. Do this sooner rather than later. To delay is to send the wrong message to individuals who are committed to you and your venture, and you also run an increased risk of disagreement and even litigation. Too many entrepreneurs delay taking care of these critical "people" issues when, at the same time, they expect extraordinary effort from their team. Loyalty is a two-way street. Also, your prospective investors will expect you to have all appropriate agreements in place. If you don't, they may question your executive and managerial abilities. Your attorneys can provide you with standard form agreements that can easily be modified to meet your particular needs. Do these agreements correctly up front, and you will save time and money in the long run.

Sidebar 7.1 What Venture Capitalists Look for in a Management Team

In evaluating an investment opportunity, most venture investors look first for a strong management team. Most believe that a great idea in the hands of a second-rate management team won't be successful.

Here are some of the most frequently raised questions about the management team.

- Is there a strong leader?
- Does he or she think big enough?
- Is there a strong technical leader?
- Is there a strong business leader?
- Does the team listen well? Or are they defensive?
- Will they take feedback in a positive way?
- What type of culture would the leader create?
- Are the leaders adaptable?
- Are they passionate for a particular idea, or for making the company successful?
- Will the team be willing and able to intellectually adapt to other ideas if the current plan doesn't work?
- Do the team members understand and accept that they may not be the right team to drive the company in the long run?
- Will the leader and team be able to attract "A" players?
- What are their values?

Sidebar 7.2 Truly Great CEOs and Mentors

Few venture capitalists, if any, have a better reputation than does John Doerr, a partner in the prominent Silicon Valley venture capital firm of Kleiner Perkins Caufield & Byers (www.kpcb.com). Over the years, John has worked with countless entrepreneurs and has shown a Midas touch in backing numerous successful high-tech start-ups, including Lotus, Sun, Netscape, Intuit, and Compaq. Regarding a topic of great importance to him, he describes the most important personal characteristics of truly great CEOs and mentors.

- *High IQ and energy*—a strong communicator and educator
- *Integrity, quality, work ethic*—intellectually honest
- *Openness*—"The best idea wins."
- *Background*—get great experience, seek out great models and mentors
- *Team-building*—grow, delegate
- *Communication*—inspire and listen
- *Ego*—humility and humor
- *Extra points for humor*

He advises college students and others seeking career advice to look for the best CEOs and mentors—those with the characteristics listed here.

In listening to him talk about this list of characteristics, it's clear that the most important one is integrity. "Integrity is a binary state—you either have it, or you don't." If you don't carefully guard it, "it can slip through your cupped hands like water, never to be retrieved." Always speak the truth—one advantage is that you don't have to remember what you said.

Sidebar 7.3 Gary Kremen on the Entrepreneurial Spirit

Serial entrepreneur Gary Kremen, successful founder of several start-ups, including match.com (sold eventually to CitySearch Ticketmaster) and NetAngels (merged with Firefly, sold to Microsoft), has these views of the entrepreneurial spirit.

- Build for the team every day.
- Solve your boss'/shareholders' problems every day.
- Prove yourself every day,
    - to your customers
    - to your team
    - to your business model (i.e., the economic value of the customer MUST be more than the cost to acquire and support that customer).
- People hiring concepts:
    - A desire to win must be the most important thing in the entrepreneur's life—more important than family, personal health, hobbies, etc.
    - If an individual's aggregate personal risk profile is not high enough, get rid of him or her now.

Sidebar 7.4 Powers and Duties of the Board of Directors

The corporations code of the state or country where your company is incorporated will set forth the specific powers and duties of your board of directors (commonly called "the board"). The following discussion is therefore general in nature and intended simply to give you an overview of this area. You should rely upon local law and your attorneys.

The business and affairs of your company are handled by the board of directors, and all corporate powers must be exercised by the board or under its direction. The members of the board don't act individually; rather, they make decisions as a body. The powers and duties of the board of directors are broad and include the following.

- electing the officers of the corporation and determining their duties and compensation
- establishing corporate policy
- declaring dividends, issuing securities, redeeming shares, and the like
- approving the company's budget
- approving the adoption, amendment, or repeal of the corporation's bylaws
- approving various significant business transactions, such as material contracts, leases, and financial arrangements
- approving mergers and acquisitions and, in general, all other major corporate transactions

In addition, the board of directors, in accordance with local law and the bylaws, may establish committees of board members that have authority to act on behalf of the board in certain areas (such as compensation or audit).

The bylaws of the corporation will specify the procedures for how the board of directors works, including topics such as the following: regular meetings of the board; special meetings of the board; what constitutes a quorum; notice of meetings; meetings by telephone; actions by unanimous written consent; and minutes of meetings.

The day-to-day functions of the corporation are carried out by the officers of the company, in accordance with the policies and direction established by the board of directors.

Sidebar 7.5 Five Things a CEO Should Not Say at a Board Meeting

Ruthann Quindlen, a venture capitalist and author of *Confessions of a Venture Capitalist: Inside the High-Stakes World of Start-Up Financing*, advises that there are five things a CEO should avoid saying at board meetings.

1. "Our competitors are way behind."

   Quindlen sees underestimating the competition as a common mistake. So is belittling them. Too many CEOs have dismissed a competitor at a board meeting and then had to eat their words at the next meeting after the competitor has announced a significant new product or partnership. The board may question your judgment if you aren't objective about the competition. Also, competition is a moving target, and you should always assume your competition is working on things that you are not aware of.

2. "If that's the way the board feels, maybe you should get someone else to run the company."

   This is simply an emotional reaction and tends to kill rational discussion of the issues. It will cause the board to question your judgment and maturity. Also, it may cause the board to think for the first time about replacing you, which is perhaps what you feared most.

3. "I know we're behind plan, but a cutback now would hurt morale."

   This is Quindlen's personal favorite. The company is in trouble, has missed milestones, and is running out of cash. However, the CEO is most concerned about employee morale. Don't worry about what employee morale will be when the company hits the wall and goes out of business! We have seen many CEOs ignore the obvious—that if you are not proactive in managing cash, it will manage you.

4. "[silence]" (when what's needed is a statement that the CEO made a mistake or bad decision.)

   Quindlen sees this as a sin of omission, rather than of commission. Although it may be difficult, take responsibility for your mistakes and move on. Your board will respect you for your maturity.

5. "I have some surprise bad news."

   "The only objectionable part of this statement is the word 'surprise.'" A start-up has its ups and downs, and bad news is part of the game. You must share concerns with the board *early*. If you wait too long, they won't be able to help.

Sidebar 7.6 Interoffice Relationships

If you or anyone else in your start-up wants to date someone at work, here are some ground rules.

- Before fishing off the company pier, ask yourself whether, if worst comes to worst, you're willing to find a new job. If not, consider signing up for a dating service.
- Check whether there's an official dating policy at your workplace. In some cases, you could be required to report any budding romance directly to your boss or Human Resources.
- Set some ground rules with your sweetie. What will (and won't) happen if you break up?
- Think twice before going public. The gossip mill thrives on this sort of thing, even more so if this isn't your first fling at this workplace.
- Absolutely no sex at the office. The rest of us shouldn't have to be afraid to set our half-eaten jelly doughnuts down on the conference table.
- No messing with the interns.

Adapted from Sara Steffins, *Contra Costa Times* (and reported in *San Jose Mercury News*, May 12, 2001).

8

Evaluate Markets and Target Customers

It is better to select an audience and fit products to it than find a product and fit an audience to it.

—Freeman F. Gosden, Jr.

Traditional Business Model

The traditional business model strategy for starting a firm suggests that you

- stake out a niche market in which you will have dominance from the start
- serve your market through increasingly better customer service and support
- develop a refined grasp of your market's distribution channels
- create product identity, company identity, and customer loyalty
- establish insurmountable barriers to entry by competitors

Although a niche market is typically small, you should select a market segment that is as large as possible and yet

- is defensible
- is one you can eventually *dominate*
- is one in which you will not be competing with the big boys

Your first task, then, is to establish a niche market in which your technology and product can profitably play. To do that, you need to know your customers and markets.

Customers and Markets

Customers

When launching your start-up, you must have at least a vague idea of whom your first customers could be. Your persistence and enthusiasm do not guarantee that these customers really exist. Some start-up entrepreneurs have no idea to whom they will sell their first product or service, what the customer will pay, what problems will be solved for the customer, or what the customer's alternatives are. Even worse, more than one entrepreneur has believed that everyone will want to buy his product. Not since *Life* magazine has anyone sold anything to everyone, and even *Life* was forced to discontinue publication after decades of success. Unless you have a legal or de facto monopoly, like Microsoft in operating systems for personal computers, don't plan on selling to everyone. Today, markets are more specialized; customers demand products and services that will deliver exactly the benefits they require. In order for your technology to result in a successful product, you must identify a realistic, specific target audience—a niche. You must have a crystal clear vision of your customer.

Know Your Customers

Before launching your company, you should get to know some of your customers personally. Talk to several potential customers about your planned product or service, and emphasize that you want to know how you can help solve their problems. One hint: do not sell too hard. Let the customer do most of the talking (if he or she will). Listen well. Ask for elaboration or clarification on any point on which he or she seems hesitant or searches for words to describe. In your own words, repeat what you believe the potential customer said: "If I understand you correctly, you feel..." Then listen again for a confirmation or clarification.

Some general questions to ask are as follows.

- What problems do you need solutions for?
- Why does our product appeal (or not appeal) to you?
- Is there anything you see that is unique about our product?
- What should this product cost, and how could you justify the investment to purchase it?
- Who in your organization would be involved in evaluating our product and deciding whether to purchase it? Can you describe this evaluation and purchasing process?
- When would you need delivery? Would you be interested in acting as a beta test site (for preproduction evaluation)?
- How will your needs change in the future?
- What are your concerns or worries about our product?

- Will you be a repeat buyer if you are satisfied, or would you only need one of these products?
- What are your alternatives if you do not buy our product?

The key to your success will be an unrelenting focus on your customers. It is the customer who will ultimately determine whether you win or lose. Customers are not hungry pigs that will eat anything you put in front of them. Treat them with respect, and never take them for granted. The venture investor's *kiss of death* (i.e., a decision not to invest) most frequently goes to entrepreneurs who don't know their customers in depth.

Empathize with your customers. Look at your product and company through their eyes. Recognize that prospective customers are interested in your product not for its own sake or for your sake, but only for how it will solve significant problems for them. The *technologist's curse* is to talk excitedly about the wonderful features of the new product and, without realizing it, bore the prospective customer to death in the process. To connect with customers, you must articulate, in language they understand, both a clear understanding of their problems and a practical solution that offers them a high benefit-to-cost ratio. What is the *value proposition* for the customer? Does your product eliminate a major pain of the customer? How are you going to help the customer make more money? How are you going to save them money? Your product must solve real problems in a significantly better way, in the customer's eyes, than all competitive products. Invest up-front the time to understand the customer's situation in depth.

Your Customers as Risk Takers

You should recognize that your early customers, in buying your new product or service, could be taking risks as great as the risks you face as an entrepreneur. What if your product doesn't work as advertised? What if you go out of business and they are left stranded without a working solution, without customer support, and without a future product migration path? Consider how Exodus/Global Center, hugely successful at first, went into a death spiral when customers worried that web servers might not be supported if Exodus/Global Center went out of business.

When things don't work out, some employers, intentionally or unintentionally, punish the individuals who choose the new untried path. Betting on your start-up can be a *career limiting move* for these individuals. Over the last three decades, many have learned that, "No one gets fired for buying from IBM." In this millennium, many would say, "No one gets fired for buying from Microsoft." Companies like Cisco and Hewlett-Packard work hard to be seen as sources that are "safe" to buy from. You need to recognize this phenomenon. It affects your product and sales strategy as well as how you communicate with prospective customers and their representatives in trying to address their needs and concerns. Also, you should prefer and try to identify customers and individuals who are *early adopters* of new products. If you're dealing with a company that never takes a chance, why waste your time?

Understand the particular risks that your product brings to your prospective customers. Rigorously consider what will happen to the customer if your product doesn't work or if you go out of business and aren't there to provide support and product improvements. At one end of this risk spectrum are products that can have a catastrophic impact on the customer's business if they don't work right, perhaps even causing the customer's business to shut down. In these catastrophic cases, the typical relationship between customer and supplier is broad, deep, closely integrated, and very visible throughout the customer organization. A lot of customer (and vendor) time goes into each phase—evaluation, contracting, preparation, installation, testing, and operations—and there's an extraordinary level of commitment between the two organizations, from left to right throughout each organization, and from top to bottom. Both companies see the relationship as a major partnership, and integration efforts are difficult to undo or replace.

At the other end of the risk spectrum are products that have only an isolated, minor, and short-term impact if they don't work. One or two people may be somewhat annoyed, but the buyer's career is not on the line. The relationship has little or no visibility beyond a few people, and the product may even be a commodity product for which there are easy substitutes.

You need to know where you are on this risk spectrum as you write your business plan. The real risks to your customers are likely to have profound impacts on the structuring and operation of your business, and understanding them will help you to

- develop realistic times for your particular sales cycle
- develop risk-reducing measures and answers to expected customer concerns
- if appropriate, arrange for a backup supplier of your product or a source code escrow for your software (if you're a software company), or for a larger, established company to guaranty continuity of services if your start-up fails
- hire the right marketing and sales professionals

Try to understand your customer's point of view, especially when it comes to adopting new technology. Numerous factors go into the "change decision" facing customers as they consider new products and services, and most of these factors are ignored by vendors. Many dot-com companies and old-line companies wasted hundreds of millions of dollars in building independent B-to-B (business-to-business) exchanges or marketplaces for particular vertical industries. The broad concepts seemed wonderful and powerful, but the vendors grossly underestimated how difficult it would be for the players to change their behaviors.

Your Customers as Innovators

Appreciate and welcome the substantial product innovations that can come from your customers. Alfred D. Chandler, Jr. and James W. Cortada's anthology *A Nation Transformed by Information: How Information Has Shaped the United States from Colonial Times to the Present* punches holes in the myth of the heroic and visionary inventor who always has to convince recalcitrant customers and markets of the value of the new product or new technology. Essays in this anthology show how, especially in the early stages of new technology, many great advances are due to the synergistic innovations of both the inventor and the customer. Sometimes, the innovations of the customer are even more important. The point is that you need to listen to your customers! Don't take them for granted or assume that you have all the answers. Your customers are gold, and you should treat them as such. You should especially value customers who are willing to work with you and who embrace change rather than avoid it.

Markets

Beyond examining individual customers, you will want to look at the overall market characteristics for the product or service being offered.

- Is it a high-growth market?
- What are the market opportunities and risks?
- Are there many competitors in this market?
- What are the barriers to entry?
- Does your company have a market niche to itself?
- Will your market endure over time?
- What are the risk factors for failing?

These critical customer- and market-related issues are addressed in more detail in Ch. 9. Professional investors, such as venture capitalists, will scrutinize market issues as part of their due diligence process prior to committing any funds to your start-up. They may be in a better position to perform such evaluations than you are, since they have access to expensive market research studies and industry association reports (not to mention their extensive network and investment experience). If you can confer with your start-up's potential investors early on, you may uncover some very pertinent market information. This does not mean that investors will do the work for you. You have to research and understand your potential markets. It can be very embarrassing if, for example, your potential investor asks about a competitor of which you are unaware.

Competitive Market Analysis

In addition to identifying a healthy, growing market, you need to carefully evaluate your competition within this market to make sure you have a perceived distinctive competence. Figure 8.1 illustrates most of the important questions you should be asking as you evaluate different markets or analyze how a particular product idea might work.

Your business plan, discussed at length in Ch. 10, will contain the results of your analysis. You need to be able to give an account of other industry participants and prove that you have either a distinct competitive edge or a viable niche to yourself. You should compile a profile of each competitor (keep a separate file for each, noting niches served, market share, etc.) and a tabular comparison of the strengths

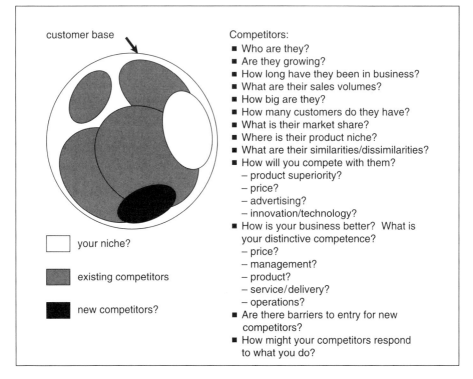

Figure 8.1   Competitive Forces in Your Marketplace

and weaknesses of each competitive product and company. A matrix with this information is both useful and common.

In your analysis, do not

- assume there is no competition
- miss any major players
- underestimate the strength of competitors
- ignore potential new competitors
- get so fixated on the competition that you become paralyzed or lose sight of the
  strategy you believe in

On the other hand, you should

- be aware of competitors' product plans and market strategies
- develop your own marketing strategy for counteracting existing and new competitors
- make perfectly clear to yourself and to your investors (in your business plan)
  what exactly will make your product better (i.e., how you will compete)

Marketing vs. Sales

Many people confuse marketing with sales. Sales is dealing directly with customers and is a developed art form. *Marketing* is enticing customers to consider buying a product and is an acquired discipline. More broadly, marketing is frequently characterized by the "four Ps," to which we explicitly add our own "S" for service, making it the "four Ps plus S." Although "service" should be included in the definition of "product" (the first "P"), this important element is so often ignored or glossed over that it is explicitly added here as the "S." The "four Ps plus S" then are

- product (what to sell)
- place (where and how to sell—distribution channels)
- price (how much to sell for)
- promotion (how to raise awareness, gain acceptance, and make people want to buy)
- service (service, warranty, and upgrade policies)

Marketing decisions determine what products a company is going to develop and sell, how those products will be positioned, to whom they will be sold, how they will be priced and distributed, and how their existence and features will be communicated to the market. Having the right products at the right price, as well as the right programs to effectively and profitably sell those products, is fundamental to any business.

Many entrepreneurs make the mistake of not charging for their product from day one. If you don't charge a fair price for your product from the beginning, you run the risk of not knowing if your customer likes it and will ever buy it.

There are two distinct branches of marketing, and the business world largely ignores this important distinction. The two branches are

- marketing the products you have
- figuring out what products you need to develop and sell in the future

Each branch requires a different skill set of the marketing professional—a person may be good at one but not the other, and it's the rare individual who is good at both. The first type of marketing (i.e., marketing what you have) is sometimes referred to here as *tactical marketing* (some call it *sales-related marketing*), and the second type is sometimes referred to here as *strategic marketing* (some call it *product marketing*). The important point here is not the terminology, but rather that you should be aware of the distinction and think about what the implications might be for your particular situation. For example, a particular marketing professional may be great at marketing ice to Eskimos, but he or she may have very little talent in figuring out what Eskimos really want.

Marketing Strategy

How are you going to enter the market, obtain a niche, maintain a market share, and achieve your stated financial projections? Figure 8.2 illustrates the infrastructure you

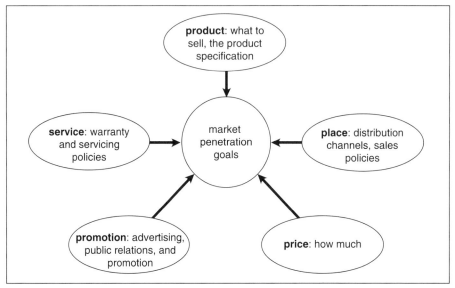

Figure 8.2   Marketing Strategy—the Four Ps Plus an S

must build to support your marketing goals. Taken as a whole, this will be your marketing strategy, and it will find its way into your business plan.

The definition of your product (the first "P" in the previous discussion) is critically important and is the subject of Ch. 9. Let's assume you have a pretty good idea of what your product will be. Then, based on your analysis of Fig. 8.2, some additional marketing questions you need to ask are

- What is the sales appeal (special qualities or uniqueness) of your product or service?
- How will you attract, maintain, and expand your market?
- What are your priorities? (Again, do not think that everyone is your customer. You cannot be everything to everyone.)
- How will you reach decision makers?
- Will you sell via salespeople, in-house staff or manufacturing representatives, direct mail, telemarketing, or trade shows?
- To whom will you sell—value-added resellers (VARs), systems integrators, or original equipment manufacturers (OEMs)?
- How, where, and when will you advertise—in trade journals, in magazines, or on television?
- How will you generate leads? How many leads are needed per sale? What is the cost per lead?
- How will you use your website and the Internet?

- How will you measure the effectiveness of your various marketing initiatives? What are the metrics? What milestones and dates will you set to determine whether to "fish or cut bait" for a particular product?
- How long is your selling cycle?
- How big will your orders be?
- How will you pay commissions?
- In what areas of the country will you concentrate?
- What are your prices, volume discounts, and dealer discounts?
- Will you be involved in price wars?
- How will you package and present your product?
- How will you collect your receivables?
- What services, warranties, and guarantees need to be offered? How will they be priced and provided?
- What product upgrades will be offered, and how will they be priced and provided?

As you can see, the marketing side of your business will consume a lot of your time. You can hire a marketing manager to take some responsibility in these areas, but as the CEO you have the ultimate obligation to make sure your business can sell, as well as make, an exceptional product.

Marketing Do's and Don'ts

Here are a few marketing tips.

- Don't underestimate the time required to establish a network for sales and distribution.
- Don't attempt to fill too many unrelated market gaps.
- Don't try to justify customer price by the cost to produce.
- Do justify price by the value to your customer.
- Do promote the marketable differences of your product.
- Do develop attractive packaging and establish brand recognition and loyalty among your customers.

Naming Your Company

In selecting a name for your company, pick a name (a brand, really) that will stand the test of time and convey the right image to the world you are targeting. This topic is included in this chapter on marketing because name selection should be driven primarily by marketing considerations. Who are the customers and other key constituencies you are concerned about? What image do you seek?

Avoid a name that is too cute or trendy. During the dot-com craze, thousands of companies had "dot-com" in their names, and thousands more used "net" or "planet" as part of their names. Because so many companies pursued this naming strategy, the names were weak and almost generic. When the bubble burst, countless companies switched to more traditional names, at some expense and with some confusion in the marketplace.

Here are some additional tips for naming your company.

- Choose a name that is easy to pronounce and has no ambiguity as to pronunciation.

- The name should be unique and may also be somewhat suggestive as to what your company does.

- The name should not be so precisely descriptive that it runs the risk of becoming inaccurate, misleading, or dated in the future, as your business grows and changes.

- The name should be pleasing to the senses and easy to remember.

- The name should be easy to search for on the Internet. (For example, exclusive use of general words in a company name makes company lookup almost impossible. General Computer Systems would be a terrible name for a new company.)

Of course, check to make sure the name doesn't conflict with another company's name or brand. Your attorney can check to make sure the desired name is available.

The vast majority of start-ups should focus on branding the company, not the product. Products come and go, but your company will remain. Many large, successful companies also focus on the company brand and not the names of particular products. Examples include AOL, Microsoft, Dell, and Amazon, and you can think of many more. Consistent with this, in many situations it makes sense for a start-up's first product to include the name of the company. Netscape's first product was Netscape Navigator, and Netscape became very closely identified with the Internet. As an entrepreneur, you will naturally be very focused on your first particular product, and you thus may make the mistake of branding the product, rather than your company. So take some time to form an overall branding strategy that makes sense, and select a brand for your company that will stand the test of time.

Leverage Technology and the Internet to Understand Your Customers and Markets

Be creative and smart in using new tools and technologies that can help you understand your customers and markets better, faster, and at lower cost. Major advances will continue to be made in the development of web-based productivity tools and processes that offer sales and marketing professionals a competitive advantage in obtaining, analyzing, and exploiting information relevant to their businesses. The wise use of information technology, with the Internet at the core, has increasingly become a focus of enlightened CEOs at companies large and small, and you should lead the charge at your start-up.

Validation

It is absolutely essential that you *validate* your product or service in the marketplace. Do not underestimate the amount of time and effort this requires. As the CEO of the company, you have a key role here. Yes, you want the best strategic marketing person in the world on your team and driving this effort, but you, as the CEO, must also satisfy yourself that the company is on the right track. This will involve talking with far more customers and prospective customers than you can imagine. Although you won't have enough time to perform all the important tasks that should fall to a CEO, you must make time for this important top priority. Validation is not a squeaky wheel that demands grease—still, you must attend to it on your own volition, before it topples your cart.

It would be incredibly demoralizing for you and your team to spend enormous time and resources on creating and launching your new product, only to find that no one was buying it. This happens frequently with start-ups and is probably the most common management mistake leading to company death. The importance of understanding your customers, the competitive environment, and your basic business model cannot be understated. You must empathize with the customer, get inside the customer's mind, and listen carefully. Examine carefully, with a good measure of skepticism, the key assumptions your team may be making. Be aware of *groupthink* among your team members, which can lead to poor decision making.

The extra time spent on this validation process will be worth gold. Even if it confirms you are on the right track, it will almost certainly lead to various tweaks of your strategy, or important refinements or changes in your product, which may make the difference between pretty good success and an enormous win for your company.

9

Define Your Product or Service

A rat trap? A rat trap? I thought you said you wanted a cat trap!

—Terry Furtado, Mechatronic Technologies, Inc.

Most people, especially engineers, believe they need to invent a perfect new product to start a business. This is not so! The sections on market pull and technology push in Ch. 4 emphasize that you should strive for superb execution in developing and marketing a perhaps less-than-exceptional product for which there exists a market, rather than for less-than-exceptional execution in developing and marketing a superb product for which there may be no customers without missionary sales efforts. Ideally, of course, you will have the best of all worlds, developing an exceptional product and doing an exceptional job in marketing it to an existing market.

The purpose of this chapter is to understand a little bit more about

- choosing the right product for your start-up
- marketing and competitive-analysis considerations in light of your chosen product
- exceptional product attributes
- producing your product

Choosing the Right Product

You will notice that this section discusses only products. This is because, in a sense, a service is also a product. Ideally, if your business provides a service, it can be replicated and marketed much like a product and, also like a product, it can represent a high-growth, high-profit-margin opportunity. In general, when the word product is used in this book, it means either a product or a service.

The term *growth* is the key word here and is discussed in detail in Ch. 5. A service business is a perfectly acceptable way to create wealth so long as it is a growth business. Many franchises fall into the category of service businesses, but the operation of one is not likely to be a high-growth opportunity. It follows, then, that the way to make money is not by buying franchises (unless you buy lots of them), but by selling them.

Assuming you have selected a product with which to start your business, do not forget the concept of service altogether. Rather, you must develop a solid strategy for the servicing of your product, and then stick with it. Good service is an extremely powerful differentiator, as Davidow emphasizes in *Marketing High Technology: An Insider's View*.

> The key is to convert great devices into great products. When a device is properly augmented [with service] so that it can be easily sold and used by a customer it becomes a product.

It is worth noting that very successful companies, such as IBM, have knowingly sacrificed technology leadership at times in order to attain service leadership. The combination of excellent service and a good basic product usually works better than does the approach of selling a poorly serviced, exotic, high-technology product.

It is also noteworthy that several developments (most of which are Internet-centric) have contributed to a tremendous expansion of opportunities to develop and offer services, sometimes at the expense of traditional products. Many start-ups have creatively based their business plans on such new developments and have helped shape new industries. For example, see Sidebar 9.1, Rapid Growth in Opportunities to Deliver Services.

Change creates opportunity. Be alert to major new trends that may present opportunities for you and your start-up. Try to exploit the natural advantages of a start-up, which include agility and lack of legacy problems. Creatively view the landscape. There may be a novel way for you to grow rapidly and profitably.

Finding Good Product Ideas

Studies by Edward Roberts of MIT indicate that most high-technology product ideas for new companies come from positions held with previous employers (source organizations) of the start-up's founders and key employees. Most entrepreneurs get an idea for a product or service based on their current or prior employment.

During the dot-com madness, many entrepreneurs picked their ideas almost out of thin air, rather than basing them on prior employment experience or any other valuable well of experience. For example, some people created Internet retail start-ups for various products (such as pet supplies) without any retail experience, other than the fact that they had occasionally purchased cat food.

Other sources of product ideas are customers, customer-sponsored research and development, and product line evolution. Market- and customer-oriented product ideas usually prove to be the best. In fact, ASK Computer founder Sandra Kurtzig says in her book *CEO: Building a $400 Million Company from the Ground Up*, "Virtually every ASK product evolved from discussions with and suggestions from our customers."

If you don't yet have your own company, you obviously don't have customers with whom you can talk, but you can talk with a range of people who might become your customers. If you're reading this book, you probably have some entrepreneurial ideas you've been kicking around. Whatever the area of interest, try to meet with people already involved in it. Don't operate in a vacuum—get out into the real world.

Competitors are also a source of new product ideas. Microsoft is especially adept at monitoring the activities of its competitors and other innovators for new ideas. You, of course, don't have the resources and clout of Microsoft with which to attack a competitor head on, but your analysis of the current landscape may suggest a new product twist or market niche that could lead to success.

Attendance at technical conferences and trade shows is always a rewarding, if exhausting, exercise, and you will see the latest products being offered at these forums. These events are great opportunities to network, ask a lot of questions, and creatively find and explore ideas for new products.

You should also subscribe to all the trade and business magazines and websites related to your technology area in order to keep abreast of new competitive products and trends. Most of these magazines are free, controlled-circulation publications and, of course, the enormous amount of good information available on the Internet is mostly free. To obtain higher-level magazines such as *Electronic Business*, you may have to fill out a longer reader qualification form, but information about you and your start-up should easily entitle you to a free subscription. You would typically fall in the lowest "check-the-box" answer for various questions on the form; for example, "less than $25 million" for company revenues, "under 100 employees" for number of employees, and you make all purchasing decisions for your start-up.

Finally, subscribe to a few general business periodicals such as *Inc.* magazine, *Business Week*, *The Wall Street Journal*, and *Success*. *Wired* may also appeal to you. *Forbes* is probably too Fortune 500 oriented, and *Entrepreneur* may be too blue-collar, small-business oriented for your tastes.

Means to an End: Do You Sell the Drill Bits or the Holes?

Apply your technology to develop a product that delivers a benefit to your customers. The most important lesson for an engineer to learn is that one does not sell technology, one sells benefits. It's been said that "the hardware store owner does not sell drill bits, he sells holes!" You must first find the needs in your market—then you can design and develop your product. Again, your company must be market- and customer-driven and technology-fueled. This is not to say that you need to be marketing driven. A good product that fills a compelling need and delivers a compelling benefit can be sold with normal marketing effort. You will note that almost all discussion on selecting a product takes us back to marketing principles—not to state-of-the-art technology.

Do Not Confuse One Product with a Business

Many engineers have a good idea for a single product. Your market analysis will tell you whether or not you will be able to grow a business based on a single product. In almost every case, though, you will need to identify a family of related products in order to build a solid business. Always be thinking in terms of a product family and growth potential. This simple observation is often overlooked in the excitement of a start-up.

It is a good idea to have two folders on your desk and on your computer labeled "next year" and "five years out." As they come to you, put ideas and thoughts in these folders for future analysis. Keep clippings, too, of articles that relate to your technology and marketplace. Brainstorm, and constantly consider new products your company could develop and produce. At any given time, innovative corporations, such as Minnesota Mining & Manufacturing (3M), derive more than 30% of revenues from products produced in the previous five years. 3M lives by the slogan, "We are forever new." Many large, successful companies in computers, electronics, telecommunications, and other high-technology markets get more than 50% of their annual revenue from products introduced within the previous three years. Follow the successful models.

Marketing and Competitive Analysis Considerations

Product Positioning and Your Competition

The temptation to develop a particular product based on your technology fuel must be viewed in light of product positioning analysis. Figure 9.1, motivated by Francis and Heather Kelly's *What They Really Teach You at the Harvard Business School*, illustrates that a successful product must have a perceived benefit to the customer over other similar products in terms of price and/or performance (as evidenced by feature differentiation).

Competing on the basis of cost alone is clearly an option. Commodity products such as personal computers, components for personal computers, web hosting fees, bandwidth, and caching services may gain market share primarily on the basis of price. If a technology enables you to produce a needed product at a cost advantage, then it is a reasonable candidate for your start-up's first product. Cost advantage alone will not guarantee you a market presence, however. Even if you could develop a software program equal in functionality to Microsoft Word or Excel and sell it at half the price, it would not take off. Notwithstanding a judicial determination that it violated antitrust laws, Microsoft has the ability and desire to do whatever it takes to kill its competitors. This difficulty in competing on the basis of price alone, of course, does not apply only to Microsoft. Reflect upon how your competition may

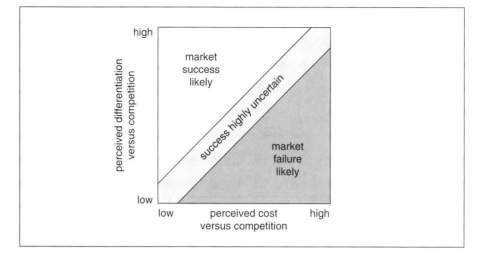

Figure 9.1   Perceived Cost vs. Perceived Differentiation Model

respond to your initiatives. They may be more willing and able to lower prices than you think (or even to give away the product—consider what happened in the browser battles between Netscape's Navigator and Microsoft's Internet Explorer). Also, even if competitors don't adjust their pricing, there typically are some hard and soft issues that make it difficult to unseat an incumbent. Customers usually have a certain level of comfort with the familiar and may perceive a better deal with the entrenched incumbent due to subjective factors such as customer service, future product upgrades, and switching costs. Never forget: perception is reality.

Competing based on perceived differentiation of product features and performance is your alternative. Differentiating features may be solely product related and highly visible, and there are many examples of these. Three-dimensional data representation and charting capabilities were added to the traditionally two-dimensional spreadsheet program. *Graphical display cell phones* replaced *alpha cell phones*, which in turn replaced those that were just numeric. Self-updating antivirus software was more compelling than static versions of such software. Or, differentiating features could be less tangible, such as your company's reputation, service, delivery, training, and product support.

Figure 9.2 is merely a single rough snapshot of the complex Internet service provider (ISP) market, and you may look at the market differently. Several product features and performance measures, along with company considerations, are lumped together to arrive at the very subjective positioning that is shown. There are hundreds of ISPs of all sizes. Many have failed, and the industry is rapidly changing. Therefore, the purpose of Fig. 9.2 is simply to introduce the concept of visually representing a product's (or company's) position in the market. There certainly are many other ways to slice and dice the ISP market. For example, the *X*-axis in Fig. 9.2 could represent

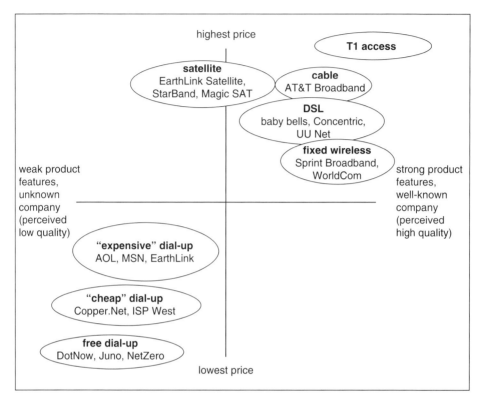

Figure 9.2   Positioning of Internet Service Providers (ISPs)

just one of several variables of interest, and a separate diagram (sometimes called a *scatter diagram*) could be prepared for each variable. Such variables of interest in the ISP market might include

- speed (both download and upload)
- reliability and service
- availability in the market (e.g., some products are available in only a few locations and some have been widely rolled out)
- perception of the vendor
- negative product features (e.g., pop-up ads, limited access time) and so forth

Also, you might further segment the analysis, depending on whether the product is intended for business or home use.

Before you launch a start-up with your product, plot its positioning with regard to your competition and verify that there will be sufficient perceived benefits in cost and features.

When you analyze your product's positioning, you'll also need to consider the issue of vendor stability from your customer's point of view. How big a risk is your customer taking in doing business with your start-up? What is the pain level if you go out of business? In some markets this is of little concern. In other situations it's a deal breaker. Many large companies bent over backward in the late 1990s to do business with high-tech start-ups, but the bursting of the Internet bubble turned things sour. Large companies that suffered when some of their start-up partners died now look especially carefully at a vendor's stability. As a result, there are some markets that simply are not viable for start-ups. This is discussed more in Ch. 8, in the section entitled Your Customers as Risk Takers. You cannot spend too much time carefully listening to your customers and really understanding their needs and perspectives.

Maintain Patent Protection or Other Proprietary Advantage

If there are technical reasons why your product can deliver better benefits to customers, and if those technical advantages can be protected through trade secrets, copyrights, or patents, your potential investors will be pleased to hear it. These types of protection can provide entrepreneurs with an opportunity for a head start on their competitors, along with a period of time during which they alone can handsomely profit. Many prescription drugs fall into this category. While they are under patent protection, the manufacturer can often charge aggressive prices for those products in heavy demand. Look at your product ideas in this light and try to identify similar opportunities.

Evaluate your proposed product against the competition. One rule of thumb is that, in order for a customer to switch camps, a new product should have 5 to 10 times the advantage over an existing product in terms of price and/or performance. A popular story illustrates this point. Ely Callaway, a 72-year-old former textile tycoon and newcomer to the golf business, catapulted his eight-year-old Callaway Golf Company from a tiny specialty outfit selling mostly novelty clubs into the fastest-growing golf club maker in the country. Callaway explained in a *Business Week* interview,

> You've got to create a product that is demonstrably superior to what's available in significant ways. And—most important—it has to be pleasingly different. That's all there is to it. Simple.

His golf club was more than twice as expensive as a normal driver, but it had a much sought-after larger sweet spot due to its revolutionary design consisting of a larger head with better weight distribution.

At the same time you are working hard to develop and protect your intellectual property, you need to respect the intellectual property rights of others. Investors don't like to invest in problems. A proposed venture investment can die on the vine if your investors learn, in the due diligence process, that you have misappropriated the ideas or technology of a competitor (especially a former employer) or otherwise acted in a cavalier fashion with respect to the rights of others.

Play in a Large Enough Market

One of the biggest mistakes engineers can make is trying to start a business in which they will develop a specialized product with a worldwide market potential of only a couple of million dollars. Not only should your target market segment be large enough to sustain your company, it should also be healthy and growing.

You've heard that venture capitalists want very large markets. That's true, but there's more to the story. Venture capitalists really want the individual companies they invest in to become very large. Viewed this way, a large, growing market becomes the means to an end, and not the end in itself. Many investors use a simplistic formula to evaluate how big your venture could become.

(market size)(market growth)(your venture's contribution) = size of your venture

Note carefully: In the investor's eyes (and in your eyes also), all three factors on the left side of the equation are critical—not just any two. At the same time, the one factor over which you have the most control is the third factor, your venture's contribution. Just because your market is large and growing doesn't mean your venture will be successful. To prosper, your company must make a large, valuable contribution in that market—and your valuable contribution must be crystal clear to your prospective investors, or they won't invest in you. Think about it. Investors have choices. If they want to play in an identified attractive market, they will choose to invest in the company they believe will make the biggest contribution in that market. Your job is to convince them that you are the horse to bet on in that race.

Recognize That Markets and Competitors Are Moving Targets

Markets and competitors don't stand still. Without becoming obsessed or excessively paranoid, role play and reflect upon what your competition may be working on. In developing their plans and projections, many companies mislead themselves by using only current information about a competitor's products, costs, and pricing. An experienced duck hunter knows he has to shoot ahead of the duck if he wants to eat duck. Venture investors are especially skeptical about competitive advantages that can be effectively wiped out by the stroke of a competitor's pen (e.g., a price reduction).

Avoid Playing in a Marketing Market

Marketing-driven companies (such as ones selling cigarettes, food products, or perfume) thrive not only on the quality or uniqueness of their products and services but also on their unique methods of promoting and selling their products. This is not the market you should be in.

You may have a technical idea for a new razor blade that will work better than any on the market. To sell this razor blade, however, you would need to compete against giants who spend tens if not hundreds of millions of dollars to introduce such new consumer items. As a technically oriented entrepreneur, you should stick to items that do not compete in the everyday consumer market.

Identify Concrete, Real Customers

If you can list the names and phone numbers of two to five people who, when asked, "Would you buy this product for this price now if it were available from this person?" would respond "Absolutely, yes!" then you are on the right track. Having these customers lined up will do amazing things with regard to investors' receptions of your business plan. In fact, some of these potential customers are good candidates themselves for seed-level funding sources.

It is also important that you understand the buying cycle of your customers. Many big-ticket items are dearly wanted by customers, but the customers have to budget for them. This can easily add a year or more to a purchase action. The uncertainty of capital expenditure cycles, which ultimately influence buying behavior in every industry, is also a factor.

Be Careful of Disruptive or Revolutionary Technologies

Chapter 4 discussed the importance of being market-driven in determining what products your company develops, and the difficulties in trying to penetrate a new market with a new product. (See Table 4.1 and the related discussion.) However, if you have what you believe is a truly *revolutionary* or *disruptive* technology, don't lose your enthusiasm—just be especially careful in how you proceed. You must be rigorous and critical in looking at your particular situation. One problem you face is that customers for your novel product may not even exist (or they may be difficult to identify), which means you can't talk with them to get the critical market information you need up front.

Partnering early with a large potential customer such as Cisco or IBM may be the best solution, if you can do it, provided that the large potential customer is willing to explore very different (and probably much less expensive) alternatives to the products they currently use. This will help you immensely in determining your product's specifications and whether there will even be a viable market when you're ready, and it will help give your start-up credibility. However, make sure your product is salable to lots of customers and doesn't become a "one-off" special that meets only the requirements of your large partner.

If you are especially interested in learning more about disruptive technologies, read *The Innovator's Dilemma*, by Clayton M. Christensen, who coined the phrase. With a case study focus on the disk drive industry (and other examples), he explains how and why dominant companies, notwithstanding their large budgets for product development and their focus on customers, frequently lose the marketing battle to new competitors with innovative products. Disruptive technologies often create lower-end products that are not fully appreciated or valued by the existing, mainstream customers (or the dominant suppliers). These new products, however, may be attractive to new or emerging markets and may evolve over time into innovative offerings that take over the older, mainstream markets. Mr. Christensen draws a distinction between innovations that are *disruptive technologies* versus those that are *sustaining technologies*, and he explains in detail why dominant companies are good at exploiting sustaining innovations but frequently fumble the disruptive opportunities.

A venture capital firm can be helpful when it comes to exploiting disruptive technologies, if you can attract a good one. On the plus side, they may be attracted to the possibility of a very big win, and their experience and contacts can be invaluable. However, they are not interested in funding long-term research efforts. Rather, their approach would be to try to help you *validate* the technology and market by setting up meetings and perhaps tests with some large potential partners. A key goal here for the venture capitalist would be to understand and minimize the market risk as soon as possible, which they see as the biggest risk faced by new ventures. Again, they are not interested in simply funding research. Yahoo! is a good example of a company that successfully offered disruptive technology.

Don't Compete with Microsoft

Venture capitalists avoid any market space that Microsoft occupies or is likely to target. From time to time, Microsoft even announces its plans to enter certain markets, which serves as a warning to potential competitors to stay away. Yes, there are examples of companies that have successfully been sold to Microsoft, but it's dangerous to assume that Microsoft will buy your company. They may prefer to annihilate you. Also, a few companies (such as McAfee and Norton in the operating system utilities market) have successfully competed with Microsoft, but those exceptions are perhaps due to Microsoft letting their competitors have the market segment without a major battle.

Of course, there are many markets that are dominated by one or two competitors, and Microsoft is simply used here as the most compelling and vivid example. (See the section entitled "Rule of X" Competitors in Ch. 5 for more about this.) Also, the admonition not to compete with Microsoft is often used generically, referring not specifically to Microsoft, but rather to the particular dominant competitor (say, Giant Incorporated) that is entrenched in your target market. So, the prospective investor who advises you not to compete with Microsoft may be referring to another company, or he may simply be telling you, in general, to be careful about competing with the big boys.

A market that is dominated by a few large competitors sometimes has room for a few profitable specialist companies. If your plan is to become a specialist company, you need to be especially clear in your strategy and execution.

Make Your Product Easily and Clearly Understandable

Many engineers concoct elaborate product ideas. That is, when asked, "What do you intend to develop or sell?" they need 15 minutes to answer.

You must be able to describe your product and its benefits with utmost clarity. As one venture capitalist is fond of telling his courting entrepreneurs, "When you tell me what your product does and why someone needs it, I want to hear an answer that's as clear as if you were describing the function of a parking lot; everyone knows what parking lots are used for, and why they are needed." If you cannot describe your product in simple, understandable terms, it is unlikely that your potential customers will even know that they need your product.

Exceptional Product Attributes
Developable and Producible in a Timely Manner

Heavy investment in manufacturing plants and equipment, such as that required in semiconductor manufacturing, is risky and expensive. On the other hand, products with low manufacturing costs, such as software, can be difficult to manage in terms of product development and maintenance. Make sure that you do not select a product that will take too much time and money to develop and produce. Again, to yield high returns on investment you need to attain rapid profitability.

Time to market is critical in this atmosphere of time-based competition. You need to be able to bring your first product to completion in a short time frame. Kurtzig of ASK Computer stated the case well in her book *CEO*.

> The faster my rudimentary product hits the market, the more money my potential users would save—and, of course, the faster I'd begin earning royalties. I didn't want to fall into the R&D trap of trying to create the perfect mousetrap. The trick is to be in the marketplace just as the demand for it is accelerating.

High Gross Margins

Software is probably one of the highest gross margin businesses an engineer can start. Because you are small and have limited capital, you need to be able to rapidly produce your first products at low cost and sell them for an aggressive price.

Substantial Collateral Revenue

A good product generates revenue from collateral items such as service and maintenance contracts, accessories, updates, data subscription services, and operating supplies. You want your customers to keep coming back to you.

Clear Distribution Channels

Before making a final decision to sell a particular product, it helps to visualize how that product will ultimately be marketed and sold. For example, if your product will sell for $50,000, it will most likely have to be sold through direct sales representatives. That means hiring and training an expensive staff of sales people who will draw salaries for a long time before sales generate enough contribution margin (gross profit) to cover salaries and commissions for the sales force. A product selling for less than $5000, on the other hand, will almost always have to be sold through distribution channels. That is, you would engage either independent distributors (who technically buy the product from you, and take title to the product) or independent sales representatives (who represent your company's products, as well as other competitive products, perhaps). Either way, you will give up typically 40% of the sales price for their efforts. While this seems expensive, being able to identify and use a known, proven distribution channel that will readily accept and promote your product will be very helpful. Proof of an existing distribution channel will also be a selling point with your investors.

Many a start-up has launched a great product, only to begin a very long, missionary sales effort that took the company under. Time is money, and trying to establish an in-house sales force or enlist a reluctant distribution channel can cost you plenty. Produce a product that you know can be readily sold.

Producing Your Product

Assume now that you have zeroed in on a good product idea. You have talked to possible customers and established to your satisfaction that there is a large and growing market where this product can solve real problems and meet real needs. This product could also be the basis for a lucrative product family. Compared to the competition, you seem to be well positioned and protected. The product is easy to describe and its benefits are obvious. It can probably be developed and produced rapidly and it has the potential for high gross margins and substantial collateral revenue. Now you have to lay out the plans for actually producing your product.

Statement of Requirements

The initial step when devising a development plan for your product will be to give the product a very specific description. This can be done by generating a *statement of requirements* document. This document describes the general requirements of your product and is to be used by engineering, marketing, and sales personnel during the product development, testing, and market introduction stages. Although this document is primarily a marketing statement, it covers engineering topics too. Much of this information can be extracted directly from a well-researched and well-written business plan. A good number of start-ups neglect to produce this document, which should not take more than one month to generate if the overall business is well planned. Start-ups lacking a carefully planned product description usually pay the price by heading off in a wrong direction or no particular direction. The statement of requirements gives your development team the direction it needs to make progress without your constant supervision. Figure 9.3 is a sample outline for the statement of requirements document adapted from a successful developer of an industrial system.

In the interest of better communication and improved productivity, you should use online tools to develop and maintain the statement of requirements as well as the other documents identified in the following sections.

Functional Specification

Following the generation of the statement of requirements, a *functional specification* document should be produced. This is more of an engineering than a marketing

What is the product?
    features
    applications and uses
    benefits delivered
    needs met
Market analysis and requirements:
    competition
    pricing
    Who is the user?
    Who makes/influences the purchase?
    What are likely sales channels?
    marketing communications and public relations literature
    distribution channels
Product requirements:
    competitive positioning
    target production costs
    Who installs the product?
    training and field support requirements
    customer support requirements
    warranty policy
    upgrade policy
    user, reference, installation manuals
    product packaging
    copy protection policy (for software)
    maintenance considerations
    expected product life
    release schedule (alpha, beta testing, first release, etc.)
    future product enhancements and extensions
Functional requirements:
    performance requirements (responsiveness, accuracy,
     reliability, mean time between failure, etc.)
    systems requirements
    human factors
External requirements:
    environmental requirements
    office, factory, etc.
Other requirements:
    regulatory requirements
    international and export considerations

Figure 9.3   Sample Statement of Requirements Outline

document, and it states in greater detail the requirements relating to the product's function (but not the product's form), such as

- how fast a machine must process parts, or how fast software must execute instructions or perform mathematical calculations
- how accurate or precise a computation must be
- how repeatable a mechanical part's positioning must be

- how a device or program must be controlled by an operator and what operating options must be presented
- how long an instrument must operate before calibration is required
- how heavy a device can be
- how much space a product may occupy

Figure 9.4 is an abbreviated sample outline for a typical functional specification document, adapted from a successful developer of an industrial system.

Terminology
Hardware platform
Operating system
User-interface standards
Help system
Input devices supported
License enforcement or control
Product features (an itemized feature list related to
    the application)
Documentation, comment, and annotation facilities
Cross-reference facilities
Debugging support
Fault detection and handling, and error recovery
Cut-and-paste interfaces
Language specifications
Instructions supported
Limitations and restrictions
Program inputs and outputs
Operating environment
Reliability considerations
International language version considerations
Development notes

Figure 9.4   Sample Functional Specification Outline

The functional specification can turn out to be a crucial document. If it is too vague, the customer will use it as a hammer against you. What started out as a bicycle could turn into a Mercedes (both are vehicles with wheels that transport a passenger from point A to point B), and you (the designer) could be required to pay for the upgrade.

A really good functional specification will be broken down into as many subspecifications as one can reasonably think of. In addition, it will have three performance target specifications (the data often being listed in three columns) as depicted in Fig. 9.5. For this reason, a functional specification is often also referred to as a *performance specification*.

performance level		
Level 1	Level 2	Level 3
what the customer thinks he or she really wants *minus* a few questionable features that would cost quite a bit to develop	what the customer thinks he or she really wants	what the customer thinks he or she really wants *plus* a few extra desirable features that would cost very little extra to develop

(row labeled vertically: function)

Figure 9.5   Performance Specifications

In regard to Level 1 in Fig. 9.5, be cautious. This is a danger area for technology companies. The developing company's engineers have been known to get together with the customer's engineers and begin adding bells and whistles ("Gee, if we just tweaked this a little bit here, it could do this, too!")—significantly increasing costs and development time without having management pass along a price increase to the customer. Also, there's a substantial risk that a standard product becomes a special product, with profound negative implications regarding company schedules, morale, production costs, margins, support, and so forth. *Feature creep* can be a killer—the difference between success and failure. Remember that the road to Hell is paved with good intentions.

For Level 3 in Fig. 9.5, make sure you look at how much time was added due to the development process as well as how much that process added to the cost—and price your product accordingly. Cost overruns occur when no one does a realistic cost analysis or time analysis or when no one updates the figures.

As illustrated in Fig. 9.6, the statement of requirements and the functional specification represent only two of the important stages involved in a good product design and development methodology. Some of your documents will be living documents. That is, they will never be entirely completed and will always be changing. Yet it is important to be diligent in producing and maintaining these vital documents that state what the product is supposed to do, and why. Producing drawings, sketches, and more detailed designs will further propel you toward understanding the product development task ahead. Without such documentation, you run the risk, over time, of slipping into producing what is easy, convenient, or interesting to produce—not what you know your customers want, need, and will buy!

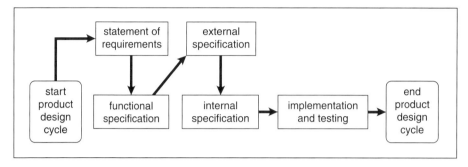

Figure 9.6   Product Design and Development Methodology

External Specification

You probably do not need to get into this level of planning at business launch time, but you should know that an *external specification* document is often developed to translate the "whats" in the functional specification into more specific "hows." The external specification states everything about the product that can be seen, felt, measured, or touched by the customer—that is, observed externally.

For example, if a functional specification says to keep the weight under 25 pounds, a corresponding external specification might stipulate that a frame be made of lightweight aluminum. Statements of speed requirements might translate into the types of motors to be used, and statements of accuracy required might translate into the specification of the use of air-guided, frictionless bearings. For software, the external specification might consist of pictures of all menus, displays, dialog boxes, and so on, with which a user would interact to perform the function specified. For Internet applications, one might specify what environment the pages would work in (e.g., the client would need to use IE 6 or newer, with Java Virtual Machine enabled, and so forth).

Internal Specification

The internal specification document explains how you will accomplish the external specification. The customer typically does not see or care about this level of detail. For example, in software products, an internal specification might stipulate the language and data structures to be used, along with the names and behavior of major routines, objects, modules, and so on. For hardware products, actual component-level decisions are made, down to the part number level if possible.

The internal specification should come last, but unfortunately it is often the first step in a start-up's product design effort. It is tempting to get started on building it without knowing what the "it" is and what "it" is supposed to do. Writing internal specifications (or worse, building your product prototype) before you understand what benefits the product must deliver by solving what customer problems is an error in judgment.

Implementation and Testing

The *implementation and testing* step should be unambiguous. At this stage there should be no more questions about how well the product is to operate, what parts it will use, or how everything interconnects. If the preceding specifications are implemented properly, the rest should be simple, and major milestones should be met on schedule. Of course, adjustments may be required because nothing can be precisely specified in advance and market needs frequently are moving targets. However, make certain that any modification or addition to an approved specification is subject to a change procedure that involves marketing and other appropriate higher-level sign-offs. (See the section entitled Managing the Change Process.) Be sure the best job possible is being done on each level and that the tasks are being undertaken in the proper order. It is amazing how many companies try to start by "hacking" a product without following any design methodology. Most of these enterprises are likely to fail.

If your start-up seems to be working from the bottom up, watch out! You cannot build a product from the pieces until you know what it is supposed to do in some detail. Most inventors are not good product development engineers. If your engineers do not understand the essential role of marketing's input in product specification and do not practice a *top-down method* (also known as the *waterfall model*) of specifying, designing, and developing a product, the business may fail even if the product idea itself is fantastic.

One alternative to the traditional top-down method is a *rapid prototyping* methodology whereby, through iterative experimentation, one converges on a satisfactory design. Although the traditional waterfall method is more popular, this rapid prototyping method has found some success in today's rapid time-to-market environment, especially in software projects where many of the hows have to be discovered through experimentation. This method is often justified on the basis that many software engineers and programmers are not very manageable anyway and tend to produce whatever they find challenging and of interest at the moment. While there may be some basis for that reasoning, it is still essential that the programmers in this case have a keen sense of what the market needs. Those businesses that have successfully used rapid prototyping follow the rule that designs (prototypes) are to be reviewed often, with marketing and development working closely together.

Advocates of rapid prototyping assert that it helps create a much better understanding of user requirements. Based on the users' initial requirements (provided by marketing), a small system is created. The users then make further suggestions, and another iteration is created, and so forth. This can help reduce the risk of development team *isolation*, where developers may implement designs and solutions without knowing if they are really usable and what customers want. This process can also accommodate changing user needs more easily. Whether or not rapid prototyping will work well for your start-up depends not only on your particular product development project but also on the skills, experience, and methodology of your development team. You need to understand how your team works best.

Sometimes a *skunk works* is allowed to exist. This is a slang term for an unofficial effort that is allowed to exist more or less out of sight. Unfortunately, out of sight means without much management direction and control. This model might work in some start-up situations where each employee is an exceptional team player, communications are superior, and there is a good sense of the market. If you choose to operate a skunk works, you had better be an active participant.

Managing the Change Process

The Functional Specification section discussed the risk of feature creep and, specifically, the risk that your engineers and your customer's representatives will decide to add new bells and whistles to your product design. This concern is just one example of why you need a *change process*—a practical procedure to manage any proposed change to a specification or other product document.

The change process should apply to each of the five steps discussed in the preceeding section.

1. statement of requirements
2. functional specification
3. external specification
4. internal specification
5. implementation and testing

You need a written procedure (which can be quite short) that specifies which individuals must approve any proposed modification to a specification or design document before the modification is implemented. The specific approvals may vary for each of the five steps.

Create a practical process that works well for you and your team. Large organizations, of course, spend a great deal of time and money on project management and have personnel dedicated to this important function. They use programs that track everything in great detail—all with the goal of producing better products in a shorter time frame at a lower cost. They use various forms and the required sign-offs are clearly stated. For example, regarding any proposed change to a specification, many large organizations use an *engineering change request* (ECR) form, which leads to review by appropriate personnel and then to an *engineering change notice* (ECN) to the specification, assuming the change is approved. Of course, you don't have the luxury of a team of professionals dedicated to this work, and it would be overkill for your start-up in any case. For software projects, you will of course use basic automated version control software such as Microsoft Visual SourceSafe, and perhaps you will use automated team and project management software such as Microsoft Project or Microsoft SharePoint collaboration technology.

Your goal should be to strike a balance that works well for your start-up environment. A key goal should be meaningful communication throughout the organization. When something changes, what else changes? What are the impacts? For example, you can see how a change to the top-level document (the statement of requirements) is likely to have a ripple-down effect through the other documents, plus possibly an impact on schedules, product costs, and so forth.

You definitely want to encourage creative thinking and new ideas. A good change process, properly explained and implemented, will not get in the way of creativity. Rather, it will encourage and reward creativity, and you'll end up with less friction among team members and a better product.

Sidebar 9.1 Rapid Growth in Opportunities to Deliver Services

The Internet has been a key catalyst in a huge growth in services, some of which has occurred at the expense of traditional products. Many entrepreneurs have worked hard to exploit these new business opportunities and have helped shape new industries.

For example, in the late 1990s there was tremendous growth in the number of *application service providers* (ASPs), both large and small, which managed software-based solutions at a central data center and distributed them over a variety of networks to their customers at multiple locations. (Later, *web services* assumed a similar prominent role and promise.) Customers who outsource their *information technology* (IT) functions in this ASP manner typically pay for the desired applications and services on a monthly rental basis. This ASP model offered many advantages to ASP customers, including

- a reduction in *total cost of ownership*
- a reduction in capital expenditures for IT, due to the outsourcing
- an increased focus by the customer on its core competencies
- better customer visibility on expenses, due to the rental model
- better IT performance, including improved security, scalability, reliability, and flexibility
- improved access by the customer to its information anytime, anywhere
- increased focus by the customer's IT personnel on key internal issues

Unfortunately, many companies simply labeled themselves ASPs to take advantage of the hot ASP market, without having the necessary business infrastructure, understanding, and experience to successfully deliver the ASP advantages to their customers. The failure of many of these so-called ASPs gave the industry a bad name—to such an extent that the term *application service provider* may not even survive. However, many highly competent, customer-focused ASPs did very well, since the basic ASP model makes sense.

Many companies have dramatically changed their pricing and revenue models to take into account some of these developments. For example, it has become very common for software providers (Microsoft, Oracle, etc.) to rent out software (for so much per month) versus charge a one-time licensing fee for the use of a particular software product. Antivirus software, with frequent updates to handle new viruses, is now commonly paid for on a subscription basis versus an up-front fixed fee.

The monthly revenue stream associated with some of these developments can do wonders for a start-up's income statement and cash flow. For example, a three-year contract with 36 monthly payments (versus a one-time spike in revenue) helps take the unpredictability out of revenue forecasts. Layer upon layer can be added to the revenue stream, as new customers are brought on board and existing customers sign up for expanded services. The resulting steady growth in revenue, coupled with the increased predictability, is very appealing to investors.

10

Write Your Business Plan

It's not the writing that's difficult—it's the thinking.

—James Leigh

Form vs. Content

This is the longest chapter in the book, not because writing a business plan is complicated in itself, but because the business planning process (content) behind the writing (form) is. Determining the appropriate form of your plan—which topics to include, in what order, and with what emphasis—is important. Even more important, however, is that the content of your plan convey an intimate understanding of what will make your business succeed. Much of this chapter's subject matter involves the content as well as the form of your business plan.

Types of Business Plans

First, there are two types of business plans.

- a general *planning and funding document* (targeted at outside parties) written to plan for the launching of the business and to raise funds

- an *operational business plan* (targeted at your management team and board of directors) written to monitor and control the growth of the company, with a view to aligning everyone's efforts to achieve stated company objectives (this document should be periodically updated)

In launching your start-up, you will be working with a general planning and funding document, and therefore that is the document addressed in this chapter.

Other than your last will and testament, the most important document you will ever write is your business plan. (Some would say that your business plan is even more important because your will won't matter much if you don't create wealth through your start-up!) A business plan gives birth to your start-up. It enables you and your team to envision and plan how the business will be run and to raise funds. Because both you and your investors have similar questions, one business plan serves both parties. Later, your operational business plans (which can be less comprehensive) will enable you to monitor, plan, and adjust to changes in the growth of your business.

Getting Started

Chapter 6 describes the financial stages of a company's growth. It is important to understand that there are also five operational stages to your company's growth. C. Gordon Bell's *High-Tech Ventures: The Guide for Entrepreneurial Success* clearly describes these well-recognized operational stages, as illustrated in Fig. 10.1.

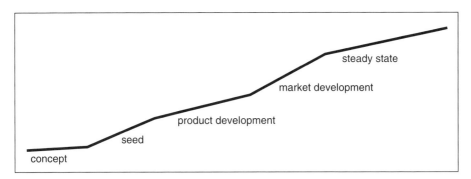

Figure 10.1   Operational Stages of Company Growth

You will be writing your business plan during a concept stage, before you have received outside funding. During a good part of this period you may still be employed.

The *concept* stage is the period during which you and your founding management team develop an idea and write the plan to implement that idea. The financial purpose of the plan is to seek funds for seed-stage testing and refinement of the idea. In some cases, the seed stage can be skipped.

In the *seed* stage your ideas are refined and an even more detailed business plan may be written for the start-up funding round.

In the *product development* stage your product is developed, tested, and refined before any real sales are made.

The *market development* stage begins when the product is sold. During this stage your start-up becomes profitable.

Steady state is reached as the business matures and sustains itself. The business should still be growing at this time, and the original investors may decide to exit or cash out.

Find a Team and Write a Plan, or Write a Plan and Find a Team?

You are encouraged to build your founding team as soon as possible. If you cast the vision and establish the mission together, you probably will be more successful. A 25-year study of high-technology companies by MIT professor Edward B. Roberts shows that multiple founders increase a start-up's chances for success. Larger founding groups start with more capital, generate more sales earlier, and can work more hours. In one subgroup of 20 young companies, 63% of those with more than two founders performed better than average, while only 20% of those with one or two founders exceeded average performance.

Not only will you need help to write a good plan, you will need help in raising funds. Therefore, it is a good idea to team with partners who can assist you in attracting funds. Investors do not throw money at glossy business plans; they invest in teams with plans to exploit market opportunities. This subject is also discussed in Ch. 7, which deals more extensively with creating winning management teams.

When to Write the Plan

When do you write the business plan, and with whom? If you are currently employed, can you take the time and energy to write your business plan and not have a conflict of interest or commitment with your employer? During the plan-writing phase you will need to conduct extensive research, talk to potential customers and investors, and understand your market better. Rarely can all this be done successfully on a part-time basis.

Silicon Valley trade secrets and unfair competition lawyer James Pooley addresses the legal implications of when you must leave an employer.

> You may feel that planning your move while you're still working for the company is somehow unethical. Deliberate, careful planning of your new enterprise is neither illegal nor immoral. Unless you are independently wealthy, you must do it while you still have an income and before you burn any bridges. As long as you don't actually begin your competing business or start recruiting your team from your employer's staff while still on the payroll, you should be clear.

Of course, you can't use any of your employer's trade secrets even in developing your plan. In the same vein, you should use only your personal resources (computer, supplies) and work on your plan only on your own time, while you continue to put full effort into your paying job. A final warning: if you have signed a non-compete contract or you are an officer or manager in your current job, you need early advice from a qualified lawyer.

The start-up scenario illustrated in Fig. 10.2 shows that at some point in time you must quit your job and dedicate yourself full time to engineering your start-up. It is for this reason that there are thousands of voyeurs and would-be entrepreneurs who will never start that business they constantly dream of. It indeed takes quite a sacrifice and risk to start your own business, especially for the first time. For this reason, many start-up founders are people who have been fired or come from other failed start-ups. In fact, many people claim that the purpose of starting your first business should be to really achieve success in your second. Of course, many start-up founders come from successful start-ups. Viewed from this perspective, if you are not yet sufficiently committed to quit your job and launch your dream, maybe you should consider joining someone else's start-up as a key employee or cofounder.

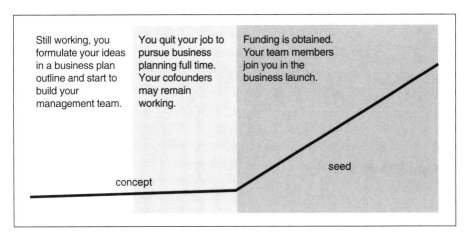

Figure 10.2   Start-Up Scenario

How Long Should It Take to Write Your Plan?

You should plan to spend 3 to 12 full-time months in the unfunded concept stage of your business while you write your business plan and launch your start-up. In his book *Writing Business Plans That Get Results,* Michael O'Donnell says, "A typical time frame for writing a plan would exceed 300 hours over one to six months, depending on how much time can be devoted to the research and writing." In the Ronstadt's Financials software package, Robert Ronstadt and Jeffrey Shuman state that "[in] our experience [the time required to write a business plan] ranges from 100 hours to nearly 2000 hours." The length of time will vary depending on the complexity of your business and how specifically you intend to use the business plan. If your company's future depends upon raising significant funds from venture investors, then your plan must be excellent and compelling, and it will take more time to prepare. Your founding team members, as you convince them to join your venture, will of course help you to write the plan. As the CEO, however, the burden is squarely on your shoulders to take the risk and ensure that the plan gets written.

We frequently encounter entrepreneurs who are having trouble writing their business plans. Some complain specifically about *writer's block*. See Sidebar 10.1 for some tips regarding this vexing issue.

How Long Should a Plan Be?

Professional venture investors look unfavorably on a business plan that has the weight and feel of a book. Since these busy investors receive far more plans than they have time to read, do yourself a favor by taking the extra time to make your message clearer and shorter.

Recognize that a well-written, concise plan typically takes more time to write than a long one. The extra time you spend in tightening your message will not only aid communication, but will also help you improve your business strategy.

A plan that is too long is similar to a person who insists on talking too much. People with limited time (which includes *everyone* you are trying to reach) are turned off.

Accel Partners (www.accel.com), a top-tier venture capital firm in Silicon Valley, offers the following advice.

> The plan should contain the business concept, the marketing, production and technology elements, the backgrounds of the principal founders and how much money will be required. The more specific the plan, the better—both for the venture capitalist now and you later on. *Ironically, experience has shown that the longer the plan, the lower the likelihood of success.* (Emphasis added.) The concise articulation of a simple but powerful concept for an innovative solution to an emerging but important unmet customer need is the hallmark of a good business plan.

When the plan is too lengthy, it's usually because the entrepreneur hasn't yet settled on a compelling strategy and is simply trying to do everything. Focus is missing.

A typical venture capital firm may receive from several hundred to a few thousand business plans per year, and on average it will fund only a handful of these. Most firms have a relatively small, flat organization and simply don't have the time to respond to each entrepreneur who submits a plan. Many plans don't even get reviewed, and in fact many firms don't even maintain a log of plan submittals. This is another reason why a concise professional plan is much more appealing than a lengthy one. Also, entrepreneurs do need good referrals in order to have their plans considered—many venture capitalists will tell you that they can't think of a single company they funded in the last few years that wasn't referred to them by someone they knew and respected. Simply sending your plan via Federal Express does not improve your chances and should be discouraged.

Some people have asserted that you don't need a business plan to raise money—just a great concept, a dozen or so PowerPoint slides, perhaps a strong executive summary, and good contacts. This view was heard more frequently during the dot-com madness. Although many companies did get funded in 1998–2000 without a comprehensive business plan, that was the rare exception even then, not the rule. In any event, strong, concise business plans are needed now more than ever.

Assuming you wish to seek professional venture money, a good target length for your business plan is perhaps 20 to 25 pages, plus an appendix. The plan summarized in Sidebar 10.2, A Strong-Management/Strong-Market Business Plan, is about that length (excluding the resumes and financial projections).

Essential Tools

You probably already own and use a personal computer (Apple or PC) with word processing and spreadsheet software. If you don't, or if you feel the system you have is inadequate for the work ahead, you must go shopping. Having a professional work environment with essential tools of the trade will make a big difference in your attitude and productivity. An excellent printer and a fast Internet connection are strongly recommended. Your business plan should reflect both good form and good content. Ignore the form and you will lose many potential investors. You know it makes good business sense to dress for success, so dress your business plan as well; it is an extension and reflection of yourself. Like a resume, it introduces you and says, "This is the very best I can do; now, do you want to talk to me further?"

Sidebar 10.3, Business Plan Writing Aids, reviews some commercially available software products that help you create your business plan. You should consider them.

Good Business Planning

There are dozens of good business plan models and actual business plan samples to be found in literature or online. If you have access, try to rummage through other private business plans to find examples that are especially relevant to your start-up situation. By now you should be networking with potential team members who have access to a variety of business plans.

Rummaging through other private business plans to which you have access can be dangerous if it results in illegal misappropriation of another's trade secrets. Be sure not to violate confidentiality agreements when you do this. Your purpose in reviewing other specific examples of successful business plans, of course, is to help educate yourself about how to organize and write your own business plan, not to misappropriate product ideas or other information for your company.

Following are some business plan basics and good sample outlines.

Business Plan Basics

This book is built around six elements of a successful start-up business.

- management team
- markets and customers
- products
- plans
- funding
- luck and persistence

These success elements map into the four principal substantive sections of any business plan.

- management team
- marketing and sales
- products
- financial projections

Your business plan must clearly cover these critical sections, and there are several variations in format. As you choose a plan format, never lose track of the following basic elements and messages you need to present.

- Include an executive summary compelling the reader to study the plan.
- Introduce a management team that will guarantee success in the venture.
- Demonstrate a market opportunity that gives this business a distinct competitive advantage. You should state who will buy your product and whether it is in a new or existing market. (Chapter 8 discusses more extensive material that should be included in your plan.)
- Describe a product that is producible and merchantable (state whether this is a new or existing product), preferably with patent or other intellectual property protection.
- Give financial projections that satisfy return-on-investment objectives, are achievable and believable, and obviously do not violate rule-of-thumb sanity-check ratios.

The Executive Summary

The most important part of your business plan is the *executive summary*. It appears at the beginning of your plan and is what most prospective investors read first. Unless it presents a clear, compelling picture of your venture and the investment opportunity, investors are unlikely to read the rest of your plan. Thus, you can view the executive summary as a traffic light—you want your reader to see green (not red) and decide to take the next step with you.

The executive summary should be two to three pages long (two is better). It should be enticing, causing the reader to want to learn more.

The executive summary is not a preface or introduction to the plan. It's a summary, and thus can stand alone if necessary—you should draft it with that in mind. Investors sometimes request that just the executive summary be forwarded, not the whole plan.

The reader should be able to read the executive summary in a few minutes and get a clear snapshot of your business, your product or service (its sustaining advantages and why customers will buy it), the environment in which you operate (markets and competition), and your strategy and plans to ensure success. A summary chart showing your projected revenues and income over five years is helpful. The executive summary thus encapsulates the key points of your business plan, not the details.

The conventional wisdom is that you should write the executive summary last. The logic underlying this wisdom is that you can't summarize something until you know what that something is.

However, you may find it best to write the executive summary first. This approach can be useful if you are having trouble writing the plan itself—which in turn is likely to be caused by an unclear strategy, or a strategy that is simply too broad. Approaching the executive summary this way, you are forced to focus on the most important strategic points, and you avoid the secondary clutter that gets in the way of clear thinking. You should not try to write your business plan until you know what your central strategy is—and the executive summary is one tool that can help you crystallize that strategy.

Plan Emphasis

Emphasis in a business plan is usually put on either the management team or the growing market opportunity. Decide what you are offering to your investors and structure your plan accordingly. If your management team is inexperienced and this is your first business launch attempt, you must focus on your unique market opportunity and how your high-technology product will make the business successful. Sometimes, personnel resumes are buried in a plan. Since many investors want to read about the management team first, if this material is hard to find, your plan may not go very far. If you have a successful management track record, on the other hand, or your combined management team looks very appealing, definitely highlight this asset as the first and most visible section of the plan by placing it immediately after the executive summary. See Sidebar 10.4, One Venture Capitalist's Perspective on Plan Emphasis.

Different investors have differing postures on the relative importance of a management team versus a growing market opportunity. You will often hear statements such as, "we invest in people, not ideas; we assume the product idea can be built," "the market is number one," or "lack of a management team is the number one company killer."

If your start-up has a strong management team and if you are playing in an attractive, growing market, then the Genus example illustrated in Sidebar 10.2 should suit you well. You can make your plan short and compelling, especially if you have a strong story to tell. Like a powerful person speaking in a soft voice, a concise business plan forces everyone to listen attentively. A plan that is too comprehensive, discussing every operations detail, can come off like a not-so-powerful person who is trying too hard. You are selling yourself, your team, and your unique market opportunity, not a used car. Prepare and present your plan accordingly.

There exist dozens of comprehensive outlines for the general planning and funding type of business plan. Also, venture investors sometimes offer a description or outline of what they like to see. Three outlines are presented in this chapter. The detailed, lengthy, comprehensive plans are not recommended. If nothing else, the items your investors will be looking for (people, financial projections, and unique market opportunity) will be too difficult to find within a long plan. However, you can use these more detailed plan outlines as checklists to see that nothing important has been missed.

Business Plan Outline

Tim Berry, founder and CEO of Palo Alto Software, Inc. (which develops and markets BusinessPlanPro™), suggests the following order for the main components of a standard business plan.

1. *Executive Summary*—a page or two of highlights, which is written last
2. *Company Description*—legal establishment, history, start-up plans, and so on
3. *Product or Service*—description of what you're selling, with a focus on customer benefits
4. *Market Analysis*—showing that you know your market, customer needs, where they are, and how to reach them
5. *Strategy and Implementation*—specific management responsibilities with milestone dates and budgets, with ability to track results
6. *Management Team*—description of organization and key management team members
7. *Financial Analysis*—including, at the very least, your projected profit and loss statement and cash flow statement

The vast majority of people who use BusinessPlanPro, as well as the vast majority of people who use JIAN's BizPlanBuilder™, do not intend to seek venture capital financing. Both products address a much broader array of businesses than those relatively few that are of interest to venture investors.

JIAN's BizPlanBuilder suggests the following business plan outline.

A. Executive summary
B. Present situation
C. Objectives
D. Management
E. Product/service description
F. Market analysis

    1. Customers

    2. Competition

    3. Focus group research

    4. Risk

G. Marketing strategy

    1. Pricing and profitability

    2. Selling tactics

    3. Distribution

    4. Advertising and promotion

    5. Public relations

    6. Business relationships

H. Manufacturing

I. Financial projections

    1. 12-month budget

    2. 5-year income (profit and loss) statement

    3. Cash flow projection

    4. Pro forma balance sheet

    5. Break-even analysis

    6. Sources and uses of funds summary

    7. Start-up requirements

    8. Use of funding proceeds

J. Conclusions and summary

K. Appendix

Adapted from JIAN BizPlanBuilder™, with permission (www.jian.com).

Venture Capitalists' Typical Business Plan Contents

The following business plan outline includes the information venture capitalists typically expect to see. (For more ideas, see Sidebar 10.5, What Crosspoint Likes to See in a Business Plan.)

A. Executive summary with five-year milestones

B. Product or service description

C. Business strategy overview

D. Marketing and sales plan

    1. Market size, projected growth, and segmentation

    2. Competitors and their market shares

    3. Strategic positioning and marketing plans

    4. Channels of distribution

     5. Sales strategy and five-year sales forecast

     6. Customer references or references on market potential

  E. Operations plan

     1. Development and engineering programs

     2. Manufacturing and materials programs

     3. Facilities plan

     4. Product service or maintenance programs

  F. Management and key personnel

     1. Organization

     2. Detailed resumes with personal references

     3. Staffing plan

     4. Stock option plan or incentive program

  G. Financial statements and projections

     1. Historical and current financial statements

     2. Annual projections of income statement, balance sheet, and cash flow for next five years

     3. Monthly projections of income statement, balance sheet, and cash flow for next one or two years

     4. Existing shareholders and ownership percentages

  H. Proposed financing

     1. Amount and terms

     2. Postfinancing capital structure

     3. Use of proceeds

  I. Appendices

An attractive business plan will exhibit

- a talented management team with entrepreneurial skills
- a large market need with high growth potential
- a unique and/or proprietary technology
- sound and executable plans
- attractive financial returns (perhaps returns of 10 times over five years)

Keys to your success will be

- *Vision*—You need a clear vision of what the company should be.
- *Commitment*—You need the commitment to work hard to succeed.
- *Focus*—You need to focus on the task at hand.
- *Execution*—You need superb execution of your plan.

A Business Plan Checklist

The following checklist has been used in a number of successful high-technology engineering start-up opportunities. Again, in preparing your business plan, do not attempt to cover every item listed; use this checklist to verify that you have not missed any important topics for your business situation.

A. Executive summary
   1. Objective of the business
   2. Background and unique opportunity and market
   3. Management team
   4. Products
      a. Initial
      b. Future
   5. Marketing strategy
   6. Producing the product
   7. Investment sought and return
   8. Use of proceeds
B. The company's objectives
   1. Origin of business idea and mission
   2. Current status; immediate and long-term objectives
   3. Meeting a new/existing market's needs
   4. Raising seed money
      a. Mission statement (must be clear, precise, and compelling)
      b. Approach for initiating new organization
      c. Time schedule for starting the business
      d. The unique opportunity
      e. Description of business objectives in clear, simple, nontechnical terms
      f. Long-range objectives
      g. Short-range goals
      h. Character and image of business
C. Background and the market opportunity
   1. The competition
   2. A growing market
      a. Meeting competition
      b. Market growth data
      c. Competition (include in appendix any compelling printed material, such as analysis of strengths and weaknesses, plus the competitors' URLs)

    d. Who buys product now, for what, where, and when?

    e. Needs and wants of intended market segment

    f. Market survey data used to develop plan and select market niche

D. Personnel

  1. Qualifications to run the business individually and as a team

  2. Organization of the business at present

  3. Organization of the business after funding

  4. President and CEO

  5. Marketing manager

  6. Treasurer

  7. Secretary

  8. Engineering management

  9. Board of directors

 10. Resumes of management team (select a consistent, powerful format)

 11. Organization chart (prefunding, postfunding) of officers, board of directors, key employees

E. Product description

  1. First product

  2. Design drawing (attached—investors love to see pictures, sketches, and drawings in business plans)

  3. Functional specifications

  4. Sample (mock-up is acceptable) advertising brochure including sketch or photo

    a. Description of product with drawings, sketches, pictures, or illustrations

    b. Desirability, advantages of product

    c. Present state of the art, trends, predictions for your place or niche

    d. Patentability or uniqueness of product. (Do not include too much technical information in your business plan. Specifically, technology-related details that you consider trade secrets probably should not be included in your business plan. Business plans frequently circulate far beyond your wildest dreams.)

    e. Describe a family of (future) products (one product usually does not make a business)

F. Marketing and sales strategy

  1. Distribution arrangements

  2. Direct sales, rentals

  3. Sales channels, costs, and relevant metrics for sales personnel (e.g., calls per week)

4. Unique promotional concepts

5. Delivery, field support, and maintenance emphasized

6. Marketing approach (market segment and distribution channels)

7. Basic selling approach (lead generation, cost per lead and cost per sale, lead generation time, and sales cycle time)

8. Market share expected over time. (By the way, overestimating this number has discredited many financial projections.)

9. List of three to five people who will buy your new product. (Get their names and permission to call them; many investors rely heavily on potential customer testimony for their due diligence.)

10. Pricing

11. Strategy for use of Internet (include in the above discussion as appropriate)

G. Development and operations plan

1. Personnel staffing requirements

2. Facilities and equipment required to develop and manufacture product

3. Make versus buy strategy

4. In-house production and subcontracting

5. Development required. (Keep this to a minimum: investors want a product fast! However, if time plans are not realistic, problems will quickly develop as milestones are missed.)

6. Operations and manufacturing considerations unique to the product

H. Historical and current financial statements

I. Financial pro formas

1. Assumptions. (State these clearly and explicitly. Format your financial templates so you can easily change any assumption and have the effects immediately filter throughout all spreadsheets. Spend time setting up your spreadsheets right.)

2. Profit and loss projections for next five years

a. By quarter, years 1–2

b. By year, thereafter

3. Cash flow, and sources and uses of cash for next five years

a. By quarter, years 1–2

b. By year, thereafter

4. Balance sheet for next five years

a. By quarter, years 1–2

b. By year, thereafter

5. Return on investment: compute this as a sanity check but do not include in plan. (This is explained later in this chapter.)

    6. Break-even chart

    7. Fixed asset acquisition schedule by month (item and amount)

J. Capitalization plan

    1. History, funding plan, capitalization, and current ownership

    2. Authorized, outstanding, and reserved stock, warrants, and options; loans and other financial transactions

    3. Capital needed

    4. Use of proceeds

K. Summary and conclusions

    1. Unique opportunity

    2. High-risk, high-reward investment

    3. Investor qualifications

    4. Time schedule for funding

L. Appendix

    1. Articles from trade journals (but only if they are compelling)

    2. Competitors' URLs

    3. Resumes (if not included in body)

    4. Product design drawings, photos

    5. Sample brochure (dummy acceptable)

    6. Customer references

Adding or Highlighting Sections

Before you write your plan, it is important that you take time to prepare an outline and customize that outline to fit your situation.

If you attempt to include all of the topics suggested thus far in this chapter, you will have a plan that is much too long and too difficult to assimilate. Identify the aspects that are most important to your business' success and document those. For example, if your start-up will be capital intensive, a capital equipment acquisition schedule and cost sheet would be exceedingly useful in addition to the standard financial pro formas.

One start-up business had a customer list of five Fortune 100 companies from earlier contract work, and added a section to its business plan describing the close relationship and noting that these five companies were signed up to beta test the start-up's product. Here were good references that could be checked during due diligence, along with important evidence that this start-up had a head start. Everyone looks for such an advantage. Of course, do not list a company as a customer unless that company is in fact a current customer (i.e., it is actually paying you money for your product). Expect that serious prospective investors will call your customers during due diligence and uncover any misrepresentation or fudging you might have done. If you lose credibility with a prospective investor, you will have zero chance of getting funding, no matter how strong your plan may be.

Another company was modeled after others in a very successful industry (although they were not to be direct competitors). It added a section entitled "Why We are a Good Investment," which tabulated sales levels and company valuations over a period of time for these model companies. Investors clearly understood these success models, and it made the start-up's pitch more understandable and credible.

A third company had not only a strong management team, but also an active and capable board of directors who truly helped to manage the business. It had a section in its plan entitled "Management and Board of Directors."

Are your product development plans especially complex, or are you proposing to develop a complex process? If so, you will want to convince your investors that you can get there in a reasonable time frame, since rapid profitability is the key to high return on investment. You could consider adding a more detailed section on schedules and milestones.

Identify the strengths and selling points of your business proposal and promote them in your business plan. Identify any perceived weaknesses in your venture and adequately defend them. Make sure this important material is highlighted in your executive summary and is easy to find in the body of the plan. Use existing guides or outlines to assist you and to help you check for completeness, but do not let them bind you.

Classic Problems

Your new venture could fail for several reasons. In preparing your business plan, be on the lookout for the following classic problems.

- inadequate market knowledge
- ineffective marketing or sales approach
- inadequate awareness of competitive pressures
- potentially faulty product performance
- rapid product obsolescence
- poor timing for the start of a new business
- undercapitalization due to unforeseen operating expenses, excessive investment in fixed assets like buildings or land, or other financial difficulties
- weak management team (which is generally the most fatal of all shortcomings)

Use Standard Ratios

Use standard and expected ratios in your financial cost estimates, subject to the comments in the next paragraph about *ratio convergence*. For example, if the expenses for marketing and sales in your industry typically run 16–17%, you will have some explaining to do if you show less than 10% or more than 20%. Sophisticated investors examining your financial projections will take you for an amateur if you are too far off the mark on common expense ratios and cannot explain why. The same goes for revenues and gross and net profit margins. Study the financial statements of benchmark companies in your industry to find numerous ratio examples.

Please note that ratios for your start-up will have virtually no meaning in the early years of your start-up. In the early years, when your revenues are zero or very small, the ratio of any category of expense to those revenues will be very large (e.g., several hundred percent, or even infinite in the case of zero revenues). Thus, for example, the larger companies in your comparison group may have a marketing-to-revenue ratio of perhaps 15%, but your ratio in year two is 850%! So why use these ratios at all? Well, many start-ups don't. However, ratios are a valuable tool and it's more a question of how you use them. Specifically, your financial projections over three to five years should show your ratios *converging* to industry average ratios as you move to that point in time when your projections show profitability and a more stable financial picture for your start-up. You can call this *ratio convergence*. Before then, during ramp-up, when revenues are modest and you're investing in the future, the ratios will definitely be "out of line." Here are two additional related points.

- You may have excellent reasons why your ratios don't converge to industry averages. For example, your particular strategy and business model may call for a higher or lower development effort than that of the industry average. That's fine. The key is that you need to think through these issues and plan accordingly. Use industry averages as a guide, but don't blindly follow them.
- When a sophisticated investor asks you why certain expenses appear out of line with the industry, you'll then have an intelligent answer, and you'll find that your conversation with this investor will be more productive and positive.

Just for example, here are some hypothetical ratios.

For selling, general, and administrative (SG&A) expenses as a percent of total revenue,

- You do some research and find that three large, stable companies in your industry spend about 35% of total revenues for SG&A costs.
- Two smaller companies in your industry spend about 45% of total revenues for SG&A, but they are not currently profitable.
- You find studies showing that SG&A expenses are typically higher for technology-based companies, and that the specifics depend much on the product distribution model that is used.

For gross and net margins as a percent of total revenue,

- You find that gross margins for the largest three companies in your segment exceed 60%.
- Their net margins (i.e., after-tax profit, as a percentage of revenue) exceed 10%.
- The two smaller companies in your industry have gross margins under 50%.
- Their net margins are currently negative (i.e., they are losing money).

For annual revenue per employee,

- If you are a software company with a high gross margin, annual revenues per employee of $300,000 or more may be fine.

- On the other hand, if you sell a hardware product that is priced like a commodity (i.e., with very low gross margins), you are likely to need annual revenues per employee to be greatly in excess of $1 million.

- This ratio of revenue (sales) per employee is very important. You need to obtain industry figures for your business to make sure your plan makes sense.

- You should take trends into account. For example, annual revenues per employee in the electronics industry have climbed dramatically in the last two decades, due in great part to productivity improvements. Your projections five years out should reflect such relevant trends. Figure 10.3 shows the strong gains in productivity over several years for one broad industry group.

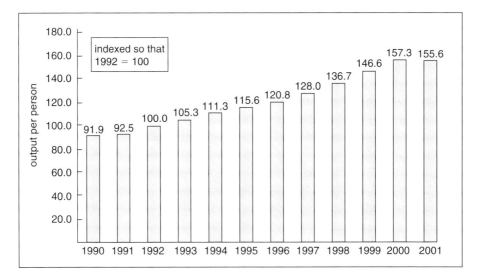

Figure 10.3   Productivity Gains in the U.S.—Output per Person (Manufacturing, Durable Goods)

There are several other ratios you should consider, including research and development (R&D) expenses as a percentage of total revenue.

Are you projecting revenues or profit margins above or below investor expectations? Miss these marks and your plan could be quickly dismissed.

Using the Internet, it is not difficult to obtain information on these ratios. You should be able to obtain copies of business plans from your associates and team members. You should also evaluate several annual reports of young, growing public companies in your industry. The various reports that public companies are required to file with the Securities and Exchange Commission (SEC) are available through the SEC system known as EDGAR (visit www.sec.gov/edgar.shtml). Several commercial websites also provide free, real-time access to EDGAR reports.

Looking Like an Amateur

It is difficult not to look like an amateur if you admittedly are one. Most engineers attempting their first start-up will not have had the operations and business experience needed to prepare a first-class business plan, attract capital, and pull off the execution. This is why it is important to build a strong management team to help you launch your start-up. As discussed in Ch. 2, if your real strength and passion is engineering, you might even want one of your team members to be the CEO while you take on the position of engineering vice president.

Understanding Financial Statements and Projections

The *balance sheet*, *income statement*, and *cash flow statement* are the three basic financial statements that must be clearly understood by the start-up entrepreneur. They represent the financial history of your company to date, and they also are the basis and form for your projections into the future. If you rely on someone else to generate these statements for you, you will not understand them and you will not be able to defend them. Even worse, you will not be able to use them to manage and control your business.

If you wonder why a fresh MBA gets paid a lot of money to run a company while engineers seem to be relatively underpaid and have to struggle to get promoted, the MBA's understanding of financial controls is part of the answer. While it takes no genius to get an MBA degree (most engineering degrees are harder to earn than most MBAs), the MBA usually has the financial edge. It may make sense for you to attend some college classes in finance and accounting before you try to start your own company. Your investors will be looking for someone with financial control skills to help prepare your projections and run your business. Even if one of your team members is financially experienced, all founders will benefit from familiarity with financial terminology and procedures.

See Sidebar 10.6, Some Pointers About Your Financial Projections.

Working Backward

As you start to prepare the financial projections for your business, it is tempting to work backward from the answers. For example, you may have figured out that in five years you'll need to have revenues of $100 million and 10% post-tax profits in order to allow your investors to obtain a compounded 25% return on their investment. If you iterate through a spreadsheet to calculate the required sales price of your product, sales quantities, and so on to meet these goals, all you have are numbers that work in the model, not in the market. It is reasonable to calculate these numbers as a sanity check, but do not prepare your financial model this way.

Get Good Data

The hardest part of preparing financial projections is not in the mechanics but in getting good data. "Garbage-in, garbage-out" is an old computer programming expression that doubly applies here. For instance, in the preceding example, you must determine your sales price from the market. What people will pay for your product is based on what benefits it delivers to them and what alternative products cost. You must clearly understand your market and competition before you can create your financial plans. Engineers in particular tend to ignore the marketing side of a business, figuring that sales problems can be dealt with later.

Do Not Ignore Your Own Data

After you know what the market will pay for your product, you can look at your cost-of-goods and backward-computed required price to see if you have a viable business plan. If you do not, you must seriously rethink whether your business is viable or not. Keep in mind that the most important purpose of the business plan is to convince yourself that this is a reasonable thing to do; selling your ideas to investors is secondary. Your goal is to build a very successful business, not just raise money from investors. If you start a business for which your numbers initially tell you that you will fail, you will almost certainly fail. It is likely that the initial business plans of many failed start-ups indicated a flaw that was ignored.

Writing a business plan forces you to consider every aspect of your proposed business. Any information you put into the business plan should confirm and reinforce information you relied upon earlier. Resolve any discrepancies to your satisfaction before proceeding.

The Three Most Important Financial Statements

The three most important financial statements are

- balance sheet
- income statement (or profit and loss statement)
- cash flow statement

These "big three" (discussed in the three following sections) are at the core of accounting, and that's where you should focus if you are not that familiar with accounting.

Please note that the accounting principles reflected in all of these financial statements apply to both the past and future. It's really a simple point, but since a company knows (or should know!) the actual numbers for its past financial performance, the financial statements covering the past are often called *historical* financials, or simply the *actuals*, whereas, the company's best estimates of what it will achieve in the future are called *projections* or *pro forma statements* (or simply the *pro formas*). (As discussed in Sidebar 10.7, we prefer the term "projections" over "pro formas.") In one case you know the numbers, and in the other you are trying to predict the numbers—but in either case the same broad accounting rules apply, and the presentations will look quite similar. Your financial projections, of course, will be an especially important part of your business plan, and you'll see that several of the tabulations that follow in this chapter are in fact projections, or pro formas. For more background on this topic, see Sidebar 10.7, What Are Pro Forma Financial Statements?

A typical new business has no financial history, and thus, in the beginning at least, deals only with projections. One labor-saving approach for a raw start-up is to prepare the projections in reference to "months 1, 2, 3…," and "years 1, 2, 3…," rather than in reference to specific months and years (e.g., January, or 2005). Typically, the contemplated start date is based on some "green light" event, such as venture funding. If you've applied this approach to your projections, you won't have to spend a lot of time recasting them in the event of a delay.

Balance Sheet

The *balance sheet* financial report is sometimes called a *statement of condition* or *statement of financial position* because it represents the state of the business at a *point* in time. This snapshot of your business differs from an *income statement*, which summarizes activity over a *period* of time. A balance sheet shows the status of your company's assets, liabilities, and owners' equity on a given date, usually the close of a month, quarter, or year. One way of looking at your business is as a mass of capital (assets) arrayed against the sources of capital (liabilities and equity). Assets must always equal liabilities plus equity.

Your balance sheet lists the items that make up the two sides of this equation. To efficiently analyze a balance sheet, you need to compare it to prior balance sheets (e.g., to see an improvement or degradation in various positions and ratios) and other operating statements (e.g., profit and loss, sources and uses of cash, etc.).

The sample balance sheet shown in Fig. 10.4 indicates the level of detail you should strive for. The actual numbers in this sample are relatively meaningless and are included only as examples. (In the real world, for example, the actual or projected numbers for "cash" and "office equipment" will not remain the same from year to year.) Your business needs will dictate what values should be inserted. Lines with zero amounts should be included so your reader will not think you missed something. In addition to projected balance sheets for the end of each of your first five years, you will also want to prepare quarterly balance sheets for the first two years. Some investors will insist that you prepare these quarterly balance sheets. Again, your worksheets should be assumption-based, allowing you to quickly enter different estimates to immediately see the results as they filter throughout all your linked financial pro formas.

	Year 1	Year 2	Year 3	Year 4	Year 5
Assets					
Current Assets					
cash	$10,000	$10,000	$10,000	$10,000	$10,000
investments	$1,800	$2,700	$4,050	$6,075	$9,112
accounts receivable	$29,500	$47,200	$75,520	$120,832	$193,331
notes receivable	$5,000	$5,000	$5,000	$5,000	$5,000
inventory	$45,000	$60,750	$82,013	$110,717	$149,468
total current assets	$91,300	$125,650	$176,583	$252,624	$366,911
Plant and Equipment					
building	$175,000	$175,000	$175,000	$175,000	$175,000
office equipment	$62,000	$62,000	$62,000	$62,000	$62,000
leasehold improvements	$18,500	$18,500	$18,500	$18,500	$18,500
less accumulated depreciation	$0	$0	$0	$0	$0
net property and equipment	$255,500	$255,500	$255,500	$255,500	$255,500
Other Assets	$0	$0	$0	$0	$0
Total Assets	$346,800	$381,150	$432,083	$508,124	$622,411
Liabilities and Owner Equity					
Current Liabilities					
short-term debt	$13,500	$13,500	$13,500	$13,500	$13,500
accounts payable	$22,500	$29,250	$38,025	$49,433	$64,262
income taxes payable	$1,500	$1,500	$1,500	$1,500	$1,500
accrued liabilities	$0	$0	$0	$0	$0
total current liabilities	$37,500	$44,250	$53,025	$64,433	$79,262
Long-Term Debt	$22,000	$19,800	$17,820	$16,038	$14,434
Owner/Stockholder Equity					
common stock	$250,000	$272,340	$307,526	$363,199	$451,370
retained earnings	$37,300	$44,760	$53,712	$64,454	$77,345
Total Liabilities and Owner Equity	$346,800	$381,150	$432,083	$508,124	$622,411
Ratios					
current ratio = (total current assets/total current liabilities)	2.43	2.84	3.33	3.92	4.63
quick ratio = (cash + accounts receivable + notes receivable/total current liabilities)	1.19	1.41	1.71	2.11	2.63

Adapted from JIAN BizPlanBuilder™, with permission (www.jian.com).

Figure 10.4   Balance Sheet

Income Statement

The *income statement* is a summary of the revenues (sales), costs, and expenses of your company during an accounting period, typically a month, quarter, or year. The income statement is sometimes called a *profit and loss (P&L) statement, operating statement, statement of profit and loss,* or *income and expense statement.* Look at the annual reports from a variety of public companies until you become comfortable with the various names and formats for the income statement. It is the easiest of the three statements to comprehend.

The sample income statement in Fig. 10.5 shows what you should strive for as a summary statement. Since this figure illustrates a less detailed income statement by year for five years, you will also want to prepare a more detailed statement by month

	Year 1	Year 2	Year 3	Year 4	Year 5
Sales					
product or service A	$58,000	$95,700	$157,905	$260,543	$429,896
percent of total sales	58%	61%	66%	69%	72%
product or service B	$22,000	$28,600	$37,180	$48,334	$62,834
percent of total sales	22%	18%	15%	13%	11%
product or service C	$20,000	$32,000	$45,000	$67,500	$101,250
percent of total sales	20%	20%	19%	18%	17%
total sales	$100,000	$156,300	$240,085	$376,377	$593,980
Cost of Sales					
materials	$21,500	$33,325	$51,654	$80,063	$124,098
percent of total sales	22%	21%	22%	21%	21%
labor	$31,000	$44,950	$65,178	$94,507	$137,036
percent of total sales	31%	29%	27%	25%	23%
overhead	$18,500	$24,050	$31,265	$40,645	$52,838
percent of total sales	19%	15%	13%	11%	9%
total cost of sales	$71,000	$102,325	$148,097	$215,215	$313,972
Gross Profit	$29,000	$53,975	$91,988	$161,162	$280,008
gross margin	29%	35%	38%	43%	47%
Operating Expenses					
selling costs	$2,000	$2,500	$3,125	$3,906	$4,883
percent of total sales	2%	2%	1%	1%	1%
research and development	$2,800	$3,780	$5,103	$6,889	$9,300
percent of total sales	3%	2%	2%	2%	2%
general and administrative	$4,100	$4,102	$4,103	$4,105	$4106
percent of total sales	4%	3%	2%	1%	1%
total operating expenses	$8,900	$10,382	$12,331	$14,900	$18,289
percent of total sales	9%	7%	5%	4%	3%
income from operations	$20,100	$43,593	$79,657	$146,262	$261,719
percent of total sales	20%	28%	33%	39%	44%
interest income (expense)	($5,000)	($4,999)	($4,998)	($4,997)	($4,997)
income before taxes	$15,100	$38,594	$74,659	$141,265	$256,722
taxes on income	$5,889	$15,052	$29,117	$55,093	$100,122
Net Income	$9,211	$23,542	$45,542	$86,172	$156,600
percent of total sales	9%	15%	19%	23%	26%

Adapted from JIAN BizPlanBuilder™ with permission (www.jian.com).

Figure 10.5   Income Statement

and quarter for the first year and by quarter for the second year. The financial program you choose to use will undoubtedly have linked schedules for various items on the income statement, so you will see the supporting data in greater detail as you drill down through the supporting schedules.

Notice how much easier your tabular data is to comprehend when you make it into a graph as shown in Fig. 10.6. Figure 10.6, of course, is merely an illustration, and a typical start-up actually generates some losses and negative cash flow in the early periods. Good business plans should be highly pictorial and easy to read.

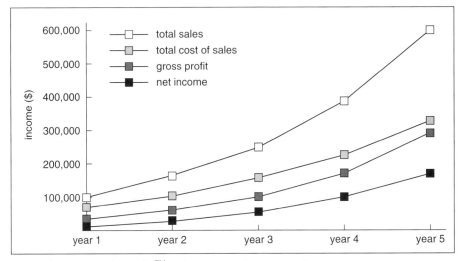

Adapted from JIAN BizPlanBuilder™, with permission (www.jian.com).

Figure 10.6   Plot of Income Statement

Many people are confused by the terms *revenue* and *income*. In a business situation, revenue denotes the gross figure, namely the sales from the business. Income denotes the net figure: the sum remaining after expenses (cost of goods sold and other expenses) have been deducted from the revenue. This net amount represents the *profit*, or *income* of the business, and it is also sometimes called *earnings*, especially in financial circles—as in *earnings per share* (which is the total profit, or earnings, of a company, divided by the total number of shares of stock outstanding). See Table 10.1, Various Definitions of Revenue and Income.

Table 10.1   Various Definitions of Revenue and Income

general terminology	salaried terminology	business terminology
gross revenue	salary or personal income	sales income or revenue
less cost of providing goods or services	less cost-of-services-provided ($0)	less cost-of-goods-sold (COGS) ($ > 0)
equals income	still equals income	equals profit or income

There are many different accounting, financial, and common definitions of these terms, and gross income can certainly mean the same thing as revenue in some contexts. Do not be embarrassed if you find yourself confusing the two. Perhaps because salary is often informally equated with personal income, many first-time entrepreneurs correspondingly confuse what one might call a business' sales income (i.e., its revenue) with the business' income. If you study the definitions given in Table 10.1, the confusion quickly dissipates. In a simple salaried situation, you have no deductible costs associated with producing the services for which you are paid. Thus, your revenue for working is equivalent to your income.

Cash Flow Statement

The *cash flow statement* is the most difficult of the three principal financial statements to understand. It includes the sources and uses of cash, and it results from an analysis of all the changes that affect the cash account during an accounting period. You can master the cash flow statement with practice and disciplined study of each line item.

Sometimes called the *sources and uses of funds statement* or *sources and applications of funds statement*, this statement allows you to analyze the changes in the financial position (represented by the balance sheet and the income statement) of your business from one accounting period to another. These statements are required in the annual reports of all public companies, and it is suggested that you study a few of them.

To understand the cash flow statement, you first need to know what *working capital* is. Working capital is equal to current assets minus current liabilities, and it finances the *cash conversion cycle* of your business. The cash conversion cycle includes the time required to convert raw materials into finished goods, finished goods into sales, and accounts receivable into cash.

If you are unfamiliar with any of the preceding terms or with concepts such as depreciation and net income, you should buy a pocket dictionary of finance and investment terms. The sources and uses of funds statement has two parts.

- The sources of funds part summarizes the transactions that increase working capital, such as net income, depreciation, the issue of bonds, sale of stock, or an increase in deferred taxes.
- The uses of funds (or applications of funds) part summarizes the way funds are used, such as for salaries, marketing campaigns, the purchase or improvement of plants and equipment, the payment of dividends, the repayment of long-term debt, or the redemption or repurchase of shares of stock.

Figure 10.7 shows a sample cash flow statement. Athough it's illustrated here as a less detailed yearly statement for just the first three years, you would prepare a statement by month or quarter for your first two years, as well as yearly statements for five years.

Many people break out a simple cash flow statement (i.e., a projection) by month or quarter for the first year or two (illustrated in Fig. 10.8), which gives a clearer picture of net cash balance over time (which is of significant interest if you want to quickly see that you can make every payroll). Data from June through November are suppressed in this figure to improve readability.

Figures 10.7 and 10.8 represent two different ways of analyzing and presenting cash flow. Figure 10.7 essentially starts with income (from the income statement) and adjusts it for noncash items, like depreciation, to arrive at operating cash flow.

	Year 1	Year 2	Year 3
Source of Funds			
income after taxes	$54,500	$163,500	$490,500
depreciation and amortization	$22,000	$22,000	$22,000
operating cash flow	$76,500	$185,500	$512,500
increased long-term debt	$40,000	$40,000	$40,000
issuance of stock	$100,000	$50,000	$100,000
total source of funds	$216,500	$275,500	$652,500
Use of Funds			
marketing and advertising	$25,000	$37,500	$88,000
salaries	$15,000	$15,000	$60,000
facilities	$65,000	$70,000	$90,000
capital equipment	$18,000	$22,500	$101,000
research and development	$20,000	$40,000	$85,000
operations expenses	$22,500	$23,500	$66,000
cash dividends	$0	$0	$0
increased working capital	$51,000	$67,000	$162,500
total use of funds	$216,500	$275,500	$652,500
Summary of Changes in Working Capital			
decreased cash	($20,000)	($20,000)	($47,000)
increased accounts receivable	$32,000	$30,000	$181,000
increased inventory	$40,000	$58,000	$52,500
increased accounts payable	($16,000)	($16,000)	($39,000)
decreased notes payable	$15,000	$15,000	$15,000
increased working capital	$51,000	$67,000	$162,500

Adapted from JIAN BizPlanBuilder™, with permission (www.jian.com).

Figure 10.7   Cash Flow Statement

Figure 10.8 focuses directly on cash (e.g., it starts with cash receipts, not "income"), and it also conveniently shows "beginning cash" on the top line and the ending "net cash balance" on the bottom line. (Of course, the ending cash balance for one month (e.g., January) automatically becomes the beginning cash balance for the next month (e.g., February).)

Again, it is helpful to show your reader this data over time in a graphic format. One useful presentation is to show, by month, the plot of total cash receipts, total cash disbursements, and the net cash balance.

Break-Even Analysis

Since becoming profitable as soon as possible is the most important goal you can meet if you want to optimize the valuation of your business, you and your investors will

	Jan.	Feb.	Mar.	Apr.	May	Dec.
beginning cash balance	$10,000	$44,174	$32,317	$19,459	$10,950	$46,061
Cash Received						
sales	$31,500	$34,650	$38,115	$41,927	$46,119	$89,873
interest income	$44	$193	$141	$85	$48	$202
sale of stock	$50,000	$0	$0	$0	$0	$0
proceeds of bank loan	$0	$0	$0	$0	$25,000	$0
total cash received	$81,544	$34,843	$38,256	$42,012	$71,167	$90,075
Cash Disbursements						
accounts payable	$15,800	$16,748	$17,753	$18,818	$19,947	$29,993
advertising	$1,200	$1,200	$1,200	$1,200	$1,200	$1,200
commissions (10% of sales)	$3,150	$3,465	$3,812	$4,193	$4,612	$8,987
salaries	$2,500	$2,500	$2,500	$2,500	$2,500	$2,500
equipment lease	$125	$125	$125	$125	$125	$125
equipment purchase	$1,995	$0	$3,000	$895	$18,500	$4,400
office lease	$3,000	$3,000	$3,000	$3,000	$3,000	$3,000
short-term loan repayment	$15,000	$15,000	$15,000	$15,000	$15,000	$15,000
other expenses	$3,100	$3,162	$3,225	$3,290	$3,356	$3,854
tax payments	$1,500	$1,500	$1,500	$1,500	$1,500	$1,500
total cash disbursements	$47,370	$46,700	$51,115	$50,521	$69,740	$70,559
net cash balance	$44,174	$32,317	$19,458	$10,950	$12,377	$65,577

Adapted from JIAN BizPlanBuilder™, with permission (www.jian.com).

Figure 10.8   Simple Cash Flow Statement

want to know when your business will break even. *Breakeven* occurs when sales equal costs. A break-even analysis determines this point by computing the volume of sales at which all fixed and variable costs will be covered. All sales above the break-even point produce profits; any drop in sales below that point will produce losses. A break-even analysis is a rough but important gauge of the volume of sales you need in order to attain profitability. The break-even point for an imaginary company is shown in Fig. 10.9, based on the data in Table 10.2. (Table 10.2 shows the data for three scenarios—optimistic, realistic and pessimistic—and Fig. 10.9 illustrates the realistic case only.)

Fixed costs are costs that remain the same regardless of the sales volume. They include items such as rent, management salaries, utilities, insurance, real property taxes, and depreciation. *Variable costs* are costs that change directly with the amount of product produced. They include items such as raw materials and direct labor (whether employee or contractor) to produce the product.

Again, it is important that you prepare a break-even chart similar to the one shown in Fig. 10.9. Nothing is more frustrating than trying to see what numbers mean in tabular form. All modern spreadsheet programs support charting from your raw data. For example, each of the charts you see in this chapter was created in just a few minutes using the data in the example financial pro forma spreadsheets.

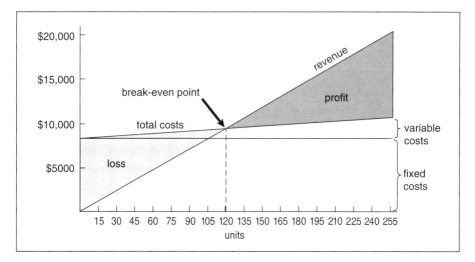

Figure 10.9   Break-Even Analysis Chart: Realistic Case

Table 10.2   Break-Even Analysis

	per month optimistic	per month realistic	per month pessimistic
fixed costs			
administrative costs	$225	$563	$1,406
R&D investment	$2,800	$4,200	$6,300
selling costs	$2,100	$3,150	$4,725
total fixed costs (TFC)	$5,125	$7,913	$12,431
variable costs			
cost of goods sold	$4,490	$6,735	$10,103
total variable costs (TVC)	$4,490	$6,735	$10,103
pricing & unit sales variables			
selling price (SP)	$79.00	$79.00	$79.00
number of units (U)	600	500	400
variable costs per unit	$7.48	$13.47	$25.26
break-even unit volume	72	121	231
gross profit	$37,785.00	$24,852.00	$9,066.00

Adapted from JIAN BizPlanBuilder™, with permission (www.jian.com).

Investors' Hurdle Rate of Return on Investment

It is to your advantage to know what measures investors use in determining which companies they will invest in, how you can compute these measures, and how you can use them to evaluate and help sell your business plan. If your venture's rate of return on investment does not equal or exceed your investors' *hurdle rate* (i.e., the minimum or required rate of return set by the investor), your plan will not be given further consideration. The following four sections elaborate on this all-important perspective of professional investors.

Basic Terms

Once you understand several related terms, you will have the vocabulary to play the investment game as it pertains to funding your start-up. The subject of finance can get very involved, but all you need to learn are the basic terms. They are all defined in relation to one another, and most of them boil down to one concept: discounting cash for the time-value of money. More advanced concepts such as the capital asset pricing model (CAPM; takes into account risk), the optimal capital structure (OCS; determines the optimum proportion of debt and equity), and the weighted average cost of capital (WACC; the average rate of return that capital investors expect the company to earn) can be left for graduate school.

Present value (PV) defines what one dollar is worth today (namely, one dollar). More important, it is the value today of a future payment or stream of payments, discounted at some appropriate compound interest or *discount rate*. For example, the present value of $100 to be received 10 years from now is about $38.55, using a discount rate of 10% interest compounded annually. This simply reflects the time-value of money. Ignoring taxes, if you were to put your savings in a risk-free, 10% annually compounded savings account, it should make no difference to you if you received $38.55 today or $100 in 10 years.

I = cash invested at the beginning of a holding period

PV = discounted value of a future payment or series of payments

Future value (FV) is simply the amount to which an investment will grow at a future time if it earns a specified interest that is compounded annually. It can easily be shown that the FV of an initial investment, I, compounded annually at rate i for n years is

$$FV = I(1 + i)^n \qquad\qquad\qquad [\text{I}]$$
$$= \text{cash yielded at the end of an investment holding period}$$

Cash-on-cash return (COC) is the simplest measure of an investment return. It is widely used to describe venture capital investments.

$$COC = \frac{FV}{I} \qquad\qquad\qquad [\text{II}]$$

As you can see, COC does not take into account the time-value of money. Therefore, investors often describe their performance goals in terms of COC and a period of time. For example, if you hear that an investor expects a 10-times (10X) return in five years, that means COC should equal 10 after a five-year holding period.

So, if the invested amount is $1 million, the investor expects or wants to receive at least $10 million in five years.

One can easily compute the actual annual compounded rate of return, i, achieved by a particular COC return over a period of n years from the preceding equations. Just use your financial calculator.

From Eq. I,

$$(1+i)^n = \frac{FV}{I}$$

Substituting Eq. II,

$$(1+i)^n = COC$$
$$(1+i) = COC^{1/n} \qquad\qquad [III]$$
$$i = COC^{1/n} - 1$$

Thus, in the example of COC = 10 in n = 5 yr,

$$i = (10)^{1/5} - 1$$
$$= (10)^{0.2} - 1$$
$$= 1.584893 - 1$$
$$= 0.584893$$
$$= 58.4893\%$$

Under the *net present value* method (NPV), the PV of all cash inflows from an investment is compared against the initial investment, I. The NPV is simply the difference between PV and I.

NPV determines whether an investment is acceptable. To compute the PV of cash inflows, a discount rate called the *cost of capital* is used for discounting. Under this method, if NPV > 0 (or equivalently, PV > I), the investment should be made.

Rate of return, or *return on invested capital*—usually called *return on investment* (ROI)—is equivalent to the *internal rate of return* (IRR) needed for the net present value of one's investment to be zero. Any financial calculator will spit out that number. This is sometimes a difficult concept to understand. Working through a few examples in a finance textbook will make this relationship clear.

Thus, IRR is the discount rate at which the present value of the future cash flows of an investment equals the cost of the investment. When the net present values of cash outflows (the cost of the investment) and cash inflows (returns on the investment) equal zero, the rate of discount being used is the IRR.

When the IRR is greater than the investor's required return on investment (called the *hurdle rate* in capital budgeting), the investment is acceptable.

An investment can profitably be made when the IRR exceeds the cost of capital.

Investors May Examine Your Financials First

Some venture capital investors will assign a junior assistant (who may be part-time and may be an MBA student) to first examine your financial pro forma documents (informally referred to as your *financials*) before they'll spend a lot of time working to understand your business (i.e., your market, your product, and the strength of your team). This is done with the thought that if your numbers do not reflect the return needed to meet their ROI hurdle criterion, they will not invest in your start-up. For this reason alone, you must do your best in preparing your financial projections.

Because the investor's ROI depends on his or her percentage equity ownership and price per share paid (items yet to be negotiated), ROI cannot be calculated solely on the basis of the business plan financial pro forma projections.

You could make some assumptions and compute ROI for a given investment scenario and include this in your plan, but most people do not. Including investors' ROI in your financial section forces you to make an assumption as to the valuation of your company, and many investors prefer that you not do that for them. Although including this information might seem to make sense—to prove that you know this is a good investment—do not do so. If you want VC's money, play by their rules. In oral presentations to VCs, be prepared to respond to questions concerning ROI.

Valuation

Investors want to calculate their ROI themselves based on their valuation calculations and using their methods, and they probably figure that in doing so they have a little edge on you. Calculating an investor's ROI is akin to computing someone else's income taxes without knowing their income (because investors will discount your projected revenues to a level they feel is attainable, and you will not know what discount they used). Because no two people would likely give your company the same valuation independently, calculating an ROI for your investors is indeed presumptuous. Chapter 17 contains information essential to your understanding of how investors put a valuation on a company (the methods differ widely). Only when you understand how much your company is worth to your investors can you begin to estimate how much equity you should give up for your seed or start-up capital. Without this knowledge, you may just have to settle for a rule-of-thumb explanation for any proposed pricing, and your stock will likely be underpriced. Unfortunately or not, supposed rule-of-thumb valuations have funded more companies than you might imagine, and many investors do not run ROI calculations at all.

Even though you will not include ROI in your plan, you must calculate it to make sure your plan will not be rejected for that reason. It is surprising how many entrepreneurs neglect to compute ROI.

A company's ROI can be expressed as a percentage earned on the company's total capital (its common and preferred stock equity plus its long-term funded debt), calculated by dividing total capital into earnings before interest, taxes, and dividends. It should be easy enough to calculate ROI for a company. But, however useful this number might be as an overall measure, it does not answer the individual investor's question, "Should I invest in this company?"

When an individual investor computes his or her ROI, the thinking is, "How much will my return be in compounded annual terms, in so many years, when I cash out?" To figure this out, one needs to know

- How much is paid per share at year 0?
- What can a share be sold for at year N?

From these two valuation-related numbers, you can see that ROI is the internal rate of return (IRR) needed for the net present value of one's investment to be zero. Any financial calculator will furnish that number.

- Given a target IRR, one can compute the purchase price per share needed for an assumed cash-out price and holding period.
- Given a target IRR, one can compute the cash-out price per share needed for a given purchase price and holding period.
- Given a target IRR, one can compute the maximum holding period one can tolerate in order to cash out at an assumed cash-out price for a given purchase price.
- IRR can be computed by setting any other target variable and making estimates of the others.

Your potential investors will attempt to compute your company's future valuation, figure in their required percentage ownership, and determine what would be a fair purchase price reflecting a judgment of current valuation. Again, Ch. 17 contains detailed information to enable you to attempt this same feat.

Table 10.3 shows an investor's IRR for several investment scenarios. Your task is to show that your company will generate such good profits so rapidly that the investor's hurdle rate of return on investment criterion can be met without needing to acquire an unreasonable percentage of your company in the seed or start-up round.

Table 10.3 shows cash flows from the investor's pocketbook. Assume that $10 is paid per share in year zero. For simplicity, no additional cash exchanges hands during years one through four. In year five, anywhere from $10 to $150 is returned to the investor at cash-out time. The investor's corresponding IRR is shown in the right-hand column.

How Big Does My ROI/IRR Need to Be?

Obviously, investors would like to hit only home runs. Ideally, an investor would get 10X his or her money back in five years, which, as shown in Table 10.3, represents a 58.49% annual compounded rate of return. In reality, the average and median numbers are usually lower. While venture capital fund returns may turn out to be single digit, venture capitalists still will not invest in any single venture unless they see 5X to 10X returns (40–60% annual returns) due to the fact that some investments will fail and others will not perform as well. At the same time, one superstar investment in a fund that yields a 50X or 100X return will make up for many losing bets in that fund.

Table 10.3   IRR for Given Cash Flow

year 0 ($)	year 1 ($)	year 2 ($)	year 3 ($)	year 4 ($)	year 5 ($)	IRR (%)
(10)	0	0	0	0	10	0.00
(10)	0	0	0	0	11	1.92
(10)	0	0	0	0	12	3.71
(10)	0	0	0	0	13	5.39
(10)	0	0	0	0	14	6.96
(10)	0	0	0	0	15	8.45
(10)	0	0	0	0	16	9.86
(10)	0	0	0	0	17	11.20
(10)	0	0	0	0	18	12.47
(10)	0	0	0	0	19	13.70
(10)	0	0	0	0	20	14.87
(10)	0	0	0	0	25	20.11
(10)	0	0	0	0	30	24.57
(10)	0	0	0	0	35	28.47
(10)	0	0	0	0	50	37.97
(10)	0	0	0	0	70	47.58
(10)	0	0	0	0	100	58.49
(10)	0	0	0	0	150	71.88

Over the long haul, venture capital funds have been expected to get at least 25% returns, meaning that they would triple their investment in five years. Even before the Internet boom, returns of 40–50% were not uncommon at times. Whatever the expectations, actual returns have varied greatly over time, of course. Returns were high in the late 1980s, much lower (even single-digit) in the early and mid-1990s, and then explosively high in the late 1990s and into 2000. When the Internet bubble burst, actual average returns quickly turned negative as valuations dropped precipitously, and an unusually high percentage of start-ups died. As for the survivors, investors realized that they would need to stick with their investments longer than originally expected—and you can imagine that an additional couple of years' holding period drastically lowers returns.

Exit Strategy

More and more entrepreneurs are including a section in their business plan that recommends a preferred exit strategy; for example, acquisition by a large company that is also a strategic partner. Your investors will also have their views as to exit strategy. Venture capitalists, for example, usually will want to see a cash-out event in a few years. Because entrepreneurs are rightly focused on getting their ventures going, they often don't give any thought to whether (and if so, how and when) the business might be sold. You should.

Private Placement Memorandum

In addition to a business plan, a company that is planning to raise money by selling securities may also be required to prepare a *private placement memorandum* (also called a PPM).

Securities laws are complex and technical. There are several exemptions from federal registration requirements, and the one you rely upon will help shape the contents of the PPM. You definitely should talk with your attorney before you start preparing a PPM, and he or she should review drafts of it. Sometimes the PPM is prepared in such a way that it *wraps around* the business plan.

Whether or not a PPM is required, you must disclose all material risks and information relating to your business in the business plan and/or private placement memorandum. State and federal securities laws contain broad antifraud provisions that make an issuer of securities liable for either a misstatement or omission of a material fact in connection with the sale or offering of the securities. These antifraud provisions apply even if the offering is exempt from registration.

In effect, a PPM is both a selling document and a disclosure and legal compliance document. Thus the tone of it may turn out to be not quite as positive as company management would like.

Even when a PPM is not required to establish an exemption from registration, it can help provide protection against claims brought under the antifraud provisions of the securities laws, in addition to greatly reducing the chances of any such claim even being made.

Due Diligence File

You definitely should set up a *due diligence file* (also called a *backup file*) that documents the justification for statements made in the offering documents (e.g., the business plan and private placement memorandum). For example, if you claim you have license rights from a third party to use certain key technologies, you should put a copy of the license agreement in this file. Keeping careful records will help you prepare a better business plan, improve your communications with prospective investors, and greatly reduce the risk of a fraud claim.

Conclusion

As you can see, a well-planned business requires a lot of homework. If you understand all the issues explained in this chapter, you are indeed very well prepared to proceed. If your start-up does not have a well thought-out business plan, you may be taking a big risk. You will have presumably generated more information by this time than you thought possible, and will know whether to proceed.

Sidebar 10.1 Writer's Block

It's quite common to hear intelligent, energetic entrepreneurs say that they under-stand and love the strategy for their new venture but are having trouble writing the business plan. Some of the most frequent complaints are

- the writing is taking too much time
- the writing is difficult, even painful at times
- the team is rarely happy with what gets written
- there are too many rewrites, and the plan never gets finished

If that sounds familiar to you, here are a few observations and tips.

- *Beware of the unclear strategy*—The most common reason for the com-plaints cited is that the company's strategy is simply not clear. The CEO and the entire team may believe that they have a wonderful strategy to make the company successful but, in fact, there simply is no clear strate-gy, and no one can clearly articulate it.

- *Eliminate the kitchen sink*—If every good idea is included in the plan, plus the kitchen sink, the strategy will lack focus, and thus can not be called a strategy at all. Under these circumstances, writing a compelling business plan becomes impossible.

- *Do your homework first*—If your strategy is not yet clear, recognize that it's too early to write the detailed plan. Don't waste your time trying. You've got homework to do first. Why describe every twig and branch of a tree if you're not sure what species of tree you have, or whether it's even a tree?

- *Define the strategy*—Get the team together and focus crisply and cre-atively on the strategy. Whiteboards are useful. So are PowerPoint over-heads and an outline. Describe the lack-of-focus problem and identify the key strategy issues to be resolved and the homework that needs to be done. Your goal is to develop a strategy that can be summarized in a few pages. Using overheads to present and rigorously review the strategy can help focus it. Contrary to conventional wisdom, you may benefit from writ-ing the executive summary first.

- *As CEO, take responsibility*—The CEO is typically the best person to write the business plan, or at least to drive the process. Sometimes there is someone else on the team who is more gifted in doing the actual writing. In any case, put one person in charge. If it's not the CEO, that's fine, but the CEO must not abdicate his or her responsibility as CEO to ensure that the right strategy is set and that a professional business plan gets written.

- *Overcome writer's block*—Even when the strategy is clear, writing the business plan can be difficult work, and some people do in fact face writer's block. Tim Berry of Palo Alto Software notes that writer's block is the number one reason for entrepreneurs to visit their site (www.bplans.com) to view a wide variety of sample plans. Also, there are many good resources and tips available on the Internet for overcoming this general problem. (Just type "overcome writer's block" or similar words into Google or another search engine.)

Sidebar 10.2 A Strong-Management/Strong-Market Business Plan

Bill Elder, founder, chairman, and CEO of Genus, Inc., has been with the company more than 20 years. Genus, a successful public Silicon Valley company that manufactures critical deposition processing products for the global semiconductor industry, was incorporated in 1981. It raised $9.5 million of venture capital in just four months based on the strengths represented in a short business plan. To give yourself a feeling of the importance of strong management and unique market opportunity, look at the following summation of their plan.

section title	number of pages	comments
executive summary	2	It is compelling and powerful.
marketing analysis	15	This section is comprehensive (the only setion with subsections); it appears first, and it comprises a full one-third of the plan. It is illustrated with many charts and touches on sales and characteristics of the industry. It also lays out the unique market opportunity. ■ history ■ direction ■ market data ■ similar equipment ■ target markets ■ competitive analysis ■ target market forecast ■ sales level and strategy
product analysis	4	This section contains enough information to describe what the product will do, but says nothing about how it will be developed or invented. Technology alone is not being sold here.
operations plan	1	It is obviously assumed that the members of the strong management team, with their proven track-records, can administer operations.
management and key personnel	8	Three two-page resumes for the president/general manager, the VP of finance, and the VP of engineering, plus an organization chart succinctly says it all. These managers have performed before and investors know they will perform again. No mention is made of any key engineers who might actually design the product.
financial data	12	Essential and basic information—standard financial pro formas along with ■ bookings/backlog forecast ■ capital/leasehold plan ■ staffing plan This section tells investors how much money the business is going to make and when, and also what will be spent to make it happen.

Summary of Genus, Inc., business plan used courtesy of William W. R. Elder, Chairman and CEO of Genus, Inc.

Sidebar 10.3 Business Plan Writing Aids

There are several software products available that may assist you in preparing your business plan. For your consideration, here are two.

- BusinessPlanPro™

  This product is developed and marketed by Palo Alto Software. You can get further information about it at www.paloalto.com and www.bplans.com. According to PC Data, this product outsells all of its competitors combined. The company sells tens of thousands of copies per year.

- BizPlanBuilder™

  This product is developed and marketed by JIAN Tools For Sales, Inc., located in Mill Valley, CA. BizPlanBuilder is the original business planning software, with many success stories and financing results, as well as PC World's "Best Buy" award. It incorporates flexible Excel financial workbooks, as well as one-page sensitivity analysis, business valuation, and an investor deal calculator. Go to www.jian.com for more information.

These products cost under $100 and take you through the process of creating and assembling the various elements of a business plan. Specific text templates and numerous options are included, and you can and should substitute your own text. Sample plans and lots of helpful tips and explanation are included. BusinessPlanPro includes over 250 sample plans.

BizPlanBuilder provides an outline of what should be in a section, and then gives sample text you could use—which is very specific to the type of business. There are many samples to choose from. The latest version of BusinessPlanPro asks you a series of "yes or no" questions and then, based on your answers, proposes a plan outline plus visuals. Such products help you generate text and visuals, such as charts and tables.

Both products are designed for a very wide range of businesses, from barbershops to advertising agencies, from retail stores to ski resorts. Please note that the majority of entrepreneurs who use these products do not intend to seek financing from venture capital firms or other professional venture investors, and that the majority of companies that use these products are not high-growth, high-tech companies.

You are off on the wrong foot if you intend to prepare your business plan by simply using boilerplate text in a cookie-cutter approach. These business plan tools are exactly that—tools—and they are not intended to be a substitute for thought. Venture capitalists are likely to be turned off by business plans that smell of boilerplate. At a minimum, entrepreneurs preparing high-end business plans for professional venture investors could use these products as checklists of topics to be covered.

BizPlanBuilder uses your installed Microsoft Excel and Word applications to open files within the product's program engine. BizPlanBuilder provides three sets of financial tools, which vary in complexity, and the user can select the level of complexity that is most appropriate.

Although some users have been disappointed somewhat with the financial tools in these products, both Palo Alto Software and JIAN have many financing success stories and satisfied customers, including many business schools and their students. The formulas and links in an integrated set of financials can be quite complex, and some entrepreneurs may prefer to also use QuickBooks.

The hard copy books that are included with these two software products are quite comprehensive and useful. Included with BusinessPlanPro are two books: *Hurdle: The Book on Business Planning*, by Tim Berry (the founder and CEO of Palo Alto Software), and *On Target: The Book on Marketing Plans*, by Tim Berry and Doug Wilson. Included with BizPlanBuilder is *Handbook of Business Planning*.

Lots of good information about business plans and the process of creating them is available on the Internet. A good place to start is www.franchises.about.com/cs/businessplans.

Anyone who has created and managed a company that offers business plan software will have some strong thoughts on the subject. The following perspective is from Burke Franklin, the founder and CEO of JIAN.

Building a business requires more than just an idea and a plan. For a moment (and you may need to refer to this moment often), put yourself in an investor's position—what would YOU want to know about a business before you invested in it? We often recommend investing an amount of money in a friend's business just to get the mental, physical, emotional, and spiritual experience of investing precious CASH in someone else's business. Now, more than ever, you must be convincing to the bone. Also, expect that intelligent people with money will want to feel comfortable with you and your answers. You will find that, no matter who you are and what you are doing, you're going to need answers to these basic questions:

- Who are you?
- Why are you in business?
- What is the opportunity here?
- What is the current situation in the world?
- How big is the market?
- What will you sell?
- How is your business structured?
- How will you make money?
- Who else is doing the same thing?
- How do you compare?
- Who are your most important customers?

- How will you reach and inspire them to buy from you?
- Do you have any strategic partners who will help?
- Who are the people running your business?
- What experience do you/they have?
- Who else are you working with?
- Who are your advisors? Who is on your board?
- Where are you today?
- What have you accomplished?
- How much money do you need to start/grow?
- What will you do with the money?
- What's the deal?
- How much money will investors make?
- When and how will investors make their money back?

Your Executive Summary will either inspire an investor emotionally or not (that's how most of us make decisions). This will only open the door to further discussion and exploration. With investors getting so many requests for capital, they want to see very quickly the gist of your business. The rest of your plan must provide the whole story with proof, logic, and the introduction to the people who will be responsible to build and run the business.

Sidebar 10.4 One Venture Capitalist's Perspective on Plan Emphasis

Michael Moritz, partner of Sequoia Capital, a Menlo Park, CA firm, offers these opinions and words of advice.

> In selecting an investment it's all in the timing. Investments in ASPs who peddled third-party software, for example, resulted in big losses, whereas today's ASPs that offer proprietary hosted software are showing early signs of promise.

> We ask where is the market, where are the customers [with open wallets], where are the customers' pain points, what is the solution [and how long will it take to develop, ship, and recognize revenue?], how defensible is the intellectual property (IP), are gross margins substantial, and who is the management?

It is interesting that this statement puts less emphasis on management than most. Management and markets, not necessarily in that order, are usually listed as the two most important factors in evaluating a business opportunity.

> First, the market must be right! We want to achieve scale in a few years. We've learned that great management in a mediocre market often yields an uninteresting company. Ultimately, however, management must be of high quality, and we must see an exit strategy.

> We look for unexploited niches [supply management software in an ever-increasing outsourced and Internet connected world].

> We want to see a substantial market potential, a proprietary product or service, existing channels of distribution, and high gross margins.

Moritz cited software as having good gross margin potential; hardware has less potential—disk drives, for example, look unattractive at 28% gross margin (unless one captures over 50% market share).

> Depending upon the business, we're looking for gross margins that are between 40–70% and operating margins that are between 15–20%.

> After the last financing round, 25–30% of the stock should stay with management. This still holds true today. Management without incentive does not hunger for success.

> Our objective is to turn every $1 million into $10 million.

> We will typically spend one to two months on due diligence before we invest in a start-up.

> Different areas are hot at different times; we like components (semiconductors and optical devices), systems (computing and communications), software (application, network, infrastructure), and services (professional and consumer).

Moritz offers the following comments on the business plan.

Business Definition/Company Purpose

The one-liner.

> We're not suggesting a glib tag line or a superficial sound bite. Nor is the one-liner a substitute for the substance that ultimately must be provided in the business.

> The one-liner is a way to very quickly position your company in one's brain with an immediately relevant frame of reference.

> The definition of your business and its purpose should fit on the back of your business card. Your ability to succinctly articulate this will communicate volumes about your understanding of your business. It says that you have the potential to successfully recruit, lead, and sell.

Business/Technology Problem

Who cares?

> Who in the customer's organization really suffers from this ailment? (Hint: it's not the CIO or CTO.) Know the people who will be recommending, approving and/or using your product. Make sure your company is selling to the people who really control the budgets.

So what?

> Is what your company will be building and selling a "must-have" or a "nice to have"? Demonstrate that the customer/user has an acute pain that causes real agony. Put it in terms of wasted capital expenses or operating expenses, missed application/service revenues, manual/complex/error-prone/time-consuming processes, and so on.

Company/Product Solution

> Given the pain, yours must be the 10,000 mg antidote. Developing a product or service that customers absolutely need—so much so that they'd be willing to pay you as a development partner—is a good way to build the foundation of a long-term business.

Market Size

> The number of customers, with the kind of pain diagnosed, should add up to at least a $1 billion market (or have the potential to grow into this). Demonstrate

> - a *Total Addressable Market* (TAM), based on a top-down analysis of the total number of customers (with assumptions as to number of units, "seats," etc.) in the entire market who could buy the product. This is reflected in dollars of total spending for your product category in the market. This is all measured in dollars, of course, and typically is projected over five years with current customer spending in the first year and projected spending based upon a category growth rate percentage – i.e., a *compound annual growth rate* (CAGR).

- the *Served Available Market* or *Served Addressable Market* (SAM), which is a subset of TAM, and is based on the segment(s) of the total market that you intend to address over the years of your forecast (with estimates of adoption, number of customers, units, "seats," etc). This is an estimation of total spending for your product category in your segments over five years.

- the *Share of Market* (SOM). While you can't go after the whole pie on day one, show that the first slice you'll go after locks you into the customer for the rest of the pie. Subsequently, show the Share of Market (SOM), which is your percentage projection of what share of the SAM your company can reasonably achieve—relative to the competition and in-house projects—over this same five-year period.

Competition

If the pain is agonizing, as you've claimed, then yours is not the only company with a prescription. Competition is good. It validates a market. Just don't be fifth to market in a field of five. There are incumbents, start-ups, and internal customer projects. Demonstrate your differentiation versus each and your barrier to entry versus each.

Product Development

Demonstrate that your solution is hard to do, but that you've figured it out because of the team and the IP. Unveil the solution. Start with the product configurations, and then go to the underlying architecture, the component parts and, finally, the IP/patents. Also, show that you know the development milestones and that the product releases are realistic.

Sales and Distribution

Show that you know how to build the business, price the product to value (not cost of goods sold), and ramp revenue. Product configurations, pricing, sales model, and partners must be mapped out. Keep in mind that the model you serve up will be compared against the market size, type of customer, sales process and financials.

Team/BOD

Demonstrate that the cofounders and early employees possess deep domain experience and have a record of success in the market you're going after. Their personal styles should be confident, but modest. Founders should know what they don't know. A-list founders are sought because they tend to recruit an A team and have the ability to set the DNA right in the first 100 days. A void in the management team is better than having a B-player, who insists on a title.

Financials

This is truth-telling time. Do the financials reflect the plan just described? Include it all. Hide nothing. You need a profit and loss statement over three to five years, cash flow statement, and cap table. Are you frugal and do you know when, where, and how much to spend in order to get to cash flow positive? Do you know how to ramp up revenue? Are gross margins between 40–70% and operating margins between 15–20%? Are you realistic about the challenges of building a company and the obstacles to market penetration? In short, do you know your business?

Sidebar 10.5 What Crosspoint Likes to See in a Business Plan

Think big, act small, and increment your way there.

—Crosspoint Venture Partners

Some venture capital firms offer their views as to what a business plan should contain, along with other helpful information about how to contact them. Crosspoint Venture Partners (Woodside, CA, and Irvine, CA) (www.cpvp.com) speaks to the entrepreneur this way.

Tell us how you intend to build your company. A business plan should contain the following.

Business
Describe your company, business goals, product or service concept, and positioning.

Team
Introduce your team with full resumes including information on existing board members and advisors. What are your hiring plans?

Product
What product or service will your company offer?
What's different or unique about your offering?
What customer problem does it solve?
What is your sustainable competitive advantage?
Who are your current and future competitors, and how is your product better?

Market and Sales Strategy
Describe your customer and your target market.
What is the total market size?
What is your sales strategy and proposed sales channel?

Capital Needs and Existing Capital Structure
How much money will your company need?
Describe the existing ownership of the company.

Financial Projections
Provide current financial statements and proforma statements of cash flow, profit and loss, and balance sheets on a monthly basis for two years and annual projections for three additional years.

Sidebar 10.6 Some Pointers About Your Financial Projections

- You DO Need Financial Projections.

  Many entrepreneurs say they don't have time to prepare financial projections and, in any case, it's a waste of time because projections are simply guesswork, plus the world changes so quickly. Well, you will need them if you plan to raise money—whether from angels, venture capitalists, corporate investors, banks, or anyone else other than your mother (and even she may tell you to do them).

  When asked about the biggest mistakes made by entrepreneurs in preparing their business plans, venture capitalists typically list unrealistic projections and assumptions among the top two or three culprits.

- You Also Need Financial Projections for Reasons Other than Raising Money.

  This point is even more important than the previous point. Preparing your projections will force you to look critically at your business model, strategy, and underlying assumptions. Your projections are also a tool that helps improve team communication, the setting and tracking of milestones, and team performance. Do you really expect to recruit that "A" candidate for the open vice president of sales position if you don't have financial projections?

- Others Will Track Your Projections.

  As time moves on, your actual financial results (e.g., sales, profit) can be compared to your financial projections. Expect your investors, directors, key employees and other interested parties to make these comparisons. You should too.

- Don't Leave Out the Cash Flow Projection.

  In addition to projections for the income statement and balance sheet, be sure to include the third key piece, the cash flow projection. Professional investors and lenders will expect to see this. Remember that "cash is king"—you need to project and manage it in order to avoid a potentially fatal cash crunch. The cash flow projection will help you take corrective action and also identify how much additional financing is likely to be needed in the future and when.

- Three to Five Years of Data is Usually Sufficient.

  Projections usually cover a period of three to five years. Venture capitalists and other professional venture investors typically expect to see five. Other third parties such as lenders are likely to be satisfied with three years. If a longer time frame is needed, you can provide it. A common approach is to prepare the projections on a monthly or quarterly basis for the first year or two, and on an annual basis after that.

- Be Practical About the Detail in Your Projections.

  There's definitely a balance as to the amount of detailed information you prepare and present. Don't get too swamped by the details, especially as you look further into the future. Don't specify how many pencils you plan to buy in year three. Also, expect to present less than you prepare. Third parties will usually be satisfied with top-level categories of income and expenses without all of the backup detail. Too much detail can make it difficult for them to understand your projections.

- Yes, There is an Element of Gamesmanship Involved.

  You may have read that some companies, including large ones like Intel, have backed away from long-range planning (say, three or five years) to focus more on the identification and rapid exploitation of opportunities that arise in a quickly and ever-changing business environment. Since your start-up's environment is likely to be even more volatile than that of a large company, you may conclude that you shouldn't prepare long-range plans. However, since your investors will want financial projections (and will usually run ROI analyses with the numbers you provide), you need to prepare them. If you intend to play the game, you need to exhibit some understanding of the rules of the game. You may prefer to look at this as a matter of "pleasing the gods," and that's fine. Also, please note that companies like Intel do develop plans to exploit the particular opportunities they choose to pursue, much like a start-up would.

- Include Your Significant Assumptions.

  The important assumptions underlying your financial projections should be footnoted or included on a separate sheet, and you must be prepared to explain and justify them. For most start-ups, the most important assumptions are those underlying the revenue projections. It is simple to use an Excel spreadsheet and arrive at whatever revenue numbers you want, but are those numbers based in the real world? If you show a revenue ramp of 30% per year, for example, how and why will that happen? What assumptions are you making about sales channels? What specific customer validation do you have? If your revenue growth is based on an increase in the number of salespeople, what assumptions are you making about their recruitment, training, and productivity (revenue per salesperson)? If you are counting on increased advertising, what assumptions are you making about conversion rates? What assumptions are you making about product mix and pricing?

  As for the date that the revenue stream starts, many plans simply show this at nine months in the future, without credible supporting information. Well, what are the underlying assumptions and justifications for this critical date? Typically, revenues don't start until many significant activities have successfully taken place, such as strategic marketing research; product definition; product development and testing; manufacturing; marketing and sales; shipping; billing; and collection. You need to determine reasonable time frames for each of the steps that apply to your business. For example, regarding product development, before you can set a schedule, you need to understand the real scope of work and the type and number of engineers and other personnel that will be needed. You may show this in the number of months required, where, for example, "hiring, orientation, and programming" might be 1, 1, and 5.

Most investors know that the assumptions are the most important part of pro forma financial projections. A key purpose of the assumptions is to make the reader believe the numbers, by understanding what they are based upon. Stating the assumptions aids communication in many ways. For example, you are likely to benefit when knowledgeable people tell you why they disagree with particular assumptions you made.

Other assumptions might relate to cost of goods sold; headcount (including totals for employees and independent contractors); payment and collection cycles; income taxes; and so forth. In many situations you might logically assume that some expenses should converge to an arbitrary percentage of sales at some point in your start-up's life, based on an industry average.

- Make Sure the Numbers Tie Together.

  Double check your math and the underlying assumptions, and make sure everything ties together correctly. For example, all of your assumptions and projections regarding product development efforts need to be reflected correctly in all appropriate expense categories and in head count. Sloppy work can be a killer. Omitting a category of expenses, such as amortization of capital equipment or interest on an outstanding loan, will make you look amateurish and may raise questions about your competence and perhaps even your integrity.

- Include Projections in Your Executive Summary

  You should include a very brief summary of your projections in the executive summary of your business plan. This may simply consist of revenue and net income by year. If appropriate, you can easily add a few of the major expense categories.

Sidebar 10.7 What Are Pro Forma Financial Statements?

The Latin phase *pro forma* roughly means "for shape" or "for form." It originally described doing something in a specific manner (e.g., filling in a form) for the sake of the process itself. The term is now used in a variety of ways in commerce and finance, and its meaning frequently deviates substantially from the Latin. So forget the Latin. For example, in some usages pro forma really means "provisional" or "a preview"—such as in a pro forma invoice or a pro forma claim (meaning that the official invoice or claim will be sent later).

Regarding the subject matter of this book, the focus here is on two uses of the term pro forma.

- Pro forma—referring to your *projections*

  When you write your business plan, you will prepare not only historical financial statements (to the extent your start-up has a financial history, of course), but also projections as to what you expect your business to achieve in the future. These forward-looking projections are sometimes referred to as "pro formas." So, you may prepare a pro forma income statement, a pro forma cash flow statement, and so forth. Unlike the pro formas discussed in the following section, your pro forma projections are a very important tool in helping you run your business. However, since the term pro forma can be ambiguous, for clarity it's recommended that you use the term "financial projections," or simply "projections," rather than "pro forma."

- Pro forma—referring to historical financials not prepared in accordance with GAAP

  This meaning of pro forma applies almost exclusively to public companies, not to start-ups. However, because you are likely to encounter this usage, the following discussion is included to help eliminate some potential confusion.

  Federal securities laws require public companies to file with the SEC financial statements that are prepared in accordance with GAAP (generally accepted accounting principles) and are accurate, truthful, and complete. However, some companies also present pro forma financial results that aren't prepared in accordance with GAAP, the true purpose of which is to project and paint a more favorable financial picture of the company. These hypothetical results are likely to appear in corporate press releases announcing earnings, and they typically are rosier than the official financial results filed with the SEC.

  The SEC is not a big fan of this practice but it did virtually nothing to curtail it until the wave of accounting scandals hit in the early 2000s (see Post-Enron SEC Reforms).

Pro forma reporting is reminiscent of the drunk leaning against the lamppost—he's using the lamppost for support, not illumination. Don't expect to ever see a company voluntarily prepare pro forma financials that show the company in a less attractive light than what's been shown by its GAAP statements. Nevertheless, the use of pro forma financials does not mean that the company has "cooked its books" (i.e., lied about the numbers and created bogus financials). Rather, the pro formas may be totally accurate—the problem is that the company has some story it's trying to spin, and that, if there's no consistency in how such pro formas are prepared, it can be difficult for the reader (e.g., an investor) to make meaningful comparisons with prior reporting periods or with other companies.

One common use of such pro formas is to present corporate earnings recalculated under a "what if" scenario. What would our earnings be if we excluded certain types of cost? The most common one is EBITDA, which is "earnings before interest, taxes, depreciation, and amortization." (Many financial experts argue that EBITDA is an acceptable tool to analyze and compare profitability between companies and industries because it eliminates some financing and accounting decisions.) During the dot-com craze, the practice got much worse, and there was even a list of 17 expense items that might be excluded to arrive at the income figure! At least one commentator referred jokingly to "earnings before all expenses." Well, when it comes to accounting, the better view is that investors are not attracted to someone who thinks, "If I had some peanut butter, I'd have a peanut butter sandwich, if I had some bread."

Stick with GAAP. Don't play cute games with accounting. Never lie.

Post-Enron SEC Reforms

Numerous accounting scandals at large companies in the early 2000s (e.g., Enron Corp., WorldCom Inc., Global Crossing Ltd.) put a bright spotlight on regulatory reform, and you can expect more heated political discussion and even some reform in the years ahead. In 2001, the SEC warned investors to be wary about companies that use pro forma reporting. In late 2002, the SEC adopted various rules to tighten financial disclosures by companies, with the goal of improving public confidence in the stock market and the integrity of corporate accounting in the U.S. Among these new rules is a requirement that companies that use pro forma reporting must ensure that the information is not misleading or false.

Frank Torres, a legislative counsel for Consumers Union, which publishes Consumer Reports magazine, noted, "It is a sad commentary on the state of corporate America that the government had to take this action. The proposed rules simply require that corporate executives tell the truth and not mislead investors, comply with accounting standards, and make disclosures in plain English."

11

Funding Issues

Business? It's quite simple. It's other people's money.
—Alexandre Dumas

Investment Criteria

Investors determine how much money they will invest based on your minimum needs, considerations of return on investment, and considerations of risk. Obviously the best opportunity (i.e., highest return) with the lowest risk will attract the most funds. This is why your business plan must reflect your very best effort, and why you should have already made progress in building your management team. You are selling an opportunity, and the evidence of this opportunity and your potential for success is reflected in the essential elements of your business plan as detailed in Ch. 10. A marketable business plan will clearly reflect

- a unique market/business opportunity
- as complete a management team as is practicable (and note that venture investors prefer to go with experienced people who have made money for investors before)
- attractive, large markets and a high likelihood of selling and distributing successfully to identified customers

- defensible competitive advantages in those markets
- sound plans and the technological basis for developing and manufacturing the proposed products
- a clear vision and an operations plan for carrying out the business
- clear financial business objectives and an understanding of the funding requirements to make the venture successful (largely the subject of this chapter)

From a prospective investor's point of view, one litmus test of your investment opportunity is, "Would I want my entrepreneurial best friend or sibling to work at this company?"

Cheap Start-Ups Are Finished

Unfortunately, the days are past when you could start a high-technology company in your garage or spare bedroom and grow to be a leader in your industry without significant external funding. Stories beginning, "Founded in 1939 in a Palo Alto garage by Stanford electrical engineers William Hewlett and David Packard..." are history. Yes, every company really starts in the mind of one or two key entrepreneurs, but if your goal is to create a dominant, high-growth, high-technology company, you will almost certainly need outside funding. Of course, there are some fortunate individuals who actually made a lot of money (perhaps even a few million dollars) in an earlier start-up and are using part of that to fund their new venture. In any case, increased competition demands a more professional approach if you are to successfully compete for scarce venture capital and other sophisticated investment resources.

A well-known general partner of a prominent Silicon Valley venture capital firm has stated, "There will be no more successful stand-alone start-ups." By this he meant that because competition is now so strong and so global, a successful start-up must from its beginning have plans for strategic partner relationships with customers (for product specification and distribution), manufacturers (for low-cost manufacturing), and other parties who can help exploit the particular opportunity.

He concludes,

> The rules have changed. While the pace of start-ups has actually turned up, we see more experienced teams starting ventures. Start-ups need at least two initial venture investors plus plans for follow-on financing. The big opportunities—and there are big opportunities, such as in the life sciences, communications and software—are still there.

Experienced venture investors realize that a company's chances of success can be greatly compromised if they invest too little cash. If they believe in the opportunity and your company's team and plan, they may encourage you to raise more money and then use it to shorten the time frames for achieving major milestones.

Looking for Seed Cash

Your business plan pro forma financial documents should tell you how much cash you will need to get your venture to the break-even point (i.e., where your revenues will balance your expenses, both calculated on a cash basis). However, this amount of needed cash may not represent what you should have to start. Realistically, you may have trouble raising that much seed cash. And, if you did raise that much cash, you might have to give up too much equity to do so. Even if you raised enough cash to take you to breakeven, you would need even more cash to finance growth after that. So how much money should you seek to seed your venture, and from whom?

How Much Money?

It really is impossible to specify an exact number here without knowing more about your business plans. Many small software companies are entirely funded by custom development contract work from one or more of their customers. This strategy gets a prototype built without giving up any equity. Usually, though, additional funding will be required. It is extremely important that you never run out of cash; that would be your worst nightmare.

Ideally, you would like to have enough cash to operate for at least six months (see your cash flow statement). Nine to 12 months is even better, since you must start raising additional cash well in advance of the time you need it, and you do not want to interrupt your development schedule to go fund raising any earlier than is necessary. Realize, however, that you will always be raising funds until your company is self-sustaining, or at least it will seem this way to you. A high percentage of entrepreneurs who successfully raised money will acknowledge that it took a lot longer than expected, and that following the dot-com bubble it took much, much longer, especially for initial rounds of financing.

You can make a good rough estimate of how much you will spend monthly based on head count alone. Unless you have better regional and industry statistics available, use the rule of thumb that a business will need to spend about $15,000 per employee per month, including all overhead costs. For high-tech companies in high-cost geographic locations with large capital equipment needs, $20,000 would be a more typical target. Since you will likely have no significant income during your seed and start-up phases, your cash outlays dictate your cash needs. Therefore, for a six-person start-up operating for six months, salaries at 60% would consume about

$$\text{total operating cost} = (\text{no. of employees})(\text{no. of months})$$
$$\times (\text{cost per employee per month})$$
$$\times (\text{percentage of salary})$$
$$= (6 \text{ employees})(6 \text{ mo})\left(\frac{\$15{,}000}{\text{employee-mo}}\right)(0.6)$$
$$= \$324{,}000$$

This estimate is consistent with the fact that a large fraction of private investor initial deals are for $50,000 to $500,000, and that most seed venture capital funds typically invest from $200,000 to $1 million at the initial stage of a new company. Several additional useful rules of thumb follow.

- Have enough cash to attract key employees to the business and to look good enough to prospective creditors and landlords that you can rent space and equipment. Be able to make promises you can keep—concerning payroll, taxes, and rent—for the near future.

- If you're funded entirely through personal funds and contributions from relatives, be able to show a bank balance of at least $100,000 at the formal launch of the venture.

- If you're funded by an angel or other sophisticated investor, try to raise a minimum of $300,000 before the launch.

- If you're funded by venture capitalists, try to show a bank balance of $500,000 to $1 million at the formal launch of the venture.

Of course, the amount of funding needed varies greatly by product and industry. For an extreme example, see Sidebar 11.1, Partnering in the Life Sciences Industry.

Seed, Start-Up, and Subsequent Funding Rounds

Your seed round financing should take you through the point where you can prove your product concept. These funds may involve product development, but they rarely involve initial marketing and sales efforts to promote the product.

Although your start-up round financing will probably be a separate round following seed, ideally the two are combined so that you can concentrate on executing your plan instead of constantly looking for funding. When venture funding is tight, you would be very lucky to secure a combined seed and start-up round. Start-up round funds are used for product development and initial marketing, assembling the key management team, perhaps preparing more detailed business plans, completing market studies, and generally preparing to do business.

First-stage early-development funds are then solicited to initiate commercial manufacturing and sales. You probably will not be profitable in this stage.

Expansion financing for your second-stage, third-stage, and fourth-stage financing steps follow the start-up phase.

Venture funding for first-stage investments typically takes a double hit during the down part of the venture funding cycle. Not only does the total amount invested decline during the downturn, but the percentage of the total invested in early deals is likely to drop also. During the downturn, investors tend to focus more on their portfolio companies and less on new seed opportunities. As a result, the percentage investment in seed companies drops. According to Venture Economics (www.ventureeconomics.com), the percentage of venture funding going into first-round investments sank to its lowest level ever in the last half of 2001, accounting for only 17% of the total during that period. This percentage in first-round deals is frequently in the 25–35% range, and during hot periods of the investment cycle it may approach 50%. According to Charles Fellers, senior editor of the *Venture Capital Journal*,

You couldn't have started a company in the second half of 2001 even if you were selling tomorrow's winning lottery numbers.

Of course, lots of companies still did receive funding during this period, but the numbers were down and the odds much longer. That is what Fellers is talking about. The point here is that you need to be aware of the general funding environment facing you, whether it's hot or cold, and plan accordingly. For example, during a down period you could decide to focus on planning your venture and perhaps trying to bootstrap it without venture funding.

Milestone Funding

In *milestone funding*, a single round of funding is divided into two or more stages, and the start-up does not get the specified funding amount for each stage unless contractually agreed to milestones are met. (See Ch. 12 on term sheets for a more lengthy discussion of milestone funding.) This type of more-demanding financing is likely to occur during the down part of the venture investing cycle. During these times, many already-burnt venture investors wield more negotiating power, and they want to tighten their new deals to reduce risk.

The Nightmare: Running Out of Money

While you hope to get each round funded in a timely fashion and for an adequate amount, there will be times when you are close to running out of cash and unable to make a payroll. One reason you want to structure your business for rapid profitability is to avoid this nightmare. If you run out of cash, you will be faced with the dilemma of trying to raise funds under duress while trying to keep the doors open. To avoid this, you need to raise enough funds, get profitable fast, and keep looking for money.

Where to Get Money
Savings, Mortgages, Friends, and Relatives

A study of 600 high-tech firms by Edward B. Roberts of MIT shows clearly that personal savings provide the primary source of seed capital (see Fig. 11.1). John L. Ward, formerly of Loyola University's Graduate School of Business, stated in the October 1990 issue of *Inc.* magazine that parents constitute the largest single source of start-up capital in the country. Most likely, you will be risking your savings, and those of your loved ones, to launch your new business. Sandra Kurtzig, the founder of ASK Computer Systems, financed her $400 million business with a $2000 commission check from a previous employer and a loan from her father for $25,000.

The most successful entrepreneurs (those whose companies grow most quickly), however, initially had money from venture capitalists and angels. Once again it is emphasized that you should try to start your business with a team. Find members who can help you attract investment funds.

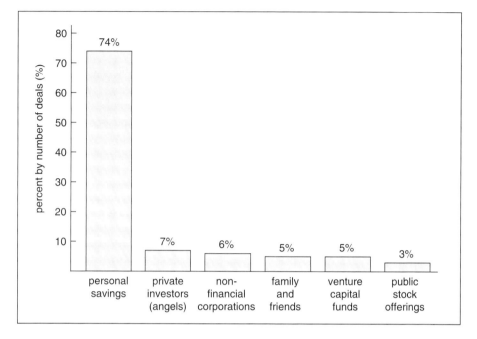

Figure 11.1   Primary Sources for Seed Capital for High-Tech Companies

Accountants and family business consultants will tell you that if you decide to borrow money from relatives, the only hope of making the loan work lies in being very explicit about the conditions of the deal in writing. Popular literature (*Inc.* magazine, etc.) is littered with tragic stories of families torn apart from misunderstandings about money loaned to business start-ups. Also, many an entrepreneur has stumbled when selling stock in their company to relatives or friends. Because entrepreneurs are typically very optimistic about their prospects, the valuation may be set much too high, and frequently the transactions are not properly structured and documented to meet legal requirements. In addition, relatives are sometimes given positions in the company that really don't make sense. Such actions may inhibit prospective investors and employees from getting involved.

Customers and Suppliers

A powerful source of capital in your seed and start-up stages can be your first customers. Getting customers to pay fat deposits up front with their orders (in return for discounted prices, for example) can relieve you of the need to raise substantial funds. Alternatively, instead of a cash deposit, you might request that your customer give you a letter of credit for a down payment that you could take to a bank and borrow against, thereby enhancing your funds and credit history simultaneously. Early customers also can provide an important revenue stream to your business if you provide them with services associated with the use of your product. Income from such services can be used to finance the continuing development of your products. At some point you might want to sell off such income substitution branches of your business to facilitate more product-oriented growth, but meanwhile, services can provide essential sources of funds. ASK Computer Systems used service bureau income to sustain itself in its early days. Largely as a result of this service income, ASK never needed venture capital.

Negotiating extended payment terms with your suppliers until your customers pay you can provide an additional cash cushion.

You may also find a customer who is willing to invest in your company by buying stock. Such investments by customers have become more common, although their popularity tends to move with general cycles in high-tech venture investments; when such investments are hot, customers are more inclined to want a piece of the action. Of course, the customer's assessment of your particular company's prospects is centrally important. Carefully think about whether and how you should approach a customer about such an investment. Although the cash infusion and indirect benefits of such an investment relationship can be huge, you don't want to unnecessarily scare a customer about your financial situation, and you also should avoid relationships that are likely to cause conflicts in the future or interfere with your business strategy.

Angels

Angels are wealthy, private-individual investors who work with start-up companies, often at the seed-level stage. Guy Kawasaki, in *Selling the Dream*, describes angels as "people who share your vision and provide *wings*, such as emotional support, expert advice, and sometimes money—as a mother bird uses her wing to shelter her young."

According to many venture capitalists, there are two types of angels—(1) casual, amateur angels who invest once in a while on an opportunistic basis and who typically don't provide support other than their invested cash; and (2) full-time angels who invest for the long-term, are better connected and more experienced in start-ups, and are able and willing to provide value in addition to their cash. The distinction is important. Venture capitalists strongly prefer to deal with the latter group.

Angels may be doctors, lawyers, other professionals, or successful entrepreneurs and businesspeople. In recent years there has been tremendous growth in funding by successful entrepreneurs and businesspeople. They typically seed start-ups with a few tens of thousands of dollars up to hundreds of thousands of dollars. Angels often are in a position to give you good business advice, usually as members of your board of directors. Also, they will often inject funds into your business on more favorable terms than would some venture capital firms. You will find angels in all walks of life, and it is often up to you to structure and propose a deal to them. Most angels, unfortunately, will not be in the best position to introduce you to the next round of investors.

By accepting angel money, you hopefully will have started your business with a knowledgeable resource and minimal dilution. However, some angels repel venture capitalists; venture capitalists often prefer not to invest along with certain people, so be careful that your early angel is not an albatross. If there is good chemistry here, the new money can live with the old money—the venture capitalists and seed investors can share board seats and vote together. This is more likely if the seed investor is a veteran angel, but it is quite unlikely when inexperienced relatives and friends are involved.

Despite all the attention paid to venture capital firms, angels annually invest in many more companies than do venture capital firms, and the total dollar amount invested each year by angels is typically greater than the amount invested by venture capitalists. This has been true for a long time. In the early 1990s, angels backed more than 30,000 new and emerging businesses a year with about $10 billion, while venture funds backed only about 2000 with $2 billion, according to a study by William E. Wetzel, professor of management and director of the Center for Venture Research at the University of New Hampshire, reported in the *Wall Street Journal*, June 4, 1990. In 1999 Evanson & Beroff estimated that there were about 250,000 angels and that they were investing about $20 billion annually. Another estimate, by Robert J. Robinson, coauthor of *Angel Investing: Matching Start-Up Funds with Start-Up Companies*, did place venture capitalist investments ahead of angel investments in the year 2000 ($50 billion versus $30 billion).

However, angels, while they may be easier to catch, can also be harder to please. Investors must typically be prepared to inject additional funds equal to, double, or triple their initial investments, and they will have to ride the company through rough times. Many angels do not have the investment experience to realize that these things will happen, while venture capitalists are almost always more experienced and able to adapt, and their funds are more heavily financed. Unlike venture capitalists, who may have worked with start-ups for years, inexperienced angels often cannot provide essential business advice. Venture capitalists are in tune with the specific markets they invest in. However, seasoned angels also know what to expect.

Angels who overprice seed deals may seem a delight to you, but to a venture capitalist looking at your start-up round, that may be reason enough to pass you up. If a venture capitalist does come in for your second round of financing and then re-prices the deal (i.e., lowers the price), your angel will get diluted more than expected.

Private Stock Offerings to Several Investors

As you investigate approaching a few angels for seed or start-up capital, you may be tempted to try selling stock in your company to an even larger number of individuals. A private stock offering is sometimes made through the drafting of a Rule 504 private placement memorandum that allows you to raise up to $1 million without too much trouble from the Securities and Exchange Commission (SEC). If you attempt this, you'll most definitely need to work with an experienced lawyer. Table 11.1 summarizes the major exemptions to registration with the SEC and includes comments on how they work.

Securities laws are complex. This chapter highlights only some of the key provisions and concepts, with the goal of helping you become more familiar with the landscape and thus work more effectively with your legal counsel.

Table 11.1 Summary of Certain Exemptions from Federal Registration with the SEC

	exemption limit	limit number of investors	documentation required
SEC Rule 504	$1 million	none	Disclosure document must be cleared by one or more U-7 states; SEC Form D must be filed after sale.
SEC Rule 505	$5 million	none if all investors are accredited[a]; 35 if nonaccredited	SEC Form D if investors are accredited; if not, Form S-18
SEC Rule 506	none	35 experienced[b] investors; no limit on accredited investors	Form S-1 for experienced investors; Form D for accredited investors
1933 Act 4(2)	none	fewer than 25	whatever attorney deems necessary to protect exception
1933 Act 3(a)(11)	none	none if all reside in the same state	Varies from state to state. Company must keep good records on investors and use of proceeds to protect exemption.

[a]*Accredited investors* are institutions or individuals with at least $200,000 in annual adjusted gross income or with a net worth of at least $1 million. The $1 million net worth does not include the worth of a personal residence.

[b]*Experienced investors* are people capable of evaulating the merits and risks of a prospective investment.

Source: Drew Field/Direct Share Marketing, San Francisco. Reported in *Inc.*, December 1991.

Any company that wishes to offer to sell stock or other securities to the public must comply with both federal and state securities laws. The company must either properly register with both the SEC (a federal agency) and state regulatory agencies, or proceed under exemptions (both federal and state) from registration. Almost all venture financing is done under one or more exemptions, and the most commonly used SEC exemption for the first round of financing (i.e., the sale of stock to founders and other investors) is Rule 504. The word "exemption" does not mean that the process is simple or that you can ignore legal requirements. To the contrary, unless you are careful to make certain everything is done right, you will be in violation of federal and state securities laws, and the consequences can be very ugly.

SCOR Financing

Almost all of the 50 states have adopted a funding process for small businesses known as SCOR (small corporate offering registration), which is intended to make it easier for small businesses to raise start-up and growth funding by selling debt or stock to the public. SCOR was enacted by the states as a counterpart to federal securities laws that were intended to reduce the regulatory burden placed on small businesses trying to raise money. Also known as ULOR (uniform limited offering registration), SCOR enables small companies to go public and raise up to $1 million during any 12-month period, without using a brokerage firm. Although SCOR offerings suffer from the absence of an active aftermarket for the underlying securities, the process is reported to work well where there is already a large group of customers or employees who are potential investors. Unlike a private placement, SCOR does not limit the number of accredited or nonaccredited investors to whom the securities can be sold, and is sometimes viewed as a "registration by exemption" and a hybrid between a private placement and a public offering.

For a SCOR offering, companies and their securities attorneys usually rely upon Rule 504 of Regulation D for the SEC exemption from the registration requirements of federal securities laws. SCOR does not eliminate the need for specialized legal counsel, and you should talk with your attorney early about whether SCOR even makes sense for what you wish to do. If you are trying to raise less than $1 million, it is possible that SCOR will work for you.

Many people believe that SCOR created more problems than it solved. Certainly, many companies tried but failed to raise money this way, and many raised much less than intended, at too high a cost.

Selling stock in your start-up company is a very difficult thing to do; also, your stock will have no market, and you and your new company will have little reputation to attract such investors. Although many firms exist for the sole purpose of helping you make these private placements, even they tend to have limited success for the average engineer starting his or her first company. Also, there have been numerous complaints about many of these consultants. Save such excursions for your second start-up, when you become famous from your first success, or at least wait a year or two until your company has a track record. Selling stock may be an exciting idea, but it is not practical for you now. Save your time and more than a little money.

Finally, do not make the mistake of thinking you can bypass or disregard the securities laws; the penalties are severe. Also, watch out for things like rules against advertising investment opportunities. As noted above, you need specialized legal assistance, and you should seek it early in your planning.

Venture Capitalists (VCs)

Venture capital firms are a kind of funnel that gathers money from limited partners and then distributes funds to a large number of carefully selected growing businesses. The venture firm managers, known as general partners, raise this money from pension funds, insurance companies, university endowments, corporations, wealthy individual investors, and the like.

In the early 1990s, a typical VC fund raised $50 million from limited partners and invested in up to 35 companies for several years, and sometimes longer than 10 years.

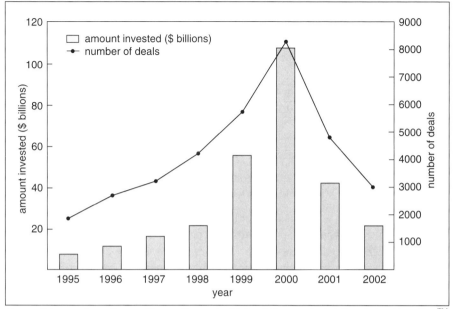

Source: PricewaterhouseCoopers/Venture Economics/National Venture Capital Association MoneyTree™ Survey

Figure 11.2   Venture Capital Investments (1995–2002)

Throughout the 1990s and into this century, the VC industry grew tremendously, with large increases in the number of funds, the size of each fund, and the average investment per company. The number of companies that a fund invests in has not changed much during this period. By the end of that time (the end of the fund), the companies either will have succeeded (returning a profit to the fund through a public stock offering or sale to a larger company) or they will have failed and been written off.

According to VentureWire (www.venturewire.com), in spite of the sharp drop in venture investing following the dot-com bubble, venture capital firms were still able to obtain major commitments to their new funds. In 2000, a record year, 250 firms raised $70 billion in new venture capital funds (including 18 funds of at least $1 billion), and in 2001, 200 new venture funds raised $55 billion (including 15 of at least $1 billion).

VC firms can make money in three ways: management fees (which in effect provide venture capitalists with a substantial monthly draw), carried interest, and stock price appreciation after a company goes public. Annual management fees up to 3% were once considered standard, but many limited partners have more recently negotiated much lower fees. The *carried interest* (or *carry*) is the percentage of profits that the general partners of a venture fund receive out of the total profits realized by the

fund. A 20% carried interest is quite typical, although some top-tier VC firms negotiated a 30% rate during the entrepreneurial explosion in the late 1990s. Additional
profits come from appreciation of the public stock from companies going public before funds are distributed to the limited partners, although such stock may also decline in value.

Sandra Kurtzig, who grew her business completely without venture capital funds,
expresses her opinion on venture capitalists in her book *CEO: Building a $400 Million
Company from the Ground Up*.

> Nowadays it is venture capital that keeps you in business in the early going. But venture
> capital is impatient money, and I doubt many venture capitalists would have stuck with
> ASK as it continued to redefine itself in its first four years. Not having venture capital
> means never having to say you're sorry.

If you decide to go after venture capital for your company, it is critical that you look
for the right chemistry with your investors. According to Ajit Shah, general partner at
Worldview Technology Partners (www.worldview.com), venture capitalists show dis-
respect when they take credit for success and simply refer to a company in which they
invest as "my company." ("The Smart VC: Mercenary or Revolutionary?," *Red Herring*,
July 18, 2001). He notes,

> A great venture capitalist connects with a CEO and his management team to help build
> something of value.

Shah says he will measure his own success as a venture capitalist by what CEOs say
about him after they have worked with him for several years.

According to Venture One, total venture capital investment in 2001 dropped by
65% from the prior year, to $32 billion—still the third highest total in history and a
multiple of the funding levels only a decade earlier. The total for 2002 was almost $20
billion—but still the fourth highest total ever.

Remember, the venture capital business is cyclical. It is essential that you keep
abreast of these trends so that you do not waste time chasing improbable funding
sources. This information will also be extremely valuable to you in setting realistic
expectations for your start-up. There are many industry-specific publications that you
might want to consult.

Very often, a company founder finds it exceedingly difficult to raise funds, especially from sophisticated venture capital sources. Despite the connotation of the name,
venture capital is not the reckless business of throwing money at speculative deals. A
significant amount of due diligence goes into evaluating an investment option, and
risk is always carefully calculated and factored into the structure of investments. Investors want assurances that they will get a return on their investment. As stated previously, they want to see a management team that has performed well in the past and
that will do so again in the future. They want to see you working in markets that are
growing and in which you have distinct competitive advantages. They are interested

in proprietary technology that offers that competitive advantage, but not in technology for technology's sake.

Sophisticated investors also want to see product prototypes—evidence that you can produce what you say you can. In short, they want to bet on a horse that looks like it will cross the finish line. But how can you demonstrate this confidence without expending initial funds? Since you cannot, you get some angel's or relative's money and do your best, thinking that soon you will really impress the pros. Ideally, your initial seed funds will produce a believable product prototype and you will be ready to shop your business plan.

It is best to get a seed-level venture capital firm involved in your business at the earliest date possible. It will have the networking connections to assist you in getting your second round of financing, and will help see that all subsequent financing rounds are equitable. Getting a quality investment firm involved from day one, however, probably will require that you have formed a complete and experienced management team including at least one individual who was successful in an earlier start-up. Again, if you try to do everything yourself, the growth of your business will likely be limited.

Corporate Investors

In most years, corporate investors invest much more in start-ups than do venture capitalists. Corporate investors can be companies of any size, but the larger ones, companies like Cisco, Intel, IBM, Oracle, and Hewlett-Packard, provide most of the dollars from this investor sector.

As used herein, the term "corporate investors" does not include banks, which are creditors, not investors.

There are two principal reasons why corporations invest in start-ups.

- *Strategic value*—The start-up offers some actual or perceived strategic value or synergy relating to the corporation's core business or future product direction. Hewlett-Packard, for example, may invest in companies that directly or indirectly help increase the sale of its core products.

- *A high rate of return on its investment*—Like venture capitalists and other investors, corporate investors want to make a lot of money.

Most corporate investors would say the first reason, *strategic value*, is the more important of the two, but both are really needed to make the transaction successful in the long run. Because the corporate investor is looking at more than just rates of return, you may be able to negotiate a better deal with a corporate investor who sees a strategic fit than you could with a venture capitalist. In this vein, at least one study indicates that the cost (as a percentage of equity given up) of capital provided by corporate investors to start-ups is only about one-half of the cost of capital provided by venture capitalists.

The point here is *not* that you should simply prefer a corporate investor over a venture capitalist. Rather, the point is that you definitely should consider this alternative and identify the corporations that might have a strategic interest in your company. Then do your homework. Here are some considerations.

- Your corporate investor may be interested in buying your company later. This exit strategy or event is more likely than an IPO.
- An investment by a corporate investor may make you very unattractive to its competitors and to certain market segments. For example, you may not be able to sell your product or services to Dell if Gateway has invested in you.
- A corporate investor may, for reasons totally unrelated to your company, be more likely than a venture capitalist to stop supporting your company or to stop making this type of investment at all. For example, if your corporate investor's core business suffers a major downturn and employees and expenses have to be cut, it may be very difficult or politically unacceptable for it to continue supporting your company. The attention and priorities of the corporate investor's management may simply change very quickly.

Corporate investments became especially popular in the late 1990s and into 2000, during the dot-com craze. Companies saw the hot IPO market and the fortunes being made in a short period of time by entrepreneurs and venture capitalists, and they wanted huge returns also, so they jumped in. Many of the resulting corporate investments made sense, and many didn't. One of the longer-term corporate investors is Intel, which through Intel Capital has actively made strategic corporate investments for more than a decade, and at one point before the downturn had a venture portfolio valued at more than $10 billion.

Many entrepreneurs prefer corporate money over venture capitalist money. For one experienced view from the trenches, see Sidebar 11.2, Gary Kremen's Corporate vs. Venture Capitalist Investment Lesson.

Shopping vs. Selling Your Business Plan

Shopping a plan in the venture capital trade means sending it out to too many investors at the same time. Although rapid growth has caused the venture industry to be less closely knit than it was, it is not at all unusual for these people to share information about potential deals. If you give your plan to multiple venture sources at the same time and they know about each other, it may be that no one gives you the attention you are looking for, since each wants to invest time on deals that they likely can close on if they become interested. Similarly, if your plan has been in circulation for a long time, it will be labeled as shopworn. No one wants to spend time evaluating a plan that 100 other investors have passed on. This section is about how to sell your business plan without overshopping it.

Experienced venture capitalists in Silicon Valley offer the following formulas for how to get started in business and how to approach a venture capitalist.

Getting Started

- Plan on establishing a serious partnership with your investors and your management team that will last at least five to seven years.

- Make the firm decision to start a business; your start cannot be contingent on "ifs" and "maybes."

- Get the support of your family (this is absolutely essential).

- Establish very clearly your *raison d'etre* (your unique contribution and business mission).

- Identify the market opportunity, develop the product definition, and build the founding team. (The importance of building a team cannot be overemphasized.)

- Write the initial business plan.

How to Approach a Venture Capitalist

- You should first select no more than three to six venture capital firms whose investment profiles fit your start-up's needs, and be sure that each has a good philosophical fit and compatible style with your team and business.

- It is essential that you obtain a personal introduction from another investor, entrepreneur, accountant, or lawyer.

- Determine if there are any conflicts. (Venture capitalists will not invest in competing companies. They want to focus all their assistance on just one competitor and avoid any conflict of interest.)

- Bring a business plan and personal references to the first meeting.

- At the first meeting, give a brief overview of the plan and identify the key reasons for your success (this is not the time to go into detail). Tell them what is unique, what you have to offer that others do not, and why you will succeed.

- Arrange for follow-up meetings; expect them to take place over a few weeks.

  See also Sidebar 11.3, Some Pointers on Presenting to Venture Investors.

Venture Capital Directories

The preceding information suggests that you prudently and carefully present your plan to investors. First, make sure the investment group you are approaching invests in your type of company. You can do this by consulting some of the many venture capital directories and lists available. Following are four of the most useful and popular directories.

- One excellent venture capital directory, especially for those in Silicon Valley, is available for $100 and is updated yearly (usually in February). It is published by the Western Association of Venture Capitalists (www.wavc.net), a nonprofit association whose approximately 140 members handle almost all professionally managed venture capital in the Western United States. Although their membership roster is free, their more helpful Directory of Members is available by mail only in hard copy form. You can contact them at WAVC, 3000 Sand Hill Road, Building One, Suite 190, Menlo Park, CA 94025, (650) 854-1322. You should invest in the most current directory, since these become obsolete very quickly.

- A national directory is published annually by the National Venture Capital Association (www.nvca.org). It can be purchased online in printed form ($150) or on a CD-ROM ($300).

- VentureOne (www.ventureone.com) publishes the *Venture Capital Sourcebook*, a directory of U.S.-based venture capital firms and their co-investors. It includes contact information, assets under management, partners, and industry and round-class preferences. This resource is distributed free of charge to members of the venture community, including corporations, investment banks, legal firms, and accounting firms.

- *Pratt's Guide to Venture Capital Sources*, updated annually, is available from Amazon (www.amazon.com) for several hundred dollars.

These directories will tell you

- who the officers or partners are

- what kind of company it is and how long it has been in business

- their investment posture in terms of minimum and maximum initial investment and desired total commitment (average and maximum) over time to any one company

- the maturity or stage of company desired (seed to buyout)

- how to seek special help that can be provided in addition to venture capital

- areas of preferred investment

- areas avoided for investment

Do not begin searching for a venture capitalist without first consulting a directory. Of course, if you already have particular firms in mind, you can obtain lots of good information about them by visiting their websites.

To get an idea of the information found in a directory, see Sidebar 11.4, Sample Page from WAVC Directory.

Over the Transom

Over the transom refers to the submission of unsolicited business plans (also known as *cold deals*)—those that appear on an investor's desk without any introduction or explanation. An unsolicited business plan submitted to a venture capital firm has almost no chance of being funded.

Many entrepreneurs have wasted months sending unsolicited business plans to venture capital firms, only to get polite declinations in the mail (if they hear anything at all). To make progress in getting a business plan read and taken seriously, either you or a team member must have a reputation or name-recognition value, or be able to get an introduction.

Investors, for the most part, simply will not take the time to study a plan from an unknown entity.

Introductions Through Networking and Name Recognition

Getting introductions is difficult. This is not something you wait to worry about after you have finished writing your plan. You need to work on introductions long before you attempt to launch your own venture capital-backed company. Besides asking every friend you know who might know investors (your banker, doctor, associates, etc.) you need to make more friends. This is done through the process called *networking*.

Attending professional association and business club meetings might seem unpleasant, especially for a technically inclined engineer or scientist. But if you want to start a venture capital-backed start-up, you must play the role of a businessperson. That means going out and meeting other businesspeople, and getting your name recognized. Determine which organizations in your area would make sense for you to affiliate with, and get on their email lists.

Delivering a speech or a technical presentation (perhaps on the challenges of applying your technology) will go a long way toward opening doors. This enables you to introduce yourself to investors. If you have given a paper at a conference, make reprints and send them to 20 or 30 potential investors with a note saying that you thought they might be interested in the topic. You could email the paper as well. Writing articles for Internet publications is another excellent way to enhance your reputation. If you do these things several times over a couple of years, your name will eventually have recognition value in their minds. An investor might not remember how he or she knows you, but your name will become familiar enough to at least glance at your business plan when it finally appears.

Looking the Part

Dress for Success, by John T. Molloy, is an old book, but it contains good advice. When an investor talks to you about your business idea, does he or she see an engineer or an entrepreneur? An entrepreneur knows how to sell, and you are selling yourself now. You have to offer your customers what they want, not what you want them to want! Styles change of course, and the trend in Silicon Valley has become more informal over the years. However, you can't afford to look sloppy or poorly groomed. You need to assess what's appropriate for you and the particular environment in which you present yourself. At times it was somewhat classy in Silicon Valley to wear tennis shoes and try to start a company. It is still entertaining to incorporate fun with business, but this is only appropriate with friends.

If you obtain an interview with a potential investor, you had better look the part. In many situations, a modern, clean, pressed suit is still appropriate for a man, and a woman should wear a business suit. Investors actually say such things as "Joe (the engineer) had a really good idea and a well thought-out plan, but he was wearing goofy socks." Your commitment to projecting a professional appearance can yield a high return on your investment. This is not subterfuge; it is expected business behavior.

How you present yourself and communicate with prospective investors is the best indicator for them of how you will do in other critical relationships. Investors certainly don't want to invest in entrepreneurs who cannot communicate professionally and effectively with customers and other key third parties.

There is controversy over the "look successful—be successful" point of view. Some claim it should make no difference, but it clearly does to many investors. If you want their money, play their game.

Appearance and social skills do matter. Perhaps the best evidence for this is MIT's Charm School, where etiquette-related subjects are taught in a fun, informal setting once each year. Subjects in the past have included Nerd Love, Table Manners, and Buttering Up Big Shots. For some valuable information and amusement, just type "MIT charm school" into your favorite search engine.

If you have several members on your team, chances are that at least one could use help on some of his or her social skills. Because the issues are so personal, most people feel very uncomfortable raising them, and so they don't. Talking about the MIT Charm School can be a positive, less-threatening way to make some progress.

Unsolicited Business Plan

If you submit an unsolicited business plan to venture capitalists, you will seldom receive any comments to help you out, usually for one of two reasons.

- The investors did not have time to read or evaluate your plan, let alone send you an email or letter, or talk to you on the phone.
- They do not want to risk litigation by commenting on your plan only to have you sue them when they back someone else's plan with your ideas in it.

This leads to the topic of confidentiality and nondisclosure agreements.

Confidentiality and Nondisclosure Agreements

Since your business plan is valuable to you and you do not want any competitors to see it, you must print "confidential" on each page and treat your plan as a trade secret. You should never give your plan to anyone who does not promise (preferably in writing) to respect the document accordingly. This is good theory, but bad reality. Some investors will sign *nondisclosure agreements* (NDAs), but they are few and far between; further, they would be more comfortable with an NDA if they already knew you or the person making the introduction. For example, a well-known entrepreneur who has had multiple successful start-ups may be able to get a venture capitalist to sign an NDA in advance. However, if you submit an unsolicited plan to a venture capitalist with a cover letter or email asking that an NDA be signed before the plan is reviewed, the plan almost certainly will be returned unopened, or you may receive a communication to the effect that the plan won't be reviewed because of the NDA request, or you may receive no response at all. The reason, again, is the risk of lawsuits. Investors receive hundreds, even thousands, of plans each year and they cannot be expected to remember what information they saw where, or to whom they should not tell what.

For example, here's the NDA policy of Asset Management Company, a prominent venture capitalist firm in Silicon Valley.

> We do not sign Non-Disclosure Agreements (NDAs). We receive so many plans each week, that if we signed every NDA request, we would quickly be swamped with legal documents. Our reputation depends on our professionalism and our ability to maintain the trust of the entrepreneurs with whom we work. We will take care to keep all of your material confidential.

The last sentence of the above statement is pretty strong, and many VC firms would probably not go that far in writing. In any event, the central point here is simply that, if you require that an NDA be signed, you won't get in the front door, and you should count on your business plan or other submittal not being reviewed.

Do venture capitalists ever cross the line and unethically use information or pass it on to other parties that really shouldn't receive it? Yes, that's certainly a safe bet, even though there are no good statistics on this point. There certainly are many engineers who believe that their ideas have been stolen by investors with whom they spoke along the way. Also, some engineers believe that they've had their brains "picked" by venture capitalists who had no real interest in investing in their company, but rather were just exploring a field in which they were generally interested, or were really doing some due diligence for another company in which the venture capitalist was invested or planned to invest. It's definitely a murky area, and there are risks, especially if there are multiple venture-funded start-ups in your competitive space.

When it comes to confidential versus public information, the entrepreneur and the investor may have quite different perspectives on the same discussion or presentation. The entrepreneurial team may believe that it disclosed very valuable, original ideas and plans, and the investor may believe that the meeting was simply a high-level general discussion with no disclosure of valuable secrets or corporate jewels (and they may even think of it as just "another plan to sell dog food on the Internet"). Also, the investor may believe it provided valuable feedback and ideas, with no strings attached, and that, in any event, there was no reasonable expectation of confidentiality. There is some litigation in this area, but not much.

It is exceedingly difficult (if not impossible) for an investor to evaluate your plan without disclosing its contents to others, and an investor is not likely to worry about putting everyone in the due diligence chain under NDA for you. The sad fact is that your business plan, especially if it is good, will probably be read and copied by many others. Most of these people will have good intentions and will not purposefully deliver your plan into the hands of a direct competitor, but it does happen.

Your best defense is to withold from your business plan your most sensitive market and technical information. Save this information for one-on-one discussions with interested investors. The purpose of a business plan is much like that of a resume: it gets you the interview. You sell and close after you get the appointment. There is no need to overdisclose confidential information in your business plan or executive summary. When your discussions with the investor get to a point of very strong mutual interest, it may make sense to ask that an NDA be signed.

Negotiation Skills

Take the time to learn negotiation skills (such as Nierenberg's win-win approach to negotiating and deal making). Both sides should act and feel like winners in a funding agreement. Kurtzig of ASK was a big believer in leaving something on the table in negotiations. In her book, *CEO*, she writes,

> To get in or out of a deal, there are four things necessary for a successful negotiation: good sense, guts, diplomacy, and leverage. You need good sense to know what to ask for, guts to ask for what you want, diplomacy to know how to ask for it, and leverage to get it.

Selling to venture investors is like selling to your customers. If you find it hard to sell to one group, you're probably also having difficulties with the other.

Paying for Criticism?

A number of firms will offer to read your business plan, make suggestions for improvements, and presumably represent you to the investment community. Many advertise over the Internet and in the back pages of business magazines and newspapers. Some of these firms are legitimate, but many are just out to get your money.

It is true that you may have to pay for help with writing a good plan. There are many financial advisors who can do a reputable job assisting you with your financial pro formas, for example, if that is a weak area for you. Seek out specific advice as you need it, and pay for that, but do not pay big bucks for general advice. (It would be wise, too, to request that these advisors sign an NDA.)

It is better, however, to work with good, experienced businesspeople who will give you their money and their advice (rather than charge you for it). These individuals are the angels discussed previously. People who are truly in a position to help you become successful will share in the future riches they help you achieve, not in your precious pre-seed funds.

Prenuptial Provisions

Venture capital ratchets (powerful instruments employed by many venture capital investors to protect their percentage stake in your business) are discussed in Ch. 12. A related concept (more in your favor) involves a provision in your contract with your seed and start-up investors that will ensure that they will stick with you when you need them in the future. Although investors typically propose the terms of any deal, everything is there for you to negotiate.

The typical scenario is that you raise some seed or start-up cash from an investor, a sort of marriage is established, and off you go on your honeymoon. But what happens later in the marriage?

As mentioned earlier, your worst nightmare in a start-up is running out of money. What would you do if you were on plan, the time came to raise more cash, and your original investors no longer possessed the enthusiasm for your business they initially had? The marriage loses some of its passion. This situation can destroy a company, and it happens frequently enough that you need to plan for it in advance.

Individuals with significant financial assets frequently employ a prenuptial agreement before getting married. You should consider a similar agreement with your investors.

If you can negotiate it, insert a "pay-to-play" provision in your investment agreement that states the investor's responsibility to put in a pro rata share in future rounds of financing. Although pay-to-pay provisions are more common in later-stage financing, your first investors may agree to one. If your initial investors can, and intend to, support you in subsequent rounds, put that intention in writing, and insert a penalty for a failure to perform. Penalties can be in the form of a loss of liquidation preferences or a ratchet to severely dilute and washout shares. Also, a common provision is that investors agree that their preferred stock will automatically convert to common stock if they do not participate in the future financing. The pay-to-play provision is intended not to punish your seed and start-up supporters, but to apply financial pressure on them to set aside appropriate funds so that they can and will support you when you need them again in the future.

A Final Note

During the dot-com bubble, lots of start-ups raised lots of money from lots of venture capitalists. Many of these start-ups spent the money with wild abandon. For one account, see Sidebar 11.5, Miadora.com—Just One of Many Similar Stories.

Sidebar 11.1 Partnering in the Life Sciences Industry

Sidebar 4.1, about the life sciences industry, highlighted the long time frames from product inception to market (10 to 15 years for new drugs) and the very high risk that a particular product will never make it to market. These factors, plus the high costs discussed here, make partnering especially attractive in this industry. Kent Stormer, partner in the Silicon Valley office of the law firm of Heller Ehrman White & McAuliffe, offers the following perspective on partnering in the life sciences industry.

Pharmaceuticals, Devices, and Other Biotech

A Tufts' study, based on a survey of data from 10 drug companies, estimates that the fully capitalized resource cost of developing and taking a new drug to market is $802,000,000. While the precise figures for development costs may be the subject of debate, they are daunting and help shape the entire development strategy.

Partnering Pitfalls

To address the significant cost, time, and risk challenges and obtain the necessary support to meet those challenges, partnering with another company or companies may become appropriate, potentially involving complex partnering strategies. These strategies can include a variety of licensing and collaborative arrangements. However, in this partnering process, it is important not to relinquish too many of the company's technology rights, particularly those to the core technology. The partnering arrangement must be carefully crafted so that adequate technology remains with the company to allow it to develop and exploit future products, while still empowering the partnership for success.

Some exclusive licenses are so broad that, in essence, they amount to an acquisition by the licensee of the key intellectual property assets of the licensor. A company that is merely the de facto satellite of a larger company is not an attractive candidate for further partnering or acquisition. It is essential, in this context, not to surrender so much of the technology that the company is no longer an attractive candidate for further partnerships or, potentially, a viable and appealing candidate for an exit acquisition. Finally, it is important to take into account and make contingency plans for the possibility that the partnering may not be successful or that it may be terminated by the other party. Excessive dependence on the success of one partnership exposes the company to great risk, much of it beyond the company's control.

It is interesting to note that a paradigm shift took place around 1997, due to the realization that outlicensing too much of a company's technology could be deleterious. Before roughly 1997, smaller biotech companies sometimes viewed partnering from the perspective that "more is better." Success was measured by the number of partnering deals, and many companies fell prey to outlicensing the bulk of their intellectual property, sometimes for an inadequate payback. Valuations of smaller biotech companies were negatively affected by this phenomenon, as investors recognized that not enough had been left behind to fuel a vital enterprise. In roughly 1997, companies began to become increasingly aware of this problem. The solution lies in making such deals more selective and finely tailored for the biotech licensor.

Tailoring the Partnership

The scope of a partnering arrangement can be delimited in numerous ways, in order to retain value in the originating company and to tailor the arrangement so that it best adapts to and exploits the complementary skill sets of the parties.

- *Fields of use*—The partnering/licensing arrangement can be limited to certain fields, particularly fields that may otherwise lie fallow or that may be more effectively developed by or with the assistance of another company (e.g., partnering to develop only particular therapeutic applications of a device, but not other applications).

- *Products*—The partnering arrangement can be limited to specified products or particular types of products, rather than allowing broad access to the technology for application to any products.

- *Activities*—The partnering arrangement can be limited to certain specified activities (e.g., commercial development, or process development).

- *Geography*—The partnering arrangement can be limited to certain geographic areas. For example, a U.S. company might want to outlicense rights in the European Union or Japan to a company with particular experience in those regions.

- *Ownership of inventions*—The partners should carefully define rights to inventions and improvements generated during the partnership. Ownership of new inventions and know-how must be resolved, potentially involving cross-licenses for limited uses, options, or rights of first refusal.

- *Exclusivity*—A partnering agreement can also be limited to a nonexclusive arrangement. However, this approach may be unappealing, in some contexts, since it may discourage the partner from making a significant investment in product development if the licensor can later license the same technology, within the same field, to others. Other variations on this approach are to make the license exclusive for a stated period of time, after which it becomes nonexclusive, or to make the license exclusive so long as certain milestones are met (such as minimum annual royalties).

Elements for Partnering Success

A successful partnership often includes the following elements.

- *Aligned interests*—The partnership must be structured as a win-win arrangement, with aligned interests and significant potential gain for both companies, if the venture is successful. Perhaps even more than for most other types of agreements, the negotiations and the arrangement that emerges from a licensing or partnering deal must provide a positive collaborative springboard for the partnering.

- *Complementary skills*—The partnership must match complementary skill sets and exploit compatible interests. It should allow the company to apply its core technologies and skills, while integrating the complementary skills of others.

- *Clear, common goals*—Clarity and a common understanding of the goals, scope, and terms of the agreement, and of the roles and obligations of each of the parties, are essential. Achieving such clarity and common understanding, in turn, involves the salutary process of thoughtful joint planning.

- *Monetary incentives*—There should be appropriate monetary and other obligations and incentives (both positive and negative) for each company through, for example, milestone payments, plateaued royalty arrangements, and penalties (e.g., loss of exclusivity). Revenue stream timing can be tailored, in some cases, to meet the needs of the parties.

- *Buy-in*—Project buy-in at all involved levels of both companies, including support of upper management and support in the trenches, is essential. Early participation and tailored compensation can encourage these elements.

- *Balanced decision making*—The partnership should involve a properly balanced decision-making and strategy-setting mechanism (potentially involving steering committees with members from both parties). It is important, too, that decision-making entities of this kind be vested with flexibility and scope as to their decision-making options, including timing, formation of committees, delegation, and formats for meetings. Finally, the arrangement should accommodate mutual modifications to the fundamental structure of the decision-making entity, as developments might warrant. The importance of flexibility in this context, as well as for other aspects of partnering arrangements, is underscored by the estimate that roughly one-third of pharmaceutical partnering arrangements are cancelled or fundamentally renegotiated before their terms are up. In short, the road to a marketed product is often difficult to anticipate.

- *Communication*—Good communication is essential to a successful partnering arrangement. The arrangement should provide for a mutually supportive, systematic communication system (beginning with a positive, win-win approach during the negotiation phase) involving regular, scheduled meetings, and should also foster regular informal discussions.

- *Dispute resolution*—It can be very helpful to have a dispute resolution mechanism (short of arbitration and litigation) that involves senior management of the companies conferring and attempting to resolve issues quickly and efficiently.

- *Ownership of inventions*—The partnership agreement should provide for the clear and properly balanced allocation of rights to any new inventions and developments achieved during the partnership. For example, a company may wish to retain ownership of developments in exchange for a share of the revenues, but may allow the partner to use those developments solely in furtherance of the partnership. Clarifying ownership of and rights to intellectual property and know-how developed during the period of the partnership is particularly important. Developments in different fields can be complementary and cross-fertilize one another. They can sometimes be divided up so that each company obtains the rights to the developments within its field of interest. Also, it is often mutually advantageous to empower the partners by allowing them certain uses of these new developments in furtherance of the partnership, particularly in the case of a royalty-based license.
- *Equity or board participation*—Board participation is often more effective than is equity participation at retaining the attention and valuable input of the partner.

Funding Rounds

Multiple funding rounds may be necessary. A company should plan each round with an eye to the potential that other rounds may follow. Thus, a company should avoid unconventional arrangements that may disquiet later potential investors, or concessions (as to price or terms) that it may not want to repeat in later rounds. Even relatively conventional arrangements crafted into early financing rounds (e.g., series voting on mergers) can be difficult to modify in later rounds.

Complexity

Added complexity in the biotech arena extends the due diligence process and limits funding sources. Such complexity can result from several factors not of concern in other industries: evaluating whether a compound or device will display required efficacy and safety necessary to bring it to market; assessing whether and how quickly the FDA will grant marketing approval for it; and dealing with the inherent complexity of life sciences technology and patents.

Trade-Off of Early vs. Late Funding

Delayed partnering tends to be more lucrative for the company (due, for example, to the more advanced state of product development and to reduced risk regarding the fate of the product). However, late funding requires a greater initial capital investment by the company to develop the technology, and thus allocates more of the risk of early product problems and attrition to the company. Late funding can also leave the company in a vulnerable position, without adequate cash reserves—a situation that can be exploited by a potential licensing partner. Licensing arrangements, particularly those involving big pharmaceutical companies, commonly take 6 to 12 months to negotiate, during which time the potential partner will likely learn of the exigency, and it can deepen. On the other hand, there is often pressure from shareholders and investors to partner too early in order to obtain early endorsement of their technology. In the case of drugs, the start of Phase III studies (the stage of clinical trials just prior to seeking marketing approval from the FDA), generally involving 4000 to 7000 human subjects, is frequently a juncture where cost, and thus the need for partnering, makes a quantum jump.

Outsourcing: The Virtual Company Model

This is the "buy or make" decision. Outsourcing certain activities can enable the company to focus on its strengths and reduce infrastructure and overhead that it cannot adequately sustain and prorate over other products. A company can outsource clinical trials (e.g., through Contract Research Organizations), process development, sales, and many other necessary activities, for fixed prices that minimize the sacrifice of the company technology. Ownership of the results and intellectual property generated through such outsourcing arrangements should preferably remain with the company. Consultants can assist with the strategy and management of these activities.

Exit Strategy

It is essential to avoid granting early-stage partners veto rights over subsequent partnerings, particularly potential exit arrangements. For the same reasons, important early agreements should also be negotiated so they may be assigned in the event of later agreements and so they cannot, for example, jeopardize an exit strategy by being terminable. Properly executed collaborations can help lay the groundwork for a favorable exit with partners or others, as well as leave the door open for additional partnerships with other companies.

Sidebar 11.2 Gary Kremen's Corporate vs. Venture Capitalist Investment Lesson

How many times have you raised venture money and negotiated the investment terms? Probably 100 times less frequently than professional venture capitalists have. Because of this, VCs are in the driver's seat—it's likely they can out-negotiate and outwait you. My strong suggestion is that, if your investment opportunity is synergistic with the goals of a key corporation, you focus on corporate or strategic investors first. They are not as price-, terms-, or return-sensitive as VCs. Often times you can agree to a nonequity deal (i.e., cash for a license, distribution rights, or a right of first look at some technology you are developing).

If you focus on how you can solve a corporation's current strategic or operating problems, the corporation might be more interested than not in investing. The key here is to find the person with the capital or operating budget to invest. You are much more likely to find this person in a profitable operating division than in corporate business development. Operating people in a company frequently have more power than do general partners at venture firms.

Also, a corporate investor/partner usually gives more credibility in the marketplace than does a venture capital investment.

—Gary Kremen
founder of match.com and
several other start-ups

Sidebar 11.3 Some Pointers on Presenting to Venture Investors

Always Tell the Truth

Don't lie about the current status of your team or company ... or anything else. Investors will undoubtedly discover the truth, either in subsequent communications or in the due diligence process, should your relationship go that far. Investors who believe they have been lied to will quickly sever their discussions with you, and you may not be told why.

Avoid Puffing Up Your Team and Prospects

This really emphasizes the previous point. Experienced investors take pride in their ability to detect exaggeration or deception.

Listen Carefully and Don't Be Defensive

How you handle questions and criticism shows much about your character and management abilities. The particular answers to questions are important, but equally important is how you think on your feet and interact with someone who may be on your board of directors. As you speak, investors are consciously or subconsciously forming an opinion about your ability to communicate clearly and professionally with various constituencies—your team, the directors, partners, customers, and so on. They're asking themselves, "Is this someone we should bet on?"

Don't Pretend that All Your Projections Are Conservative

Your revenue projections should be realistic and defensible, but don't pretend that it will be easy to meet them. Explain your central assumptions underlying the projections, and avoid projections that are simply "top down" hopes (i.e., "If just one person in 1000 in Europe buys our widget, then our revenues in year three will be $250 million ... and of course we expect to do much better than that."). Explain clearly what major milestones have to be reached and when, in order to achieve your sales projections.

Be Prepared

In addition to preparing a concise presentation, critique your own presentation strengths and weaknesses.

Be Respectful of Your Competition

First, recognize that you do have competition. Some entrepreneurs claim that they don't have any competitors. This is a red flag for investors. Also, it's embarrassing to have a VC mention a competitor during your presentation that you have not identified in your plan and discussions.

Sidebar 11.4 Sample Page from WAVC Directory

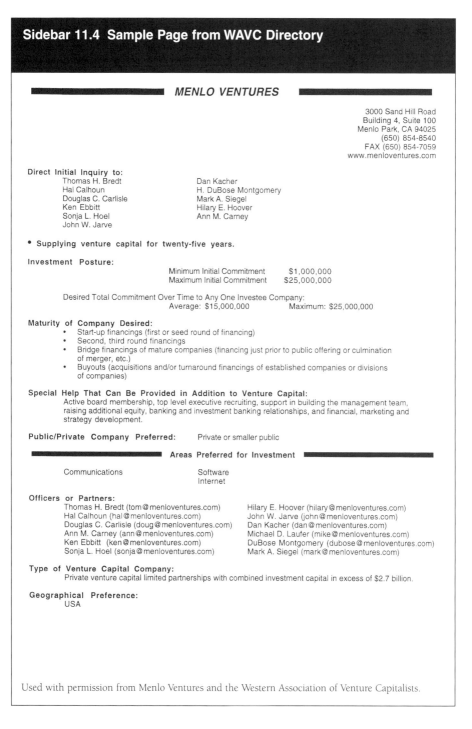

MENLO VENTURES

3000 Sand Hill Road
Building 4, Suite 100
Menlo Park, CA 94025
(650) 854-8540
FAX (650) 854-7059
www.menloventures.com

Direct Initial Inquiry to:

Thomas H. Bredt	Dan Kacher
Hal Calhoun	H. DuBose Montgomery
Douglas C. Carlisle	Mark A. Siegel
Ken Ebbitt	Hilary E. Hoover
Sonja L. Hoel	Ann M. Carney
John W. Jarve	

• Supplying venture capital for twenty-five years.

Investment Posture:

Minimum Initial Commitment	$1,000,000
Maximum Initial Commitment	$25,000,000

Desired Total Commitment Over Time to Any One Investee Company:
Average: $15,000,000   Maximum: $25,000,000

Maturity of Company Desired:
- Start-up financings (first or seed round of financing)
- Second, third round financings
- Bridge financings of mature companies (financing just prior to public offering or culmination of merger, etc.)
- Buyouts (acquisitions and/or turnaround financings of established companies or divisions of companies)

Special Help That Can Be Provided in Addition to Venture Capital:
Active board membership, top level executive recruiting, support in building the management team, raising additional equity, banking and investment banking relationships, and financial, marketing and strategy development.

Public/Private Company Preferred: Private or smaller public

Areas Preferred for Investment

Communications	Software
	Internet

Officers or Partners:

Thomas H. Bredt (tom@menloventures.com)	Hilary E. Hoover (hilary@menloventures.com)
Hal Calhoun (hal@menloventures.com)	John W. Jarve (john@menloventures.com)
Douglas C. Carlisle (doug@menloventures.com)	Dan Kacher (dan@menloventures.com)
Ann M. Carney (ann@menloventures.com)	Michael D. Laufer (mike@menloventures.com)
Ken Ebbitt (ken@menloventures.com)	DuBose Montgomery (dubose@menloventures.com)
Sonja L. Hoel (sonja@menloventures.com)	Mark A. Siegel (mark@menloventures.com)

Type of Venture Capital Company:
Private venture capital limited partnerships with combined investment capital in excess of $2.7 billion.

Geographical Preference:
USA

Used with permission from Menlo Ventures and the Western Association of Venture Capitalists.

Sidebar 11.5 Miadora.com—Just One of Many Similar Stories

The vast majority of the best professionals, including top-tier venture capitalists, actively participated in the dot-com "tulipmania." (Note: Traders in 17th century Holland drove up the price of tulip bulbs to astronomical levels in a frenzy of irrational exuberance, and when the bottom fell out of the market, thousands of Dutch businessmen were ruined.) This first-hand account about Miadora.com (online jewelry) is just one such story from that period of madness.

> We had our first $2.6 million round of funding from blue-chip VC firm Sequoia Capital and launched our site in September 1999. From the get-go Sequoia said let's get this thing up and running, have a great Christmas and IPO in May and June. That was the idea. We had a second round of capital, then a third in March totaling $46 million. Weeks after that the meltdown started.
>
> We were going to be out of cash in September, and yet we still went out and bought a company that was little more than a URL—Jewelry.com—for $5 million. We thought nothing of spending $250,000 on a single ad.
>
> Sequoia said: 'Do it! Spend the money, don't let it sit there!' We drew up a budget but never ever had a budget meeting after that. I could have spent like a drunken sailor, and nobody would have said anything to me.
>
> There wasn't a wind down. Up until the last day, Sequoia was trying to make a deal with the other jewelry dot-coms to come together, join forces and keep it going. At the eleventh hour, on Sept. 21 [2000], they had an emergency meeting and said: 'We are not putting in another dime. Close it down.' I remember that day like I remember the day Kennedy got shot.

—Richard Caniglia
Vice President of Operations
Miadora.com

Note: The company's life span was 15 months. This story was reported on Forbes.com, as well as on the controversial website f _ _ _ edcompany.com.

12

The Term Sheet—A Practical Overview

He who has the gold (that you need) makes the rules.

—The professional venture investor's Golden Rule.

It's an exciting moment when you receive your first term sheet from a prospective investor. It validates all the long hours you've put into your start-up, and you feel good. However, take a deep breath and don't get carried away too quickly—there's a lot more work ahead. You need to look at the big picture and make certain the proposed financing fits into your long-range plans. You also need to complete your due diligence and make sure that the prospective investor is a good fit for your company.

This chapter is intended to take the mystery out of term sheets. The typical first-time entrepreneur has heard about term sheets but wants and needs to learn more. This chapter will cover the key provisions of term sheets and shed some light on the negotiations. The goal here is not to make you an expert in this area. Investors don't expect the entrepreneur to be an expert on financing, but they do expect you to be savvy enough to have learned the central concepts and to be able to negotiate in a competent manner. Although subsequent financing rounds will be discussed, the main focus will be on the "Series A" financing (i.e., the first professional round, which could include angel investors, venture capitalists, or possibly corporate investors).

The first negotiations are usually directly between the entrepreneur and the investors, without attorneys present, so it's important that you understand the terminology and rules of the game. Your attorney, and possibly other key advisors, can help guide you through the process, and you should involve them early in the process.

The term sheet is typically drafted by the venture capitalist, or other professional venture investor, who prefers to use a document with which he's familiar. Of course, nothing prevents you from preparing the term sheet, and it's more likely you will do so if you're seeking money from angels or other nonprofessional investors. In any case, the term sheet is not the document that sells the company; rather, you use other tools, such as your executive summary and slide presentation, to do this. The term sheet is dry and legal—and totally devoid of sizzle.

A sample term sheet appears at the end of this chapter (see Sidebar 12.8). It is intended to be fairly representative of what you might see. As such, its purpose is not to show the latest fads in term sheet design, since these are likely to change over time. If you're lucky, you'll encounter only shorter and fairer term sheets that better balance the interests of the investors and the founders—not the much longer, draconian versions that are used by some *vulture capitalists* to pick the carcass clean if necessary.

For some practical pointers regarding the preparation and negotiation of a term sheet, see Sidebar 12.1, Term Sheet Tips.

Definition of Term Sheet

The *term sheet* (sometimes called a *letter of intent*) sets forth in summary or outline fashion the essential terms of the proposed financing of the company. In Europe it may be referred to as the *heads of agreement* (in reference to a document setting forth the *headings* of the principal terms of a proposed contract, with summary discussion of each point).

Typically, the term sheet is not a binding agreement, except that it may create a few limited binding obligations (such as an obligation to pay certain expenses) that would survive should the transaction not close. (See the section entitled Survival of Certain Provisions for more information.) The financing becomes binding only when and if a definitive written agreement is entered into by the parties. Although the term sheet is not binding, it can provide some credibility for your dealings with prospective employees, potential partners, and other parties.

The term sheet is the first step in a series of legal events leading to the consummation of a financial investment. The sequential steps in almost all situations are

1. negotiation and signing of the term sheet
2. negotiation and signing of lengthy definitive agreements in accordance with the term sheet, with such changes as the parties may agree to
3. completion of due diligence
4. the closing (i.e., everything is done, and you get the money)

Very infrequently, the term sheet is skipped, and the parties go directly to the definitive agreements. This may make sense if the parties (especially the attorneys) already know each other and have worked well together, the market and the proposed deal are quite clear, and there is a mutual desire to close the deal as soon as possible.

Also, due diligence is typically done throughout the negotiation process. For example, the investors would not even consider preparing a term sheet unless they had already performed substantial due diligence about your company, the business opportunity, the team, the competition, and so forth. Likewise, before you meet with prospector investors, you need to check them out, and you should continue this process even after the term sheet is signed.

A term sheet is typically from three to six pages long, but after the Internet bubble collapse, it became more common to see longer ones, as investors added and expanded protection clauses.

The term sheet is intended to document the nonbinding *handshake* between the investors and the company. It sets forth all key business and legal terms of the transaction, and thus it should shake out any *deal killers*. This can prevent a lot of wasted time, since there's no point in having attorneys prepare lengthy, definitive agreements if the parties are not in basic agreement on all of the major issues.

Primarily for fun, a one-paragraph term sheet appears in Sidebar 12.2.

Standard term sheets tend to become more onerous in periods of difficult financing, as venture capitalists tighten customary terms and add other provisions in order to better protect themselves.

Although the term sheet does not obligate the investors to complete the investment, a fully negotiated term sheet may give the investors enough comfort to extend *bridge financing*, which frequently uses warrants as a *kicker* for the investors. If bridge financing is extended, the term sheet will be modified to include the terms of the bridge. (Bridge financing is discussed in the Warrants and Bridge Financing section of this chapter.)

Dilution and Antidilution

The central purpose of this section is to help you understand antidilution concepts and provisions that are likely to appear in a term sheet you receive from a venture capitalist or other prospective investor.

Dilution is a word with numerous meanings, many of which go well beyond the narrower subject matter of the discussion here. In the broadest sense, existing shareholders are diluted whenever the company grants any new shares of stock (whether common or preferred), grants a stock option, issues a warrant or the like giving the recipient the right to purchase or be given stock, or otherwise grants any right that gives the recipient some claim on the assets or income of the corporation. Whenever any of these events occurs, the percentage interests of the current stakeholders are reduced, and they are therefore *diluted*. However, this very broad definition of dilution is not the basis for the *antidilution* protection sought by venture capitalists, or for the following discussion, and not all dilution is bad.

Others define and view dilution from a different perspective. A stock analyst, for example, may be concerned about whether a particular transaction (say a merger) will increase or decrease earnings per share, and only in the latter case (a decrease in earnings per share) will the transaction be considered *dilutive*. Thus, the analyst's dilution focus is not on the number of shares outstanding, but rather on earnings per share. Again, this is not the basis for the antidilution provisions that are the subject of the following discussion.

Also, don't consider dilution to be a dirty word. Whether it is or not is totally situational and depends on the particular facts. As your company grows, you in fact will be working hard to achieve many things that cause dilution, but which you expect or at least hope will be wonderful for your company. For example, you are elated when you successfully hire your new vice president of engineering and grant him stock or options. You celebrate the signing of a strategic contract with a Fortune 500 company, even though warrants to purchase some of your stock are part of the deal. You are relieved when you close a needed round of financing on fair terms, even though your shareholdings are diluted. Presumably, in each case you believe that you are increasing the value of the company, and thus you are happy with a smaller-percentage slice of a bigger pie.

Venture investors seek a variety of provisions (which are discussed in various sections later in this chapter) to protect their interests from being diluted. The main such provision typically appears in a section entitled Antidilution Protection (or the like). However, additional protection may also appear elsewhere. For example, it may appear under Preemptive Rights (also sometimes entitled Rights of First Refusal), which allow the investors to participate in future financings on a pro rata basis—and which require your attention even though the company receives the same amount of money no matter who buys the stock. The main point here is that the antidilution protection is not all neatly contained in one section of the term sheet and that you need to understand the entire picture. As for the section entitled Antidilution, it typically contains two types of antidilution provisons.

- innocuous provisions (sometimes called *structural antidilution*) that apply to all shareholders and are simply a matter of good housekeeping
- extremely important provisions (usually called *price protection*), which are typically heavily negotiated and, when triggered by a lower price per share in a subsequent financing round, give the investors additional shares of stock for no additional payment (note that, especially in the case of the ratchet, these can be a killer)

As you and your attorneys review a term sheet, one of your goals should be to clearly understand how each provision dilutes, or has the potential to dilute, your equity interest in the company. The following discussion will help you do this.

Key Provisions of Term Sheet

Type of Security

In almost all cases, the venture investor will want *preferred stock* rather than *common stock*. Accordingly, the discussion in this chapter assumes that preferred stock is the investment vehicle. Common stock as the investment vehicle for venture investors was more common in the early days of venture investing and continuing into the 1970s. Since then, preferred stock has become, by and large, the standard. Also, since the late 1980s, *participating* preferred stock (discussed in the section entitled Liquidation Preference) has become much more typical (as opposed to simple *convertible preferred*) and is probably now used in more than half of all deals.

Valuation or Price

What *pre-money* price will be put on your company? Whatever is decided, you need to be clear what assumptions you're making. Typically the pre-money valuation is *fully diluted* (i.e., it includes all of the outstanding stock of the company, plus any outstanding options, warrants, or other rights to buy stock, plus any unallocated options available in the company's stock option pool). Whether or not the option pool (both allocated and unallocated) is included in the pre-money price can make a significant difference in the effective pricing and thus the actual percentage of the company that you are selling. So be clear. For an example, see Sidebar 12.3, Who Bears the Dilution Caused by the Stock Option Pool?

Don't think in terms of price per share, even though the term sheet will include this. Rather, think in terms of the pre-money valuation of the entire company (e.g., $5 million) and the post-money valuation (e.g., $7 million, if $2 million is invested), and think in terms of the percentage of the company owned by your different constituencies.

If you had a choice, you would want a given pre-money price (say $5 million) to *exclude* the stock option pool. Done this way, the stock options dilute everyone, not just the current shareholders, and your percentage share ends up being higher. Some people refer to this as a negotiating *trick*. Rather, it is simply an illustration of how the numbers work, depending upon your assumption regarding the stock option pool, and why it's important to be clear about all your assumptions. In any case, the sophisticated investor certainly understands the difference.

Capitalization Table

A term sheet will frequently include a brief capitalization chart that shows the pre-money stock distribution and post-money distribution among the different equity constituencies (i.e., the current shareholders, the option pool, and the new investors). Many people find this visual form of presentation easier to understand.

Milestone Financing

In a *milestone financing*, a single round of venture funding may be divided into two or more stages, and the start-up does not get the specified funding amounts for each later stage unless contractually agreed to milestones are met. This is also sometimes called *staged financing* or *two-step funding*. For example, the term sheet for a $5 million investment could provide for an initial payment of $3 million, plus an additional payment of $2 million if and when the company successfully completes the prototype of its product. In this example, the price per share is likely to be the same throughout, although it doesn't have to be. Here are some additional comments.

- Milestone financing has been used for a long time, but it became uncommon during the Internet bubble when it was easier for entrepreneurs to raise money. Milestones are more likely to be used if the investor who wants them has the lion's share of the negotiating power.

- The milestones may to tied to just about anything—achieving profitability by a certain date, signing a contract with a large customer, hiring an agreed-upon CEO, successfully building a prototype, and so forth. Frequently, the milestones are some of those already provided by the start-up in its business plan, which means, in effect, that the investor wants management to do what it says it will. You need to be especially careful here, because there are lots of surprises in the world of start-ups, and things frequently take longer than planned.

- Milestones favor the investor by reducing the investor's risk. If the company doesn't meet a milestone, the investor is not required to put up the additional funding. In this case, the investor can cut its losses and run, or it can negotiate a more favorable deal before releasing the additional money. Expect to see your start-up's valuation drop if you don't meet the milestones.

- Rather than being tied to additional funding, the milestones are sometimes structured so that something else negative happens if they are not met. For example, they may be structured to provide *price protection* to the investor by automatically increasing the investor's percentage ownership of the company if the milestones are not met. This is typically done by reducing the conversion price that applies to the conversion of the investor's preferred shares into common. Sometimes the missed milestones give the investor the right to buy more shares at a much lower price. There's another possibility that should be strongly opposed—that the missed milestones give the investors control over the board of directors.

- There is another big potential negative. Since circumstances can change quickly, the milestones may cause management to pursue a certain course that, in retrospect, is not in the best interests of the company. For example, if the start-up does very well, it may be more prudent to increase marketing and engineering expenses ahead of plan than to achieve a milestone of profitability by a certain date. Or perhaps the company continues to drive to complete a certain product because that's a stated milestone, when in fact a change in product is what is warranted. This potential negative should not be ignored, and you may be able to use it to avoid milestone financing.

- Many venture capitalists prefer not to use milestones.
- If milestones are used, they need to be carefully considered and crafted. Of course, it's better to avoid them completely.

Additional Investors

Are the venture investors going to fund the entire amount of the round themselves? Or does the term sheet require you to find additional investors to complete the round? If the proposal is conditional based upon finding new investors to fill out the round (say, to invest the last $2 million in a $5 million round), you really don't have a solid proposal.

Stock Option Pool

The size of the stock option pool reserved for employees of the company typically ranges from 10 to 30% of the fully diluted capital structure of the company after the Series A investment (which includes the outstanding common, the stock option pool itself, and the Series A preferred stock sold to the investors). The appropriate size of the option pool depends upon several considerations, such as the number and type of new hires the company is planning, whether the founders and other key employees hold only common stock (meaning their shares aren't included in the option totals), the industry the company is in, the relevant importance of options in the employees' compensation arrangements, and the maturity of the company. Both management and the investors should want to ensure that there are sufficient unallocated shares in the option pool to attract the contemplated additional key hires and other personnel over an agreed-upon period of time (say, one to two years).

Experienced investors understand the importance of stock options and will not object to a pool of reasonable size. It's even possible they will want to increase the pool size proposed by management. Typically, the company and the investors reach agreement upon the size of the pool, and this is included in the term sheet. If the option pool needs to be increased later, the board can act on this, although it's possible that the investors (typically through their director representatives) will want the right to approve or disapprove the increase.

Warrants and Bridge Financing

Warrants are contractual rights that give the holder the right (but not the obligation) to buy a specific number of shares of a company's stock at a stipulated price (called the "exercise" or "strike" price) within a certain time limit or, occasionally, in perpetuity. A warrant works like an option and is often used as a "kicker" in conjunction with another debt instrument or security.

With regard to term sheets (the subject matter of this chapter), warrants are frequently used in bridge financing as an additional incentive for the lender/investor who is providing the needed interim or "bridge" financing. Such funds are intended to get the company safely to its next financing, and a warrant, in part, reflects the added risk the lender/investor is taking in this kind of financing. The lender/investor thus receives both a promissory note (convertible into company stock) and a warrant.

For example, you may hear about a start-up receiving $1 million in 6% bridge financing with 25% warrant coverage. This means that $1 million is being loaned to the company at a 6% rate of interest (with the intention that it be converted into stock in the upcoming larger financing round that the company is working on), and that the lender/investor is also receiving a warrant to buy $250,000 (i.e., 25% of $1 million) of additional stock at the to-be-determined price of the new round.

See Ch. 16 for further discussion of warrants and bridge financing.

Liquidation Preference

A liquidation preference applies in the event of a *liquidation* of the company, and you should pay attention to how liquidation is defined. In the world of venture capitalist-backed companies, it is almost uniformly defined to include both of the following.

- *A disaster situation*—In this situation, the assets of an unsuccessful company are being sold or disposed of in some fashion. (The term sheet may refer to this as a *liquidation* or *winding up* of the company.)
- *Any other sale of the company*—This typically is defined to include any transaction—such as a merger, acquisition, or sale of all or substantially all of the assets of the company—that results in the shareholders of the company not owning a majority of the shares of the surviving entity.

In rare situations, the term sheet will divide this topic of liquidation preferences into two sections: one entitled *liquidation preference* and one entitled *sale preference*. This approach could make sense if the preference terms are intended to vary for some reason. This is more likely to occur in later financing rounds than in the Series A round, since the complexities of multiple rounds may lead to varying treatment of the different series of preferred stock, depending upon whether it's an *upside* situation, on one hand, or a *disaster* or *downside situation*, on the other.

For the most traditional type of liquidation preference (i.e., the *nonparticipating* liquidation preference, discussed later in this section), the preferred shareholders need to decide, at the time of liquidation, whether to stick with the liquidation preference or convert their preferred shares to common shares. If the total liquidation distribution is below a certain dollar amount (which can be calculated), they are better off sticking with their preferred stock, and if it's above that amount, they do better by converting. The investors can easily calculate which is better for them. Of course, when investors put money into your company, they hope that ultimately, at the time of a very successful liquidity event (e.g., a sale of the company), it will be in their economic interest to convert their preferred shares into common shares and divide a huge gain with the other common shareholders on an equal pro rata basis.

There are different types of liquidation preferences, including

- *nonparticipating* liquidation preference
- *fully participating* liquidation preference

- *partial participating* or *hybrid* liquidation preference
- *multiple* or *super* liquidation preference (e.g., 2X or 4X, vs. the traditional 1X), which became more common right after the Internet bubble when many entrepreneurs viewed some venture capitalists as working hard to deserve the derogatory name *vulture capitalists*.

See Sidebar 12.4 for examples of the liquidation preference at work.

A *nonparticipating* liquidation preference is the best type for the founders and other employees holding either common stock or stock options. In the event of liquidation, the preferred shareholders are first in line among the shareholders and receive the amount of funds they originally invested, but they do not share in anything beyond that. Why would the preferred investors ever agree to a provision that results in them only getting their money back? The answer, as noted above, is that they have the right to convert their preferred stock to common stock at any time, and will do so if they would receive more on a fully converted basis (if, for example, the company's value had greatly increased).

A *fully participating* liquidation preference is much less favorable for the common stock stakeholders and should be avoided if possible. In this variation, the preferred shareholders first receive the amount they originally invested, and they then *participate* fully with the common shareholders on a pro rata *as-converted* basis in the remaining assets of the company. Since they have it both ways, they don't need to run numbers to decide whether to convert.

A *partial participating* preference, also called a *hybrid*, is a variation of the above types and can take different forms. Typically, the preferred shareholders first get their money back, and they then share the remainder with the common shareholders on a basis that is a percentage of what the *fully participating* amount would be. Another variation is that the preferred investors first get their money back, and they then participate with the common shareholders until they receive up to a multiple (say, 3X or 4X) of their original investment. You can see that the variations are endless, and many deals end up as hybrids.

A *multiple* or *super preference* is really another hybrid, but a much more extreme and really quite disturbing one. Many entrepreneurs view this as excessive greed. Under a typical variation of this *punitive financing*, the preferred investors get back a multiple (say 2X) of their investment before the common shareholders see a penny. If they invest $10 million with a 2X preference, for example, then you and the other common shareholders won't receive anything unless the company is sold for at least $20 million in *net distributable proceeds*. (The gross selling price would have to be even higher than the $20 million, since there are other obligations that stand in line ahead of the shareholders, including attorneys' fees and other expenses of doing the deal; taxes; and other creditors of the company, both secured and unsecured.) In some cases the super preference is also a participating preference. Additional rounds of financing only raise the hurdle. Some employees have gone ballistic when they realized how bad the situation really was—which raises the point that management has to invest the time to make sure its team of employees really understands the facts.

How does one explain the trend in the venture capital community, following the bursting of the Internet bubble, to demand more of these super preferences (say 2X or more)? When it comes to explaining these extreme preferences (as well as some of the extreme forms of *price-protection antidilution* discussed in the section entitled The Full Ratchet), it's certainly not a matter of fairness, and there is little supporting logic that can be offered with a straight face. Rather, the results are dictated largely by greed and raw negotiating power. When the venture capital industry is in a down part of its cycle with lower rates of return, the investors typically have more negotiating power, and many exert it. Some venture capitalists seem to bend over backward to actually deserve the moniker *vulture capitalist*, which has been around for years. Many entrepreneurs believe too many venture capitalists are thinking, "We made too many rotten funding decisions during the dot-com madness, and now *you* are going to pay for it!"

It is in your best interest to keep the Series A financing as simple as possible, and this especially applies to the liquidation preference. A solid negotiating strategy is to point out to your Series A investors that they will look more and more like common shareholders as the company does additional rounds of financing in the future—and therefore the initial terms should be kept as clean and simple as possible. Don't start with onerous liquidation preference terms that are likely to become a floor for future rounds. For example, if the Series A preferred investors receive a 2X liquidation preference, subsequent investors (who will move to the head of the line) will want it too, and maybe more.

Sometimes liquidation preferences are structured in such a way that the amount of the preference increases over time. This operates to the advantage of the preferred shareholders, of course, and to the disadvantage of the common shareholders, as well as the preferred shareholders in any prior round. One way to increase the amount of the preference is to add any *accrued but unpaid dividends* to the preference. Since companies backed by venture capitalists rarely declare any dividends, this provision rarely hurts the common shareholders. However, there are other ways to increase the size of the preference that do hurt them. For example, the amount of the preference may automatically increase by a stated percentage (say 5% or more) each year or, which is effectively the same thing, there may be a *mandatory* annual dividend (say 5% or more) on the preferred shares.

If and when there are additional financing rounds beyond the Series A, the respective liquidation priorities for the various rounds need to be addressed. Will the new investors agree that all series of preferred stock will share equally on a pro rata basis (which is called *pari passu*), or will the latest series stand first in line if there's a liquidation? The investors in the latest round have the most clout, since they are providing the new money. Nevertheless, they sometimes consent to pari passu treatment. This is more likely if they are already invested in an earlier round or if they are looking ahead to subsequent financing rounds when this issue is likely to be resolved in the same way.

During negotiations, various arguments can be made by the investors and the founders as to why the liquidation preference should be structured a certain way, but it ultimately comes down to negotiating power, not logic or fairness. Nevertheless, let's review some of the arguments.

First, it should be noted that there's no real argument as to *whether* there should be a preference—the term itself, *preferred stock*, implies a preference. Consider what could happen, theoretically at least, without a preference. Let's say the founders sell a minority position in their company for $10 million of preferred stock *without* a liquidation preference (or, which would amount to the same thing, they simply issue common stock for the cash). It is possible that they could then immediately liquidate the company and distribute the cash among all shareholders on a pro rata basis, with the majority founders receiving the lion's share, which would be more than $5 million in this example. Of course, this example is outrageous, and there's no need to go into the ethical and legal issues raised—but it does illustrate a key reason why preferred stock carries a preference.

The investors will argue that their investment is in hard cash and deserves some of the protections of debt (in addition to having the upside potential). They may say that, in addition to being first in line for repayment of the "principal," it deserves an interest component, such as a mandatory dividend or a provision that automatically increases the amount of the preference over time, as discussed previously. The founders will argue that their hard labors (*sweat equity*) are equally valuable, and that in any case the deal is not a secured debt transaction.

As for the participating preferred shareholders, founders argue that this is unfair *double-dipping*, and the investors counter that this is especially needed in some in-between situations where the founders could make a few million dollars and the investors' rate of return could nevertheless be unreasonably low. On balance, the investors' argument for participating preferred may carry more weight if the founders have been paid competitive salaries throughout—otherwise, they should be compensated for the sweat equity they put it, just as the preferred shareholders are getting their cash investment back.

Throughout, the founders should argue for the *mutual alignment of interests*. All parties are involved in the enterprise because of the tremendous upside potential, and it's a mistake to arrange things so that one group (i.e., investors in a particular series) may have an incentive to see certain things happen (such as a premature sale of the company, or an unwise liquidation) that are not in the best interests of the company or the other shareholders.

Dividend Preference

Dividend preference is *not* a key deal point, but it's included here for general information. A term sheet typically provides that the preferred stock will receive a dividend *if and when declared* by the board of directors of the company. This is largely a legal fiction, since the board will almost never declare such a dividend. The main purpose of this provision is to help make enough distinctions between common stock and preferred stock to allow the company, from a tax law point of view, to value the common stock at a fraction (frequently one-tenth at the time of the Series A financing) of the value of the preferred stock. (The lower pricing on the common stock substantially strengthens the equity incentive for the founders and other key employees to stay with the company.)

Generally, preferred stock does not have mandatory dividend rights but, as noted in the Liquidation Preference section, a mandatory cumulative dividend on the preferred stock may be used in order to pump up the value of the liquidation preference over time. In this situation, the dividend, although mandatory, typically is not paid each quarter or year but instead cumulates over time and is simply added to the dollar amount of the liquidation preference.

Redemption Rights

Redemption rights permit the preferred shareholder to force the company to *redeem* (i.e., buy back) stock in the future (most commonly five years out) at a specified price. This gives the preferred shareholder some protection (or perceived protection) if the company performs poorly, plus a possible path to liquidity where no other path appears likely.

What redemption price will be negotiated? Is it simply the price originally paid for the stock? Is it the amount of the liquidation preference? Or is it the fair market value of the stock at the time of redemption (which could be substantially above or below the original purchase price)? In the latter case, the company and the investors would either agree on the price at the time of redemption, or the price would be determined in a process that involves an outside independent appraiser.

Investors requesting redemption rights typically frame their argument as a protection for *minority shareholders* who have no control. If the company's management cannot get the company to an initial public offering or a successful sale, how will the minority investors ever get their money out? If your investors request this, you don't want any part of it. Redemption rights are likely to make it more difficult to raise capital in subsequent rounds because later investors will want their funds to be used to make the company more successful, not to cash out earlier investors. Also, you don't want to be forced to part with scarce cash at a time when you can't afford it, which is likely to be all of the time. Again, these rights violate the keep-it-simple-stupid (KISS) rule, and they set a precedent—if you agree to redemption rights in the Series A round, you will likely be forced to accept them in subsequent rounds.

There is one solid reason for you not to make redemption rights a big negotiating issue—namely, they are virtually *never* used. In fact, many experienced advisors and attorneys for start-up companies have never seen them used. (The explanation for this may be quite simple—if the company is not doing well, it won't have the money needed to repurchase the investors' stock, and if the company is doing well, the investors will want to keep their shares.) Of course, the argument cuts both ways. As the entrepreneur, you can argue that redemption rights shouldn't be part of the deal if they're never used, and the investor can counter that you shouldn't object to their inclusion if they're never used. Arguably, redemption rights, even if never exercised, give the holders some leverage down the road when they really want a better deal on something else. On balance, however, the issue of redemption rights is a tempest in a teapot.

If you must live with redemption rights, try at least to push the redemption date as far into the future as possible—7 or 10 years is better than 5.

Outside venture capitalists in a follow-on round will certainly review any pre-existing redemption rights and decide their course of action. Their choices are to

- *Do nothing*—This means they would neither object to the existing redemption rights nor demand any such rights for themselves. This is unlikely.

- *Demand the same rights*—This, at a minimum, means that additional time will be spent on negotiating the specific terms. For example, the order of exercise of the rights held by the different series of preferred should be determined.

- *Demand that the prior rights be eliminated*—This would require the consent of the *old money*.

- *Demand that the prior rights be modified in some fashion*—For example, five-year redemption rights given in a round two years in the past could be reset at five years from the current date.

Redemption rights are another example of something that wastes time and money in negotiations. Once again, try to get everyone to follow the *keep-it-simple-stupid* rule and the *alignment-of-interests* rule.

Preemptive Rights

As noted above, a *preemptive right* (also known as a *right of first refusal*) is a form of antidilution protection that entitles a shareholder to maintain his or her current percentage ownership interest in the company by purchasing, typically on a pro rata basis, his or her share of any future stock sale by the company. It is common for venture capitalists to seek this right. On rare occasions, they request the right to buy all of the shares the company intends to sell, not just their pro rata share, and this is especially troublesome.

Since the company will receive the same amount of money regardless of who buys the stock, should you care about preemptive rights? Yes, you should. Preemptive rights can slow down and complicate your efforts to raise money. One problem is that the shares first have to be offered to existing shareholders for a period of time. Another is that the new investor may want to purchase the whole amount. In general, preemptive rights do limit your flexibility. For example, they could make it more difficult for you to later bring on board a particular new venture capitalist or other strategic partner. You should avoid giving preemptive rights if you can. If you can't, the preemptive rights should contain *carve-outs* (i.e., exceptions) for shares sold or issued to strategic partners or various other parties the company does business with, including employees, consultants, directors, and service providers.

In any case, preemptive rights given to investors should automatically expire at the time of an initial public offering, to avoid a potential obstacle regarding the sale of stock to the general public.

Conversion Rights

Preferred stock in venture deals carries two types of conversion rights—one *voluntary*, and one *automatic*. The two types can be further described as follows.

- *Voluntary conversion* (also simply called *conversion* or *conversion right*)—Each of the preferred shareholders almost always has the right to convert his or her preferred stock (or any portion of it) into common stock at any time.

- *Automatic conversion*—Generally, all of the preferred stock *automatically converts* into common stock upon certain events, which usually are
  - a voluntary vote by a majority of the preferred stockholders, with all series of preferred stockholders voting together (sometimes a supermajority vote is required), or
  - the company's *initial public offering*, provided the initial public offering meets certain requirements, which usually are
    - the underwriters have firmly committed to place (i.e., sell) the entire offering
    - a certain minimum amount of capital must be raised for the company in the offering, say $20 million, and
    - the offering price per share must be greater than a certain minimum amount, say 5X the price paid for the preferred stock

Let's now look at the mechanics of how preferred stock converts to common stock. The *conversion ratio* (also called the *conversion rate*) determines the number of shares of common stock into which each share of preferred stock is converted. Initially, the conversion ratio is set at one-to-one, meaning that each share of preferred would convert into one share of common if the conversion right were exercised immediately after the financing. In the lengthy definitive agreement, the conversion formula typically is based on what is called the *conversion price*, which is initially set at the purchase price per share paid for the preferred shares. The conversion ratio is determined by dividing the original purchase price per share by the conversion price per share. So, for example, if the original purchase price is $2 per share, the initial conversion price will be set at this $2 per share, and the conversion ratio would then be $2 divided by $2, which results in "one" (which is also called *one-to-one* or *one-for-one* conversion).

The definitive agreement usually spells out in great detail (several pages of legalese) how certain events will cause the conversion price to be adjusted. For example, if the antidilution provisions kick in, then the conversion price is reduced, which means that the preferred stock would then be convertible into an increased number of common shares. Antidilution provisions are discussed in the following section of this chapter.

If there are multiple rounds of preferred stock financing, each round will have its own conversion price. For example, if the company does well, the first round conversion price might be $1, the second $3, and so forth—with the conversion price for each round set initially at the price per share paid for the preferred in each respective round. Each conversion price is then subject to adjustment in the future, depending on the terms of each respective round, which are likely to vary. Of course, the higher the conversion price, the fewer the number of common shares that will be issued upon conversion, and thus the smaller the dilution.

Upon the conversion of preferred stock into common stock, the special rights associated with it (such as special voting rights, antidilution protection, and liquidation preference) terminate, with perhaps a few exceptions (such as registration rights, discussed in the section entitled Registration Rights). Sometimes, certain rights (such as *preemptive rights*) terminate in the event of an initial public offering but not in the event of any other type of conversion. One reason for this is the desire of both the underwriters and the company that the company's capital structure and financial statements be as simple and clean after the initial public offering as is possible.

Antidilution Protection

A down-price round is a *double whammy* for the founders, but typically not for the venture capitalists. The first blow is that the lower price means more of the company has to be sold to raise any particular amount of cash. The second blow is caused by any price-protection antidilution clauses kicking in. Under the typical deal structure, the dilution is largely absorbed by the common stockholders (often the founders) because the venture capitalists frequently invest in the down-price round (thus at least getting some benefit from the lower price), and they also benefit from their antidilution protection. Perhaps one shouldn't be too surprised by this—after all, our economic system is called *capitalism*, not *workism* or *sweatequityism*!

Typically, there are two types of antidilution clauses that appear in the section of the term sheet entitled Antidilution Protection, or Antidilution Provisions, or the like. The first type is not really important at all, and the second type is extremely important and is usually heavily negotiated. The two types are

- *Structural antidilution protection*—This type of antidilution clause is straightforward, sensible, and without controversy. It does not require much attention (assuming it has nothing sneaky written into it), and it is discussed here for completeness and clarity only, simply because it, together with its more important sister clauses discussed in the Weighted Average Antidilution Protection section and the section entitled The Full Ratchet, are all generally described as antidilution clauses. It is triggered by a routine or technical *recapitalization* that is intended to treat all stakeholders the same and does not involve any insider or third-party investment. These include *regular stock splits* or *forward stock splits* (e.g., each share is replaced by two, five, or X shares); *reverse stock splits* (e.g., each share is replaced by one-half share or some other fraction of a share); and stock dividends (e.g. each shareholder receives new, additional shares based on the number of shares currently held; for example, if there is a 50% stock dividend, a shareholder holding 100 shares would receive 50 additional shares). In each case, the conversion price is automatically adjusted to achieve a fair result. The hallmark of this type of antidilution clause is that no one shareholder or group of shareholders receives an advantage or benefit to the disadvantage of others. For example, if there is a two-for-one common stock split, then a conversion price of $1.00 per share applicable to preferred stock would automatically be reduced to one-half, or $0.50 per share, which results in the preferred shareholder's *percentage interest* in the company upon conversion being unaffected by the stock split.

■ *Price protection*—The second type of antidilution clause, often heavily negotiated, is known as *price protection* for the venture investor, and it's important that you understand it. It appears in different forms, and its intent (unlike that of the noncontroversial antidilution provisions discussed previously) is definitely to give substantial advantages to certain shareholders (typically venture capitalists buying preferred stock in the round in question) at the expense of others (typically the founders, other employees holding common stock or stock options, and any other shareholders). This provision, in effect, automatically *gives* additional stock to the venture capitalist if stock is issued in a later financing round at a price per share below that paid by the venture capitalist. Of course, if the subsequent price is higher, no adjustment is made. The importance of this clause to you is that, if the subsequent price is lower, the venture capitalist (and not you) will receive additional stock, and your stock holdings will be diluted, perhaps substantially. The most common type is called *weighted-average* antidilution, and there are variations of it. Another type, the *full ratchet* (or simply, *ratchet*), is especially unfair and definitely should be avoided. These will be discussed in the following sections, but first a word about fairness.

Much could be written (and has been written) about why venture capitalists believe they need antidilution protection against later *down rounds*, and why they think such protection is fair. However, fairness has little to do with it, and it ultimately boils down to the cold reality of negotiating position and power. If you have the luxury of being courted by several eager prospective investors, you will be able to negotiate more favorable terms. However, if times are tough and you desperately need initial or additional funding, you will undoubtedly face more onerous terms. In the down part of the cycle in venture capital investing, term sheets become longer as more onerous terms and protective mechanisms are inserted. In general, the *golden rule* applies—"He who has the gold (that you need) makes the rules." However, many entrepreneurs believe that some venture capitalists, in squeezing so hard, are killing the goose that lays the golden eggs. Yes, entrepreneurs, not venture capitalists, are that goose!

Weighted-Average Antidilution Protection

As discussed in the section entitled Conversion Rights, preferred stock is convertible into common stock at a ratio that is calculated by dividing the purchase price paid for the preferred by what is called the *conversion price*. Initially, this ratio is equal to one, since the initial conversion price is simply equal to the price per share paid for the preferred. Therefore, at that time, the preferred stock would be convertible into common stock on a one-for-one basis; e.g., 100 shares of preferred (regardless of the price paid) would convert into 100 shares of common, and this would remain the case until the conversion price changes, which is where price-protection antidilution clauses come in.

A *weighted-average* antidilution clause is very common and appears in most venture capital deals. Should there be a subsequent financing round at a lower price, this clause protects the preferred investor by recalculating the *conversion price* at which the preferred is convertible into common. It's called "weighted-average" because, in determining the new conversion price, it takes into account the number of shares issued at the lower price in a subsequent round, as well as the number of shares outstanding before the new issuance. In effect, the *weighting* is based on the number of shares. This means, for example, that the conversion price is not reduced much if only a few shares are issued at the new lower price. On the other hand, the issuance of lots of shares at the new lower price will pull the conversion price closer to that associated with the new lower price.

Here is how you do the weighted-average calculation to determine the *new conversion price*.

A = total number of shares outstanding before second-round financing
(Note: There are variations of this formula that depend on what's counted in "shares outstanding." See the discussion later in this section on *narrow-based* weighted average and *broad-based* weighted average.)

B = number of shares second-round financing would have purchased at higher first-round price

C = number of new shares actually purchased at the lower second-round price

The formula to determine the new conversion price is

$$\text{new conversion price} = (\text{old conversion price})\left(\frac{A + B}{A + C}\right)$$

One can intuitively understand this calculation. For example, let's assume that

a) a total of 5 million shares are outstanding after the venture capitalist buys n shares (where, by the way, n doesn't affect this calculation) at \$3 per share in the first round of financing (Series A), and

b) 5 million shares are subsequently sold at \$2 per share in a later down round, the Series B, for a total of \$10 million

Then, on a weighted-average basis, you would intuitively expect (since 5 million new shares are issued in the second round and the same number was previously outstanding) that the new conversion price for the first-round investors would be *halfway* between the $3 price paid in the Series A round and the subsequent $2 price in the Series B round—which is $2.50 per share.

The formula confirms this.

$$\text{new conversion price} = (\text{old conversion price}) \left(\frac{A + B}{A + C} \right)$$

$$= (\$3.00) \left(\frac{5,000,000 + \dfrac{\$10,000,000}{\$3}}{5,000,000 + 5,000,000} \right)$$

$$= \$2.50 \qquad\qquad\qquad [\text{I}]$$

Yes, you intuitively thought it should be $2.50, and it is.

As another example, assume that

a) a total of 3 million shares are outstanding after preferred shares are purchased at $2 per share in the Series A round, and

b) 2 million shares are later sold at $1 per share, raising a total of $2 million, in a later down round (the Series B)

Since there were 3 million shares outstanding right before the second round and 2 million shares are sold in the second round, you would intuitively expect the new conversion price for the shares issued in the Series A round to be reduced to a point that is two-fifths of the way from the Series A price paid ($2) to the new lower Series B price ($1)—or $1.60.

The calculation confirms this.

$$\text{new conversion price} = (\text{old conversion price}) \left(\frac{A + B}{A + C} \right)$$

$$= (\$2.00) \left(\frac{3,000,000 + \dfrac{\$2,000,000}{\$2}}{3,000,000 + 2,000,000} \right)$$

$$= \$1.60 \qquad\qquad\qquad [\text{II}]$$

You intuitively thought it would be $1.60, and it is.

Note that the above two examples did not even indicate how many preferred shares were purchased in the Series A round. This illustrates that the calculation of the *new conversion price* does not depend upon the number of shares purchased at the Series A price. Of course, the benefit of the new conversion price will accrue to all the shares purchased in the Series A round.

The term *share multiplier*, defined in the following formula, may be used to measure the real benefit that accrues to the holder of the antidilution provision. (In words, the share multiplier is the multiplying factor you need to apply to the original number of common shares that a Series A preferred share was convertible into, to get the new increased number of shares of common shares that it is convertible into.)

$$\text{share multiplier} = \frac{\text{old conversion price}}{\text{new conversion price}}$$

In Eq. I, then,

$$\text{share multiplier} = \frac{\text{old conversion price}}{\text{new conversion price}}$$

$$= \frac{\$3.00}{\$2.50}$$

$$= 1.2$$

In this example, the Series A preferred shares no longer convert on a one-for-one basis. They now each convert into 1.2 shares of common stock. By applying this factor to the total number of Series A shares issued, you can easily calculate the total cost of the antidilution clause in shares. For example, if the Series A investor had purchased 2 million shares, they would now convert into 2.4 million shares of common, not 2 million, and so the "cost" to the company of the antidilution clause is 400,000 shares.

There are variations of the weighted-average antidilution formula that use different definitions of what's counted as "shares outstanding" in the *A* in the formula above. (*A* = total number of shares outstanding before the second-round financing.)

- Under the *narrow-based* weighted-average provision, only the issued common shares are counted in the "base" of shares outstanding before the subsequent lower-price round of financing.

- The *broad-based* weighted-average provision counts not only the common shares but also stock options, the preferred stock, and warrants. (The specific details of what's included can vary. For example, sometimes the whole option pool is counted, and sometimes only outstanding options are counted.)

The narrow-based approach is more favorable to the holder of the dilution protection. This is because the number of shares in the lower-priced Series B is being compared to a "narrower base" of shares (i.e., a smaller number of shares before the Series B). This means that the dilution "pull" per share toward the Series B is greater, which causes the conversion price to drop more quickly. Likewise, the broad-based approach is more favorable to the founders.

The Full Ratchet

The *full ratchet* (sometimes simply called a *ratchet*) can have a very severe impact on the founders' percentage ownership interests and is widely viewed as unfair. However, you may nevertheless encounter it in a proposed term sheet, especially since the so-called *standard terms* (which really don't exist) of many venture capitalists became much tougher following the collapse of the dot-com bubble. While still in only a relatively small percentage of deals, the full ratchet has recently been raising its ugly head more often.

How the full ratchet works is quite simple. If there is a subsequent financing round at a lower price, then the ratchet, in effect, gives the advantage of the lower price to the holder of the ratchet and puts him in the position where he would have been had he actually received the lower price in the first place.

Let's consider an example. Your first investor, Ace Ventures, buys 4 million shares of preferred stock at a price of $1 per share, for a total cash investment of $4 million in the Series A financing. Initially, these shares are convertible on a one-for-one basis into 4 million shares of common stock. Let's assume the investor has negotiated full-ratchet antidilution protection. Later, at the time of the Series B financing (or it could be any later series), your company seeks additional funding, but the best price you can get for your preferred stock is only $0.80 per share. What's the impact of the full ratchet? Regardless of the number of shares the company sells for the $0.80 price, Ace Ventures gets the benefit of this lower price. This is accomplished by adjusting the *conversion price* so that the 4 million shares of Series A preferred stock are now convertible into 5 million shares of common. (The $4 million would have purchased this higher number of shares originally if the price had been only $0.80 per share, rather than $1.00.) Please note that no new shares of preferred are issued to Ace Ventures—they still have only the 4 million shares they originally were issued, but the shares are now convertible into more common shares (5 million vs. 4 million).

The ratchet operates this way regardless of how many shares are issued at the lower price in the later round. It could be millions of shares—or it could be only one share. Yes, it's true! If, in the example above, you issued only one additional share in the Series B round at $0.80 per share, you would have 80 additional cents in your pocket, and your Series A investor in effect would have an additional 1 million shares! You now know why they got the name "Ace Ventures."

One odd effect of the ratchet is that the Series B investor needs to consider the diluting impact of the Series A ratchet on his Series B deal. The Series B investor who thinks, for example, that he is buying 10% of the company for a certain dollar amount will actually receive less than 10% due to the additional equity interest received by the holder of the Series A ratchet. So, in theory at least, the Series B investor needs to lower his price somewhat, which in turn causes the ratchet to spin out additional equity for its Series A holder—and so this cycle continues. The Series A investor, of course, can calculate the steady-state solution to which this process iterates. A key point here is that, in a typical situation, all of the dilution comes at the expense of the common shareholders (i.e., the founders).

If the dilution of the founders is too severe, it's possible that the Series B investor will walk away from the deal. Although you can't count on this, it's also possible that the Series B investor will demand, as a condition to investing, that the ratchet holder agree to reduce the ratchet's impact—the notion being that a sophisticated investor will want management to be properly motivated by a big enough piece of the pie. Of course, it's also possible that the Series B investor is the Series A investor. Entrepreneur beware!

Suppose you issued a few shares, believing incorrectly that they wouldn't trigger the full ratchet. The results could be catastrophic. Perhaps the ratchet holder would waive his ratchet protection in this particular instance, but don't count on it. This is simply another reason why the ratchet is not fair.

Sometimes a ratchet is used for a very limited time period (say 3 to 12 months) to address a particular concern. Perhaps some additional funding is needed immediately, but either there's not enough time to complete the due diligence, or some particular negative issue has just come up in due diligence. Perhaps there's a major milestone a few months away (such as a large contract with a key customer) that, if it doesn't happen, will cause the company's valuation to drop and the need for cash to become urgent. In these cases, the investors might insist upon a ratchet to protect themselves if in fact a down round is necessary during a limited time period. In such situations, the parties might agree on a ratchet clause for a short period of time, say six months, with a weighted-average antidilution clause taking effect after that.

There are a few instances where a group of investors will build a ratchet into their deal in order to help guarantee that everyone in the group will continue to support the company on a pro rata basis if additional funds are needed. The investors who do not invest in a subsequent down round would feel the full impact of the ratchet.

An expanded example of how the full ratchet works is in Sidebar 12.5, The Full Ratchet at Work. Sidebar 12.6, Comparison of Antidilution Types, is an example of how the various antidilution provisions can have widely varying results.

Whatever the type of price-protection antidilution, there should be carve-outs for certain types of transactions. The main exclusion is for employee stock option plans and other incentive arrangements. Options granted to employees and stock granted upon option exercise should not trigger the antidilution provision.

Voting Rights

In general, the common and preferred shareholders vote together on most matters requiring shareholder approval. The preferred shares are counted on an *as-if-converted* basis (e.g., if a preferred share is convertible into two shares of common, then each share of preferred is entitled to two votes).

However, the term sheet typically calls for several exceptions to the above rule. These exceptions shift some power to the preferred shareholders and are discussed in the following section entitled Veto Rights. Of course, the selection of the board of directors also involves voting rights, and this is discussed in the Board of Directors section. Those two sections should be read together with this section.

Veto Rights

Veto rights are also known as *negative covenants*, *approval rights*, or *protective provisions*. These rights are especially important to venture investors who are minority shareholders in the company and do not control the board of directors. The issue here is control, and the effect of veto rights is to transfer some power to minority shareholders. The negotiation of this issue can sometimes become quite heated. This issue and the issue of valuation are often the most heavily negotiated items in a term sheet.

Most term sheets will list specific company actions that require the prior approval of the preferred shareholders. The least-controversial items are those that would adversely affect the rights of the preferred shareholders, including

- any amendment or change to the company's articles of incorporation or bylaws that adversely affects the *rights*, *preferences*, or *privileges* of the preferred shareholders
- the creation of any new class or series of stock having any rights, preferences, or privileges superior to, or equal with, that of the preferred stock of the investors
- any change in the liquidation preference, conversion rights, dividend rights, veto rights, and so on, held by the preferred shareholders. (These rights are sometimes separately listed, even though they all are already protected by the above prohibition against anything that adversely affects the preferred shareholders. Perhaps the reason for this is a desire for clarity, plus a desire for belt-and-suspenders protection.)

The above provisions are generally acceptable because they prevent the majority shareholders (assuming the investors are purchasing a minority interest) from later simply undoing, by majority vote, the specific rights and protections that the new investors have negotiated.

Frequently, investors will also ask for veto rights regarding other actions, such as

- a merger in which the current shareholders do not have control of the surviving entity
- a sale of all, or substantially all, of the assets of the company
- an increase in the authorized number of shares of stock (of whatever type or class)
- any redemption of stock not already provided for in the articles of incorporation
- purchasing stock of, or otherwise investing in, any other business
- borrowing money or incurring debt beyond a specified level
- purchasing assets in excess of a stated dollar limit
- numerous other actions, creatively defined, where the veto rights tend to handcuff management and the board of directors

The items near the bottom of the preceding list are especially troublesome. Your main theme in negotiations should be that these matters are properly left to the board of directors to decide. Separate veto rights can split the company, cause individuals to pursue their own agendas rather than what is best for the company, and lead to unintended negative consequences in the future. They also can cause delays, due to the shareholder vote required.

In addition, the issue of how the preferred shareholders vote sometimes arises. Will they all vote together regardless of how many series of preferred stock have been issued, or will each series of preferred stock vote separately? You should strongly resist the latter, since a series vote gives a veto or blocking power to multiple groups (or even individuals), and you thus run the risk that management and the board of directors will be unduly restricted as to how the company is best run. This issue typically arises only if a particular series of prospective investors requests a separate vote for their series. This is another situation where the keep-it-simple-stupid rule and alignment-of-interests rule should apply.

Your competent legal counsel will be able to make sure that the veto rights are reasonable. In particular, counsel should make sure that appropriate carve-outs are included in the veto rights granted to your investors. For example, if there's a veto right regarding the issuance of any additional stock, then a carve-out for the issuance of stock upon the exercise of stock options must be included. Without this carve-out, such a routine issuance of stock would inappropriately require the approval of the preferred shareholders.

Board of Directors

The issues here are the number of directors on the board and how they are selected. The lead venture capitalist will generally request and receive board representation, but how many seats are appropriate? In most cases the founders retain control of the board through the Series A financing. However, if there are additional financing rounds (which is likely for a company on a successful trajectory), then it's likely you will lose control of the board at some point.

A common structure is to have a five-person board, with two seats controlled by the common stockholders (the founders), two seats filled by the investors, and an additional seat (the fifth seat) filled by an industry expert mutually agreed to by the founders and the investors (or by the four directors selected by them). Even if you have only one venture investor in the first round, the investor may want to select two directors. If you are concerned about board control, then you should think carefully about how the "neutral" fifth director is selected. The venture investors may already have a candidate or two in mind—candidates who are highly qualified, but who are also likely to be aligned with them—and it may be difficult for you to say no. As an alternative approach, you may want to independently line up your own highly qualified candidate in advance.

Even if the founders control a majority of the board seats (say three out of five), the venture investors may nevertheless feel comfortable with the situation, knowing that their likely participation in future financings gives them additional clout.

You should resist making the board too large and unwieldy in a misguided effort to accommodate all investors who might want to be on the board. Your goal should be to create a balanced, strong board that provides relevant experience, strong business judgment, and good contacts. Five is a good number and perhaps the most common. Three is adequate in the early days. Seven is getting a little large, and it rapidly gets unwieldy beyond that.

The specific arrangements regarding the number of directors and the selection process are typically set forth either in the company's articles of incorporation or in a separate *voting agreement* signed by the investors and the founders.

A term sheet will sometimes specify that a venture investor has *visitation rights*, which means that the individual, although not a director and not having any voting rights, has the right to attend and participate in all board meetings. Since established investors carry certain prestige and power with them, and since they will probably be essential participants in future financing rounds, occasionally they may feel that they don't need the actual voting power of a director.

Also, the directors selected by the venture investors will usually control the important Compensation Committee and Audit Committee. The authority to approve salaries and stock option grants does provide a certain amount of power.

See Ch. 7 for more discussion of the board of directors.

Right of Co-Sale

The *right of co-sale* is essentially an *antibailout* protection for minority shareholders that is intended to prevent key founders (and perhaps other key members of management) from selling their shares to a third party and leaving the minority shareholders still stuck with all their shares (sometimes referred to as *holding the bag*). Of particular note, this right gives the holder some protection if control of the company is being transferred to a third party. If a founder wants to sell some or all of his stock, the investors having a right of co-sale (typically the venture capital investors and perhaps other nonmanagement minority investors) can participate in the sale, typically on a pro rata basis based on their respective percentage ownership interests in the company. As for the procedure, the founder who is planning to sell his shares must first notify the investors holding the right of co-sale as to the proposed terms of sale. If the investors decide to participate in the sale, then the number of shares sold by the founder is appropriately cut back so that the total number of shares sold to the third party remains the same. In effect, the investors sell a portion of their shares alongside the founders' shares.

Co-sale rights typically have certain reasonable exceptions or carve-outs, such as sales of small amounts of stock (perhaps capped at a total of X shares in any 12-month period) and sales or transfers due to termination of employment or death. Also, co-sale rights typically terminate upon the company's initial public offering.

Co-sale rights are sometimes referred to as *tag-along rights*. Others define tag-along rights more narrowly to cover only the situation where someone's shares will be sold in a public offering pursuant to a registration statement filed with the SEC.

Also, the co-sale agreement frequently contains a *right of first refusal* that prohibits the founders from selling their shares to a third party without first offering to sell the shares to the company and the preferred shareholders on the same terms and conditions as are proposed for the third-party sale.

Drag-Along Rights

A *drag-along right* gives the holder the right to force other shareholders (typically the founders and other common shareholders) to sell their shares when there's a third party willing to buy all the shares of the company and the sale has been approved by a specified percentage of the stockholders (either a majority or supermajority). Since many prospective buyers won't buy a company unless they can acquire 100% control, the preferred shareholders may not be able to sell their shares unless the other shareholders also sell. Drag-along rights are thus a method venture capitalists use to help ensure the liquidity of their investment.

Vesting for the Founding Team

The purpose of vesting is to help ensure that you and other employees have a strong incentive to stay with the company and make it wildly successful. It's definitely not in the best interests of the investors or the company if you and other key team members can leave the company and retain ownership of all your stock. This is especially true with high-tech companies, where most of their value is reflected in their employees. Accordingly, Series A investors generally require the founders to agree to a vesting schedule for their stock, if this is not already in place. The same applies to other employees to whom stock is sold. Sometimes you may be asked to extend or otherwise modify the vesting arrangements that are already in place. Your best course is to have customary vesting arrangements already established, in which case it is highly likely the investors will accept those.

The most common vesting period is four years, with a one-year *cliff*. This means that 1/4 of your stock vests one year from the start of vesting, and thereafter an additional 1/48 of the stock vests for each month of your continued employment. There are many variations of course, but the goal should be to reach a vesting structure that fairly balances the interests of all concerned. Frequently, the founding team is given credit for all or some of the time already devoted to the company—meaning that the vesting starts at an agreed-upon date in the past, or the parties simply agree that the founders are already partially invested, say 25%, on day one. Sometimes there is no one-year cliff for the founders, and their stock simply vests on a monthly basis throughout. Sometimes the founders have a shorter vesting period, say three years. Some CEOs want, as a matter of team building, to have everyone's stock vest on the same basis—but you need not feel obligated to do so, since there may be good reasons to treat the founders differently, and each situation is different. For example, it may be contemplated that you will be replaced by a seasoned CEO at a certain stage of the company's development, in which case more-rapid vesting for you makes sense.

Change in control is another important issue. What happens to your unvested stock (and unvested stock options) when there's a change in control of your company? This is occasionally a hot topic in negotiations. If the change-in-control event triggers the immediate vesting of all unvested stock, then you would be able to leave the company with all of your stock. This is usually not in the best interests of the company or the investors. The blow to the company would be even worse if other key employees followed you out the door, perhaps to start a new venture. A device called a *double trigger* is sometimes used to balance more fairly the respective interests of the parties in this situation. Under double-trigger vesting, two things need to occur to accelerate the vesting: (1) there's a change in control, and (2) your employment is terminated without cause. Under this arrangement, the first trigger (a change in control) by itself does not accelerate vesting. However, when both triggers occur, all or a portion (say 50% or 75%) of your unvested stock is automatically vested.

In most acquisitions, the buyer is also buying the company's team, and the buyer may shy away from doing the deal if the team can leave fully vested or if the buyer has to negotiate a new incentive structure to cause the team to remain.

The vesting issues are not just between you and the Series A investors. Frequently there are issues among the founding group. For example, morale may suffer if one of the founders is able to leave with too many shares of stock. Vesting is also discussed in Ch. 15.

Registration Rights

The central issue of *registration rights* in a term sheet is the scope of the negotiated, contractual right (called *demand rights*) of the preferred shareholders to require the company to register their shares with the U.S. Securities and Exchange Commission (SEC) so that the shares can then be sold in the public market. This contractual right is important because, under securities laws, it is the company, not its shareholders, that holds the right to register its securities for public sale. Frequently, when a company does its initial public offering (i.e., goes public), the existing shareholders are not permitted by the underwriters to sell their shares in the offering. Sometimes they are permitted to sell some of their shares. The shareholders typically are eager to see their investment become liquid at some point, and the public sale of their stock is generally the most desirable route.

Whenever a company offers securities for sale to the public, it must file an appropriate form of registration statement with the SEC in Washington, D.C. The submittal is reviewed by the SEC, which may offer written comments. The SEC has several such forms of registration statements, and SEC rules define the circumstances in which each form may be used. Form S-1 is most often used when a company does its initial public offering. (Form SB-2, which is generally easier to prepare, may be available for qualifying smaller companies.) The S-1 form is the *catch-all* registration statement and must be used if no other form (such as the S-3 discussed later in this section) may be used. It is quite comprehensive, and the total costs in connection with its use are considerable. Therefore, the company will try to limit this demand right in reasonable ways. For example, the company may limit the number of times the right can be used (perhaps to only once or twice).

One question that arises regarding demand rights in a term sheet is whether the preferred shareholders will have the right to demand registration before or after the company files its initial public offering. It is quite common to give the preferred shareholders the right, after the company has gone public, to require the company to register their shares. It is much less common for the demand rights to apply before the company has gone public (i.e., the shareholders typically don't have the right to require the company to go public). The logic behind this is that the company may simply not be ready to go public. For example, it makes little sense to give some shareholders the right to compel an IPO if the underwriters won't handle or support the offering, or if the market isn't receptive to the offering, or if company management does not support it. Nevertheless, term sheets sometimes contain a provision that sets a deadline for the company to take itself public, say four to seven years, and then permits the shareholders to demand an IPO if the deadline is not met.

Demand registration rights will specify a minimum percentage (perhaps 20% or 30%) of the shareholders that are required to demand registration.

The shareholders with registration rights that demand an IPO may be subject to a *lock-up* provision that prevents them from selling their shares that aren't sold in the IPO for a period of time (commonly 180 days) after the effective date of the IPO. Even in the absence of such a contractual lock-up, the underwriters would probably require a lock-up as a condition to their doing the offering. The lock-up provision can be painful if the stock drops precipitously shortly after the offering, which happened in the case of numerous dot-com companies when the dot-com bubble burst. Of course, many other shareholders suffered in that situation, and many of those companies should not have gone public in the first place.

An *S-3 registration right* is a simpler and less expensive form of demand right. The holder of such a right can require the company to register the holder's shares on form S-3. Because the S-3 form of registration statement can incorporate, by reference, much of the information that the company has already filed with the SEC, it takes much less time and money to prepare. The S-3 form can be used by most companies that have been public for more than 12 months, provided that the aggregate market value of the securities held by nonaffiliates of the registering company (also called the *public float*) is $75 million or more.

Piggyback rights entitle shareholders holding these rights to participate in a public offering initiated by the company. The rights may extend to all or a portion of the shareholders' shares. In effect, these shareholders get a piggyback ride on the company's offering. Piggyback rights are not very controversial, and most venture investors want them. They are a convenient and cost-effective way for these investors to cash out all or a portion of their investment. Typically, the company bears the expense of such registration, although in some cases the selling shareholders agree to split the registration fees required under various state securities laws. The underwriter handling the offering usually has the right to cut back the number of piggyback shares (even to zero) if the underwriter determines that the public sale would be adversely affected. Sometimes the venture investor will argue that the piggyback shares can be cut to zero only in the case of an IPO.

Procedurally, the company notifies the shareholders who hold piggyback rights each time it plans to do a public offering, and then the shareholders indicate whether they want to be included. Because the piggyback does not add a lot of expense, the holders of these rights typically are not limited as to how many times they can participate, but the rights usually expire a few years (often five years) after the company's IPO.

So what's the main difference between demand registration rights and piggyback registration rights? It's simply that the holders of demand rights can require the company to do a public offering, whereas the holders of piggyback rights can require that their shares of stock be included in a registration that is started by the company, but cannot demand that the company do a registration.

Primary offering refers to shares sold by the company, and *secondary offering* refers to shares sold by existing shareholders. Underwriters and the new shareholders will generally prefer that the offering proceeds go into the coffers of the company and not into the hands of other shareholders, and so there may be a real practical limit as to the size of the secondary offering. In this case, there will be an issue of priority as to whose shares are included first. The venture investors who paid cash may require that their shares be sold ahead of the shares of management and other shareholders. The underwriters ultimately have much control over these matters, since they won't do a deal that doesn't make sense to them, no matter what the prior contractual obligations may be among the shareholders and the company.

Confidentiality

Venture investors do not like to sign *confidentiality agreements*, also known as *nondisclosure agreements* (NDAs). However, they may be willing to sign an NDA at the time they sign a term sheet, and in this case the NDA should survive and be binding whether or not a definitive investment agreement is signed.

Information Rights

Venture investors typically request the right to receive certain information from the company on a regular basis. Generally, you should not object to a reasonable request for items such as the company's regular financial statements (whether monthly or quarterly) or the company's annual budget (assuming you prepare one). However, you should avoid requests that

- require special preparation (e.g., the investor wants you to prepare a special report that you otherwise wouldn't)

- are too intrusive (e.g., the investor wants the unlimited right to drop by the company from time to time and talk with management or other employees)
- infringe upon the proper role of the board of directors (e.g., the investor wants the right to informally attend board meetings, or review certain contracts or transactions)

Appropriate limitations will be expected by professional investors and will not undercut the desired goal of good relations between your company and its investors.

Sometimes the information rights are limited to shareholders holding at least a certain number of shares (whether preferred shares or common shares issued upon conversion of preferred shares). This makes sense. Also, information rights should terminate upon the company's initial public offering, since the company will then be filing publicly available reports with the SEC. Plus, you don't want to be in a position of arguably providing insider information to a select group of shareholders.

Pay to Play

Although there are many variations of what is loosely referred to as *pay to play*, a pay-to-play provision typically causes preferred shareholders to lose the benefits of antidilution protection (i.e., price protection) and perhaps certain other protections (such as pre-emptive rights) if they fail to invest their pro rata share in a subsequent down round of financing (i.e., where the stock price has been lowered). The idea is to encourage the investors to support the company in the future, especially during hard times, and to earmark appropriate funds for this possibility. If preferred shareholders do not step up to the plate and the pay-to-play provision is triggered, their preferred stock, in accordance with its pay-to-play terms, is automatically converted into a new series of preferred stock that is the same as the old, except that it carries no antidilution protection. A common variation is that the preferred stock simply converts into common stock.

The specific pay-to-play arrangement applicable to a certain financing round, say the Series A round, must appear in and be part of the original agreements for that round, or it must be subsequently agreed to by the shareholders, according to whatever shareholder votes are required. For example, a group of prospective Series B investors may agree to invest only if the Series A investors first agree to amend their arrangement in such a way that the pay-to-pay provisions demanded by the Series B investors are implemented.

Many founders favor pay-to-play provisions, and so do many venture capitalists. Of course, as a founder, your first choice is that there not be any price-protection antidilution provision at all, in which case you may not need a pay-to-play provision. However, as a practical matter, it's quite possible that your venture investors will insist on some form of price protection.

Although pay-to-pay provisions are more common in later-stage financing, your first investors may agree to one. Also, pay-to-play provisions increased in popularity following the collapse of the Internet bubble.

No-Shop and No-Talk

A *no-shop* provision (also called a *no-solicit*) is really what it sounds like. The term sheet may have a provision that prevents you from actively soliciting rival bids for a stated period of time (say, 30 days). A *no-talk* provision states that you won't negotiate with any rival bidders, including both solicited and unsolicited bidders. Using provisions like these, some investors may try to restrict you, especially if they feel the investment opportunity is hot. Avoid such restrictions if you can. Be especially leery if the investor is not taking the whole round and needs to find other investors to fill out the round (in which case you don't have a real deal anyway).

Most term sheets with a no-shop or no-talk clause don't specify what the remedy is for a breach. Presumably, although somewhat unlikely, the investors could file a lawsuit seeking damages arising from the breach. Some term sheets will contain a *breakup fee*, to be paid by you if you breach the clause.

A related provision is one that tries to rush you, for example, by giving you 48 hours to accept the offer. The purpose of these provisions is to take you off the market. Be professional and decisive, but don't be that rushed.

If you have caught the eye of more than one venture capitalist, you should let the other interested parties know that you have received a term sheet, and ask them to submit a proposal if they are still interested. Although this is in your best interest, it's also a courtesy to the other prospective investors with whom you have been talking. If you don't let them know, they may be justifiably upset because you never gave them a good faith chance. You should not disclose to the other prospective investors the name of the investor that gave you the term sheet, and vice versa. Also, resist the temptation to get the competing investors together in one room to do a deal. This is an exceptionally bad idea! Whatever you do, you must behave professionally throughout, and needless delay is not your ally. There are many founders who had a proposed term sheet taken off the table because the investors thought the founders were either indecisive or were just using them to get a better deal.

Survival of Certain Provisions

As previously noted, the term sheet typically is not a binding agreement, except that it may state that certain obligations are binding and survive even if the financing does not actually occur. These may include

- an obligation to pay certain expenses of the investors (for example, the investors' legal fees up to a stated dollar amount, say $10,000)
- an obligation to pay the investors a *break-up fee* (not very common)
- any confidentiality or nondisclosure agreement (NDA) signed by the investors
- an obligation of each party to indemnify the other for any broker's fees or finder's fees for which it is responsible
- a provision prohibiting the company from negotiating with other investors for a stated period of time

Also, once the term sheet is signed by all parties, there's generally an obligation to negotiate the detailed terms in good faith. You should do so whether or not the term sheet expressly calls for good faith negotiations.

Dilution Is the Number One Business Issue

In the typical term sheet, what is the most contentious and heavily negotiated issue? It's *dilution*. It's any and all issues that cause, or may cause, the founders' percentage equity interest (typically common stock) in the company to be reduced (i.e., diluted). Unfortunately, there is no one section in the term sheet (whether called "Dilution," or anything else) that covers all aspects of dilution. Rather, provisions in several sections cause dilution or have the potential to do so. Two key sections are (1) pricing and (2) the *price-protection* language in the Antidilution section. Other such provisions are in sections with titles like: Stock Option Pool, Liquidation Preference, Dividend Preference, and Vesting for the Founding Team.

When you receive a term sheet, work closely with your experienced attorney and identify the issues that count most for you, as well as the ones that really aren't that important. Figure out your negotiating strategy and go for it. Good luck!

A Sample Term Sheet

As previously noted, venture capitalist term sheets became longer and more onerous after the Internet bubble collapse. For a chart showing the major terms and how they changed, see Sidebar 12.7, Much Tougher Investment Terms After the Dot-Com Bubble.

Sidebar 12.8 is a sample venture capital term sheet.

Sidebar 12.1 Term Sheet Tips

Remember to KISS

Remember to KISS ("keep it simple, stupid") if you're preparing or negotiating a term sheet for your first investment round. The term sheet for the first round frequently becomes the floor for future rounds, so you should try to keep it simple and clean. For example, if you give a 2X or 4X liquidation preference to the Series A investors, investors in later rounds are likely to demand and get these same rights or more. A point to make with the first round investors is that they also have an incentive to keep it simple because their interests will become more and more aligned with those of the common shareholders as time goes on and there are additional financing rounds.

Negotiate, but Don't Kill the Deal

Assuming you are comfortable with your prospective investors, your main goal is to get funded at a reasonable price and on fair terms and conditions. Negotiate, yes, but don't kill the deal. Get funded and move your company forward.

Have a Negotiating Strategy

Related to the previous point, distinguish between clauses that really don't matter and key clauses that should be negotiated. Some people negotiate each issue with equal intensity, perhaps out of habit or a misguided desire to display their prowess and tenacity. This makes no sense and is likely to leave your prospective investors with serious concerns as to your negotiating skills and common sense.

Don't Discuss Valuation Prematurely

Valuation is typically not discussed in early meetings with venture investors. You may scare off investors by tossing out a number too soon. Experienced venture investors will have a number of discussions with you and do some due diligence before they are ready to propose or discuss a valuation and offer a term sheet.

Place a Reasonable Valuation on Your Company

Many entrepreneurs make the mistake of setting a company valuation that is simply too high. Investors expect entrepreneurs to be optimistic, but the valuation should not be based on the assumption that everything will go exactly as planned and that there will be no delays or unpleasant surprises. An excessive valuation will cause many venture investors to cross you off their list, partly because they suspect you may be too difficult to work with.

Empathize with Your Prospective Investors

Try to put yourself in the shoes of your prospective investors and understand what deal points are most important to them. Try to understand how they view your company and why it interests them. Most professional investors will list on their website all of the companies in which they are invested, together with information about their investment objectives, and you can learn more from other sources.

Try to Set the Right Expectations in Discussions

Assuming the investor is interested and there appears to be a good mutual fit, try to set the right expectations with the investor regarding valuation and other key business provisions. A central goal here is to avoid receiving a term sheet that is way off the mark.

Involve Your Attorney Early and in the Right Way

Hire the right law firm, as well as the right individual in that firm. Some people will advise getting your attorney involved before you put any terms on the table. You typically should get your attorney involved much earlier than that. Certainly let your attorney know early of your plans to raise money, since he or she can help you with fundraising strategy and introduce you to a few prospective investors.

Don't Ask Your Attorney to Get You a Better Price

Don't ask your attorney in the middle of negotiations to get you a better valuation. The justification for your price must come from you and be sold by you. However, the attorney does have a key role and can help you prepare for negotiations and guide you through the process.

Avoid a Lock-Up Provision

Avoid a lock-up term sheet that prevents you from talking or negotiating with other investors. Many investors do not like these and do not insist upon them.

Avoid Cross Talk Between Prospective Investors

A prospective investor may ask you if you have other interested investors or if you have received a term sheet. You are not obligated to identify such other investors or provide a copy of any term sheet received, and you shouldn't. He will be surprised if you do. Rather, your answer should be general and as positive as possible under the circumstances. Also, it's not a good idea to get all your prospective investors together in a room to negotiate with you. This destroys any prospect of competitive bidding, and your investors are likely to overwhelm you in negotiations. For example, they will all have the common interest of driving down the price. However, if one of your investors wants to introduce other investors to you, that's quite different—this is exactly what a lead investor should do.

Learn from the Experiences of Others

Talk with an entrepreneur or two who has negotiated term sheets and successfully raised money.

Sidebar 12.2 A One-Paragraph Term Sheet

Term sheets have gotten longer in recent years. However, even in the good old days you wouldn't have seen one as short as the following, although experienced legal counsel for investors and start-ups sometimes communicate with each other in shorthand like this. Just for fun here's a one-paragraph summary of a proposed Series A investment.

> $3M for 50% of equity, fully diluted. $6M pre-money valuation. 25% option pool. Broad-based, weighted-average anti-dilution price protection. Fully participating preferred with 6% cumulative/mandatory dividend and 3X liquidation preference. Convertible into common stock at any time; mandatory upon qualified IPO. Preemptive, first refusal (re founder shares), drag-along, and co-sale rights for investors, with customary carve-outs. Investors to have two seats on five-person Board, with one outside director chosen by other four. Four-year vesting for founders and employees, with one-year cliff. Two demand rights, plus unlimited piggyback (with pro rata cutback) and S-3 registration rights. Veto rights to be negotiated. No shop for 45 days, with $5K of investors' legal fees paid by company.

Perhaps the above is perfectly clear, especially after you've read this chapter on term sheets.

Sidebar 12.3 Who Bears the Dilution Caused by the Stock Option Pool?

Let's assume you and the other founders own 7 million shares of common stock, and that you have earmarked 3 million shares of common stock for the stock option pool (including options already granted, as well as options expected to be granted over the next year or two). Let's assume you have placed a $4 million pre-money valuation on the company and, based on this valuation, venture investors are willing to pay $4 million for one-half of the company in a Series A preferred round. What are the respective ownership interests after this investment?

Well, it depends on how you define "pre-money valuation."

Case 1: If the option plan is included in the pre-money valuation.

Founders:	7,000,000 shares
Option plan:	3,000,000 shares
Subtotal:	10,000,000 shares
Series A investors:	10,000,000 shares ($0.40 per share, for the total of $4M)
Total:	20,000,000 shares

After this investment, the ownership interests are

Founders:	35%	(7,000,000 shares)
Option Plan:	15%	(3,000,000 shares)
Series A investors:	50%	(10,000,000 shares)
	100%	(20,000,000 shares)

Case 2: If the option plan is not included in the pre-money valuation.

Founders:	7,000,000 shares
Series A investors:	7,000,000 shares ($0.571 per share, for the total of $4M)
then add the	
Option Plan:	3,000,000 shares
Total:	17,000,000 shares

After this investment, the ownership interests are

Founders:	41.2%	(7,000,000 shares)
Option Plan:	17.6%	(3,000,000 shares)
Series A investors:	41.2%	(7,000,000 shares)
	100.0%	(17,000,000 shares)

You can see that a simple definition can make a big difference. If the pre-money valuation does not include the option pool (as in Case 2), then the option pool dilutes everyone (which is to your advantage), and the result is that the investor pays a higher price per share ($0.571 per share, rather than $0.40 per share). On the other hand, if the pre-money valuation does include the option pool (as in Case 1), then the founders bear all the dilution of the stock options. The main point here is that you should understand the underlying math and clearly communicate your assumptions. Sophisticated investors will certainly be clear in any term sheet they propose.

Sidebar 12.4 Examples of the Liquidation Preference at Work

In the event that a company is liquidated (e.g., sold), how the pie gets split among the various stakeholders will depend greatly on the specific terms of the liquidation preference. Here are a few specific examples that vary depending on whether the preferred stock is nonparticipating or participating, and whether the preference is a basic 1X preference or carries a higher multiple (e.g., 2X or 4X).

Basic Nonparticipating Preferred

In the event of liquidation, the holders of *nonparticipating* preferred stock need to run a simple calculation to determine whether they should stick with their liquidation preference or convert their preferred stock into common stock (and thus share on an as-converted basis). It's an easy calculation—they run the numbers both ways and pick the course that gives them the bigger piece of the pie.

As an example, let's assume that the Series A preferred investors have purchased, post-money, 30% of the company for $3 million, at a price of $1 per share, and that their liquidation preference is set at $1 per share (the price per share they paid) and is a simple 1X preference. This thus entitles them to receive the first $3 million (the total amount they paid) from any liquidation proceeds that are distributed to the shareholders. This means that the common shareholders will not receive anything unless more than $3 million is available for distribution.

The capital structure of the company is

Common shareholders	7,000,000 shares	(70%)
Series A Preferred shareholders	3,000,000 shares	(30%)
Total	10,000,000 shares	(100%)

The post-money valuation of the company is thus $10 million (which is simply the total of 10 million shares outstanding, times the $1 price per share paid in this financing round).

If, for example, the company is sold or liquidated for $15 million in net proceeds, then the preferred shareholders will receive more by simply converting their preferred stock to common stock and taking their 30% of the $15 million (which is $4.5 million). This is better than the $3 million liquidation preference they would receive if they stuck with their preference and did not convert. The break point for their decision is simply $10 million, the post-money valuation of the company.

So, in our example,

- if the proceeds are $3 million or less, the preferred shareholders take it all
- if the proceeds are more than $3 million but less than $10 million, the preferred shareholders take the first $3 million and the common shareholders split the rest among themselves

- if the proceeds are $10 million or more, the preferred shareholders convert out of their liquidation preference and all shareholders (common and preferred together) share in the proceeds on an *as-converted* basis

If there are multiple rounds, the calculations are more complicated, but the principle remains the same. Each series of preferred investors will run the numbers to decide whether it's best to stick with their particular preference or convert their shares to common.

Participating Preferred

However, if the preferred stock carries the more onerous *participating* liquidation preference, then the preferred shareholders do not have to make a choice, since they have it both ways. In the example given here, they would first receive their $3 million preference, and they then would also share (or *participate* in) the remainder of the proceeds with the common shareholders. So, if the company is sold for the $15 million mentioned previously ($15 million in net proceeds, that is), then the preferred shareholders would receive $3 million *plus* 30% of $12 million (which is $3.6 million), for a total of $6.6 million—which is much more than the $4.5 million they would receive under a nonparticipating liquidation preference. The difference, of course, comes out of the pocket of the common shareholders.

Multiple Preferences (e.g., 2X, 4X)

Whether the preference is the basic 1X or a higher multiple will have a big impact on how the pie is split. Both the nonparticipating preference and the participating variety may carry a multiple. (3X is assumed in two of the following scenarios, but the possibilities are endless.) In the good old days, a liquidation preference was usually a nonparticipating preference with no multiple. Following the dot-com crash, many investors demanded more onerous terms (preferences with multiples, etc.)—which many entrepreneurs saw as pure, raw greed.

Some Examples

The examples shown here are based on the assumed facts in the previous example (i.e., the Series A preferred investors have purchased, post-money, 30% of the company for $3 million, at a price of $1 per share). The impact of a multiple (assumed to be 3X) for different assumed company sale prices is then shown for both the nonparticipating and participating scenarios. Obviously, the possible examples are unlimited.

	net proceeds of sale of company (M = million) ($)		
	3M	9M	15M
common shareholders	0	6.0M	10.5M
1X *nonparticipating* Series A Preferred	3.0M	3.0M	4.5M
common shareholders	0	4.2M	8.4M
1X *participating* Series A Preferred	3.0M	4.8M	6.6M
common shareholders	0	0	6.0M
3X *nonparticipating* Series A Preferred	3.0M	9.0M	9.0M
common shareholders	0	0	4.2M
3X *participating* Series A Preferred	3.0M	9.0M	10.8M

It is important to note that, for all of the above scenarios, the post-money valuation of the company remains the same: namely, $10 million (which is the total of 10 million shares outstanding, times the $1 price per share paid in the financing round). Yet the real value of the company, say from the entrepreneur's perspective, varies greatly depending on the terms of the specific liquidation preference. In this regard, the "valuation" number may be misleading.

Also, the previous examples are quite simple, since they assume only one round of financing. But the principles remain the same for a more complex situation with multiple rounds of financing. Your goal here is to understand how various liquidation preferences work so that you can run the numbers and thus understand the real implications.

Sidebar 12.5 The Full Ratchet at Work

Here's a simple, fictitious example of how a full ratchet could work against you and perhaps even your second-round investors. The example assumes that the investors in the first round have negotiated a full ratchet. To emphasize the power of this financing device, here is an example that is extreme, although not by any means the most extreme.

The ratchet technique is so powerful that knowledgeable second-round investors may avoid deals that involve it, or they may at least negotiate with the first-round investor to change its terms before investing. While Investor 1 and Investor 2 may work something out, you and your management team will likely remain very disadvantaged.

Investor 1 purchases 1 million shares of Series A preferred stock for $1.00 per share, with the customary provision that these Series A shares may be converted one-to-one into common shares at some point in the future. However, the ratchet clause provides that if any shares (of any preferred series X) are ever sold for a lower price ($LP), the conversion ratio will be automatically changed from one-to-one to one-to-N, where $N = \$1.00/\$LP$. For the purposes of this example, it is assumed that management has retained (i.e., owns) 500,000 founders' shares (or one-third of the company).

The company runs out of cash, falls behind schedule, and takes the only financing deal to be found. In a very small second round, Investor 2 purchases 200,000 shares of Series B preferred stock for $0.10 per share, for a total cash infusion of $20,000. Because of the ratchet, each of Investor 1's Series A shares is now automatically convertible into 10 common shares, not one! ($N = \$1.00/\$0.10 = 10$).

If these two investors were the only capital sources for the business, $1,020,000 would have been invested, and the future ownership picture would show substantial dilution for the business founders and the second-round investor, as shown.

	shares before ratchet	perceived percent owner- ship (%)	shares after ratchet	effective percent owner- ship (%)
management	500,000	29.41	500,000	4.67
Investor 1	1,000,000	58.82	10,000,000	93.46
Investor 2	200,000	11.76	200,000	1.87
total	1,700,000	100.00	10,700,000	100.00

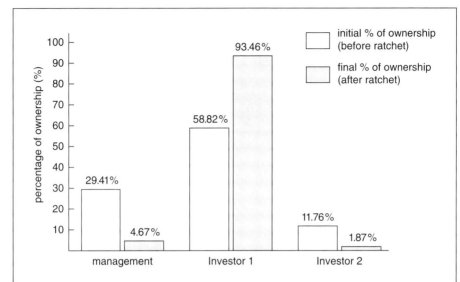

You can see from this extreme example the power of the ratchet. Management's initial one-third ownership interest would drop to under 5%, while the initial investor's interest would increase from less than 60% to over 90% at no additional cost.

Another way to look at this example is that the company in effect has sold 9.2 million shares (not 200,000 shares) for the $20,000 in cash, and that the effective price in this second round is thus only $0.0022 per share ($20,000/9,200,000 shares), not $0.10 per share.

An independent, sophisticated second-round investor is most unlikely to play this game. It is disturbing to think, however, that the first-round investor may have some direct or indirect influence on the behavior of the second-round investor, due to whatever relationships and obligations exist in the world of finance. However, what may be worse is that the ratchet would apply even if the second-round investor and the first-round investor are in fact the same person or entity. Of course, given such severe dilutive consequences as in the above example, rational founders would oppose such an investment of $20,000—although they may not have a choice.

A ratchet may remove all motivation from a management team. In some cases it may be used by investors who have decided to replace management. In any case, you can see why it's important to understand ratchets, along with the general concept of *punitive financing* (which typically refers to a round of financing in which some of the existing shareholders/founders are unwilling or unable to continue investing in the company, and those who do invest agree to do so only at a very low price, which causes major dilution for the nonparticipating investors).

Sidebar 12.6 Comparison of Antidilution Types

As illustrated here, various antidilution clauses can have widely varying results. This example is based on the following assumptions.

- Management and other shareholders own 500,000 shares of common stock. (Note: Only this total will be included in the *narrow-based* weighted-average calculation.)

- There are an additional 750,000 shares of common stock covered by outstanding stock options and warrants issued to customers and corporate partners. (Note: Along with the 500,000 shares above, these additional 750,000 shares will also be included in the *broad-based* weighted-average calculation.)

- Investor 1 purchases 1 million shares of Series A preferred stock for $1.00 per share.

- Investor 2 purchases 500,000 shares of Series B preferred stock for $0.50 per share, for a total cash infusion of $250,000.

antidilution method employed	new conversion price for series A ($)	share multiplier (ratchet factor) = 1 / new conversion price
full ratchet	0.50	2.0
narrow-based weighted average	0.75	1.333
broad-based weighted average	0.857	1.167

You could easily construct a spreadsheet for further analysis of this example or more complicated situations. The example here represents a fairly simple situation with two rounds of preferred stock financing.

Sidebar 12.7 Much Tougher Investment Terms After the Dot-Com Bubble

In the summer of 2001, Fenwick & West, a top-tier law firm in Silicon Valley that regularly works with technology start-ups, summarized the incredible climate change in venture capital financing caused by the collapse of the dot-com bubble. While certainly not intended to be a statement of what the "market" was for each post-bubble deal term, their summary captures overall the significant shift from what often prevailed during the bubble to the terms that frequently prevailed immediately after the bubble collapse.

The lengthening of the *closing cycle* in this chart reflects, in part, the fact that after the bubble, investors started spending more time analyzing the venture's business model, checking references, and completing the due diligence process.

Venture Capital Term Comparisons for First-Round Investors During and After the Bubble

term	then, it was not uncommon to see	... and after, it was not uncommon to see
valuation	$15–$100 million pre-money	$3–$10 million pre-money
investment amount	$5–$30 million	$2–$10 million
number of investors	single VC investor	at least 2 VC investors
closing cycle	1–2 months	3–4 months
closings	single tranche investment	milestone-based tranches
dividends	nonmandatory, noncumulative 8% per year	in some cases, mandatory, cumulative, payable in kind 15% per year
liquidation preference	1X purchase price, plus participation rights to 3X	for some later-stage deals, up to 3X purchase price, plus participation rights, possibly with no cap
redemption	none	at option of holders after 5 years at purchase price plus accrued dividends
automatic conversion	upon qualified IPO of $50 million, no price limit	upon qualified IPO of $25 million, and at least 5X purchase price
antidilution protection	standard broad-based weighted average adjustment	full ratchet adjustment for a period; then weighted average
board composition	2 VCs; 2 common; 1 outsider	same

(continued)

term	then, it was not uncommon to see	... and after, it was not uncommon to see
protective provisions	investor approval of: senior securities, sale of company, payment of dividends, liquidation, change of rights	investor approval of senior or pari passu securities, sale of company, payment of dividends, change of rights, change of business, incurrence of debt over specified limit, annual budgets and variances, acquisitions of other businesses, grant of exclusive rights in technology, appointment or termination of CEO
preemptive rights	right to maintain pro rata ownership in later financings	right to invest 2X pro rata ownership in later financings
most favored nations treatment	none	right to get any more favorable terms granted in later financings
pay to play provisions	often used; preferred loses antidilution protection if don't participate in later financing at lower price	more common now; preferred automatically converts to common if don't participate in later financing at lower price
first refusal rights	right to purchase any shares proposed to be sold by employees	right to purchase any shares proposed to be sold by any shareholder
co-sale rights	right to sell alongside any founder that sells shares	right to share alongside any shareholder that sells shares
drag-along rights	none	right to force all shareholders to sell company upon board and majority shareholder approval
founder vesting	standard 4-year vesting with some up-front vesting	moving to 5-year vesting in some cases
employment agreements	none	employment agreements for key founders
representations and warranties	from company only	some reps and warranties from founders individually re IP etc.

Used with permission from Fenwick & West LLP.

Sidebar 12.8 A Sample Venture Capital Term Sheet

Software Start-Up
Summary of Proposed Terms
Sale of Series A Preferred Stock

The following sets forth the proposed terms for the Series A Financing of Start-Up. This term sheet is nonbinding. Any legally binding obligation on either party is subject to the execution and delivery of a definitive stock purchase agreement and completion of due diligence.

Issuer: Software Start-Up (the "Company"), a California Corporation. The proposed transaction involves raising $4,000,000 through the issuance of Series A Preferred Stock ("Series A")

Amount of Financing: $4,000,000

Price per Share: $1.00, based upon a $4 million pre-money valuation (including option pool set forth below)

Closing: November 30, 2003

Investors and Amounts:

ABC Ventures	2,500,000 shares	$2,500,000
XYZ Ventures	1,500,000 shares	$1,500,000
Total	4,000,000 shares	$4,000,000

Types of Securities: The Series A Preferred Stock with the rights, preferences, and privileges set forth below

Capitalization Post-Closing:

Common Stock Outstanding	2,000,000	25%
Preferred Stock Outstanding	4,000,000	50%
Pool Available for Future Employees	2,000,000	25%
Total Common Stock Equivalents	8,000,000	100%

Terms of Series A Preferred Stock

Dividends: The holders of Series A shall be entitled to receive noncumulative dividends at the rate of 8% of the Series A purchase price per annum, prior and in preference to any dividend on the Common Stock. Dividends to be paid if and when declared by the Board of Directors. Thereafter, any further dividends would be allocated between the Common and Preferred stockholders on a pro rata basis, treating the Preferred Stock on an as-if-converted basis.

Liquidation Preference: In the event of any liquidation or winding up of the Company, the holders of Series A shall be entitled to receive in preference to the holders of the Common Stock an amount equal to $1.00 per share for each share of Series A, plus all declared but unpaid dividends on the Series A.

Any remaining proceeds shall be allocated between the Common and Series A stockholders on a pro rata basis, treating the Series A on an as-if-converted basis, until the aggregate return to the Series A is $2.00 per share. Thereafter, all remaining proceeds shall be allocated among holders of Common Stock on a pro rata basis. A merger, consolidation, sale of assets or other transaction in which control of the Company is transferred will be treated as a liquidation.

Conversion: Holders of Preferred Stock shall have the right at any time after the date of issuance to convert their shares into shares of Common Stock. The initial conversion rate shall be 1:1, subject to adjustment as provided below.

Automatic Conversion: The Series A shall be automatically converted into Common Stock, at the then applicable conversion price, in the event of a public offering of not less than $20,000,000 in aggregate proceeds and a price per share to the public of not less than $5.00 or upon the vote of holders of at least a majority of Series A.

Antidilution Provisions: The conversion price of the Series A will be subject to adjustment on a broad-based weighted average basis to reduce dilution in the event that the Company issues additional equity securities (other than Exempted Shares as defined below) at a purchase price less than the applicable conversion price. The conversion price will also be subject to proportional adjustment for stock splits, stock dividends, recapitalizations, and the like. "Exempted Shares" means reserved employee shares described under "Employee Pool" below and shares issued to equipment lessors or strategic commercial partners approved by the Board or in connection with acquisitions approved by the Board.

Redemption: The Company shall, upon the request of the holders of at least a majority of the Series A, redeem the Series A shares at initial cost plus accrued dividends, at any time after the 7th anniversary of the Closing and at the rate of 1/3 of the Series A per year for three years, to the extent the Company has funds legally available therefor.

Voting Rights: The Series A will vote together with the Common Stock and not as a separate class on an as-if-converted basis except:

(1) Consent of the holders of at least a majority of the Preferred Stock shall be required for any action which: (i) adversely alters or changes the rights, preferences, or privileges of the Preferred Stock, (ii) increases the authorized number of shares of Preferred Stock, (iii) creates any equity security on a parity with or having preference over the existing Preferred Stock, (iv) effects a

merger, reorganization, or sale of the Company or substantially all of its assets, or (v) effects a reclassification or recapitalization of the outstanding capital stock of the Company.

(2) The holders of Preferred Stock shall vote separately on matters that otherwise by law are subject to a class vote.

Purchase Agreement: The investment shall be made pursuant to a Stock Purchase Agreement reasonably acceptable to the Company and the Investors, which agreement shall contain appropriate representations and warranties of the Company, covenants of the Company reflecting the provisions set forth herein, and appropriate conditions of closing, including an opinion of counsel for the Company.

Information Rights: So long as an investor continues to hold shares of Series A or Common Stock issued upon conversion of the Series A, the Company shall deliver to the investor audited annual and unaudited quarterly financial statements. So long as an investor continues to hold at least 500,000 shares of Series A, the Company will furnish the investor with monthly and quarterly financial statements and will provide a copy of the Company's annual operating plan within 30 days prior to the beginning of the fiscal year. These provisions shall terminate upon a registered public offering of the Company's Common Stock.

Registration Rights: Holders of at least a majority of the Preferred Stock shall be entitled to two demand registrations (at any time after the earlier of (1) the Company's initial public offering, or (2) five years from the Series A closing) and unlimited piggyback registrations and unlimited S-3 registrations (covering at least $5,000,000 of stock), in each case with the Company to pay all registration costs (including the fees and expenses of one counsel for the selling shareholders). Registration rights will expire five years after the Company's initial public offering. Registration rights shall be transferable to a transferee of at least 15% of the then outstanding Series A or conversion shares.

Participation in Future Offerings: Investors to have the right to participate in any future sales of securities by the Company (other than Exempted Shares) on the basis of their pro rata share of all outstanding Common and Preferred shares. In addition, the Company will grant the Preferred shareholders any rights of first refusal or registration rights granted to subsequent purchasers of the Company's equity securities to the extent that such subsequent rights are superior, in good faith judgment of the Company's Board of Directors, to those granted in connection with this transaction.

Board of Directors: The size of the Company's Board of Directors shall initially be set at five. The holders of the Series A, voting as a separate class, shall be entitled to elect two members of the Company's Board of Directors, the holders of Common Stock shall be entitled to elect two members, and the fifth member shall be mutually agreed upon by the other directors.

Fees of Special Counsel: Company will pay legal fees of special counsel to investors for work in completing the documentation of this financing, up to a maximum of $30,000. In the event this financing does not close for any reason, each party shall be responsible for its own legal costs incurred to date.

Conditions to Closing: Closing is subject to completion and execution of a mutually acceptable definitive legal agreement which will contain additional provisions customary in transactions of this type, including representations, warranties, etc.

Employee Matters

Key-Man Life Insurance: As soon as possible after the Closing, the Company shall procure a key-man life insurance policy for each Founder in the amount of $1,000,000, naming the Company as beneficiary; provided, however, that at the election of holders of a majority of the outstanding Series A, such proceeds shall be used to redeem shares of Series A.

Agreements with Employees: The Company shall enter into invention assignment and confidentiality agreements with each of its employees in a form reasonably acceptable to special counsel to the investors.

Employee Pool: Upon the closing of this financing there will be 2,000,000 shares of Common Stock reserved and available for future grant to key employees under the Company's incentive stock option plan.

Employee and Founder Vesting: All employee option grants will vest over a four-year period. Twenty-five percent will vest on the first anniversary of employment; the remainder will vest monthly over the next 3 years. The "founding group" will be credited with one year of vesting as of the Closing in respect of the shares currently held, with their remaining unvested shares to vest monthly over three years. No acceleration of vesting except that each founder will be credited with 12 months vesting in the event of the founder's termination without cause or for "good reason" within six months following a change of control.

Restrictions on Transfer and Co-Sale: No transfers allowed prior to vesting except with the Company's consent. The Company shall have a right of first refusal on vested shares of Common Stock until public offering.

The investors shall have a right to participate pro rata (on the basis of outstanding shares of Preferred Stock and Common Stock) in transfer of stock by founders for value (Co-Sale Agreement).

Used with permission from Fenwick & West LLP.

4

MAKING IT PAY

Part Four of this book (Chs. 13–18) covers the most important remuneration issues for you to consider in planning and launching your start-up. You will learn to balance salary and equity rewards, learn what works and what does not, and understand what practices are followed in other start-ups. Chapter 13 deals directly with the important issue of salary and introduces the remaining (primarily equity-related) topics of Part Four.

13

Remuneration Practices for Your Start-Up

So you think that money is the root of all evil.
Have you ever asked what is the root of all money?

—Ayn Rand

Salaries

Compensation and Benefits for Start-Up Companies

How much you will remunerate yourself, your associates, and other employees in salary, fringe benefits, equity participation (usually stock options), and other perquisites depends on your needs, your cash situation, the culture you have established in your company, the financial needs (or *nut*) of each employee, and the preferences of your investors. There is always a balance between wanting to preserve precious cash and getting your due. If you do not pay fair salaries early on, sweat equity may never be fully compensated. If cash is initially tight, you might want to consider giving deferred compensation to balance cash-flow needs with the need for equitable compensation. You may have no choice. The wisest approach is to go slowly (making incremental enhancements) and keep your eye on cash flow. Remember always that "cash is king," and you don't die until you run out of cash.

Salary and Fringe Benefits vis-à-vis Stock and Stock Options

Salaries at start-ups should be reasonable and competitive. More established companies will offer superior fringe benefits that you cannot yet afford, such as retirement plans. You might think that you have to offer higher salaries to offset this difference, but this is not true. Your offsetting financial attraction is instead the potential for equity ownership that you can offer (the subject of Chs.14 and 15). However, while your salary costs can be attenuated by the offsetting value of any stock or stock options offered, this is only true to the extent that the manager or employee understands and appreciates the potential value of his or her stock position.

Virtually every potential candidate for employment with your start-up is generally familiar with the dot-com mania and bubble. Many were directly involved or have friends who were. They know that many people got very rich and that many made no money and lost their jobs. They know stories of paper fortunes gained and lost. However, most do not really understand the intricacies of equity compensation and are not in a good position to assess and appreciate the potential for wealth creation through equity ownership. Some start-up entrepreneurs choose to keep such employees in the dark, attracting them simply with good salaries and thus avoiding dilution of the equity pool. Other more knowledgeable entrepreneurs take advantage of the tremendous power of equity participation and educate their employees on this front. It is strongly urged that every start-up employee should have a potential ownership interest in the business, should know what that interest can be worth, and should be apprised monthly of the financial performance of the business. This strategy can work well to attract and retain strong team members who are dedicated to hard work to achieve their and your success.

A start-up is definitely not for everyone. In fact, it's really only right for a pretty small fraction of workers. Many will want and need the real or perceived security of a large company. That's fine. Your job is to find the right ones who want to roll the dice with you, notwithstanding the dot-com bubble. You need to openly communicate with them about the challenges and opportunities at your start-up, and speak especially to the opportunity for wealth creation through equity ownership. Of course, there are many good reasons why your employees need to know what is going on, and highlighted here is one area that is easily overlooked: they need to be able to explain things to their spouses and answer tough questions—nothing good will result if they can't.

If you have a candidate who hesitates to join your start-up (wanting extra salary for the extra risk and lack of benefits), you probably should not hire him or her. You want key managers and employees who thrive on the risk and excitement of a start-up environment and are motivated in part by visions of their stock appreciation. If it takes an excessive amount of effort and arm-twisting to get someone to join a start-up, it is generally not worth the effort because he or she will not stay with the company very long. You want people on your team who voluntarily "buy in" to the situation because that's where they want to be.

Not all small companies can afford to offer a full range of benefits to their employees. Comprehensive health care is especially expensive, and other benefits such as vision and dental care just add to the total expense. Section 125 cafeteria plans, dependent care reimbursement plans, and 401(k) plans can be relatively inexpensive ways to offer competitive fringe benefits using your employees' own money (see Ch. 18).

Six-Figure Salaries

In the 1980s people began to talk about "six-figure" salaries, and it became a personal goal for many. Throughout the 1990s and into this century, $100,000+ salaries for CEOs at venture-backed start-ups became more and more common, and the trend toward higher salaries has worked its way down the organizational chart to vice presidents and other key positions. No longer are slave wages with sweat equity the only path to moderate wealth.

Over the last several years, total compensation packages (salaries, equity, and benefits) at venture-backed start-ups became more competitive and generous. The packages became even more attractive during the dot-com explosion, when well-funded start-ups were competing aggressively for talent. Wherever you are in the business cycle, count on professional investors to realize that competitive compensation is a key factor in attracting and retaining outstanding employees.

In considering salary levels, it's helpful to distinguish between two broad groups of start-ups,

- start-ups that have not raised any significant funding, which simply cannot afford to pay competitive salaries or any salaries at all
- start-ups that have successfully raised a significant round of financing, which can afford to pay salaries

If you are in the first group, your goal must be to somehow get funded and get to the second. In an environment where execution time and growth are critical, you need to attract and retain the best team possible, and you need the resources to do that.

With the exception of the seed-level start-up funded exclusively by the founders' and their relatives' hard-earned cash, successful start-ups generally do not neglect wages for the founding and key management team. Since you and your key employees might never realize a penny's worth of gain on your stock or stock options, it is important to place liberal, reasonable salaries high on your list of ways to retain the best team.

There are numerous free online resources that will help you set up an equitable compensation plan, and these resources get better each year. See the Resources Available to Start-Up Entrepreneurs section of this book for some recommendations.

When presenting a job offer, be certain that the potential employee appreciates that his or her compensation includes both monetary and nonmonetary elements (i.e., stock options and benefits are forms of compensation).

Signing Bonuses

Especially when labor markets are tight, many well-funded start-ups offer signing bonuses to new employees. These bonuses are separate from stock option grants. They generally go to upper- and middle-level employees, but they may also extend to programmers and other employees when dictated by market conditions. There's frequently a provision that the employee has to repay the bonus if the employee leaves the company before a specified date. A survey by the American Compensation Association found that the bonus was paid in one lump sum at the time of hire 60% of the time. In the remaining 40% of the cases, the cash bonus was split, with part paid at the time of hire and the remainder paid after some fixed period of employment (say 6 or 12 months). Especially in pre-IPO situations, many key executive recruits are able to negotiate very substantial cash signing bonuses and other benefits.

Severance Packages

It's helpful to view severance packages in two broad categories.

- those that are agreed to in advance on a case-by-case basis with individual employees (who typically are key, senior employees)
- those that are determined unilaterally by a company at the time it is laying off employees

Most discussion in the media concerns the latter type, with a focus on how generous (or stingy) the company decides to be, or can be. Many employees who lost their jobs in the dot-com downturn received only their final paychecks, including payment for accrued vacation, but did not receive any severance benefits beyond that. Other companies gave each terminated employee two or more weeks of severance pay, plus an additional week's pay for each year of service. Most companies use length of service to determine the severance payments, and since the measure is weeks of pay, the more highly paid employees receive more cash. Start-ups generally have no specific severance policy. Although it may be tempting for you to put in place and announce up front a more generous policy, be careful, because you may simply not be able to afford the cash drain later at the time when you have to cut expenses and people.

Many heavily recruited senior executives are able to demand and negotiate a severance package up front that specifies what cash payments and other benefits they will receive in the event their employment is terminated. You may find yourself negotiating such a package with a key candidate you want to bring on board. With some creative effort, you might be able to reduce or eliminate the requested cash payments by increasing the equity participation.

Salary Extremes

You want to attract and retain good people at a low cost. At the same time, you will be tempted to hire superstars and pay whatever is necessary to attract and keep them. However, you will need to maintain perceived equity across the company. If some employees think their salaries are inequitable, you can expect less work output from them, and your more valuable employees may show their feelings by leaving the company.

The fact that you need to maintain equity does not mean that you have to pay all employees on the same scale. Rather, it is important that employees perceive that the criteria used to determine how they are paid are fair and that those same criteria are applied across the business.

It has been said that you cannot win the remuneration game. You can go to great lengths to reward one outstanding employee who might still feel underpaid even after an exceptional salary action. Further, if and when other employees find out, the consequence may be that everyone feels underpaid.

Keeping salaries confidential in a small company is virtually impossible, although most CEOs try their best. Also, most employees desire and expect confidentiality regarding their compensation. Legend has it that Steve Jobs, after he founded NeXT Computer, Inc., posted all salaries on a bulletin board, but with mixed results.

Pay for Performance

Keep salaries competitive and in line with industry standards. Reward exceptional performance continuously—primarily with additional stock options (see Ch. 15). On occasion, hand an exceptional employee a check for, say, $1000, perhaps grossed up to cover taxes. Some CEOs try to hand out these mini-rewards as nontaxable employee expense reimbursements (sort of like dipping into a big petty cash drawer), but that practice is not recommended. If the IRS does not catch you, your auditors might when they need to get clean financial statements for investors or a distant initial public offering. Above all else, you need to be honest. Would you want to work for someone who isn't?

Look at each individual to see what motivates him or her, and use the appropriate vehicle for handing out effective rewards. For example, one key employee had a reputation for driving a junk heap, and he frequently fixed flat tires in the company parking lot. One day after the employee met an important deadline, the CEO had a local garage install four new tires on the employee's car. That gesture cost only a few hundred dollars, but it clearly said to the employee that his performance was valued.

Headhunters

Until you receive substantial venture financing, you won't even consider using *search firms*, also known as *executive recruiters* or *headhunters*. Even after you receive funding, you may not want to use them because you'll always have one eye on conserving cash.

Venture capitalists, however, use search firms quite extensively in connection with their portfolio companies, and they may insist that you use one to fill certain key positions. It may be hard to say no, since it's "their money." Also, you may be criticized later if you take too much time on your own trying to find the right new hire, or if the person you hire doesn't work out. There's no venture capital rule stating that you won't hear, "We told you so!" or, "That CEO just doesn't listen!"

Search firms work on either a *contingency* or *retainer* basis. The major difference between the two arrangements (or between the two types of search firms) is that a contingency firm is entitled to payment if and only if it fills an open position, whereas a retained firm requires payment whether or not the search is successful. Because special arrangements are sometimes offered or negotiated, the line between the two types of arrangements (and the two types of firms) is frequently blurred. However, the assistance that a top-tier retained search firm offers, especially one that has worked with and guided numerous venture-backed companies, can be invaluable. The best retained search consultants become closely familiar with the client company and its people, culture, market, and strategy, subsequently leveraging their networks, as well as providing an objective, experienced approach to the search process.

The cost of a contingency search is typically 15–30% of the annual salary of the person being hired and, as noted previously, the search firm receives nothing if the position is not filled. The cost of a retained search may be up to one-third of the annual compensation package (including bonus), and an up-front payment (usually one-third) is typically requested.

Contingency search firms usually work on entry-level or mid-level positions. Their compensation in dollars is less, and they quickly source many resumes. But don't expect a high level of quality in the services provided or in the resumes received. Typically, these firms do not take the time to understand your business or your particular needs. In contrast, retainer firms usually work on higher-level positions (perhaps $100,000+ in annual salary) and invest significantly more effort into the process. They take the time to learn about your business and the position's particular requirements, and focus on quickly identifying a targeted short list of excellent candidates. They also interview candidates, thus serving effectively as a buffer in the process.

Working with an executive search consultant is all about building a sense of trust. "Select a consultant that you feel comfortable with, regardless of firm association," says Rick Gostyla of the executive search firm Spencer Stuart. "Bottom line, it's the relationship and personal chemistry that matter most."

For some helpful tips, see Sidebar 13.1, Working with Executive Recruiters Successfully.

Using retained search is quite common—almost pro forma—among venture capital firms seeking the best talent to serve as board members; chief executive officers; vice presidents of sales, engineering, or operations; or in other key executive and management positions. The executive search firm Spencer Stuart handles over 3000 searches each year, over a quarter of which are for venture-backed portfolio companies.

Search fees may often be negotiated. A search firm looking for a long-term relationship and repeat business may be willing to reduce its fees or take a portion of its compensation in stock options or warrants.

Assuming that your start-up can't afford a search firm or that you've simply decided not to use one, here are some tips to help you find the right people on your own.

- Use the Internet extensively. Post your positions on several of the popular sites that connect employers with employee candidates, such as Monster.com, Jobs.com, and HotJobs.com.
- Post your open positions on your website.
- Offer cash referral awards to your employees.
- Surprisingly, ads in newspapers still work in targeted locations for certain positions. So don't ignore this tool.
- Look to your competition for good candidates.
- Use your network of personal and business contacts. Ask your board members and investors to help you fill open positions.

Many people don't know how to effectively use their networks to find excellent employee candidates. A key is to make it easy for the people you contact, giving them a clear "call to action." Let them know that they can help you even if they don't have a particular candidate in mind and even if they don't understand the field or position in question. One effective approach is to put together a succinct message (not exceeding one email screen, with links if appropriate) with relevant information about the opportunity and the position you wish to fill, which the recipient can easily forward to some of his or her contacts who may know such a person or something about the field. Point out how easy this is to do, and ask the recipient to do it. The right person is typically two or more steps out in the network (which is why it's called *networking*), and there is a beautiful, unpredictable nature to the process of how people and jobs get connected. For example, you might hear, "A friend of my cousin's neighbor put me in touch with the right person."

Equity Ownership: Stock and Stock Options

Stock grants (see Ch. 14) and stock options (see Ch. 15) are major sources of future potential wealth for you and your employees. Many start-up entrepreneurs vastly underestimate the power of these instruments. Study the next two chapters closely if you are unfamiliar with the mechanisms and practices of stock grants and stock option grants (as most engineer-entrepreneurs are). In terms of direct financial payback, understanding and applying these equity-related concepts are every bit as important to your success as being customer- and market-driven.

Form of Equity Incentive Vehicles—an Umbrella Plan

The most common legal style is to draft one plan document (say, 10–15 pages) that governs various equity incentive vehicles under one roof or umbrella, typically including

- Incentive Stock Options (ISOs), also known as "statutory" options or "qualified" options

- Nonqualified Stock Options (NQSOs)
- Restricted Stock Purchases

You might view this plan document as an umbrella or master plan document. It will be called something like, "Acme, Inc.'s 2003 Equity Incentive Plan," and it requires approval by your start-up's board of directors and shareholders. The year simply refers to the year the plan was adopted, and the plan will remain in effect for many years after that. The typical plan sets forth the parameters and legal requirements that apply, including

- *its purpose* (which of course is to provide incentives)
- *the number of shares available under the plan* (which can be increased later if needed)
- *eligibility requirements* (which vary depending on whether it's an ISO, NQSO, and so on)
- *administration* (by the board of directors or a committee appointed by the board)
- *the legal and practical details* (the "nuts and bolts"). These detail how the plan works. For example, in the case of options, these passages will cover type of option, exercise price, exercise period, method of payment for the stock upon option exercise, termination, limitations, legal and tax considerations, and so forth.

The plan document refers to various other standard agreements and forms that will be used to implement the plan. These include the stock option agreement, the option exercise agreement, and the restricted stock purchase agreement, among others.

Other Compensation

Other equity- and wealth-building vehicles (see Ch. 16) and fringe benefits (see Ch. 18) complete the remuneration spectrum. One needs to consider this entire spectrum when formulating a workable compensation policy.

Employment Contracts

While Ch. 18 covers the basics for employment contracts for yourself, try to avoid giving extraordinary protection or rights to any others. Investors do not like these complications, which can be the cause of severe cash drains if you need to shake out non-performing team members. In particular, with rare exception, you should not agree to employ anyone for any particular period of time; all employment should be *employment at will*, which means that either the company or the employee has the right to terminate the employment at any time, with or without cause.

To avoid misunderstandings and to reduce the chances of litigation, you do need written agreements with everyone who works for you, including both employees (whether full-time or part-time) and independent contractors. Your attorneys have many standard form agreements that they can easily tweak for use in your company, and the legal expense for this routine work is not great. The types of agreements and their form can vary, and they may include a short employment letter (1–3 pages), a stock option agreement, a restricted stock purchase agreement, and the like. Whatever the form, the agreements are intended to clarify the relationship, which benefits everyone, and they will also protect the company by covering such key topics as employment at will, confidentiality of company information, and the company's ownership of all intellectual property resulting from the relationship.

Sidebar 13.1 Working with Executive Recruiters Successfully

Hopefully, in most cases you will be able to find and hire the right key people through word of mouth and the networks of your venture investors. However, given the demand for top talent and the complexity of the search process, you and your board of directors may decide to turn to an executive search firm for help in successfully finding a new CEO or other key senior person. If you do, here are some helpful hints from Richard A. Smith and Jonathan Visbal, of the executive search firm Spencer Stuart, that will vastly increase the likelihood of search success.

- *Avoid the "bait and switch."*

  Within the professional services marketplace, it is common practice to have a "selling partner" pass off new business to junior associates for execution. For many segments of the professional services marketplace this model is successful for both firm and client. Not so in the executive search world. Public market pressure and other factors have forced several large firms toward a highly leveraged model that stresses selling partners and junior back-room executors. If you're not careful, you may place the critical responsibility of recruiting a key executive into the hands of someone you've never met. Bottom line: success requires direct interaction and calibration with the specific individual leading the search. Injecting a middleman into the process only dilutes communication.

- *Choose the "realist," not the "optimist."*

  To close the deal, many search professionals think they must portray a strong sense of optimism, stressing how easy the search will be and that they already have several candidates in their "back pocket." Beware! As much as you would like to believe them, senior-executive searches are typically extremely challenging. Success requires someone who can understand and help navigate the likely obstacles. Look for the search professional with a strong perspective on the advantages and challenges likely in your search, and in particular, look for a realistic perspective based on industry-specific experience.

- *Retain a surrogate in the marketplace.*

  One of the critical values an experienced executive search firm brings is surrogacy. This is the ability of the firm, and in particular the executing consultant, to represent your company positively in the marketplace. In today's highly competitive market for talent, there is no substitute for a knowledgeable consultant representing your company, signaling to the marketplace the importance of the search, and perhaps more importantly, being able to gain the trust and peer-level respect of the candidate pool. A brand is perhaps a search firm's greatest asset. Well-known search firms can leverage their brand credibility to get calls returned and have the company's story heard.

- *Beware of "container" fee structures.*

  One recent trend is the emergence of *container fees*, a type of executive recruitment that is part contingency and part retainer. In a container search, partial payments are made by the client regardless of search outcome, with the final payment being contingent upon completion of the search. While this structure can be seductively attractive, the difference is in the level of commitment. In a fully retained search, the firm is committed to a solution, no matter what challenges may arise. In contrast, a "container" search firm may be committed to little more work than a contingency firm would be, after which it may respectfully discontinue efforts if an appropriate candidate cannot be found. This outcome can be devastating. By the time the company is able to re-engage another firm (assuming it is able to do so), it has lost three to four critical months and will have to pay nearly twice the price to complete the search. Remember the observation about bacon and eggs: The chicken is involved, but the pig is committed! Make sure your recruiter is committed as well.

- *Demand critical assessment, and evaluate it carefully.*

  Selecting the right CEO or other key person requires much more effort than simply filtering resumes or relying on gut feel. Success requires a critical evaluation of each candidate under consideration, an examination of behavioral competencies, and an analysis of not just intellect or industry exposure, but of emotional intelligence. Not only should the firm be able to quickly identify prospects for the position, but each candidate should also be critically evaluated against the position's required competencies. This evaluation should be communicated to clients in clear and actionable correspondence. Do not accept mere regurgitation of a candidate's resume. Demand a deeper level of evaluation and use this as a guidepost in your assessment of candidates.

- *Calibrate early and often.*

  When working with the industry's top executive search recruiters, you're not just paying for the identification of warm bodies, but for valuable business advisory services. Many clients hire a search firm expecting it to simply return in four weeks with the best candidate. Unfortunately, this process often fails based on lack of alignment among the client, search consultant, and marketplace. The search professional should first assist in a thorough assessment of the skills and competencies required, not only for the executive to be successful, but to fully augment and integrate successfully with the current executive team. There should also be frequent communication between the consultant and the client, with a view on the market (i.e., what position or company attributes are viewed positively, what attributes candidates are concerned about, and which pockets of the market are most interested and why). This feedback will help align expectations between the firm and the client as the search progresses, and will also enable the search consultant and client to discuss potential changes midstream. In turn, this synergistic communication will best calibrate the role to more effectively target appropriate market segments as well as develop the most powerful, positive message for the marketplace.

14

Stock Ownership

A pessimist sees the difficulty in every opportunity; an optimist sees the opportunity in every difficulty.

—Sir Winston Churchill

Stock ownership is the clear differentiator of the start-up company. It is the quintessence of entrepreneurial activity. With stock, you have a kind of ownership and pride in an enterprise that cannot be replicated in any Fortune 500 company environment. You have a deeper stake in the business, more potential wealth, and correspondingly more risk. Most start-up entrepreneurs have little experience or training to guide them in the areas of stock ownership, grant, and award practices. A careful reading of this chapter and the next will arm you with the knowledge necessary to leverage the power of equity to make your business a success in the way it is best measured—in the wealth generated for the start-up's founders and other stakeholders.

There are really two different perspectives in time from which you will want to address the distribution of stock and stock options. As a founder/owner, you view the new company as being yours because you (and your family and friends) provided the initial capital to get the company going. Also, you personally provided a lot of *sweat equity* to get it going. The business eventually gets to the point where it needs additional investment capital. Since you, as the founder/owner, own all or at least the lion's share of the company (at least initially), your objective is to bring in additional funds with as little dilution as possible. Founders/owners look at stock in their company as their investment capital.

Later, as a founder/employee, you can no longer think of the company as yours, assuming that you have raised capital by selling stock. It really belongs to your investors, since they may own, say, 75% or more of the stock after two or three rounds of financing. From this point of view, your new objective is to negotiate as good a deal as possible for yourself and your associates.

Table 14.1 provides an overview of the basics of stock and stock option practices. Stock and stock options are perplexing subjects. Key features of each type of stock and option are characterized in terms of the advantages and disadvantages of each type to the employer and to the employee. The remainder of this chapter and Ch. 15 provide more detail.

Risk-Reward Scale

First you need to understand more about the various stock weights that you will arrange to put on the reward side of your start-up risk-reward scale, as shown in Fig. 14.1.

You are starting your own business, so you will be the owner, right? Perhaps—if you intend to remain a small business. However, Ch. 5 establishes several reasons why a high-tech start-up needs to grow. With rare exception, growth requires capital, and that implies the presence of investors who will give you needed funds only in return for an immediate or optional equity interest in your company. Banks will not lend a

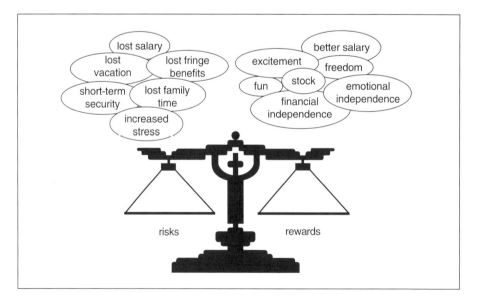

Figure 14.1   Start-Up Risk-Reward Scale

Table 14.1 Stock and Stock Options

event type	employee advantages	employer advantages	employee disadvantages	employer disadvantages[b]
stock grants				
gift of stock	Immediate voting rights. Stock is free.[a] Stock in hand is easier to keep. No conditions for ownership	Gets a more loyal employee. Book expense, which reduces profits, and may save taxes.	Tax liability. Repurchase agreement.	Dilution of ownership. Book expense, which hurts paper profits.
grant of right to buy stock immediately[c]	Immediate voting rights. Stock is cheap. Stock in hand is easier to keep. No conditions for purchase.	Gets a more loyal employee. Gets small amount of additional capital.	Tax liability. Repurchase agreement. Need to buy immediately.	Dilution of ownership. Book expense, which hurts paper profits.
type of stock granted				
restricted	Section 83(b) election can reduce future tax burden.	Can buy back stock if employee does not meet performance or vesting conditions.	Repurchase agreement. Pay some income tax up front if purchase price is below fair market value.	
transferable (generally cannot be done in start-ups)	Can dispose of shares anytime, subject to applicable securities laws.		Immediate tax liability.	Loss of control of stock.
other stock acquisitions				
purchase (investments)	Immediate voting rights. Very high ROI possible. Can sell shares anytime, subject to applicable securities laws.	Gets additional capital.	Need higher salary, and/or invest hard-earned cash.	Increased number of shareholders.
via provision of property	Can dispose of shares anytime. Immediate voting rights. Sophisticated investment. Tax-free exchange possible.	Gets needed property.	Some investment risk.	Dilution of ownership.
stock option grants				
incentive stock options (ISOs)	No income reportable (no tax) on grant or exercise. Options exercisable in any order. Taxed only when stock is disposed of. Vesting schedule may be negotiable.	Does not show as an expense, thus does not hurt paper profits. High likelihood option will not be exercised by employee. Exercise schedule not negotiable.	No voting rights until exercised. Taxed when disposed of. Many IRS requirements to qualify: option price ≥ fair market value; must exercise ≤ 10 years from date of grant; must be employee to exercise or exercise < 3 months after termination; need cash to exercise options before they expire; high risk of losing options. Exercise schedule is not negotiable.	Possible future dilution of ownership.
nonqualified stock options (NQSOs)	Options exercisable in any order. Vesting schedule negotiable. Exercise schedule may be negotiable.	Gets a more loyal employee. Book expense, which reduces profits and may save taxes.	No voting rights (until exercised). Taxed when exercised. Taxed when disposed of.	Possible future dilution of ownership. Book expense, which hurts paper profits. Exercise schedule negotiable.

[a]The IRS will not recognize stock grants as gifts in the classic sense—stock will most likely be treated as compensation to the employee (so he will owe income tax on its value); therefore, it is technically inaccurate to say the stock is free.
[b]On a *fully diluted* basis, all of these events dilute ownership.
[c]Founders' stock is usually in this category, with the purchase price set very low (e.g., $0.01 or $0.001 per share).

start-up money unless the entrepreneur personally secures the loan with personal assets (such as a house), so you probably will be stuck with co-owners in your business. Your founding team and other key employees will be critical to your success, and it is essential that they are all motivated by a share of the ownership of your business, which is assumed here to be a corporation. (See Ch. 20 for a discussion of why a corporation is the most popular form of legal entity for a high-tech start-up, especially one that intends to raise money from venture capitalists.)

Ownership in a corporation is reflected in shares of the company's stock. The founders of the business will almost always be granted cheap founders' stock, also known as *cheap stock*. Cheap stock can also be issued to other employees who come on board in the early days of the company, before the value of the stock has risen much. Employees who join the business later, after the company and its stock are more valuable, will usually be granted stock options, which give them a chance to participate in the success of the company without having to invest cash. (See Ch. 15 for more information about stock options.)

As noted above, the general rule is that high-growth, high-tech start-ups require outside investment capital. Another general rule is that such start-ups also need to reward and motivate their employee teams through the use of equity incentives. For the views of an expert in employee ownership, see Sidebar 14.1, Five Tips from Dr. Beyster.

Ownership Interest over Time

Other stockholders will eventually own a good portion of your company and, through increased value of their shares, will participate in the profits. While you may eventually also distribute cash dividends as a form of profit sharing, in your first years you will not even think of wasting precious cash for that. In fact, with rare exception, the most successful high-tech start-ups do not distribute cash dividends, even if they have lots of cash. (They prefer to use the cash to continue expanding the business.) So what do you need to know about stock ownership in order to launch your business successfully? Figure 14.2 shows qualitatively how stock ownership interests might change over time as your business grows.

In the beginning, the company you launch is clearly yours, and you call the shots. You may very well be the only stockholder, hold every office your secretary of state requires, and be the only board member. You own a very big piece of a very small pie. As you bring other founders, key employees, and investors on board, however, the picture changes greatly. The value of the company (the increasing area of the pie) and your percentage ownership (the ever smaller percentage slice) will depend greatly on a number of factors. Your hope and goal, of course, are that your small piece of a big pie will be worth a lot more than your big piece of a small pie.

How Many Shares Should You Grant?

The total percentage of stock owned or claimed by management and employees (including stock options) may be 15–30% after the last round of financing, and much less than that after an IPO. The founding CEO at the time of an IPO may own 2–5%, although 1% or less is not uncommon. In periods of declining returns on venture capital funds (where valuations are lower and venture capital terms get tougher), you can expect an even smaller portion for management and employees. At least one well-known venture capital fund tells entrepreneurs in advance that its general model is 80/20. Management and employees will likely get 20% or less.

As the founder, you could initially own about one-half of all the stock granted to the cofounding team, and you could own as much as one-third of the total stock allocated to the management-employee pool (i.e., the noninvestors' shares) after the final round of financing (see Fig. 14.2). These numbers will vary widely, and will depend greatly on who else cofounds or joins your business.

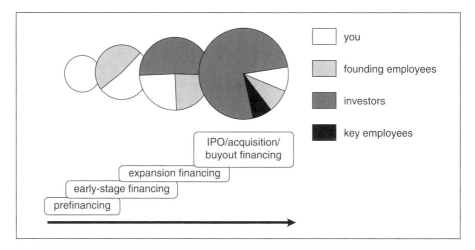

Figure 14.2   Business Ownership Interest over Time

The absolute number of shares you should grant an employee or cofounder will be determined in part by the established price per share. At the beginning, the number of shares initially distributed and the pricing of these shares is completely arbitrary; only percentages really matter. One approach is to price your stock so that each founder has something approaching 1 million shares. This is a very powerful psychological threshold, as people can see their million dollars more clearly if they have a claim on 1 million shares of your stock. Even junior employees will be able to visualize their tens of thousands of shares being worth significant amounts. Anyone who thinks about it for more than a moment will realize that the number of shares really does not matter, but even you will be heartened by the thought of owning millions of shares of stock. Venture capital investors understand this psychology as well and will often encourage you to play this penny stock game. When you take your company public in the future, the underwriters who handle the offering will want the stock price to be in a customary range (typically $10–$20 per share), which means you may have to do a reverse split, significantly reducing the number of shares each employee claims. If not handled properly, this can cause employee animosity (even though the stock split will not change anyone's percentage interest in the company). Of course, it's also possible that a stock split will be needed to get the price per share into the desired range, and this would make everyone happy.

A customary pricing approach is to sell the founders' stock initially at a very low price, say $0.01 or $0.001 per share. This fraction-of-a-penny approach can be more exciting since it results in more shares being distributed to your founders and emphasizes the possibility of a real home run. Prominent Silicon Valley venture capital firms, for example, on occasion make returns of 200 or 400 to 1 on their investments that result in hot IPOs, although these big home runs are relatively uncommon, of course. Since returns of 300 or 400 to 1 are not unheard of, why not hand out a million shares worth a penny each that some day might be worth several dollars each?

Some entrepreneurs maintain a major ownership for years, even after the company goes public. In 1986, for example, Microsoft Corporation went public at an IPO price of $21 per share. At that time, founder Bill Gates still owned 43% of the company, and his 11 million shares were worth $234 million on the day of the offering. Many stock splits later, the Microsoft shares he retained along the way hit a high-water mark of $79 billion (a 337-fold increase over their value at the time of the IPO). Microsoft stock subsequently dropped significantly from its high point and, after the terrorist attacks in 2001, Gates' Microsoft stock was worth only $32 billion. The legendary Dave Packard and Bill Hewlett retained a significant percentage of Hewlett-Packard for many years after it went public, and they endowed foundations worth several billions of dollars. Others will own less than 1% after years of work, which they may feel is not enough.

In her book *CEO: Building a $400 Million Company from the Ground Up*, Sandra Kurtzig of ASK Computer said of her company's day of public offering,

> For the 546,550 personal shares I sold, I was to receive a check for $5,580,276. And I still owned more than 3 million shares of ASK stock, 61% of the company.

Like a baby, you give this entity birth, and as it grows and matures it will grow into its own. Enjoy and prosper from the journey and the destination of this child!

Common and Preferred Stock

Preferred stock owners have certain advantages over common stock owners. The owners of preferred stock have a first claim on the assets of the company (after debts have been taken care of) should it ever be necessary to liquidate the company. When it became much harder for entrepreneurs to attract funding following the collapse of the dot-com bubble, some venture investors insisted that their liquidation preference be increased from the customary 1X to a higher muliple, even up to 4X. (4X means that the preferred stockholders would receive back four times their investment amount before the common shareholders would receive a penny.) Some preferred stock issues also carry a dividend payable every year on every share before any dividends can be paid to common stockholders. Further, if the preferred stock is cumulative preferred, then any dividends not paid in previous years would accrue and must be paid in full before the common stockholders could get a penny in dividends. For these reasons, preferred stock usually has a higher valuation or market value than common stock.

In some cases where investors or insiders have attached unreasonable, expensive dividend rights to their preferred stock holdings, the common stock can be predicted to have virtually no present or future value, barring some miracle in the fortunes of the company. However, such burdensome dividend rights (so-called *mandatory* dividends) are generally not imposed by professional investors. More commonly, a venture capitalist's term sheet will provide that the preferred shares being purchased are entitled to a cumulative dividend "if and when declared." The "if and when declared" language is important, and is largely a legal fiction, since the board will almost certainly not do this. One reason for this type of language is to create legal distinctions between the common stock and preferred stock so that "cheap stock" (common shares, or stock options on the common) can be issued to employees at a much lower price than the preferred without triggering the imposition of income taxes.

It is for these reasons that your investors, if they are at all sophisticated and if they contribute any substantial amount of money, will almost certainly demand preferred stock, and will require you to hold common stock.

A rule of thumb is to assume that one common share is only worth between 10% and 50% of one preferred share, depending upon the preferred dividend policy and the maturity of the start-up. The 10% figure is generally used in the early stages of a start-up before any major value-enhancing milestones have been achieved, which means, for example, that if the preferred is sold to investors in the first round of financing for $1 per share, then options on common stock issued at about that time could reasonably have an exercise price of only $0.10 per share. (This is a 10-to-1 difference in the value between the preferred and common, and some companies have even used a 20-to-1 ratio in the early stages.) As a start-up achieves success and moves closer to an IPO, the spread between the common and preferred would be reduced. Generally, each share of preferred stock will be converted into one share of common stock just before the company goes public or is sold, at which time their values become equal. (The conversion ratio for preferred stock almost always starts out at one-to-one, but is subject to possible adjustment under the applicable negotiated terms governing the preferred. See the term sheet discussion in Ch.12 for more about this.)

As noted previously and in Ch. 20, venture capitalists will expect to buy preferred stock in your corporation. Assuming you plan to seek money from such investors in the future, it is important that you not do things along the way that will make these efforts more difficult. In particular, the financial and legal "stuff" needs to be done right. Prospective investors prefer to invest in people who have taken the time to understand the rules of the game—people who "know what they're doing." A prospective investor may walk away from a start-up that has too many *clean-up* problems. Plan ahead. Don't create problems that shouldn't be there.

For example, many companies stumble by issuing common stock (rather than preferred) to a group of outside investors in the first round. Although this may appear to make sense for the founders (because, in the event of liquidation, there would be no preferred shareholders standing first in line to receive the liquidation proceeds), it is not the customary way of structuring the financing, and it can create problems. One problem is that your employees then would be granted stock options at a price that's much too high. This is because the pricing couldn't benefit from the substantial pricing spread (say 10-to-1) between the preferred and the common, simply because there is no preferred. The result is likely to be new key employees who are unhappy because the option price is too high or because the options become *underwater options* if there's a down round in the future. Although it may be counterintuitive, you want your key employees to have options with a price that's as low as possible. Another problem is that your first-round investors are likely to get upset when later investors get preferred stock and they didn't.

Authorized and Outstanding Shares

When you and your lawyer incorporate your business, your *articles of incorporation* ("articles"), also called *certificate of incorporation*, will specify the number of shares of common stock and the number of shares of preferred stock that the corporation is *authorized* to issue, together with the rights and privileges of each class of stock. The articles may also create various *series* of each class of stock, or this may be done later as needed by a simple amendment to the articles. For example, a series called "Series B Preferred Stock" could be created when your start-up does its second outside financing round. In states that allow *blank-check preferred stock*, you can simply specify in the articles that classes or series of preferred are authorized, with the rights, preferences, and privileges of each to be determined by the board of directors from time to time. This avoids the necessity of shareholder action each time you wish to create a new class or series.

The number of authorized shares can be any number and is likely to be quite large, say 10 or 20 million shares, and a number much larger than what you have current plans to use. Also, if at any future time you want your company to sell more shares than what is authorized, an amendment to the articles will easily accomplish this. The authorized number of shares is also quite meaningless, and it only temporarily specifies how many shares can be sold or otherwise issued in the future. Do not use the number of authorized shares to compute anything.

The number of shares sold or given to people is the number of *outstanding shares*, or *issued shares*. In calculating your present percentage ownership of the company, divide your share holdings by the number of outstanding shares. To estimate your percentage ownership at some future point in time, divide your current share holdings by the sum of the number of shares currently outstanding and any authorized shares that you estimate will be issued between now and that point in time (for example, to raise money or to accommodate the exercising of stock options).

Another important concept is the calculation of shares outstanding on a *fully diluted* basis. In this case you also take into account all outstanding preferred stock, stock options, warrants, and any other instrument that can be converted into common stock of the company. You simply calculate the number of common shares that each of these outstanding equity obligations is convertible into, and you add these numbers to the total number of common shares outstanding. The result is the total number of common shares outstanding on a fully diluted basis. If you only take into account some of these other instruments (only the preferred stock, for example), you will arrive at a *partially diluted* total. In all cases, when you're using numbers, make your assumptions clear. So if an investor asks how many shares you have outstanding, you may say, "we have 5 million shares outstanding on a fully diluted basis." The word "diluted" comes from the fact that whatever you're talking about (e.g., company earnings) becomes diluted when you spread it over more shares.

Acquiring Stock

One can generally buy stock at fair market value at any time once a business is underway, subject to federal and state securities laws, of course. Initially, founders usually will divide up the business according to the perceived value each member is expected to bring to the party, independent of how much total cash is provided. Founders providing extra cash (i.e., more than their share) can simply be treated in part like investors. One also can acquire an option (which is a right, but not an obligation) to buy stock in the future, usually at a discounted price.

Founders' Stock

When launching your start-up, you will grant to yourself and your founding team shares of stock called founders' stock. However, this does not mean that the shares are free from a dollar point of view or free from conditions and restrictions. Also, the term "founders' stock" has no special legal meaning, and the shares you issue to Joe will look the same whether or not you choose to call him a founder. Since people are proud to be considered founders, and since it really costs you nothing to do so, you should err on the liberal side in deciding which key early people will be considered founders. It can be very motivating.

For Founders

Although "founders' stock" has no special legal significance, it does carry some meaning in the business world. Founders' stock is loosely defined as "cheap stock" (received when fair market value is near zero). Founders' stock is usually available only to those who create or found a business and is granted in proportion to one's potential contribution. It is often purchased for a nominal sum or a token amount with little or no income tax liability. Its purchase is made just after incorporation and before the infusion of substantial outside capital, when the value of the company is very low.

For Key Employees

A key employee whom you hire later but choose to treat as a founder may still be granted cheap founders' stock even after the infusion of outside capital. However, there will be income realized from the IRS' point of view, and the employee must pay taxes if the stock is purchased at a price less than its fair market value. Although your company could gross up a paycheck to help the employee pay his or her taxes, this is not done frequently in practice because of the impact on cash. Therefore, from a practical income tax point of view, cheap founders' stock is only readily available before the business is substantially capitalized and before any events or achievements have caused the valuation of the company to rise significantly.

Dollars

Founder shares are sold primarily to distribute ownership in the business equitably. Price is an issue only to the extent that, after founder shares are issued and before financing can be obtained, the company must end up with sufficient capital to be viable. Though many state laws specify no minimum level of capitalization, your lawyer will likely recommend that you and your cofounders scrape together at least a few thousand dollars at this step. He or she wants to be paid, as will many new service providers you will be engaging very soon. If you do not start with sufficient capital, you will find yourself lending money to the business very soon.

Anyone (including yourself) who lends money to a start-up, especially if the loan is not secured by other assets, should be compensated with a very high interest rate (like junk bonds) or with an option to convert the loan into equity in the future. Take some caution, however, in compensating yourself with a high-interest-rate loan. Several items to be aware of are as follows: the high interest rate may violate applicable usury laws; if the lender is also a corporate officer or director, charging a high interest rate may be a breach of fiduciary duty and open the door to a shareholder suit; high interest may run afoul of IRS rules on reasonableness; and the interest income could be treated as disguised wages, perhaps making the company liable for penalties for failure to withhold FICA (Federal Insurance Contribution Act), FUTA (Federal Unemployment Tax Act), FWT (federal withholding tax), and so on.

Vesting and Repurchase Rights

Imagine that you and your founding team have come to an agreement as to the distribution of founders' stock among the team members. Now, what happens if some of these key people leave the business: they quit, are fired, or become ill? Will they simply retain all their founders' stock and eventually benefit from the future years of labor of those remaining behind? This could happen if you do not impose some restrictions, including *vesting* and *repurchase rights*. It is wise to use a lawyer experienced in this area. Also, try to get someone on your board of directors who has experience in start-up businesses.

Putting appropriate *restricted stock agreements* in place will help clarify the under-standings and expectations of all team members, in addition to giving them comfort. Also, any problems in this area (such as a large chunk of the founders' stock being held by people no longer working at the company) will come out later in any due dili-gence by a prospective investor, and could cause problems. To the extent the prob-lems are fixable, the investor may require restrictions or modifications to be agreed to by everyone after the fact, in which case you may have less control over the outcome. It's better to be proactive and do things right from the beginning. This improves your chances of success, and gets you better results in the long run. It also makes you appear more competent.

Consideration for Stock Grants

If you are using the sale of founders' stock to substantially capitalize your business, you may find a few cases of financial hardship among your founders and key employees. For such individuals, the company might lend them the money they need to purchase their stock, and this loan might be forgiven over time in whole or in part as they acquire longevity with the company. Some key employees negotiate not only forgivable loans (which they never have to repay) but also zero interest (or forgivable interest) loans. The same goals could be accomplished by the individuals signing promissory notes for the purchase amount.

However, in all cases, you want to make sure, under applicable law of the state where the corporation is incorporated, that the individual is giving valid *consideration* for the shares being purchased. State law typically excludes some forms of considera-tion for these shares. For example, *future services* of the individual to the corporation usually cannot be counted, and promissory notes and loans may be acceptable con-sideration only in limited circumstances. The experienced attorney handling your incorporation can advise you on this.

Also, depending on the amount of the loan and other factors, the IRS may impute interest (with the rate depending on the situation) on zero interest loans and promis-sory notes. If you do not actually pay interest to the company, the company could be considered to have received the imputed interest (when it actually received none).

The numerous massive corporate scandals (Enron, etc.) are likely to continue fuel-ing legal reform efforts relating to corporate governance and executive compensation, including loans to directors, officers, and other employees. Although the principal focus of reform is on public companies, private companies should also expect to be affected.

Restricted Stock Grants

The shares you will be granting can be "restricted" in two senses of the word, and you need to be aware of both.

Transfers Restricted by Securities Laws

State and federal securities laws dictate to whom outstanding shares in a corporation can be resold, under what conditions, and at what times. If you or your employees have received a stock certificate for the shares granted to you, these shares probably have not even been registered with the state of incorporation (depending upon the number and kinds of shareholders and the amount of capital accumulated). Since all shares have legal restrictions on their transfer, you can expect unregistered shares to be even more restricted. Thus, you should not be surprised to see printed on the top of your certificate in big bold letters and red ink something like the following.

> IT IS UNLAWFUL TO CONSUMMATE A SALE OR TRANSFER OF THIS SECURITY, OR ANY INTEREST THEREIN, OR TO RECEIVE ANY CONSIDERATION THEREFOR, WITHOUT THE PRIOR WRITTEN CONSENT OF THE COMMISSIONER OF CORP-ORATIONS OF THE STATE OF CALIFORNIA EXCEPT AS PERMITTED IN THE COM-MISSIONER'S RULES.

There will also be several rules printed on the back of your certificate in very small type, making reference to obscure sections of legal code understandable only by lawyers schooled in federal securities laws and your state's securities laws. The bottom line is that, short of dying, you probably cannot sell or otherwise transfer your stock to anyone except the company, or possibly other qualified and sophisticated investors or shareholders. However, your major concern will be with the more common meaning of the word "restricted," as described in the following section.

Transfers Restricted by Agreement

In general, you and other employees will enter into an agreement or agreements (several pages long) that set forth various restrictions, rights, and other terms and conditions that apply to your stock. The agreements may be entitled Restricted Stock Purchase Agreement, Shareholders Agreement, or the like.

Typically, the company has the right to buy your stock (usually called a *right of first refusal* or *right of refusal*) should you wish to sell or transfer any stock to a third party. The agreement will spell out the procedures and details as to how this works, and it should exempt some transfers (e.g., a transfer of stock to your family trust). Also, the company will typically have the right to buy your unvested shares should you leave the company, and the agreement will set forth the details. Various other restrictions may be included, and the agreement will also state that the stock cannot be sold or transferred except as permitted under federal and state securities laws. Many of the terms of the agreement are negotiable.

Future Tax Liability on Restricted Shares

If one receives restricted founders' shares or other restricted shares, no tax is due immediately, because the shares are subject to repurchase by the company. However, you may have to pay income taxes when any of your restricted shares become tradable or are not subject to a substantial risk of forfeiture. Therefore, in the few years after you receive your shares, you may be in for quite a surprise as you become vested. At the time of each vesting, the difference between what you paid for your shares and their new current fair market value is taxed to you as ordinary income, even if you do not sell a single share. In fact, it may not be practical or legal for you to sell shares at that time even if you wanted to, but you will still owe taxes. Unfortunately, that holds even if the stock later becomes worthless. However, there is a solution for these problems—see the following section on Section 83(b) elections.

Section 83(b) Election

Fortunately, you can partially or completely avoid the preceding tax liability problem (and almost everyone who is aware of this alternative does so) by ignoring the transferability limitations and risk of forfeiture, and electing, under Section 83(b) of the Internal Revenue Code, to immediately pay tax on the difference between the fair market value at the time of grant and the amount you paid for your restricted stock. This tax will be zero if the price paid for the stock is equal to its fair market value, which is typically the case for companies that have recently been formed. If less than fair market value was paid, then the difference is subject to taxation (with the resulting tax likely to be small, assuming the start-up's valuation is still low). When you use this election procedure, any future appreciation will be taxed not when the restrictions lapse (i.e., as you become vested), but when you dispose of the stock. Note that there is a distinction between selling stock and disposing of it. Disposition is broader and includes gifting it to someone else. Tax laws change frequently, though. By the time you decide to sell your shares, the tax laws will probably have changed—which is why it is important to work with your attorney and a tax advisor in this matter.

In summary, by taking the Section 83(b) election, you might pay a small tax up front (or no tax, which is more likely), but in return you will postpone payment of significant future taxes if the fair market value of the stock rises. The one drawback to a Section 83(b) election is that if you lose the stock by selling it back to the company under a forfeiture (repurchase) provision, you may not be able to offset any income recognized when you made the Section 83(b) election. However, the rules in this area are subject to change. Assuming you paid fair market value for the stock, this drawback does not apply.

While perhaps not as common, the 83(b) election can just as easily be taken as a preventive tax measure to reduce the risk of paying taxes earlier than necessary for nonqualified stock options (NQSOs), which are discussed in Ch. 15. In this case, upon exercise of the option, if the stock purchased is still subject to a substantial risk of forfeiture (this is not usual), you can similarly make an 83(b) election within 30 days of exercise to recognize the compensation at the date of exercise rather than at the time the risk lapses. If the fair market value of the stock is expected to rise during the risk period and you expect to hold the stock after the risk lapses, making the election may be advisable since it could minimize the amount of taxable compensation received. This is particularly true if the risk will expire during the same taxable year in which the option is exercised.

To reduce the perceived mystery of taking the 83(b) election, study the typical form letter for the state of California, of the type that your company's attorney should complete and submit for you, reproduced here as Fig. 14.3. You should use the services of your company's attorney to ensure proper execution and handling of this critical document, since a clerical mistake can cause significant tax problems for you and other employee shareholders. Also, it is fairly common that the receiving tax office doesn't properly record what was submitted, and an experienced attorney has good procedures in place to handle this. Within 30 days of receipt of your shares, this letter must be properly delivered to the IRS and the appropriate state tax office. Also, your attorney will advise you that you need to attach a copy of this letter to your federal and state tax returns (thus explaining the gain you chose to recognize at the time you purchased your founders' stock or exercised your NQSOs). In addition, you typically need to coordinate the preparation of the 83(b) form letter with your company, because income recognized to the employee becomes an expense recognized to the company, and the fair market value should be agreed upon in order to make the amounts agree.

Transferable Shares and Vesting

Transferable shares are those without transfer restrictions as discussed previously. You own them free and clear, and they could be sold the next day if a suitable buyer could be found, provided you comply with applicable state and federal securities laws. Of course, when you incorporate your business, you could grant to yourself all the transferable shares you want, up to the limit of the number of shares you authorized the business to issue. However, when investors, cofounders, or knowledgeable key employees join the game, they will want you to change the rules. They will want your shares to be subject to vesting, probably over a four-year period. Although a five-year vesting period at one time was common on the East Coast, four-year vesting (frequently with a one-year cliff) is now the most common arrangement throughout the country.

There is not much reason for a start-up company to give any employee a stock grant free of vesting restrictions. If you did, the employee would be free to move on to another job, and perhaps sell the shares later for a handsome profit. The main purpose of vesting is to create a strong incentive for the employee to stay with your company and work hard.

The preferred shares you sell to your investors will, of course, be transferable, since your investors are giving you full consideration for them. There is typically no vesting requirement placed on these shares. Of course, by agreement the preferred shareholders are likely to be subject to certain restrictions, including first refusal rights, and these shareholders, like everyone else, cannot transfer the shares except in compliance with state and federal securities laws. Sometimes intellectual property rights such as

<u>Election Under Section 83(b)</u>
<u>of the Internal Revenue Code of 1954</u>
<u>and Section 17122.7 of the California Revenue and Taxation Code</u>

The undersigned taxpayer hereby elects, pursuant to the above-referenced Federal and California Tax Codes, to include in his gross income for the current taxable year, the amount of any compensation taxable to him in connection with his receipt of the property described below:

1. The name, address, taxpayer identification number and the taxable year of the undersigned are as follows:
   NAME: TAXPAYER:_____   SPOUSE: _____
   ADDRESS: _____
   I.D. No.: TAXPAYER:_____   SPOUSE:_____
   TAXABLE YEAR:_____
2. The property with respect to which the election is made is described as follows:
   _____ shares of _____
3. The date on which the property was transferred is:_____
4. The property is subject to the following restrictions:

   The shares are subject to restrictions set forth in an agreement between the Corporation and the registered holder, a copy of which is on file at the principal office of the Corporation.
5. The fair market value at the time of transfer, determined without regard to any restriction other than a restriction which by its terms will never lapse, of such property is:
   $ _____
6. The amount (if any) paid for such property is: $_____

The undersigned has submitted a copy of this statement to the person for whom the services were performed in connection with the undersigned's receipt of the above-mentioned property. The transferee of such property is the person performing the services in connection with the transfer of said property.

<u>The undersigned understands that the foregoing election may not be revoked except with the consent of the commissioner.</u>

Dated:_____   Taxpayer: _____

The undersigned spouse of Taxpayer joins in this election.
Date: _____   Spouse: _____

Figure 14.3   83(b) Election Form Letter

patents or trademarks will be exchanged for shares, and these shares, likewise, would have no reason to be ownership restricted. Similarly, you may try to conserve funds by paying some of your service providers shares instead of cash and, likewise, it probably would not make sense to attach a vesting requirement to these shares.

In the event that you receive transferable shares that are free of any risk of forfeiture, any difference between the fair market value and the purchase price of such shares would be taxed as ordinary income (e.g., as compensation for service), as would seem fair.

Make sure you execute your stock grants properly with the assistance of your attorney. Otherwise, an irregularity may, in the future, force you to sell your founders' stock back to the company at your original cost of almost nothing. This happened in 1980 to some of the founders of Genentech, Inc., a very successful biotechnology company that raised $35 million in its initial public offering.

Sidebar 14.2, Playing on Employee Desire for Stock Ownership, illustrates the importance of understanding the nature of vesting and other conditions involved in acquiring value from stock and stock options.

When and How Often to Grant Stock

To your cofounders and key employees you will want to provide as much motivation and express as much confidence and expectation as you can up front. On day one, grant to yourself and your key employees and founders as much stock as you think will be fair, assuming they will perform as projected in your business plan. This is all the better reason to assemble the team first and then write the plan, as opposed to writing a plan and then looking for a team. That way (as discussed in Ch. 10) everyone will have bought into the performance objectives in advance. Then, if employees exceed expectations or the plan, consider granting more shares in the future, but in the form of options (as explained in Ch. 15).

One case where the model of front-loading stock grants fails is when you have a strong technical person in whom you are entrusting unproven management responsibility—someone who may not work out as a manager, but could remain as a strong technical contributor. In such a case, grant 75% of the stock you had in mind on day one, and plan to enhance that with options equal to the remaining 25% if he or she proves worthy of your trust. Resist the temptation to restrict vesting of founders' stock contingent on an individual's occupying a certain position at a future point in time. Things will change too rapidly to see that far ahead, and vesting based on anything other than time of employment will likely serve to misdirect energy and focus. On the other hand, people in key profit and loss positions can be promised stock or stock option bonuses if they meet or exceed profit and revenue goals. This may be a better form of vesting. It is important to review stock positions at least annually to preserve fairness and maintain motivation. You started your business because you had a passion and motivation, and you need those same feelings instilled in every one of your employees.

On rare occasions you may be tempted to consider accelerating the vesting period on options for some of your key employees as an additional reward. This is generally discouraged, since you want to keep the pressure on and minimize potential dilution. If you try to be fair, you will generally make the right decision. Never burn a bridge; you will likely be working in some relationship with your associates and investors again in the future.

The Alantec Litigation

The relationship between the founders and the venture investors can become quite divisive and acrimonious when the business is not doing well. Althought relatively rare, litigation may result. For a discussion of a prominent case brought by company founders against several Silicon Valley venture capital firms, see Sidebar 14.3, The Alantec "Washout" Litigation.

Sidebar 14.1 Five Tips from Dr. Beyster

Dr. J. Robert Beyster, the founder of both the Foundation for Enterprise Development and SAIC (Science Applications International Corporation), offers several tips for start-up entrepreneurs.

1. To succeed in fiercely competitive times, your employees must care about the success of your business as much as you do, to feel and act entrepreneurially. There is no better way to do this than to give them a stake in the equity.

2. Focus on developing the strongest, most successful company that you can. If you can do this, your personal wealth will follow.

3. Teach your employee shareholders to understand the business side of your operations, not just the production side. It's not enough that they *hope* their stock value grows; they need to know what *they can do* to drive that value.

4. It is fitting and fair to base the size of each employee's equity stake on their personal contribution to the growth and development of the company.

5. A sense of ownership—and the commitment, drive, and motivation that flows from it—comes not from owning shares alone, but from a sense that one has an ownership status that is to be respected. Build a company culture that treats employee shareholders as partners in enterprise, encouraging them to take initiative and assume authorship of what they do.

Sidebar 14.2 Playing on Employee Desire for Stock Ownership

In one start-up that I was involved in, two of us were having dinner, discussing the fortunes each of us was to make if the company's predicted sales were achieved that year. Our stock would soar in value for sure!

While I understood clearly my well-documented stock option position in the company, my friend, who was from Australia, did not really understand how U.S. securities laws, tax laws, and other such esoterica operated. He was confident, however, that he owned a good piece of the pie, and that he would share in the goodies. After all, the president had told him that he was a partner in the company. Well, the enterprise was not legally a partnership, but rather it was a corporation, and so that term lacked substantive meaning. However, it sounded good to my friend.

Upon further discussion, it became obvious to me that this gentleman had been granted not founders' stock but stock options (he did not own stock in the company as he had assumed), and he certainly had no idea when he would be eligible to buy the stock, for how long he would be eligible, and at what price he could purchase it.

—Mike Baird

Sidebar 14.3 The Alantec "Washout" Litigation

The Alantec lawsuit settled for $15 million while the jury was still deliberating its verdict, and there's a rumor that the jury would have awarded about triple that amount if the case had not been taken out of its hands. This "washout" case sent ripples through the venture capital community and caused investors, board members, and legal counsel to consider more carefully how "down rounds" and "washout" financings are handled.

In the Alantec case, the two founders brought legal action against several Silicon Valley venture capital firms that had funded the company through several financing rounds. The plaintiffs alleged various causes of action, including fraud and breach of fiduciary duty, and they asked for both compensatory and punitive damages. At the core of their case was the argument that the venture capitalists who served on Alantec's board of directors had issued stock to themselves and others (including new management) at a price well below fair market value. On the other hand, the defendants argued that the company had missed several key milestones and was close to bankruptcy, that no new source of financing could be found, and that their efforts to rescue the company were fair and reasonable.

What happened? In 1990, after two rounds of preferred stock financing, the founders owned 8% of Alantec (taking into account both the common and the preferred stock that had been issued), and the venture capitalists owned the rest. It's noteworthy that the founders owned 90% of the common at this point (more on this later). Several months later, after the founders had left the company, additional financing rounds reduced the founders' ownership interest from that 8% to less than one-hundredth of one percent. Several years later, in 1996, Alantec (a Silicon Valley manufacturer of computer networking equipment) was sold to Fore Systems, Inc., for approximately $800 million. The plaintiffs subsequently filed their lawsuit, and the case was settled in 1997 after 18 days of trial.

From a defense point of view, the case had what litigation attorneys refer to as "bad facts." The financing in question required the approval of each class of shareholders, and especially troublesome was the way the company obtained the approval of the common shareholders. After the board meeting in which the directors approved new financing at $0.05 per share, the company and its attorneys wrestled with the issue of shareholder approval. The problem was that the old management held 90% of the common stock. The solution devised was to issue lots of immediately exercisable stock options to new management, allowing them to exercise the options and outvote old management. The minutes of the earlier board meeting were then revised to include board approval of this creative solution. During the trial this board meeting became known as the "phony board meeting."

There were other "bad facts." The common shareholders were given no advance notice of the financing, and they had no real opportunity to participate in the new financing. Promissory notes that the new management signed when they bought their common stock were later forgiven.

Also, the defendants decided to rely upon an "advice of counsel" defense, which caused the waiver of the attorney-client privilege. As a result, the company's attorneys could be called as witnesses at the trial, and their notes and records became available to the plaintiffs. The plaintiffs apparently were helped greatly by testimony showing animosity toward the founders, as well as the use of colorful language in written notes, such as comments about the need to "wash out" the founders who held too much stock. Also, it's been said that board documents included a comment that the founders' percentage would be so small (0.007%) that it would require scientific notation.

Litigation of this type is fairly unusual, partly because the community of professional venture investors is quite "clubby," and problems are typically resolved behind closed doors without publicity. By way of comparison, litigation involving intellectual property and employee terminations is much more common for startups.

Since you may hear about Alantec or this type of situation, it won't hurt you to have some familiarity with it. It gives you a point of reference in thinking about what could happen if your company performs poorly.

Because the Alantec case was settled by the parties, it is not a legal precedent. It's also worth noting that cases like this tend to be very fact specific, meaning that each one is different. However, the case did cause the venture capital community to pay more attention to an important aspect of its business. Here are a few observations.

- The Alantec investors may have been too aggressive in setting a low valuation. Would it not have been wiser to leave something on the table for the founders?

- Attorneys for start-up companies and venture capitalists have become more careful about how they handle possible conflicts of interest among the various players, including the various classes of stockholders and the directors.

- Antidilution clauses usually are part of the mix. Typically, preferred shareholders benefit from antidilution provisions and common shareholders don't.

- An independent new investor in a round (versus an insider-only round) gives some assurance that the pricing is fair, and it may make sense for the new investor to be the lead investor. In Alantec, only insiders were involved in the new financing.

- The board of directors should help ensure that the funding process is fair, and everything should be properly documented. The board should plan ahead and act long before the time the company is expected to run out of money; it should not wait until the last minute when financing alternatives are more limited and less attractive. Were all reasonable financing alternatives considered? Did the founders have an opportunity to participate in the round? (Whether this is practical and whether the founders have the financial resources to participate is another question.) Should a special committee of the board get involved and consider alternatives? Did the board take reasonable steps to determine that the pricing was fair?

People have different perspectives on things like this. From the investors' perspective, the company is being "rescued" … and from the perspective of some founders, they are being "re-screwed."

Don't be paranoid. Venture capitalists do not invest in companies with a view to later doing a down round or imposing a washout. They, like you, want your company's value to rise dramatically and continuously. However, many (most, really) start-ups fall short of their business plan goals, and the investors frequently are faced with an unpleasant situation and difficult decisions.

15

Stock Options

May fortune favor the foolish.

—Kirk (Star Trek IV)

Stock Option Grants vs. Stock Grants

What is the difference between stock and stock options? Stock is printed on fancy paper that feels and looks like money, while stock options are typed on cheap 20-pound office stationery. Beyond that, here are some substantive differences.

- A *stock option* is an agreement to allow, but not obligate, someone to purchase shares in the future at a specified price. A stock option can be exercised only after it has vested and before it expires. Another drawback to an option is that it has to be exercised within a stated number of days (typically 90) after your employment terminates. Also, if you're an *insider*, even if you've exercised a stock option, you may face additional restrictions as to when you can sell the stock, and the same applies to stock you own.

- Employees who join a start-up later in the game will typically receive stock options with an exercise price that is substantially above the price of the founders' stock, assuming that the fair market value of the stock has risen in the meantime. (When stock options are granted, they typically are priced at the then fair market value of the stock.) This is to be expected, and it relates to the respective risks taken by the founders and the employees who join later. However, the point here is that these more expensive options are less likely to ever pay off since they have a higher probability of being *underwater stock options* (i.e., the stock price is below the exercise price) when the optionee is able to exercise them.

- *Stock*, on the other hand, while it almost certainly will entail some tax liability if granted at a discounted price (based on the spread between its fair market value and the discounted price), and even though it may also be subject to vesting and other restrictions, has long-term potential value that is easier to realize. Once you've earned it, you keep it even if you leave the company (subject, perhaps, to the company's right to repurchase it), and it may later appreciate in value. Of course, it's also possible that your ownership interest will be substantially diluted at some point in the future or that the stock will decline in value.

- One strong point for stock options is that you can never lose money on them if you *flip* them (i.e., you exercise the option and sell the stock at the same time), or if you otherwise handle them wisely. Viewed this way, options have the potential for an infinite rate of return on the cash invested (zero). With stock, on the other hand, you can lose 100% of your investment, however small, if the company goes out of business or otherwise does not perform well.

- If you never exercise a stock option, you don't have any annoying tax and accounting details to take care of—the option just expires.

- Stock options carry no voting rights, but shares of stock do.

- Many stock options are never exercised (and thus are lost forever) because they are under water at the end of their exercise period.

Stock options are the most widely used and most popular mechanism by which employers make it possible for employees to participate in the future increased valuation of the company. The number of shares you will grant to an individual in your stock option plan will reflect that person's perceived importance and potential contribution to your enterprise. Vesting schedules will be established so that as time passes (four years typically), and perhaps also when performance targets (profitability, personal objectives, etc.) are met, the employee becomes eligible to exercise his or her options.

Table 14.1 provides a convenient overview of the basics of stock and stock option grants.

When to Grant Stock Options

Chapter 14 dealt with the issue of stock ownership: primarily when and how to grant founders' stock to yourself, your start-up founders, and your first key employees. It was established that a stock grant is an appropriate vehicle to motivate and reward an individual contributor before substantial capitalization of the business. Chapter 14 also showed that after the business is substantially capitalized, cheap stock is more difficult to grant without encountering adverse tax consequences. Thus, it was suggested that stock options are a more appropriate vehicle for motivating individual contributors after funding. In this chapter you will learn about the kinds of stock options available, and how and when to grant them. As with stock grants, important concepts such as vesting and tax consequences are also covered.

How Often to Grant Stock Options

Usually, the options you will grant to an employee upon employment are the only options you will grant to that individual unless his or her responsibilities increase or his or her performance has greatly exceeded your expectations. Some people think of stock options as a kind of yearly bonus. They are not too far off, since at many larger, more established companies, key employees and executives are often granted options on small amounts of stock annually as a reward for a job done well and as an incentive to stay with the company for a few more years. You can do this also, but at most start-ups, larger amounts of stock options are usually granted upon employment, and then little or none are granted after that.

One common exception is to grant additional options about the time the employee has become fully vested in the options originally granted (for example, after four years of employment if the employee's original option grant vested over four years). The idea is that valuable employees should at all times have some unvested options to give them an incentive to stay longer with the company.

In start-up companies where options are granted yearly, proportionally fewer options should be granted annually, and the primary effect is to extend an employee's vesting period. This approach is not as effective, though, since the potential to make a financial killing is not as obvious to the employee in the earliest days when the need to motivate your people is at its highest. Also, options granted later are likely to have a higher exercise price, which means that the potential gain for the employee is less. Other start-up entrepreneurs like the incremental grant approach because it allows rewards to more closely track changes in the perception of an employee's importance and contribution to the company over time. In any case, enlightened management regularly reviews the amounts of stock options issued to employees and makes adjustments based on perceived inequities.

On How Many Shares Do You Grant Options?

This is a very negotiable issue. The more an employee knows about options and business valuations, the more you will likely have to grant to satisfy that individual.

It is important that you start off with a pool of shares for all founders, employees, and future hires. Then, work out a one- or two-year plan showing the average number of shares to be granted per employee, declining over time as the price per share goes up. Be a little stingy, since you have a fixed pool to work with. Although it's possible later to increase the size of the option pool, any increase is likely to be quite limited and targeted for future hires, especially if you have sophisticated venture investors whose approval is required. Think about the relative number of shares per key employee. It may not be fair, but tradition has it that percentage share ownership decreases rapidly from each level from the top to the bottom of the company.

A rule of thumb for a start-up is that the percentage share ownership decreases by about a factor of two or three for each level from the top of the organizational chart to the bottom. So the CEO would typically receive about two or three times the number of shares of each person on the level right below him (typically vice presidents), who in turn each receive about two or three times the number of shares of those on the next level below, and so forth down the chart. This is a very rough estimate for early-stage start-ups. Actual share distribution varies widely in actual practice, depending on several factors including the type of company and team; the stage of the company's development; the particular experience and skill set of each team member; the rest of the compensation package for each member; and the expected level of individual contribution and effort. For example, if you recruited Steve Jobs to be your CEO, you would have to give him a lot more stock than two or three times what your vice presidents got. Also, the share distribution often drops off more quickly at the lower levels in the company, and some companies do not even offer any ownership interest to employees at the bottom of the chart. Our strong bias is that a high-tech company should provide an equity incentive, however small, to all employees, as well to many of its outside consultants and partners.

For employees clearly in the same level in the organization (for example, all of your senior computer programmers), you might consider granting stock options proportional to salary to build some equitable treatment into your compensation structure.

It's not uncommon for a group of entrepreneurs, say two or five or even ten friends out of college, to want to divide the company's ownership equally among themselves. Although this egalitarian structure seems fair and sensible at first glance, it is not what venture capitalists expect to see, and you should be aware of this if you intend to raise venture financing from professionals. Since the responsibilities and expectations placed on the CEO's shoulders are much greater, the CEO should receive a much larger share, and it's likely that there should be distinctions made among the rest of the founders. The key is to take a tough, analytical look at your particular situation, with the goal of creating a structure that will work into the future—a structure that is not likely to require subsequent "fixing" when professional investors get involved.

Although stock options are the main topic of this chapter, you need to look at the total equity incentive (both founders' stock and stock options) for each person in determining the fair allocation of ownership interests. Your founders are likely to hold 100% of their equity incentive in the form of founders' stock, and your later employees are likely to hold only stock options. The preceding rule-of-thumb discussion is based on the total number of shares involved, whether in the form of stock options or shares of stock.

For a key employee, someone on whom you are betting the future of your company, one rule of thumb is that you should grant stock options whose fair market value is equal to one year's salary. In calculating the fair market value of one share of stock, it is important to use the latest preferred share price even though you will be granting options on common shares. This takes into consideration the fact that the preferred shares will convert to common shares someday if the business is successful. The employee thus hopes to multiply this value by 10, just as the investors hope to multiply by 10 (or much more) the value of their preferred stock investments if your company is one of their few home runs of the season. Thus, a $50,000 salary level employee can clearly see a $500,000 potential on the horizon, and your $100,000+ vice presidents can see their million dollars or more.

To summarize, look at employee positions, levels of responsibility, and individual abilities to contribute to the future increased valuation of your company when deciding the number of shares upon which options will be granted.

Once in a while a rare, knowledgeable employee will be able to do his or her own due diligence on your start-up (much like an investor would) and might be in the position to reasonably argue for a much larger grant based on a different view of the future. Is not a 5X return on investment more realistic for your business? In such situations you can grant the employee more stock if you think he or she can help you achieve your goals. The more knowledgeable employees are about valuation methods and option practices, the more practiced they may be in start-ups, and thus the more valuable they may be to you.

Some CEOs believe that staff members should receive stock equal to half their salaries. Applying this or a similar rule of thumb may build credibility for you if it results in your compensation structure being perceived as fair by most of your employees. If you have some sort of a defensible formula, you will avoid dissension in the ranks. An engineer who makes 10% more salary than another might not need to have exactly 10% more stock, but he or she had better not have less stock unless you have a pretty good reason! Consider the advice of your board of directors, which presumably is experienced in this area. It has been said that you can never win the remuneration game, so do the best you can and be sensitive to the needs and perceptions of others. You are not a Fortune 500 company, so you do not have to have detailed policy manuals and formulas in this area to guide your every move. Recognize who the key players and contributors are, understand what motivates them, and dispense the appropriate rewards as needed.

The bounding parameter in granting stock options is the rule of thumb that was previously mentioned, which is that after the last financing round, management and employees should own or have claim to between 25–30% of the business. There is an unfortunate trend these days, however, that reduces this target level. On the other hand, founders typically would prefer, if possible, to retain effective control (50+%) after all outside financing has occurred and all stock options are taken into account. This is not always possible.

If you keep in mind the preceding basic ideas, it will soon become obvious how many options to grant to your employees. It is recommended that you be as generous as you can with your associates, but be realistic. Start out low for most employees, and leave room to give more to performers who do exceptionally well. You alone are not going to make your business worth $100 million. Many entrepreneurs hold tightly onto control, never giving anyone else a piece of the action. While some succeed in this stinginess, most would come out further ahead if they were more generous.

Stock Options as Part of a Total Package

Although the focus of this chapter is stock options, you should consider them in the broader context of the total compensation package offered to each employee. (See Ch. 13 on remuneration practices and Ch. 14 regarding stock.) This is an important and perhaps obvious point. For example, your founders who already own cheap founders' stock will typically hold all or most of their equity incentive in that form, and they may be granted few or no stock options. The calculations in the previous section regarding stock option grants must take into account the total equity incentive for each employee. In general, the founders purchase founders' stock at a very low price, say $0.01 or $0.001 per share, and later employees receive stock options.

Your stock option plan and option grant practices will therefore take into account the total package of benefits for each employee, including stock, stock options, cash compensation, and other benefits such as medical and dental coverage. Sometimes, adjustments in stock options are needed. You may have a key employee who is willing to work for less cash in exchange for additional stock options. Other employees may have a monthly cash need that is somewhat outside the range you can afford. In making adjustments for such people, you need to balance each package in a way that is fair to each individual as well as the whole team. A person who wants to forego some cash compensation should receive more in stock options, and this will generally be viewed as fair. Also, the benefit of this to your cash flow can be important, especially in the early months of your start-up, and the risk-taking, entrepreneurial spirit of such individuals can be very valuable and infectious.

Two Kinds of Stock Options

There are two kinds of stock options you need to be familiar with: *incentive stock options* (ISOs) and *nonqualified stock options* (NQSOs). Until recently, the most common option type for employees was ISOs, but you need to understand clearly the advantages and disadvantages of each in order to avoid any serious mistakes. Also, there are situations where ISOs simply cannot be granted (e.g., to consultants, board members, and other nonemployees). This section will review each.

Incentive Stock Options (ISOs)

Under an ISO plan, one is granted the option (i.e., the right, but not the obligation) to purchase shares in the future at a given price, usually the fair market value of the

stock on the date of grant (established by the board of directors, if there is no market). Following are some salient features of ISOs.

- No ordinary income is reportable on option grant or option exercise (although
  alternative minimum tax may be due because of option exercise). ISOs are taxed
  only when the shares are sold or otherwise disposed of.

- If requirements are met, gain on the sale is a long-term capital gain. These ISO
  requirements include

  - The option price must equal or exceed the fair market value of the stock at
    the time the option is granted. Also, an employee who owns more than 10%
    of the outstanding voting stock is not eligible to receive an ISO unless the
    option price is at least 110% of the stock's fair market value at the time the
    option is granted, and the option is not exercisable later than five years from
    the grant date.

  - The option, by its terms, must not be exercisable later than 10 years follow-
    ing the date of grant.

  - The option must be exercised while the grantee is an employee, or within
    three months after termination (one year if the employee is disabled). There
    have been cases where individuals, in good favor with past employers, have
    arranged to be employed (albeit on a very part-time basis) in order to retain
    their incentive stock option rights, while moving on to other full-time
    employment. This is something you might want to consider as part of your
    severance agreement before you join. Again, the advice of legal counsel in
    formulating a valid plan is essential. (You can see from this that ISO exercise
    schedules cannot be negotiated for one of the most important periods — that
    following employment.) You could negotiate for a maximum exercise sched-
    ule of 10 years for those years in which you are employed.

  - The maximum value of shares that an employee may be granted options on,
    in any calendar year, is $100,000 in fair market value of the stock at the time
    the options are granted. However, if you are granted less than $100,000 in
    any year, a partial carryover may be utilized in subsequent years.

  - The stock must not be disposed of within two years after the option is grant-
    ed, or within one year after it is exercised. If the shares are sold prior to the
    end of these time periods, a *disqualifying disposition* occurs so that the options
    are then treated as *nonqualified options*. The amount by which the fair market
    value on the date of exercise exceeds the price paid is then deemed to be
    (ordinary) income. This may or may not be important, depending on the
    current state of the capital gains tax.

ISOs became the staple of key employee compensation when the Tax Reform Act
of 1981 made this device attractive to employees by reducing the tax rate on capital
gains. ISOs are especially popular because they permit employees to purchase cheap
common stock in the future without triggering a taxable event.

In practice, many option holders (regardless of the type of stock option they hold) simply exercise their option and then immediately sell the stock received. (Of course, the gain is then simply the difference between the option price paid and the sale price.) This practice, commonly known as *flipping*, eliminates one of the potential benefits of ISOs, namely long-term capital gains treatment. However, flipping also effectively eliminates exposure to the stock price dropping after option exercise, and it also eliminates the need for the optionee to come up with cash to buy and hold the stock. Flipping requires that there be a ready market for the sale of the stock (e.g., the company is a public company whose stock is publicly traded). Regarding the risk of the stock price dropping after exercise of an ISO, see the section entitled Alternative Minimum Tax—the ISO Trap.

Nonqualified Stock Options (NQSOs)

Stock options are called *nonqualified* if ISO provisions are not specified in the stock option plan (i.e., NQSOs don't *qualify* as ISOs under U.S. tax law, which is where the term *nonqualified* comes from). The value of nonqualified options is considered taxable income on the date exercised (as measured by the spread between the option price paid and the fair market value of the stock on the date of exercise). In addition, the granting of NQSOs itself can trigger a taxable event if the fair market value of the underlying stock exceeds the stated exercise price (which is not the usual case) and there is no risk of forfeiture (which, again, is not the usual case). Furthermore, if the NQSO has an ascertainable fair market value, the value of the option less any amount paid by the employee is taxable as ordinary income in the first year that the employee's right to the option is freely transferable or is not subject to a substantial risk of forfeiture. In contrast, recall that ISOs generate taxable income only when the shares are disposed of. This subject gets so complex that even experienced tax lawyers trip up here and need to go back to original source materials to answer individual questions. Do not try to figure it all out by yourself. Consider this chapter to be only an introduction.

Review the Section 83(b) Election topic in Ch. 14 to see if you need to take preventive tax liability action for your options as well as your founders' stock.

Option Vesting and Exercise Schedules

The typical stock option plan (which is usually part of a broader "equity incentive plan") provides for flexibility that meets legal requirements but is broader than the typical standard terms offered by the company (which you might view as "company standard"). This means your company may have the power to approve exceptions in a particular case that go beyond the company standard. For example, a key new hire who is badly needed may have the negotiating power to receive both faster vesting and a longer period for exercising the option in the event of termination of employment. However, because tax law is complex, legal counsel for the company should review and approve any exception to the standard stock option plan before it is implemented.

In practice, almost all employees receive options that have the same vesting and exercise terms. Most of your new key employees will be told what the company offers and will simply accept those terms. Indeed, most employees do not even know that they have to vest in their options or that they will have limited time periods to exercise options. In general, if a company makes an exception, it does not make it public.

The mere fact that you have some flexibility does not mean you should use it liberally or at all. Bear in mind that venture investors will prefer that all of your key employees be locked in by the more stringent standard terms, which provide a stronger incentive for these key personnel to stay with the company and work hard.

In vesting options, like in vesting stock, the same rules of thumb apply. The most common vesting, once called *West Coast* vesting, is four-year vesting with a one-year cliff (i.e., 25% vests after one year, and then the rest vests monthly on a straight-line basis for three more years, which means that an additional 2.0833% vests each month for the 36 months). Five-year vesting was once common on the East Coast (i.e., 20% vested after one year, and 20% vested each year after that for four more years.)

During the dot-com era it become quite common for companies to allow employees to immediately exercise all their options, notwithstanding the limitation of normal vesting schedules. This is commonly called *pre-exercising* the option, and it's also sometimes referred to as *reverse vesting*. In any case, the idea is to start the clock running on the holding period for the stock so that the employee may benefit more quickly from capital gains treatment, versus ordinary income. In effect, this allows the option to be fully exercised even though it's "unvested." The employee is then issued restricted stock that is subject to the vesting (i.e., the company has the right to repurchase any unvested stock if the employee's employment is terminated before the end of the vesting schedule). Note that the Section 83(b) election has its role to play here. Of course, since there's always the risk the stock will drop rapidly in value, this device of pre-exercising the option probably makes more sense for early stock that is dirt cheap (i.e., the amount of cash paid for the stock is very small, and the employee can afford to lose it all). However, during the dot-com period, many individuals in fact lost major sums of money when they pre-exercised their options, paid lots of cash for the stock, and lost all or part of it when the stock dropped in value. Given this sad history, pre-exercising stock options became much less popular.

Exercising Options—an Interesting Twist

Here is an interesting note. Even if one had options on cheap stock, exercising those options could inject much-needed capital into a company—more than reflected by just the exercise price of the stock. One interesting case involved Fortis Corporation's CEO, who had an opportunity to exercise nonqualified stock options on 750,000 shares for one-hundredth of a cent per share. A $75 investment would bring him about a $7.5 million gain at a current market price of $10 a share. The company would benefit because exercised options become part of the company's compensation costs, reducing taxable profits and thus taxes. So, even though the company does not sell the exercised shares at market value, it still benefits, thanks to the tax code. This assumes of course that the company has significant taxable income to start with.

The Future of Stock Options

The perceived benefits of stock options can vary greatly over time, as well as from individual to individual, even if there are no changes in applicable law. During and at the top of an upswing in stock prices, stock options generally become more popular and desired. More employees want them when they see entrepreneurial friends and associates reap the benefits and perhaps buy a new car or even a new home, or more, with stock option proceeds. When the markets are down and stock option "windfalls" are more rare, stock options become less popular. Some of your best employees will have a longer term, perhaps more enlightened, view of these things, and will want even more options when their pricing is low and they are less popular.

Looking back, the effect of the Tax Reform Act of 1986 on stock options was clear for major corporations. Many of them eliminated incentive stock options or, in the case where both incentive and nonqualified options were offered, dropped the incentive options. However, other companies figured the preferential tax rate on capital gains would come and go, making incentive stock options attractive again. In addition, because the need for cash to pay tax on nonqualified options at the point of exercise often encouraged executives to sell their stock quickly, public companies that wanted to encourage executives to hold stock for long periods of time tended to stay with incentive stock options. Later changes in tax laws also helped make ISOs more popular. Some larger companies emphasized cash compensation rather than options.

The dot-com era caused a lot of publicity and discussion about actual and perceived problems with stock options (and stock), and further significant changes in U.S. tax law can be expected. The International Accounting Standards Board has already proposed (in 2002) rules requiring companies to count stock options as a company expense that is subtracted from income. Although these rules would not apply to U.S. companies, it appears likely that the rule-making body in the U.S.—the Financial Accounting Standards Board (FASB)—will adopt similar rules.

Because of the "AMT ISO trap" problems that exploded during the dot-com era (discussed in the section entitled Alternative Minimum Tax—the ISO Trap), most tax advisors began to discourage the strategy of exercising ISOs and holding the stock. Also, the granting of NQSOs (as well as founders shares) to more people became more common.

Stock options will continue to play a major role in young companies.

Administrative Details

Your outside law firm should handle all administrative matters regarding your company's stock and stock options. Don't try to do this yourself, and don't simply hand it off to your part-time bookkeeper or corporate secretary. A careless mistake can cause major headaches, and you don't want to do anything that looks amateurish to outside investors or may kill a deal. Law firms with a high-tech practice are able to handle all this easily and cost effectively, since they've done it many times before and have standard documents and good procedures already in place. You should understand what's going on, but your limited time is best spent elsewhere. Do set a high standard for your law firm on these employee matters, and if they are not efficient and timely, either make sure they correct the problem immediately, or find a new law firm. You want your employees to know that you take these employee benefits seriously.

A Comparison of Tax and Accounting Effects on ISOs and NQSOs

Tables 15.1 and 15.2 present a summary of the salient tax and accounting effects of ISO and NQSO grants on the company and on the employee.

Table 15.1   Tax Effect on Company

type of stock option	tax effect on company upon:		
	grant	exercise	sale of stock
NQSO (No reverse vesting; i.e., shares are fully vested at exercise.)	No tax effect (in general).	Employer may deduct amount of ordinary income recognized by optionee; that is, the difference between fair market value (FMV) at exercise and exercise price. The employer is required to withhold taxes on the amount of ordinary income recognized in order to take the deduction.	No tax effect.
ISO	No tax effect.	No tax effect.	Employer may deduct amount of ordinary income (if any) recognized by optionee. No withholding tax is required. If sale occurs within two years from grant or within one year from exercise, employer may deduct ordinary income equal to spread that existed at exercise. No deduction if sale occurs more than two years from grant and more than one year from exercise.

Table 15.2   Tax Effect on Employee

type of stock option	tax effect on employee upon:		
	grant	exercise	sale of stock
NQSO (No reverse vesting; i.e., shares are fully vested at exercise.)	No tax effect (in general).	Taxable on ordinary income equal to *spread* at exercise (i.e., the difference between FMV of stock at exercise and exercise price). This amount is subject to withholding.	Taxable on capital gain equal to difference between sale price and FMV of stock at exercise.
ISO ■ Optionee must be employee (as opposed to director or other independent contractor) continuously from grant to the date three months before exercise (12 months in case of disability). ■ Plan must be approved by shareholders. ■ Maximum option term is 10 years (5 years if optionee owns more than 10% of total combined voting power of all classes of stock). ■ Option price is at least 100% of FMV at grant (110% if optionee owns more than 10% of stock). ■ Of all options held by an optionee that vest in the same year, only the options covering the first $100,000 worth of stock qualify for ISO treatment. The value of the stock is measured for this purpose at grant.	No tax effect.	No tax effect, except for possible alternative minimum tax on spread. A tax advisor should be consulted for alternative minimum tax consequences.	If sale occurs within two years from grant or within one year from exercise, then taxable on ordinary income equal to spread that existed at exercise plus capital gain equal to difference between sale price and FMV at exercise. No withholding is required. In general, ordinary income will not exceed amount of gain realized (sale price minus basis). If sale occurs more than two years from grant and more than one year from exercise, then taxable on long-term capital gain equal to difference between sale price and exercise price.

Note on accounting effect: The accounting effect on the company is the same for NQSO as it is for ISO. Options with an exercise price equal to at least 100% of FMV of stock at the time of the grant generally produce no compensation cost at any time. However, options with performance-based vesting (as opposed to service-based vesting) may be subject to accounting treatment as stock appreciation rights (SARs), with the result that increases in stock FMV must be expensed in each reporting period while the option is outstanding. An accountant should be consulted on this issue. Options with exercise price below 100% of FMV on the date of the grant produce compensation cost equal to the discount, which can be amortized over the vesting period for each option.

Alternative Minimum Tax—the ISO Trap

Out of a sense of fairness, the Alternative Minimum Tax (AMT) was created in the U.S. in 1969 to ensure that wealthy taxpayers using various tax shelters would pay at least a "fair" or "minimum" tax. The AMT system shadows the regular income tax system and uses different deductions and tax rates. A U.S. taxpayer is required to calculate both AMT and regular income tax—and then pay the greater of the two taxes. In effect, the AMT, if it applies, constitutes additional taxes that taxpayers pay on top of their regular taxes. Twenty-eight deductions or write-offs (so-called "preference" items) such as property taxes, state and local taxes, and personal exemptions, are not allowed under the AMT calculations, and in their place a flat exemption is applied ($45,000 for a couple). Discussed here is only the AMT's possible impact on the exercise of incentive stock options (ISOs). Nonqualified stock options (NQSOs) are not subject to the AMT.

The AMT is discussed here because it has a major unintended negative consequence—the "incentive stock option (ISO) trap"—which has financially devastated many entrepreneurs, and because it illustrates well the importance of understanding the financial and legal terrain in which you, your company, and your employees and other stakeholders operate. This is not, of course, a complete treatise on this complex area of taxation.

The AMT is triggered whenever a taxpayer exercises an incentive stock option (ISO) in one year and holds the stock into the next year. The paper profits as of the day the option is exercised (i.e., the fair market value of the stock on the date of exercise, less the option price) is a tax preference item under AMT, even if the stock price drops dramatically later—and that's the trap! You may owe taxes far in excess of the subsequent depressed value of the stock. In effect, countless people had to pay taxes on "phantom" gains—gains they never had in their pockets.

If the stock is subsequently sold and there's a capital gain, the taxpayer will receive a credit with respect to that gain for the amount of AMT previously paid. But for many taxpayers, the damage has already been done, and they are financially ruined. Also, the reported losses may be used as offsets against other capital gains you report and, if there are losses left over, they can be carried forward to future years. However, it could take many years for the losses to be used this way, and many taxpayers will never be able to use them. Assuming that the AMT rate is 28% and the capital gain rate is 20%, in many cases the actual tax on the sale of ISO stock is 28%, and an 8% alternative minimum tax credit carry-forward is made available for the future. This can be used in other years when the regular tax exceeds the AMT.

The biggest damage occurred in 1999 and 2000 when thousands of high-tech workers wittingly or unwittingly encountered large AMT bills when they exercised incentive stock options and held the stock into the next tax year. By holding the stock for at least one year, they planned to take advantage of favorable long-term capital gains rates (20%) that may apply to ISOs, rather than having the gain taxed at ordinary income rates (then up to 39.5%). (For the sale of ISO stock to qualify for this favorable capital gain treatment, the taxpayer must wait at least two years from the date of option grant and at least one year from the date of exercise before selling the stock.) This is not just a problem of the rich. Many middle-income taxpayers encountered financial disaster when stock prices dropped precipitously, and they owed taxes far in excess of the ultimate value of their ISO stock. For an illustration of this trap, see Sidebar 15.1, The AMT ISO Trap—A Hypothetical Example.

As previously noted, most tax advisors, in view of these problems, began to discourage the strategy of exercising ISOs and holding the stock.

The number of taxpayers subject to AMT has grown at a surprisingly rapid rate, but it may literally explode under the tax plan put in place by the George W. Bush administration. AMT now does not just make sure that the mega-rich have to pay a fair share of income taxes. It now extends into middle-income America and below, and this trend will continue. Approximately 1.5 million taxpayers were expected to owe the tax in 2001, which was a large increase over prior years. Under the Bush tax plan, many tax experts predict that the number of AMT taxpayers will increase to 36 million by 2010, a number that is about double what the number would be without the Bush plan. Perhaps this should not be a surprise since the Bush plan was designed to funnel more than 50% of the tax savings to the top 1% of all taxpayers. Also, the flat exemption used in the AMT calculation was not indexed for inflation, which over time causes many more taxpayers to be subject to AMT.

The "Wash-Sale" Trap

As noted previously, the AMT on ISOs is not triggered if the stock received upon option exercise is actually sold in the same tax year in which the ISO is exercised. Realizing this, many taxpayers sold their stock by the end of the year in order to avoid a huge AMT bill on the ISO exercise, even though the stock price was depressed, and then quickly bought back the same number of shares (presumably because they remained bullish on the company's prospects).

However, this strategy ran afoul of complex, largely overlooked *wash sale* tax rules, and the taxpayers faced an AMT based on the original paper gain, but with some additional salt rubbed in—the paper gain was not taxed at lower AMT rates (e.g., 28%), but rather was taxed as ordinary income at rates that then ranged up to 39.5%. The general tax rule is that it's a "wash sale" if you sell stock at a loss and buy substantially identical securities within 30 days before or after the sale—it's as if the sale never occurred. Many financial advisors unwittingly advised their clients to buy back the stock this way, unaware of the overlooked IRS rule on wash sales, and some large firms (Ernst & Young, for example) have issued national alerts about the rule.

Helping Your Employees Understand Stock Options

Surveys show that most employees holding stock options have a poor understanding of how stock options really work. According to an OppenheimerFunds, Inc. survey, almost half (47%) of employees with stock options knew "little" or "nothing at all" about exercising them, and more than half (52%) knew "little" or "nothing at all" about the tax implications. Three-quarters were unfamiliar with the Alternative Minimum Tax, and a surprising number (11%) had already let an option expire when it was "in the money" (i.e., the stock price was above the exercise price). The point here is that you can serve your employees well by helping educate them about this important topic and encouraging them not only to read and understand the stock option documents your company provides, but also to take advantage of many excellent resources on the Internet.

Sidebar 15.1 The AMT ISO Trap—a Hypothetical Example

In 1996, Mary Entrepreneur, a mid-level employee in Watch-Us-Fly.com, received an incentive stock option (ISO) to buy 10,000 shares of Watch-Us-Fly stock at $1.00 per share. Watch-Us-Fly lived up to its name, and the company went public a few years later.

In 2000, when the stock hit $120 per share, Mary exercised her ISO and paid $10,000 for 10,000 shares of Watch-Us-Fly stock. On paper her stock was worth $1,200,000! She held the stock into the following year (which triggered the AMT calculation), intending to hold the stock long enough to take advantage of the lower long-term capital gains rates. Unexpectedly, she found herself owing $350K in AMT taxes for 2000. (Note: this is an approximation, since the AMT calculation is complex and depends upon the particular situation.)

However, in the meantime the stock price plummeted to $10 per share, and her 10,000 shares are now worth only $100,000—far less than the AMT taxes she's obligated to pay. She is financially ruined.

She notes sadly and ironically that of all the companies she has worked for, Watch-Us-Fly is the first and only one where the stock options were worth any-thing—and they ended up destroying everything for which she had worked a life-time.

16

Other Equity and Wealth-Building Vehicles

The future will not just happen if one wishes hard enough. It requires decision—now. It imposes risk—now. It requires action—now. It demands allocation of resources, and above all, human resources—now.

—Peter F. Drucker

To this point it has been established that you, as the founder of your own business, will have a significant stock ownership in your business through a founders' stock grant. In addition, it is possible that you and your board of directors may have granted you additional options on stock contingent upon meeting performance objectives.

This chapter will explore other vehicles for building wealth as your business grows and prospers. You will want to consider some of these vehicles for your key employees and fellow management team members as well. Some of the vehicles described here may be especially well suited for rewarding key players who are not founders.

A large majority of early-stage venture-funded companies rely mainly upon stock (see Ch. 14) and stock options (see Ch. 15) as their main workhorses in providing equity incentive to employees. In this sense, the vehicles discussed in this chapter are the exception rather than the rule, and they are covered here because the entrepreneur should have some general familiarity with them. Depending upon your particular situation, one or more of them may make sense now or, as is more likely, they may be appropriate only when your company is larger and more mature. Be creative in adapting these equity and wealth-building vehicles to your start-up where appropriate. For one creative example, see Sidebar 16.1, Founders Retain Control Through Foresight.

Unrelated Stock Purchase

You always have the option of buying into your business just like one of your investors. Some entrepreneurs decide against this option, preferring not to put all their eggs into one basket; that is your choice. But consider how infrequently an excellent investment opportunity comes along in which you really believe, in which you have deep, inside knowledge of the situation, and which can be highly leveraged. If this is a good deal for your investors, it could be a good deal for you too. In fairness, however, it should be noted that your investors have the safety of diversification, whereas you do not, assuming that you are not independently wealthy with lots of assets outside your start-up. If you do not feel that confident about your proposed business, why start it? Instead, go back to the drawing board until you have it figured out. Launching a successful company is difficult enough; do not compound your problems by starting something you do not believe in 100%.

Sophisticated investors want you to have a lot of skin in the game. There are many people who say they want to be entrepreneurs but who do not want to risk anything. These people are not really entrepreneurs, and experienced investors can spot them. Many investors want you to have more than your time on the line. Are you really committed 100% to your start-up? There is a balancing process here, and only you can decide what's right for you. On one hand, you shouldn't even be involved in the venture if you don't believe in it 100%. On the other hand, given your family situation and where you are in life, it may not make sense to risk all the financial assets of your family, since success is never guaranteed.

These decisions about risk are very important, and they are entirely yours. Step back occasionally and look at the big picture, with the goal of making personal financial decisions with which you are comfortable. If you are married, your spouse should also be involved in this process.

One useful exercise is to carefully think through the benefits of additional wealth, versus the pain of losing what is ventured. Don't let greed cause you to see only the upside. As an example, let's say you personally have $500,000 in assets, and that you have the opportunity, by risking all those assets, to make an additional $500,000. Such a gain would be wonderful, a real pleasure. However, if you lose the $500,000, the pain of this loss would undoubtedly be much more than the pleasure of gaining the same amount, especially if your family suffered. This phenomenon comes up in different ways. For example, if your company goes public, you may have the opportunity to take some money off the table. Let's say that your stock is worth $2 million but the price is expected to be volatile. Even though you are optimistic about your company's prospects, the pain of losing that $2 million, which is always possible, will be much greater than the pleasure of seeing it grow to $4 million or even more. There are countless entrepreneurs who regret not taking some of the gain when they had the chance, and setting it aside in a more secure investment. If that strategy is right for you, do it, and don't feel disloyal in any way to the company—after all, you earned the money.

If you like the idea of investing in your own company but are short on cash, consider setting up a stock purchase plan for yourself and your employees. It will help the cash flow of the business and allow everyone to increase their ownership without sacrificing precious savings.

Even before establishing a full-blown stock purchase plan for all employees, you can set up a special deal for yourself to acquire more stock in your new company. You will have to negotiate with your board of directors, since the board establishes remuneration policy for the officers of your company, which includes yourself. As part of your compensation package, obtain the right to buy preferred shares of stock in your company at fair market value (just like any investor). This stock can be issued monthly or quarterly, and the cost can be effectively deducted from your paycheck. You may need to be paid a higher salary, or eat into your savings a bit, to keep making your mortgage payment. But where else can you invest relatively small amounts of money in a start-up company that you obviously have a lot of confidence in, especially if you are not a sophisticated investor, as is required in most states? As a founding employee, you should be legally entitled to purchase stock in your company if the company is willing to sell it. Keep in mind that venture capital investors legitimately like to keep the number of preferred stockholders to a minimum to avoid complications in subsequent rounds of financing.

How much stock should you purchase? Assume that you want to accumulate additional stock that will one day make you worth an extra $500,000. Since you are betting that the stock price will increase by a factor of 10 over the next five years (as are your investors), you need to acquire about $50,000 worth of stock in the next two or three years. Thus, you might purchase $2000 worth of stock each month for the next two years. You may be able to pay yourself the $2000 extra in salary to make this relatively painless, but how could the company possibly afford that? Because the cash flows directly back into the company as you pay for your stock, all this does is cause the company to suffer some dilution.

Even if your board of directors does not agree to raise your salary, you could also try to live on $2000 less. Purchasing stock in your company is worthwhile. You will have the stock cleanly in your pocket (without any risk of losing it) because, like an investor's preferred stock, there is no vesting. Be aware that most investors will want to pay you what they consider to be a fair salary and have you reinvest part of that. Therefore, it is up to you to negotiate what is fair these days. See Ch. 13 for more information on remuneration practices for start-ups.

If you have a board of directors that looks unfavorably on increasing your salary, there are other options. If you do not have any additional savings that you can invest, get creative. How about taking out a loan from your own company? Consider anything to buy an additional block of stock now to hold free and clear. The private placement memorandums and footnotes to financial documents of the small start-up companies in this country are littered with sweetheart deals. If you do not act, do not ask, and do not try, all you will have is your vested founders' stock—and you may deserve more.

Tax-Free Exchange of Intellectual Property for Stock

The technique addressed in this section is fairly commonly practiced. One way to avoid paying any tax at the time you obtain shares, whether they are restricted or transferable, is to exchange intellectual or other property (technology, business plans, patents, etc.) for stock in a tax-free exchange. This method often works only during a new, fresh, tax-free incorporation. The most typical situation is that the technical founders (and others) who have been developing the product and technology transfer all of their rights in the relevant intellectual property to the new company in exchange for stock.

For example, the intellectual property assets of a sole proprietorship may be exchanged tax-free for stock in a new company, at fair market value; then the new stock can be held for later sale. Your basis for the value of your assets must be realistic, and you may realize a taxable gain here! This is a complex issue requiring the assistance of a tax attorney. Many founders and key employees of a start-up will have some property of true value, which can be transferred to the company in exchange for stock of equal value. If you are not launching your start-up today, consider obtaining some legitimate and valuable patents now, on your own, to exchange for stock in the future. It is again emphasized that you should work with a lawyer and a tax advisor to make sure that what you propose is legal and will accomplish the desired tax consequences.

Investment Through the Provision of Real Property

In theory, you should think of yourself as an investor in your start-up, even if you are not providing significant financial backing. Through the provision of real property (or intellectual property as described in the preceding section), you can obtain the ownership you need on advantageous terms.

If you find yourself in the position of having to provide your own seed capital, consider providing property instead of cash. If you decide to invest property to obtain a piece of your company, follow the professional investor's example. If you have property or could buy some that the start-up needs, do not trade it outright for stock (never for common, perhaps for preferred). Instead, lease the property to the start-up in exchange for a consideration that will include an ability to acquire a future interest (stock) in the company. This is preferable to lending the company the money and then worrying about security on the loan, or purchasing stock and worrying about it becoming worthless. If the company needs to use your money or other property for developing a new process, have rights to the process assigned to you, and give back conditional rights to use the process for future stock in the company. The difference between the preceding arrangement and simply investing in the company will become apparent if the company runs into financial trouble. Having unencumbered title to tangible assets will provide you protection. Through careful analysis of how you are going to invest in your start-up, you may find yourself very comfortably positioned; indeed, you will be a true owner of this business.

To execute such an elaborate plan, you must think and act like a venture capitalist, perhaps with the assistance of an experienced venture capital lawyer. Expect to meet some resistance from the sophisticated investors on your board of directors, who do not receive these demands from every entrepreneur they run across. Enjoy the process, and learn from it. Otherwise, you may find yourself feeling less like a founder and more like an employee by the end of the year.

Warrants

Warrants are certificates, usually issued by the company, that give the holder the right (but not the obligation) to buy a specific number of shares of a company's stock at a stipulated price (called the "exercise" or "strike" price) within a certain time limit or, occasionally, in perpetuity. A warrant, in effect, is an option and is often used in conjunction with another debt instrument or security. Warrants are used by many start-ups, as well as large companies.

Warrants are frequently issued in conjunction with rounds of financing, as leverage and protection mechanisms for the investor and, if exercised, as future sources of capital for the company. They are frequently used in bridge financing as an additional incentive and reward for the lender, to perhaps reflect the added risk the lender is taking in this kind of financing. For example, you may hear about a start-up receiving $500,000 in 8% bridge financing with 20% warrant coverage. This means that $500,000 is being loaned to the company at an 8% rate of interest (with the intention that it be converted into stock in the next financing round) and that the lender/investor is also receiving a warrant to buy $100,000 (i.e., 20% of $500,000) of stock at the price to be set in the new round.

Warrants are not usually used as a form of employee incentive or compensation. (If warrants were issued to employees, they would be similar in effect to nonqualified stock options.) Warrants are also more easily sold or transferred between individuals, since there are usually no vesting conditions or repurchase agreements associated with them. The financial reporting documents of many high-tech companies are littered with footnotes describing special investment situations where warrants were attached. If you have the opportunity, be creative in this area.

Some of your service providers, such as law firms, may take warrants in lieu of part or all of their fees. Also, many small companies give key customers and strategic partners warrants to purchase stock of the company as a way to help cement relationships and encourage the recipients to be helpful. Sometimes the warrants are given as "kickers"; i.e., they are over and above what you would otherwise pay or give the recipient. Also, you need to consider the possible tax impact of their use. For example, if warrants are given to customers who purchase your product, depending on the particular facts, you may have to treat the warrant cost as an expense and add it to the cost of goods sold.

SARs and Phantom Stock Plans

There's a significant legal issue that may come into play if you set up a SAR, phantom stock plan, or other similar plan. No matter what you call the plan, it may be subject to ERISA (Employee Retirement Income Security Act of 1974) if it covers too many employees, defers some payments until termination of employment, or otherwise looks too much like a retirement plan from an ERISA perspective. If you suddenly find that the plan is subject to ERISA, then you have numerous legal issues and regulatory problems to untangle. With respect to SARs and phantom stock plans, most companies try to avoid ERISA by limiting the period for cash payout (perhaps to a year) and by limiting the plan to just a few key executives.

- *Stock Appreciation Rights (SARs)*—With SARs, a company grants an employee the right to receive a cash bonus equal to the appreciation in the value of a specified number of shares of the company's stock over a specified period of time. Of course, if the stock does not appreciate, the employee receives nothing. SARs cause no dilution in equity ownership, but the payment of cash bonuses is typically unattractive to a start-up focused on saving cash. SARs come in many flexible forms and may include provisions regarding vesting, performance milestones, and forfeiture in the event of termination of employment. Also, if the company's stock is not publicly traded, there has to be a method for determining the stock price. SARs are sometimes granted in tandem with stock options, with the goal of helping the employee, upon exercise of the stock options, to be able to pay for the stock and any taxes that may be due. When used this way, they are called "tandem SARs."

- *Phantom Stock Plan*—Phantom stock is very similar to SARs, except that the phantom stock bonus typically also reflects dividends and stock splits, and in some cases the employee also receives the value of the underlying stock, not just the appreciation. Typically, SARs can be exercised any time after they vest, whereas phantom stock payments are usually made on predetermined dates. Since neither SARs nor phantom stock plans are tax qualified, they are not subject to the same rules that apply to 401(k) plans and ESOPs (unless, as noted previously, they cover too broad a group of employees, or otherwise are improperly structured, which may make them susceptible to ERISA rules), and the awards can be given on a more arbitrary basis to key employees. Typically, the bonuses are taxed as ordinary income at the time they are received. For both SARs and phantom stock, the goal is to give key employees an incentive to help increase the value of the company's stock, without giving them a real stock ownership interest in the company. These plans can be used quite successfully by 100% family-owned businesses that do not want to distribute stock outside the family.

There are numerous variations on the basic theme of making more share ownership, or equivalent compensation, available to employees. For example, the company could have a bonus plan payable in stock of the company, or payable partly in stock and partly in cash. Several terms may be used to describe some of the variations, such as

- *Performance Unit Plan*—An employee earns specially valued units at no cost based on achievement of predetermined performance targets.

- *Performance Share Plan*—An employee receives shares of stock based on achievement of predetermined performance targets.

- *Formula Value Stock Plan*—An employee earns rights to a special class of stock (not publicly traded) that is valued according to a formula such as book value.

Employee Stock Purchase Plans (ESPPs)

An *employee stock purchase plan* (ESPP) is actually a kind of stock option plan and is most frequently used by public companies.

Under the Internal Revenue Code (Sections 421 and 423), such a plan is designed to permit employees to buy stock of their employer corporation, usually at a discount, and usually through payroll deductions. Both the company and the participating employees receive favorable tax treatment, assuming the plan is qualified under the Internal Revenue Code. The plan must be nondiscriminatory and include almost all employees. Therefore, this is not a good vehicle to reward key employees for performance. Also, no option can be granted to any employee who holds 5% or more of the voting power of the company. A plan may provide that the grant of options will be based on a uniform relationship to salary. The option must be issued under a stock purchase plan approved by the company's stockholders.

- *participants*—Only employees are eligible. Options must be granted to all employees, except that the plan may exclude those employees who (1) have been employed less than two years, (2) work 20 hours or less per week, (3) work five months or less in any calendar year, or (4) are highly compensated.

- *amount of purchase*—All employees granted options must be given the same rights and privileges. The amount of stock you may buy may be limited to a percentage of your pay. The terms of the plan must provide that your right to buy stock may not accrue at a rate that exceeds $25,000 of stock in any calendar year, based on the fair market value of the stock at the time of option grant.

- *price*—The option price to you cannot be less than the lesser of (1) 85% of the fair market value of the stock at the time the option is granted, or (2) 85% of the fair market value of the stock at the time you exercise the option. Typically, the employee gets to buy stock at the lower of the two prices during a six-month period.

- *time of exercise*—If the price you pay, under the plan, is not less than 85% of the fair market value at the time of option exercise, then you must exercise the option within five years from the date it is granted to you. If the price you pay is not determined in this way, you must exercise the option within 27 months from the grant date.

- *tax treatment*—You do not realize any reportable income as a result of the grant or exercise of the option. To receive maximum tax benefits, more than two years must pass from the time the stock option was granted to you to the time you dispose of your shares, and you must have held the shares for more than six months. If you sell the stock for less than the option price, your loss is deductible as a capital loss.

Employee Stock Ownership Plans (ESOPs)

An *employee stock ownership plan* (ESOP) is a type of tax-qualified, defined-contribution employee benefit plan that buys and holds the employer company's stock. The stock is held in a trust, and participating employees have accounts in the trust. Typically, participating employees receive their benefits only when their employment ends, and their interests are subject to vesting. An ESOP has nothing to do with stock options. An ESOP offers excellent tax benefits to the company and its participating employees. Typically, the employee does not pay for the stock; rather, the company contributes cash to buy its stock from other shareholders, or it contributes stock directly, or it has the plan borrow money to buy the stock and then the company pays back the loan over time. Thousands of companies, most of which are closely held, have ESOPs, and they include both private and public companies. ESOPs are frequently used by closely held companies to buy the shares of employees who leave the company.

For several reasons, ESOPs typically don't work well for venture-backed start-ups. ESOPs, like 401(k) plans and other qualified plans, are subject to strict rules as to how they operate. For example, a company with an ESOP must make the plan available to all of its full-time employees who meet certain length-of-service and age requirements, and there are limitations regarding the distribution of benefits. Entrepreneurs and their venture investors, on the other hand, will typically want lots of flexibility in how the benefits are distributed, with executives and key employees getting most or all. It's generally better, and much more customary, for high-tech start-ups to use

- nonqualified stock purchases (the main subject of Ch. 14)
- stock options (the main topic of Ch. 15)

Also, an ESOP is more expensive, since its setup costs can be $20,000 or more, and its annual maintenance cost may be several thousand dollars.

Section 401(k) Plans

Most large companies have a 401(k) plan (or a comparable savings plan under another section of the Internal Revenue Code). A 401(k) plan allows employees, on a pretax basis, to put part of their pay into a trust that is sponsored by the company, and many companies match the employee contributions on a percentage basis, say 25% or

75%. The employees must have at least four investment choices under the plan. These plans are mentioned here, mainly for completeness, because companies can make their own stock available as one of the investment choices, and they also can make their matching contributions in shares of their stock. However, because of various tax and securities rules, it is not very practical, or common, for small companies to do this. Section 401(k) plans are discussed further in Ch. 18.

Sidebar 16.1 Founder Retains Control Through Foresight

A small model-building company in Silicon Valley owes its livelihood in large part to the special machinery it uses to produce certain essential components. Neither the machinery nor the components can be easily procured on the outside. The founder of this company had first considered the traditional method of financing the acquisition of this machinery by the company, using the $20,000 seed capital he would inject into the company. Instead, though, he crafted an agreement between himself and the company, which said, in effect, the following.

> I, the founder, will buy this machinery with my own money, and I will lease this machinery to the company for a period of five years, for a cash consideration (which roughly equals the time-value of the money), and in consideration of my right, as founder, to exchange my ownership rights in the machinery for 100,000 shares in the company at any time during the term of the lease. At the end of the five-year lease, if I have not exercised my exchange right, the company will have the right of first refusal to purchase the machinery from me at fair market value.

In this way, should the company prosper, the founder would gladly relinquish ownership rights to the machinery in exchange for the more valuable stock. On the other hand, should the company encounter financial difficulty and face liquidation, the founder would at least have unencumbered title to the machinery, which he could claim as his, and liquidate to help recover his initial investment.

Here's a tip: The entrepreneur's attorney should do a quick review of any such proposed agreement and advise the entrepreneur as to any special legal requirements (such as, in the above example, the advisability of filing a UCC form to put the world on notice of the entrepreneur's interest in the machinery, thus protecting the founder's interest in the machinery against the claims of other creditors of the company).

17

Valuing Your Equity Position

When you can measure what you are speaking about, and express it in numbers,
you know something about it.

—Lord Kelvin

Your stock's future value may easily equal 5, 10, or even 20–100 times its present value if your business is successful. But, do you even know your stock's present value? Businesses are valued all the time by investors, and prices are put on shares. Common shares are always worth some fraction of the preferred shares (since preferred shares carry special rights and preferences).

You and your board of directors will, from time to time, establish the fair market value of common shares when you declare the exercise price for options on these shares. However, this number means little. If the company succeeds and all the preferred stock is converted to common stock, the value of the common shares, in effect, steps up to that of the preferred shares. Note, however, that in determining what your stock may be worth under different scenarios, you do need to understand how the preferences work for the various series of preferred stock that stand in line ahead of your common stock. Especially with the multiple preferences (say 3X or 4X the amount invested) that became common in financings after the dot-com crash, a so-called "successful" sale of the company could result in little or no payment to the common shareholders after the preferred shareholders take their payments off the top. This is discussed more in Ch. 12. On the other hand, an IPO will usually trigger an automatic conversion of the preferred stock to common stock.

If the company fails, the common shares will likely be worthless. Since the usual presumption is that all preferred shares will convert into common shares at some point in the future, it is customary to value a company (on an *as-if-converted* basis) based on the total number of common and preferred shares outstanding. In the simplest case, after a round of financing, a company's value can be stated to be the multiple of the latest price paid for a preferred share (i.e., the price in the round), times the total number of common and preferred shares outstanding. However, this still does not answer the question regarding the value of your company prior to initial funding or just before you need a new round of funding.

Valuations at Different Points in Time

Company valuations at different points in time are interesting to consider. For example, you might want to compute value

- at launch
- at capitalization, when you first start to sell preferred stock to investors and when it is perhaps more important
- a number of years further out in the future when those investors exercise their exit strategy

For a discussion of two important terms, see Sidebar 17.1, Some Terminology: Pre-Money and Post-Money Valuations.

Valuation at Launch

The value of your company on the day it is formed is highly subjective. While its potential value is enormous, its market value is probably nil. However, your stock obviously has some value because you will not sell as many shares as each of your cofounders wants to buy (at the nominal penny per share, or whatever). What your stock is worth at this time is a futures game. When you buy founders' stock, you are buying futures. Actually it is more like options on futures—it is pretty speculative.

The valuation of the company at launch might be said to be equal to the total number of shares sold to date (i.e., your founders' shares), times a price all of you would agree would be fair for one more share to be sold to an outside investor. The value of this one new share can be, and indeed should be, equal to more than the price paid for founders' shares, since it represents all the potential future worth (discounted for time and risk) of your company as reflected by your abilities and impending contributions.

George VonGehr, managing director of Alliant Partners, notes, "The principal value-setting factor is the ability to attract some reasonable amount of financing, and in that sense the market sets the valuation."

Valuation at Capitalization

Your company probably will not be substantially capitalized at the time of distribution of founders' stock (depending upon whether a significant price was placed on the founders' stock). Typically, each founder will contribute a token amount (perhaps $1000 to $20,000) to pay for his or her founders' stock. Whether the sum of such contributions constitutes a substantial capitalization depends on the particular business. Many businesses have only a few hundred dollars in the bank after the founders' stock has been distributed. While this is discouraged for a variety of practical and financial liability reasons, it is common.

Investors can reasonably aim for future valuations at least 10X their original investments in preferred stock, or much more in the case of many raw start-ups. The minimum return they seek typically decreases for later rounds, assuming the company has made continuous and substantial progress. For example, the investors in the last round before the company is expected to go public will not expect 10X returns. This reduction in target returns is strictly the result of risk adjustment by the investor. "In later rounds where we can better evaluate customers, competitors, and the path to liquidity, we typically apply lower discounts, and thus we have lower targets for our return on investment," says Brian J. Grossi, a general partner in AVI Capital Management, a venture capital firm in Silicon Valley.

In any case, investors will work backward from estimated future values of your company, factoring in risk, to determine today's appropriate investment value. Your common stock returns can be orders of magnitude higher (a 100–1000X return or more). What really counts, however, is not how much cash you put into the business, or the number of shares you own, but rather your percentage ownership interest and the total value of the company. It is precisely this dividing up of stock ownership that is most controversial and that establishes how much equity ownership you have to give up to investors for the cash you need. While highly subjective, there exist various well-defined methods venture capitalists use.

If your business is successful, you might well expect to turn a small founder's contribution of a few thousand dollars into several million dollars. As many of your investors will do, you too can make some interesting calculations as to the possible future value of your founders' stock by looking at factors such as sales and profit margin. Much of the information needed to do this should be found in your company's business plan (although that may represent your best-case scenario).

Valuation at Exit

Your investors will be especially interested in what your company may be worth at the time of investment liquidity (e.g., public offering, sale of the company). You can see this reflected in AVI Capital's capitalization formation road map (presented later in this chapter).

Valuation Benchmarks from VentureOne Study

VentureOne is a research firm founded by David Gleba that tracks activities in venture capital and private company financings. In 1991, Gleba completed a valuation study using pricing data from 1000 private equity rounds concluded since 1987. His study was reported in *Upside*, November 1991. Although this study is now quite old, it still offers a valuable perspective on an important topic—the cost of capital for various sources of venture funding. Its value is in helping you reflect on this important issue, not in the specific numbers (since they are dated and should be taken with a grain of salt).

From his study, important valuation benchmarks were obtained in terms of

- source of capital
- stage of company development
- company industry

For rounds of more than $1 million, Gleba found that venture capital was twice as expensive as corporate cash, and corporate cash was at least twice as expensive as capital raised from an IPO. Table 17.1 shows the percentage of equity relinquished for a fixed dollar amount of investment. Keep in mind that post-start-up companies will more easily attract corporate cash, and only the more mature companies will be able to do an IPO. The earlier the stage of your company, the more expensive will be your source of capital. To translate, early-stage companies have lower valuations. This is not a big surprise, but Gleba's study also showed that for companies at the same stage of development, corporate investors still paid two to five times the average venture capital valuation because of the strategic value to the investing corporation. Corporate cash may be out of reach for your seed-level start-up, but you nevertheless will want to explore this possibility and, in any case, keep it in mind for future financing.

Table 17.1 Equity Relinquished vs. Source of Capital
(for a fixed dollar amount of investment)

capital source	venture capital	corporate cash	IPO
percent of equity given up (%)	10.8	4.4	1.7

In this study, variations from industry to industry were not insignificant. Software companies, for example, had higher valuations at start-up and lower valuations at profitability. Gleba's advice to entrepreneurs is, "Secure seed capital from individuals; seek a corporate partner early; get profitable quickly; and avoid restart [down] rounds."

Factors that Venture Investors Consider

Unless you've done it before, your discussions with potential investors regarding your company's valuation will probably seem arcane and complicated. Although Excel spreadsheets can be run ad infinitum, valuation is much more of an art than a science. The list of potential factors to be considered by investors is long. It includes

- the potential or expected return on the investment
- recent valuations of similar investments (similar type and stage)
- market valuations of similar, successful companies
- the ability to protect the company's technology (i.e., the strength of its intellectual property)
- the apparent ability to take major market share or to grow rapidly into a large company
- how willing the investors are to pay to get in the game, if they feel they are missing an opportunity
- the perceived strength of the management team (references, track record, etc.)
- the prior investors in the company (if any) and their strengths, interests, and reputations
- the current workload of the potential investors
- how "hot" the company is perceived to be

Of course, most of these factors are subjective and cannot be easily quantified and inserted into a specific, numbers-driven valuation model. Most of these factors (as well as the factors appearing on any venture investor's list) are used to decide *whether* to invest, and not to set the valuation. So, for example, if the management team is weak, the prospective investor is highly unlikely to go beyond a quick read of the executive summary. However, if the investor somehow has decided to invest, then the valuation in the first round is likely to follow the simple "formula" of the following section.

A Secret: Venture Capitalists Don't Really Use Valuation Models—at Least Not for the First Round

You can read a lot about various valuation models, and in fact several models will be discussed later in this chapter. However, don't try to put too fine an edge on this topic, for at least two reasons.

First, venture capitalists simply don't use any of them in deciding whether to invest in a particular start-up, at least not in the first round, or in setting the price if they do decide to invest. That's "the secret." Most venture capitalists don't need financial models because, "they are in the market every day and know what early-stage companies are worth," according to George VonGehr.

Second (and this largely explains the first point), although the models have a mathematical structure and precision that is appealing to many minds, everyone knows that the quality of the raw data used (projected revenues, etc.) is so subjective and uncertain that the models generate unreliable conclusions, or rather, they generate whatever results you seek. You know the saying: "Garbage in, garbage out."

This central truth applies to some extent throughout the life of the start-up, but it is especially true in the initial round of financing. So how do venture capitalists value a company?

The cynical and accurate view is that venture capitalists, assuming they've decided to invest in your start-up, do the following.

1. They determine the dollar amount of capital your start-up needs to operate for the next 12 months.

2. For an investment of that amount, the venture capitalist wants approximately 40–60% of the company.

3. That's it—there's no number three.

That's the way Gordy Davidson, chairman of Fenwick & West, sees it. Do note that if there's a set-aside for a stock option pool for management and key employees (which is customary), then this set-aside frequently comes out of the founders' share. At least that's the way the investors like to structure it. This means, for example, that if your investors are buying half of the company and 25% is set aside for the option pool, then the split is really 50-25-25 (among investors, founders, and the option pool), with the founders in effect being diluted 75%.

You may think this approach to valuation is too simple to be true. Let's explore it.

- *Your start-up must shine like a diamond.* Perhaps the most important statement among those you've just read is: "assuming they've decided to invest in your start-up." Don't read over this lightly. The simple valuation formula above comes into play *only* if you have caused investors to become very interested in your company and eager to invest. Of course, there are numerous major factors that will determine whether an investor ever gets to this point (strong management team, large growing market, compelling unfair advantage held by your company, etc.).

- *Similar prices for both winners and losers.* Venture capitalists really don't know which of the several bets they make in a year will do well, although they don't frequently articulate it this way. They put their money on several horses and hope that a good percentage of the horses run well, with perhaps a Triple Crown winner or two in the mix. That's one reason the pricing and structure of their various deals look similar. Realistically, it's difficult or impossible to predict in advance which companies will be the big winners, the average, and the clear losers. If they and other investors actually had such divination abilities, you'd see a much greater spread in the pricing of the horses in which they invested and, of course, the lead-footed trotters would never get any horse feed at all!

- *Funding does not guarantee success, but keeps you in the race.* An obvious corollary of the above is that you are not guaranteed success just because venture capitalists have invested in your company. Yes, it's a major milestone, and the financial and other valuable resources provided by your investors can help you tremendously, but the real work is just beginning. Your first-round funding is not an end, but rather the start of a significant new chapter in the life of your company. Celebrate, but only briefly, and then get back to work.

- *A good question.* You may be asking, "OK, if I'm going to end up selling about half of my company in the first round, why should I ask for less money rather than more?" Exactly! If you seek and get $1 million in return for 50% of the company, your pre-money value is $1 million, and your post-money value is $2 million. But if you seek and get $5 million, your pre-money is $5 million, and your post is $10 million. Another advantage in seeking more money is that you won't find yourself quickly back on the trail seeking more financing. Without doubt, there are limits to this point, since venture capitalists do not want to see a culture of overspending (especially not after the dot-com crash). Also, the amount of funding will usually be based on an agreed upon operating plan, not simply your request. However, you do have a degree of control over formulation of the operating plan. In the final analysis, investors do not want to see their money wasted, and you should not want to waste it either.

- *Determining the amount to ask for.* So how are the 12-month capital needs of your company determined? Interested venture capitalists will certainly consider your numbers as a possible starting point but, if they invest, they by then are likely to have made their own calculations too. Be prepared to support your numbers. For example, if you say you need $5 million, your operating plan must include a logical *use of proceeds* section tied to this amount, with supporting strategy and data that are realistic and convincing to your investors.

- *Ask for enough money.* Competent entrepreneurs more often make the mistake of asking for too little money, rather than too much. The primary reason for this is a natural tendency to underestimate the scope of work for major projects and other activities. A second reason is a human tendency to underestimate or ignore the inevitability of distractions and unexpected external events that are beyond the company's control, but which usually have a negative (not a positive) impact on resource requirements and time frames. Yes, an entrepreneur should have and project a sense of optimism and belief in the abilities of his team, but it's a mistake to assume perfect execution with no unpleasant surprises.

You may wonder then, under the simple valuation technique above, how valuations for start-ups can drop (or increase) so dramatically. Venture investing is certainly subject to swings between hot and cold markets. When the market is cold, venture investors simply put in less money for roughly the same percentage of the company, using a much tougher and leaner estimate of the cash needed for 12 months of operation. As an extreme but vivid example, the budget for Super Bowl ads is eliminated. The entrepreneur is simply expected to do more with less, and proposed expenditures have to pass through a tougher filter. So, for example, instead of receiving $5 million for half the company, the start-up may only get $3 million. An alternative approach, with a similar result, is for the investor to reduce the time frame during which the cash will be spent. For example, the investor may receive half the company for supplying the expected cash needs for a shorter period, say nine months.

Peer Group Comparisons

For various comparison purposes, including valuation, venture capitalists frequently identify a *peer group* of companies for each of the start-ups in which they invest or have a serious interest. Ideally, a group of "pure play" companies in the start-up's target market, or in a similar or adjacent market, can be identified. Peer group companies are typically public companies, although private companies may also be used if good financial data, including valuation, are available. The goal is meaningful, accurate comparative data against which the start-up can be measured.

Various financial ratios are calculated for the peer group, and these are then used to value or benchmark the start-up. If valuation is the goal, then the ratio of market capitalization to various other financial measures for the peer group will be used, such as market capitalization to sales, or market capitalization to earnings, or market capitalization to cash flow. These ratios are then applied to the start-up. Typically, it's the start-up's projected future performance, not its current performance, that is used in these comparisons. The various comparisons allow the venture investor to "triangulate" on a reasonable valuation for the start-up, or to set a potential valuation range. Discounts or premiums may then be applied to the result to take into account special factors (e.g., a private vs. public discount, a premium for control of the company, a discount to reflect a higher valuation for the industry leader in the peer group).

Investors may also apply multiples based on completed M&A (mergers and acquisitions) transactions.

Please note that investors also make peer group comparisons for purposes other than valuation. For example, they could see if your gross margin figures are in the ballpark by comparing them to those of your peer group.

If the peer group used by your prospective investor is doing exceptionally well, that will help move your financing forward. On the other hand, investment deals on the verge of closing may suddenly collapse if the peer group experiences a sudden big drop in the stock market. For many reasons entrepreneurs may see this as unfair or irrational, especially if they believe, "we don't even compete with that peer group!" For more information about the methodology of peer group comparisons, see Sidebar 17.2, Future Value of the Start-Up—Collecting and Using Data.

See also Sidebar 17.3, What Percentage of the Company Value Is Yours?

More Commonly Used Valuation Methodology

Several years ago, Dr. James L. Plummer, president of QED Research, Inc., in Palo Alto, CA, compiled a comprehensive book on the subject of venture capital valuation techniques, based on his exhaustive survey of valuation methods used by almost 300 venture capitalists. You may refer to his *QED Report on Venture Capital Financial Analysis* for essential details. The essence of many of the valuation methods reported is based on the time-value of money—that is, some sort of discounted cash flow analysis. Since

Ch. 10 covered these valuation basics, the following are highlights of the more common valuation methods reported by Plummer. (See also Sidebar 17.4, Some Less-Common Valuation Methods, as Reported by QED.)

The Conventional Venture Capital Valuation Method

The conventional method is a simple present-value computation (refer to Ch. 10 for the basic calculations). This computation is based on an investor's estimate (probably discounted from the numbers presented in your business plan) of

- your current revenue, R
- your expected annual rate of growth of revenue, r
- the number of years to liquidity, n
- the expected after-tax profit margin at the time of liquidity, a
- the expected price-earnings ratio as of the liquidity date, P
- a discount rate appropriate for the investment stage, risk, and illiquidity, d

It can easily be shown that the present value, V, is computed as

$$V = \frac{R\,(1 + r)^n\,aP}{(1 + d)^n}$$

You will find that P, the expected price-earnings ratio as of the liquidity date, is likely to be much higher if liquidity is associated with an IPO versus an acquisition or management buyout (MBO). It is important to note that investors using the term *rate of return* (ROR) are in fact talking about the conventional VC method. This bit of information might be worth a lot to you when you enter your negotiations with a venture capitalist and the subject of valuation methods comes up.

Please note that an investor may do multiple present-value calculations using this conventional method, each based on a different set of assumptions. For example, the investor may calculate the present value of your company using different revenue stream projections, with low (pessimistic), medium (expected), and high (optimistic) forecasts being the most common.

The First Chicago Method—Alternative Scenarios

The First Chicago method employs the same analysis techniques as the conventional venture capital method, except that three different outcome scenarios are considered and given probability weightings. The First Chicago method was originated by Stanley C. Golder of First Chicago Corporation, and many venture capital firms use it. The three scenarios are "success" (IPO or attractive sale), "sideways survival," and "failure" (liquidation). For example, if your company is predicted to have the present values and associated probabilities shown in Table 17.2, your First Chicago method present value will be the sum of weighted present values as shown.

The First Chicago method is a very powerful and intuitive technique for explicitly accounting for the risks associated with a venture investment. It has the advantage of forcing the investor to consider the three major "outcomes" for any business, and to assign probabilities to each.

Table 17.2   First Chicago Method for Valuation

	success scenario	sideways survival scenario	failure scenario
expected present value	$10 million	$1 million	$0.5 million
probability of scenario	50%	30%	20%
weighted present value	$5 million	$0.3 million	$0.1 million
First Chicago method valuation (sum of weighted present values)		$5.4 million	

The Fundamental Method—Present Value of the Future Earnings Stream

The conventional venture capital method and the First Chicago method both focus on one point in time in the future: the liquidity date. The fundamental method, in contrast, looks at multiple years in the future, both before and after liquidity. The total present value of the company is the sum of the stream of after-tax earnings during, for example, the first 10 years, plus the present value of the estimated residual value of the earnings stream beyond year 10, when your growth rate levels out. This forces the investor to look at a more complete story of your company's future. For this method to be valid, it cannot be used for short streams of earnings; the analysis should be carried out beyond the period of assumed supernormal growth.

Revenue Multipliers (Value-to-Revenue Ratios)

A revenue multiplier is a factor that can be multiplied by the revenue of a company to obtain a rough estimate of the value of the company. Revenue multipliers are used because their simplicity allows them to be applied quickly.

Revenue multipliers vary tremendously depending on

- the annualized rate of growth of the company
- the investment stage the company has reached
- the product sector it is in
- whether revenue is being measured on a leading basis (the next 12 months) or on a trailing basis (the last 12 months)

The *QED Report* contains 40 QED curves that adjust the size of the revenue multipliers for each of these factors.

The revenue multiplier method is widely used, despite its weakness of not taking into account variations across industries in such factors as profit margins, required capital intensity, R&D required, and differing lead times for R&D, marketing, and production. Plummer presents additional quantitative feedback from venture capitalists about how revenue multipliers are used in practice.

Table 17.3 summarizes the popularity of the principal valuation methods described in this section.

Table 17.3 Popularity of Principal Valuation Methods

	primary method	secondary method	seldom used	not used
conventional VC method (%)	68	20	5	7
fundamental method (%)	6	25	28	41
First Chicago method (%)	16	28	18	38
revenue multiplier method (%)	11	29	31	29

Plummer reports that revenue multipliers are used as a primary valuation method more in the early stages of investment. This method may be appropriate for your start-up. Since start-up companies have little, if any, profit margin, it is natural to look at valuation techniques based on estimates of revenue. As your company matures, it will be more natural to measure its value based on earnings-oriented methods.

As noted previously, investors frequently employ peer group comparisons in using revenue multipliers.

Capitalization Formation Road Map from AVI Capital Management

Many venture capital firms have customized a capitalization model for their own internal use in evaluating companies and tracking progress. Brian J. Grossi, general partner of AVI Capital Management, advises,

> It is of critical importance to plan potential sources of capital beyond the seed commitment that would sustain the company growth through liquidity (i.e., IPO or sale of the company). AVI uses this information in planning a viable investment scenario that balances the financial expectations and desires of the founders and management, the internal-rate-of-return criteria for AVI, and expected internal-rate-of-return criteria for investors participating in later rounds.

An example of AVI's capitalization model (called "AVI's Capitalization Formation Road Map") is presented in Table 17.4 to help you understand the capital formation requirements of your business.

The capitalization model or road map identifies anticipated future capital needs, with a projected timeline, and ties them to important future milestones (such as product introduction, a specific revenue target, and achievement of breakeven). This helps to illuminate the probable dilution from future capital infusions and their associated

Table 17.4 AVI's Capitalization Formation Road Map

	founders establish reserves		Series A 9 months			Series B 12 months			Series C 8 months / P/R Ratio 1.05		
date	01-Jan-01		01-Jul-01		121.7%	28-Mar-02		103.4%	23-Mar-03		88.2%
($ in 000's)			pre		post	pre		post	pre		post
cap value			$1,800		$2,800	$7,000		$12,941	$32,353		$50,000
annualized sales						$12,996			$30,876		
funds raised			$1,000			$5,500			$12,500		
shares sold			1,250,000			2,750,000			2,500,000		
share price			$0.80			$2.00			$5.00		
total funds raised					$1,000			$6,500			$19,000
total shares	reserved: 2,250,000				3,500,000			6,470,588			10,000,000
total company		100.0%			64.3%			38.2%			35.0%
founders	1,500,000	66.7%		shares	42.9%		shares	23.2%		shares	15.0%
CEO		0.0%		500,000	14.3%			7.7%			5.0%
management		0.0%		100,000	2.9%			1.5%		200,000	3.0%
option pool	750,000	33.3%		(600,000)	4.3%		220,588	5.7%		829,412	12.0%
warrants											
common		0.0%			0.0%			0.0%			0.0%
AVI capital			$1,000,000	$1,250,000	35.7%	$2,000,000	1,000,000	34.8%	$1,000,000	200,000	24.5%
venture fund 2			$0	0	0.0%	$2,000,000	1,000,000	15.5%	$2,000,000	400,000	14.0%
venture fund 3			$0	0	0.0%	$1,500,000	750,000	11.6%	$1,500,000	300,000	10.5%
venture fund 4									$8,000,000	1,600,000	16.0%
corporate investor											
check:					100%	reinstate options:		100.0%	reinstate options:		100.0%
							220,588	15.0%		1,029,412	20.0%

Used courtesy of Brian J. Grossi, general partner.

	Series D 20 months		liquidity		totals 55 months total 6 months lockup			
P/R Ratio:		2.50	3.00					
			10-Jul-05	< IPO date		hurdle val. >	$292,132,469	
18-Nov-03		53.3%	06-Jan-06	< liquidity date		hurdle pr. >	$25	
pre		post	pre					
$117,571		$137,385	$342,113			if converted	liq. pref.	
$47,028			$114,038	shares	$ invested	$ returned	$ returned	ROI
							pref. > $32,500,000	
$13,500						profit > $309,612,500		
1,148,239								
$11.76								
		$32,500	$29.28					
		11,685,299	$32,500					
			11,685,299					
		34.5%						
	shares							
		12.8%		1,500,000		$43,915,758	$43,915,758	
		4.3%		500,000		$14,638,586	$14,638,586	
		2.6%		300,000		$8,783,152	$8,783,152	
	537,060	14.9%		1,737,060		$50,856,197	$50,856,197	
		0.0%		0		$0	$0	
$500,000	42,527	21.3%		2,492,527	$4,500,000	$72,974,141	$72,974,141	120%
$500,000	42,527	12.3%		1,442,527	$4,500,000	$42,233,111	$42,233,111	103%
$500,000	42,527	9.3%		1,092,527	$3,500,000	$31,986,101	$31,986,101	103%
$2,000,000	170,109	15.1%		1,770,109	$10,000,000	$51,823,785	$51,823,785	85%
$10,000,000	850,549	7.3%		850,549	$10,000,000	$24,901,669	$24,901,669	53%
		100.0%		11,685,299	$32,500,000	$342,112,500	$342,112,500	
reinstate options: 537,060		20%						

NewCo Quarterly Revenue

— company plan
-- approximation

revenue ($ in thousands)

35,000 / 30,000 / 25,000 / 20,000 / 15,000 / 10,000 / 5,000

Sep-00, Mar-01, Sep-01, Mar-02, Sep-02, Mar-03, Sep-03, Mar-04, Sep-04, Mar-05

cost of capital, and it also gives the investor (AVI) guidelines for appropriate reserve setting for the investment.

As you review the AVI capitalization model in Table 17.4, you will see "P/R Ratios" in some of the *investment phase* header boxes at the top. In the early stages, the valuation is affected by qualitative factors such as strength of management, characteristics of target market, and so forth. For later stages, the model uses multipliers to set valuation. These multipliers are similar to the QED/Plummer multipliers discussed in the section entitled Revenue Multipliers (Value-to-Revenue Ratios).

Valuation as a Black Art

Valuation, in all cases, is highly subjective. In the case of start-ups it's definitely a black art. A key point here is that all the math can create a false sense of precision.

This doesn't mean that you should ignore valuation techniques and not devote any time to understanding them. Rather, you need to develop a solid working knowledge of the main valuation techniques and when and how they might be used. Prospective investors will ask you what valuation you place on your start-up and how you arrived at it. Also, they may assign a junior person to "run the numbers" based on your numbers; if the information you supplied doesn't support an attractive investment, why should the investor proceed? So you need to make sure your financial projections make sense. Investors expect to see enough information in your business plan to allow them to run their own valuation calculations, which, by the way, they are unlikely to share with you. Also, they will ask questions about specific items, such as the assumptions underlying your revenue projections, and you need to anticipate these questions and know why they are being asked.

The Effect of Founders' Cash on Company Valuation

It would seem obvious that a founder who invests a substantial amount of capital in the seed stage could realize much higher valuations in start-up and later-stage financing rounds. This is usually (but not always) the case. The valuation that investors will put on your company can vary dramatically.

Some investors do not seem to care how much cash you personally have invested. Some do not want you to be preoccupied with losing your home, and they will pay the fair price for your business opportunity. These investors generally figure they and other outside investors will eventually own about 75–80% of your business, regardless of its financing history. They also figure that management and employees need about 20–25% of the pie to be properly motivated; you need not pay much for your slice, in their eyes.

Other investors, however, will put a high value on your sacrifice and hard-earned invested cash, which they see as a sign of your commitment to the business. It really pays to do your due diligence on your prospective investors to optimize your investment.

The Importance of Negotiation in the Valuation Process

In the final analysis, valuation comes down to negotiation. In order to maximize the chances of a successful negotiation, you need to be prepared. All elements of your business plan must reflect your viable business strategy, and everything must play well together. Have you set forth a solid case for your revenue and profit projections? Do you have solid justification for your cash requirements for the next 12 months? Are there any obvious defects that will undercut your position, and perhaps cause the interested investor to walk away? Do you and your team believe in your financial projections and other main elements of your business plan? The Boy Scouts say it best: "Be prepared." The outcome of negotiation also depends upon your negotiating position. If your prospective investor knows he or she is your only hope, you almost certainly will be looking at a lower valuation. However, if you are fortunate enough to have several suitors, your valuation will be higher, plus you'll have an increased probability of striking a deal.

Sidebar 17.1 Some Terminology: Pre-Money and Post-Money Valuations

You'll want to understand these two terms before you seek venture funding.

Pre-Money Valuation

The value of an enterprise before new money is injected is called its *pre-money valuation* (or *pre-money value*, or simply *pre-money* or *before the money*). For example, suppose that after your first year your company has 1 million shares outstanding. Of those, 300,000 (common) shares were sold on day one for $0.01 per share as cheap founders' stock, and thereafter 700,000 (preferred) shares were sold for $1.00 per share to a first-round investor. The total paid-in equity is only $3000 plus $700,000, or $703,000, but the current (pre-second-round financing) valuation will be computed to be equal to the total number of shares outstanding times the stated value of one share today (which hopefully is greater than the $1.00 price paid a year ago). If the current stockholders are only willing to sell new shares to the next-round investor at, for example, $2.00 a share, then the stockholders are setting the company's pre-money valuation at $2 million (based on 1 million shares, each now worth $2.00). If, in fact, the company's performance supported it, the current valuation could be much higher. Likewise, if the company wasted its first-round cash, its current valuation could be much lower, or even zero. Whatever value is placed on one share of stock at this time by either the stockholders or potential investors, the pre-money valuation is determined by multiplying that share value times the total number of shares outstanding (before the next financing round is completed).

Post-Money Valuation

The value of an enterprise after new money is injected is called its *post-money valuation* (or *post-money value*, or simply *post-money* or *after the money*). In the preceding example, assume that the current shareholders and the new investors agree that the pre-money valuation for this company should be $2 million (based on a current share worth of $2.00). If the new investors buy 1 million additional shares, they will contribute an additional $2 million, for a total paid-in equity of $2,703,000. Now, what is the post-money valuation? The answer is simple; it is the total number of shares outstanding after the second round is funded (2 million shares) times the current per-share valuation ($2.00), or $4 million.

Please note also that the pre-money valuation, plus the dollars invested in the current round, equals the post-money valuation. In our example, the pre-money of $2 million plus the $2 million invested equals the $4 million post-money.

Another approach to computing this post-money valuation is to impute value based on the percentage of equity purchased and the total amount paid for it. This imputed value is equal to the amount invested divided by the percentage of the venture purchased for that amount. In this example, the new investors bought 1 million shares (50% of the company) at $2.00 per share (for $2 million total), so the post-money valuation would equal $2 million divided by 0.50, or $4 million. It follows that pre-money valuation is calculated by subtracting the amount of new capital invested ($2 million) from the post-money valuation ($4 million). (In this case, $4 million minus $2 million equals a pre-money valuation of $2 million.)

It is obvious that a new $2 million investment might make a $2 million company worth $4 million. Reasoning by extremes, however, if the new investors bought only one new share at $2.00, the post-money valuation would then be 1,000,001 shares times $2.00, or $2,000,002. So you can see that a small amount of new money does little to increase post-money valuation, while a substantial injection of funds will substantially increase it.

This is why, if you tell investors that the company is worth $X million, they will be tempted to ask, "Is that before or after we make our investment?" However, they will not usually spell the question out; they will simply ask, "Is that pre- or post-money?" These terms are simple, intuitive, and logical, but lots of entrepreneurs stumble over them, only to weaken their negotiating position.

Sidebar 17.2 Future Value of the Start-Up—Collecting and Using Data

This sidebar offers additional information about some of the valuation methods discussed in the main body of Ch. 17. It discusses the use of these methods in making peer group comparisons.

Future Value of the Start-Up as a Multiple of Sales

Before settling upon any assumptions regarding the future annual sales of your company, look at your competition. Could your assumptions be realistic in your market? If your competitors are public companies, their sales information is available. The market value of a company might then be 2X to 4X its sales, but this is highly dependent upon your industry segment. The information you need about any public company is readily available online from numerous sources.

First find one or more public companies that typify your start-up. For example, if your start-up is a business software company, you should look at software companies that are closest to the particular market segment you are targeting. The *ratio of market capitalization to sales* for each of these companies will be available online, or you can easily make the calculations. The market capitalization of a company is simply the number of shares outstanding (say 50 million shares) multiplied by the market price of the company's stock (say $30 per share), or $1.5 billion in this example. If this company has annual revenues of $500 million, then its market value to sales ratio is three. Each industry, and segment within an industry, will differ. Software companies, for example, with high gross margins are often valued at 4X sales or more. Many high-growth, high-margin software companies have gone public at valuations of several times sales. Other less-explosive software companies are valued at only 1X to 2X sales. Of course, these ratios may fluctuate significantly over time due to stock market swings and other factors.

Future Value of the Start-Up as a Function of Sales, Profit Margin, and Price-Earnings Ratio

Another way to estimate a company's value is to estimate its future sales, and then apply industry standards for expected *profit margin* (PM), which is profit as a percentage of sales, and expected *price-earnings ratio* (P/E), which is price per share divided by earnings per share, or price (total market capitalization) of the company divided by the earnings of the company. As discussed in Ch. 17, it's common to use a peer group of public companies to make these comparisons.

The P/E ratio is also known as the *multiple*, and it sometimes appears as PE. Especially for publicly traded companies, you may hear about a *trailing P/E*, the calculation of which is based on the most recently reported annual earnings of the company, and a *forward P/E*, which is based on projected earnings for next year.

Let's take a hypothetical company in your peer group. It has $2.5 billion in sales, and its profits or earnings after taxes are about $200 million; thus its profit margin is the $200 million earnings divided by $2.5 billion sales, or 8%.

Let's say its stock trades at about 25X earnings (profit) per share. Thus, this company's worth (market capitalization), W, could be calculated as

$$W = (\text{sales}) \, (PM)(P/E)$$

$$= (\text{sales}) \left(\frac{\text{earnings}}{\text{sales}} \right) \left(\frac{\text{price}}{\text{earnings}} \right)$$

$$= (\$2,500,000,000) \left(\frac{\$200,000,000}{\$2,500,000,000} \right) \left(\frac{\$25}{\$1} \right)$$

$$= \$5,000,000,000$$

The value of this company is found to equal about twice its annual sales.

To take your start-up's example, assuming you are in the same industry as this peer group company and that your business will someday do $100 million annually in sales (if that is what the business plan projects), your company's future value can be estimated to be

$$W = (\text{sales})(PM)(P/E)$$

$$= (\text{sales}) \left(\frac{\text{earnings}}{\text{sales}} \right) \left(\frac{\text{price}}{\text{earnings}} \right)$$

$$= (\$100,000,000) \left(\frac{\$200,000,000}{\$2,500,000,000} \right) \left(\frac{\$25}{\$1} \right)$$

$$= \$200,000,000$$

Investors will typically discount the result for risk and lack of liquidity. Also, this future value is exactly that—in the future—so investors wanting to estimate today's value could do a present value calculation using their internal rate of return.

Sidebar 17.3 What Percentage of the Company Value Is Yours?

It is important to estimate what percentage of the total company value, W, will be yours. To do this, you need to estimate the number of shares that will be outstanding at the time your company goes public or is sold (5 to 10 years in the future), and then calculate your percentage. Your business plan should tell you approximately how many more shares of stock must be sold (and at what price) before the business is self-sustaining (review your financial pro formas). Remember, this is just a plan; the actual results can be off by an order of magnitude or more. First, compute the dilution factor. Let N be the total number of new or future shares to be sold and let O be the total number of shares currently outstanding. Then the dilution factor will be

$$D = \frac{O}{N + O}$$

You can calculate your future percentage ownership, FP, as your current percentage, CP, multiplied by the dilution factor, D.

$$FP = (CP)D$$

Then multiply your estimated FP times the market value, W, of the company (estimated in Sidebar 17.2) and you have your fortune.

$$fortune = (FP)W$$

In other words, if you obtained stock or options on 5% of the company when you founded it, CP = 0.05, and if $D = \frac{1}{5}$ (in this case we are assuming that dilution is a factor of 5; e.g., 1 million shares were issued by the time you received yours, and an additional 4 million new shares were issued afterward), your future percentage is

$$FP = (0.05)\left(\frac{1}{5}\right)$$

$$= 0.01$$

Your future worth is

$$fortune = (0.01)\,(\$200{,}000{,}000) = \$2{,}000{,}000$$

It is highly unlikely that you could achieve this wealth as an employee in someone else's start-up, which is why you want to start your own company.

Sidebar 17.4 Some Less-Common Valuation Methods, as Reported by QED

You may wish to skip or simply skim this sidebar, since it describes valuation methods that are rarely used in early-stage financing. It is included as background information that may interest some readers. Much of the information is derived from Dr. James L. Plummer, president of QED Research, Inc., in Palo Alto, CA, who compiled *QED Report on Venture Capital Financial Analysis* based on his survey of valuation methods used by almost 300 venture capitalists. (The most common valuation methods are discussed in the main body of Ch. 17.)

Adjusted Net Worth

If one simply takes the net worth of a business and makes adjustments for intangibles such as patents and goodwill, a valuation can be obtained that may be useful for businesses where fixed assets are the most important component of value. However, unless your start-up just built a $200 million semiconductor wafer fabrication facility, investors are unlikely to use this method to value your new venture. In the few cases where investors look at the market value of a start-up's assets, it typically would be for the purpose of (1) understanding the "worst case" liquidation scenario, or (2) setting a floor value under some other valuation technique that the investor is using, such as discounted cash flow.

IRS Excess Earnings Method of Valuing Intangibles

The IRS has a valuation method based on excess earnings. Your excess earnings (i.e., a rate of return realized beyond what is normal for a business of comparable risk) are used to compute the capitalized value of your assets (tangible and intangible). Again, since your new start-up will likely have no earnings, this valuation method will not be relevant for your seed and start-up rounds.

Rule-of-Thumb Ratios Applied to Before-Tax Earnings

For normal-growth, closely held companies, this is a before-tax form of the common price-earnings ratio method. It is used because it is less subject to manipulation by owners. Again, because your new start-up will likely have no earnings, this valuation method will not be relevant.

Present Discounted Value of Future Earnings Stream

By computing the present value (see Ch. 10) of the estimated future earnings stream from a business, you can arrive at a total present value of future earnings. Add to this the present value of the ending value of a company and you can compute the value of a company today. This method seems more practical than the others mentioned for a start-up, but it is based on uncertain estimates.

If anyone believed the numbers in your business plan, this present-value approach could easily be computed.

The *QED Report on Venture Capital Financial Analysis* contains the desired returns used by venture capitalists for various stages of investments. The size of the discount rate used falls dramatically from the more risky early-stage investments to less risky later-stage investments.

Price-Earnings Ratios of Comparable Public Companies with Adjustments for Liquidity

It is tempting to look at the market value (prices) of public companies with similar earnings to estimate the value of larger normal-growth, closely held companies. The error in doing so is that private companies are less liquid and thus typically have values that are 15–50% lower, and investors making such peer group comparisons (discussed previously) will make an adjustment for this. On the other hand, younger, higher-growth companies can have price-earning (P/E) ratios exceeding those of public companies. It is not unusual to see a high-growth company emerge at an IPO with a P/E ratio of 30 or much higher, while comparable older and slower-growth companies might reflect a P/E ratio of 10. The P/E ratio only makes sense for companies that are profitable (since if the earnings are zero or negative, the P/E will be infinite or negative). During the late 1990s and into this century, many companies went public without earnings, and their valuations were obviously based on other factors, including perhaps some measure of irrational exuberance.

Revenue Multipliers for Professional Practices

Companies with few assets (especially service companies, where owners can take out most earnings) are often valued on the basis of revenue. What has evolved is a set of ranges of revenue multipliers for estimating the goodwill value of professional practices. For engineering and other consulting practices with weak repeat business patterns, the revenue multiplier is often 15–25%. To this goodwill value must be added the adjusted net worth of the company, which includes accounts receivable and fixed assets. This multiplier must be adjusted upward for businesses with high growth rates.

18

Other Compensation and Start-Up Employment Considerations

The engine which drives enterprise is not thrift, but profit.

—John Maynard Keynes

A principal focus of this chapter is on you, the founder, and the fringe benefits issues that affect you and your family directly. What practical issues, such as health insurance, do you need to consider before you make the start-up plunge? In addition, the discussion will include the issue of group insurance and other fringe benefits for you and your entire company. According to Labor Department surveys, a significant majority of small businesses provide medical care benefits for full-time workers. Of course, the percentage of large businesses that do so is substantially higher (well over 90%). However, before you work on group plans, it is important to first take care of your own short-term needs.

Entrepreneurs Need Insurance

Especially if you've worked at a large company, you may be accustomed to receiving a broad package of fringe benefits, at minimal or no cost to you, that includes medical, dental, and vision insurance, long- and short-term disability insurances, and life insurance.

When you decide to launch your own business, do not overlook how new insurance premiums or the lack of insurance might affect your personal finances. If you became seriously ill or died, the consequences would be grave to you and your family. Even though you may be able to survive without dental and vision care insurance benefits, you will still need basic medical and life insurance coverage.

If you're married and your spouse is employed, review the insurance coverage (and other fringe benefits) offered through his or her employment. Understand what's covered and what's not, and plan accordingly.

Do Some Planning Regarding Fringe Benefits

Although perhaps obvious, a key point here is the need for some planning. Review your personal financial situation, and do some financial planning for yourself and your family before you launch your start-up. Whenever you start a business or leave an old employer, you must make certain that your basic insurance needs are covered without interruption.

In addition, include in the plans for your start-up a fringe benefits plan (at least a rough outline or road map) covering you and all of your employees. Of course, unless you are one of a small minority of founders who start immediately with lots of funding, your budget for employee benefits won't allow you to offer all the fringe benefits that you would like to offer. However, you can develop a general plan covering what you would like to offer and when (i.e., what events, like first-round financing or perhaps a certain level of revenue or profit, will need to occur before you can offer certain group benefits).

In addition to being cost effective, your benefits plan should be consistent with your company's values and goals. No one will expect you to offer everything at once, and it can be positive for the team when benefits are added over time. Once you receive significant venture financing, you will be able to put in place a more competitive benefits package. With rare exceptions, venture capital-backed companies offer competitive benefits programs.

Communicate with your employees and explain what you're planning to do in the benefits area and why. Get them involved. Discuss the benefits budget. After medical coverage and other high-priority items are addressed, you may still have some discretionary funds in your budget for additional benefits. It may make sense to purchase better productivity tools for employees working at home (e.g., computer upgrades, faster Internet connections). Ask your team where they think the funds should be targeted. You may get some suggestions that are quite popular and surprisingly inexpensive. Also, keep your eye open for free services that may be available in your community. For example, local hospitals sometimes offer free health fairs.

There are lots of free resources available to help you do both your personal planning and the company planning. Also, as discussed later in this chapter, for the typical start-up it makes good business sense, at a very early stage, to outsource the administration of your group benefits plans.

Use the Internet

You can easily use the power of the Internet to research your issues and obtain the insurance coverage you need. In the past, most people met with an insurance agent in person to take care of their insurance needs, whether personal or business. However, the Internet has been rapidly revolutionizing the insurance business and will continue to do so. The Internet offers convenience, privacy, savings in time and money, speed, and lots of good information. You can quickly go to different sites and get information and quotes for the insurance product you need—life insurance, health insurance, dental, vision, automobile, and so forth. You can easily look at various deductibles and options and compare prices. Insurance sites are available for both individual insurance and business insurance.

However you decide to buy insurance—whether from a human being in person or "automatically" over the Internet—you face the same question: are you dealing with one insurance company only, or with a *broker* who represents many different insurance companies? Generally, dealing with a broker is more cost effective because the broker—whether it's the human being you meet with or the automated Internet website you're on—will be able to shop several insurance companies in seeking the best deal for you.

There are many good insurance sites on the Internet that allow you to compare quotes from a multitude of insurance companies. These include

- InsWeb (www.insweb.com)
- Insure.com (www.insure.com)

Sites like these offer lots of helpful information. Individual insurance companies also have their own websites (e.g., www.farmers.com or www.prudential.com), which may sometimes have better background information about a particular topic of interest to you.

Also, the website of The American Council of Life Insurers (ACLI) (www.acli.com), which is an organization that represents several hundred insurance companies in the U.S., contains a wealth of information about insurance, including practical tips about shopping online for insurance.

In addition to using the Internet, talk early on with a prospective outsourcing partner or two, as noted in the following section.

Outsourcing Your Benefits Work

It almost always makes sense for a small company to outsource its payroll and benefits administrative work to a professional organization that specializes in these matters. The Internet has helped revolutionize how these services are best provided, and many service companies have been formed in the benefits area to take advantage of the opportunities. Outsourcing these functions has many advantages for your start-up.

- Your time and company resources are better spent focused on your core business.

- The risk of a legal violation (which is high, since the administration of these benefits is extremely complex and involves many state and federal laws that change frequently) is greatly reduced.

- If you're not an expert in the field, benefits work is very time consuming and often frustrating. (All too frequently, competent accounting or finance employees try to do this work on their own, with the misguided intention of saving money, only to waste an incredible amount of internal resources and create unnecessary frustration.)

- Company morale will be better, since your employees will have 24/7 access to their accounts and other educational resources and information, coupled with personalized access to their account representatives when needed.

- Your communications with your team regarding benefits will be more effective and positive.

- In addition to handling the administrative work, your outsourcing partner can help you design and implement the right benefits plans.

- The amount of paperwork and duplicate entry of data in different databases is greatly reduced.

There are many companies that offer these services. One is MyBenefitSource (MBS) (www.mybenefitsource.com), which is an H&R Block company that provides payroll and benefits administration services to tens of thousands of small and mid-sized companies (with the number of employees ranging from just two to a few thousand). You should easily be able to find the right outsourcing partner for you. Make sure it has a small-company focus and meets your needs. One approach is to talk with small companies in your area about their experiences with outsourcing these important functions.

Talk very early in the process with a prospective outsourcing partner or two, even before you think you are ready. You can get a lot of good free advice and ideas—both about your personal needs regarding benefits such as medical and life insurance, and also about group benefits for all employees of your company.

Life Insurance

Some forms of protection, such as proper medical and life insurance, are almost routine.

You probably already own some life insurance. Review your policies and purchase some additional term insurance if needed to cover the coming several years. If you are in good health, this insurance is cheap and comforting. Inexpensive term insurance is available through the IEEE (Institute for Electrical and Electronic Engineers) (www.ieee.org) and many other organizations. You are probably already a member of one or more of such organizations, or you can easily join if you're not. Also, as discussed previously, it's easy to get practical insurance information and quotes over the Internet.

Most group term life insurance policies from previous employers can be converted into individual whole life policies after termination of employment, but this whole life insurance is often extremely expensive, and the rates offered are usually not at all competitive. The rule of thumb is to take advantage of group term conversion options only if you are totally uninsurable. Shop around.

It is easy to put in place a group insurance plan for all your employees.

Key-Person Life Insurance

You have probably read about companies that have *key-man* or *key-person* life insurance for their key executives. Venture investors sometimes require this insurance in order to help protect their investment if you or another key person dies. The start-up company purchases this insurance and is typically named the beneficiary (i.e., the party to whom the death benefits are paid), although sometimes the venture investors insist that they be the named beneficiaries. The amount of insurance purchased usually ranges from $500,000 to several million dollars, and it may approximate the amount of the investment. It's usually term insurance because that meets the desired goals and is the least expensive.

This key-person insurance will not be of much help to your family. Some of these insurance policies do, however, include partial payment to your spouse, which is something to keep in mind in your negotiations with investors. A variation is to have the company purchase a separate life insurance policy covering you that is payable to your beneficiaries.

Health Insurance

If you are not covered by a spouse's group medical plan, you should shop for competitive medical insurance. You will want to make certain that each member of your family has medical coverage that continues without interruption.

An excellent temporary solution for many is provided by COBRA (the Consolidated Omnibus Budget Reconciliation Act of 1986). This federal law requires most employers (those with at least 20 employees) sponsoring group health plans to extend to previous employees certain existing group plan insurance benefits for 18 months (even if the employee quits) at a cost of just a few percentage points above group plan rates. COBRA coverage is typically less expensive than individual health coverage that individuals can obtain on their own. Of course, COBRA participants will usually pay more for their health insurance out of pocket than will active employees, simply because most employers pay all or a substantial portion of the group premium for their active employees. Even after the allotted time (18 months), the plan can be converted to an individual rather than a group rate, but you may get a better deal if you shop around.

Depending upon what's provided under the employer's plan, the medical benefits available to covered beneficiaries under COBRA may include

- physician care
- inpatient and outpatient hospital care
- surgery and other major medical benefits
- prescription drugs
- other medical benefits, such as vision and dental care

However, employers are not required to offer life insurance as a continuing benefit under these health insurance continuation provisions.

COBRA may provide a much-needed temporary solution to your medical health insurance needs, especially if you have an uninsurable prior condition. If you are entitled to COBRA benefits, your employer's health plan must give you written notice about your right to continue the health benefits under the plan, and you'll have 60 days to elect to continue coverage or lose all right to these benefits. Be aware, though, that many companies have been negligent in properly implementing their obligations under the law. Also, when one becomes covered by another employer group health plan, no matter how poor the new benefits may be, COBRA coverage could be cut short.

Generally, it has become easier to put in place a group health plan for all your employees. However, the process remains complex and is subject to both federal and state law. As a result, you need to check out the alternatives available in the state where you are located or have employees. An experienced broker can help you select the right health coverage. Also, to make your package of benefits more attractive to current and prospective employees, you may consider offering related or ancillary coverages, such as

- prescription drugs
- dental
- vision
- employee assistance programs (EAPs)
- chiropractic
- acupuncture
- fertility programs

In general, health insurance is the number one benefits concern for employees. Of course, a central issue is cost: what can you afford, and when. Cost sharing with your employees is one possible approach. You could, for example, have a plan that provides for the company to pay one-half of the monthly health insurance premium for each employee, with the employee to pay the other half. Another possible tool is the popular, pretax *Section 125 plan* (also called a *cafeteria plan*), which is discussed later in this chapter.

California is among the states that have tried hardest to make cost-effective health plans available to small companies and to reduce or eliminate some of the major problems in health care (such as an employee being denied coverage because of a *pre-existing* medical condition). As a result, California start-ups (with as few as two employees) have enjoyed the increased availability of flexible health plans that offer an array of choices to their employees. See Sidebar 18.1, Health Insurance for Small Companies in California—One Approach.

Whatever state your business is located in, you should benefit from the federal insurance reforms known as *HIPAA* (The Health Insurance Portability and Accountability Act of 1996). HIPAA (which includes numerous other insurance reforms) guarantees access to health coverage for small employers (50 or fewer employees) and, in general, prevents insurance companies from excluding employees or their family members from employer-sponsored coverage based on health status. Insurance companies are required to renew coverage to all groups, regardless of the health status of any member. Bear in mind that health insurance is complex and is also regulated by state law. Talk with your insurance broker and use the Internet to see what specific programs are available in your state for your company. Regarding the federal requirements and programs, a good place to start is www.hcfa.gov. This site has a wealth of information and can also point you to good sites for your particular state.

Disability Insurance

People 45 or younger are three times more likely to become disabled than to die, yet almost everyone has some life insurance and few have disability insurance. If you die it does not cost your family much money. Financially, they just have to deal with the loss of income. If you are disabled and sick, additional expenses will also be incurred.

Disability insurance typically pays, on a tax-free basis, up to 60% of what an individual earned before he or she became disabled, and does not take effect for a period of time, say 60 to 120 days, depending on the policy. The shorter the lag before the insurance takes effect, the higher the insurance premium. However, please be aware that disability policies from different insurance companies vary widely, and it is not wise to simply take the policy with the lowest cost. For example, policies define *total disability* differently. Under the fine print of a cheap policy, you may find that your particular illness or condition does not entitle you to benefits. Look for a policy that pays if you cannot work in the same capacity as you did before an illness (which is sometimes called *own-occupation* disability). Expert advise from a qualified broker is helpful. Although disabilities do not occur frequently, they do happen, and they can be devastating. If you are healthy, disability insurance is not expensive, and you should buy it to protect your family.

Asset Protection Maneuvers

The area of asset protection also needs your consideration. You probably should visit an estate planner to determine the best way for your family's assets to be held. To help prevent your family from being economically wiped out if the business fails, it might be advisable to put certain assets in trust for your spouse, or to designate those assets as separate property. Furthermore, should the business succeed, it might make sense to put some of your new company stock into trust funds for your children.

Retirement Plans

When you first launch your start-up you probably will not have a good retirement plan in place for you and your first employees.

Start-ups typically cannot afford employer-funded retirement plans that eat into limited cash. Rather, they typically rely more on flexible IRS-compliant plans that allow employees to shift a portion of their otherwise taxable income into tax-advantaged plans. For this latter category of retirement plans, set forth in the following sections is a brief overview of several types of plans—both for individuals and for companies—for you to consider. For everything there is a season.

Section 401(k) Plan

Regarding retirement benefits, most large companies offer a flexible *Section 401(k) plan* (or a comparable savings plan under another section of the Internal Revenue Code). A 401(k) plan allows employees, on a pretax basis, to put part of their otherwise taxable pay into a trust that is sponsored by the company. Many companies also match the employee contributions on a percentage basis, say 25% or 75%. The fund assets are taxed only when the employee withdraws them (typically at retirement, since there is a 10% penalty for withdrawal before age 59 $1/2$), and thus the assets in the meantime may accumulate more rapidly without being taxed. The company also receives tax advantages. It is entitled to take a tax deduction immediately for (1) the amounts contributed to the trust fund as authorized by the employee, and (2) the amount of any matching contributions by the company. Section 401(k) plans are quite flexible; for example, participating employees must have at least four investment choices under the plan. Within the maximum annual contribution limit ($10,500, periodically adjusted upward), the employee determines the amount to be contributed each pay period through payroll withholding.

The company is not required to make any matching or other contributions to a Section 401(k) plan. Thus, if it chooses not to contribute, the company's only costs will be those of setting up and administering the plan. However, it is very common for companies to include matching contributions in their plan designs in order to meet certain *nondiscrimination tests* imposed by federal tax law (e.g., one such test limits the contributions by the most highly compensated employees in relationship to the contributions of all other employees), thereby protecting the tax-qualified status of the plan. Companies have found that a properly designed matching contribution (perhaps $0.25 or $0.50 by the company for each $1.00 contributed by the employee, for the first 3% or 4% of the employee's pay) can encourage lower-paid workers to contribute to the plan and thus help ensure that the plan maintains its tax-qualified status.

Section 401(k) plans are usually for employers with more than 25 employees. Eligible employees can contribute up to 15% of their compensation, up to a maximum annual contribution of $10,500 (which is indexed for inflation).

SIMPLE 401(k) Plan

Another type of retirement plan, the *SIMPLE 401(k)* plan, may be good for a smaller company (100 or fewer employees) that would like to (1) avoid the higher administrative costs associated with a regular 401(k) plan, and (2) have a plan that automatically satisfies the nondiscrimination tests under federal tax law. The maximum salary deferral permitted per employee was set at $8000 in 2003, increasing to $10,000 in 2005, with periodic adjustments thereafter. This plan requires that the employer match employee contributions (e.g., on a dollar for dollar basis for the first 3% that each employee contributes to the plan). Although this type of plan can be an attractive benefit in competitive labor markets, you should not implement this type of plan unless your company has an adequate, dependable cash flow to fund the matching contributions each year. Also, the SIMPLE 401(k) plan requires more reporting and paperwork than does the SIMPLE IRA, discussed later in this chapter.

Types of IRAs / Increased Contribution Limits

Individual retirement accounts (IRAs) can be very important in retirement planning. Several types are discussed here. Under federal legislation passed in 2001, increased contribution limits for IRAs and Roth IRAs are being phased in over time—to $3000 in 2002, $4000 in 2005, and $5000 in 2008, with the limits indexed after that. Also, under IRA "catch-up" provisions covering taxpayers 50 and older, those limits are increased by $500 in 2002 and by $1000 beginning in 2006.

Regular IRA

Millions of individuals have set up a *regular IRA* retirement account, also called a *traditional IRA*. Effective with the 2002 tax year, the annual contribution limit was increased from $2000 to $3000, and it increases in later years. Your annual contributions may or may not be tax deductible, depending on your income level and whether you already participate in a 401(k) plan. Interest and other gains accumulate on a tax-deferred basis, and there typically is a 10% penalty for early withdrawal (before age 59 $^1/_2$).

Spousal IRA

A nonworking spouse may contribute up to $2000 annually to another type of individual IRA, a *spousal IRA*, even if the working spouse participates in a 401(k) plan through their employer. The annual contributions may or may not be tax deductible, depending on income level and whether there is participation in an employer-sponsored plan.

Education IRA

The *education IRA* allows taxpayers to set money aside for the future educational expenses of their children. Although this type of IRA was initially not as popular as expected, the increase in the annual contribution limit from $500 to $2000 (effective with the 2002 tax year) certainly helps. Setting up this account does not affect what you can contribute to your personal IRA accounts.

SIMPLE IRA

A *SIMPLE IRA* is a tax-deferred plan provided by small businesses (100 employees or fewer) or sole proprietors who do not maintain any other type of retirement plan. Both employee and employer contribute. It gets its name from its legal title, the "Savings Incentive Match Plan for Employees" (SIMPLE), and in 1997 it replaced the type of IRA known as SARSEP-IRA. Under a SIMPLE plan, employees can elect to make salary-reduction contributions (up to $8000 per year in 2003, or $9000 for individuals age 50 or older, with periodic adjustments thereafter) to the plan rather than receiving these amounts as part of their regular pay. The employer must make certain matching contributions (one option is a dollar-for-dollar match of up to 3% of employee compensation). The SIMPLE IRA has the advantage of higher contribution limits and is generally subject to the same rules that apply to a regular IRA.

Roth IRA

Contributions to a *Roth IRA* are not tax deductible. However, your gains can accumulate on a tax-free basis and, for accounts that are at least five years old, withdrawals upon retirement (age 59 $1/2$) are not subject to tax. The annual contribution limit was raised from $2000 to $3000 (for accounts opened in 2002), and contributions are not permitted for taxpayers with gross incomes above certain levels.

SEP-IRA

You may soon want to investigate setting up a *simplified employee pension IRA* (SEP-IRA) plan. This type of retirement plan is frequently appropriate for sole proprietors or small companies; it involves less paperwork than many other retirement plans and is easy to set up and administer. A SEP plan allows an employer to make tax-deductible contributions toward his or her own retirement (if a self-employed individual) and the employees' retirement without becoming involved in more complex retirement plans. As is the case for the other types of IRAs, the funds in the SEP grow tax free until withdrawal at retirement. Each participating employee sets up an IRA account, and the employer funds the contributions. The SEP rules generally permit an employer to contribute annually to each participating employee's SEP-IRA up to 15% of the employee's compensation, or $25,500, whichever is less. This dollar amount is periodically increased for inflation. Except for the higher contribution limits, the SEP-IRA is generally subject to the same rules that apply to a regular IRA.

Keogh Plan

Perhaps you already have a *Keogh plan* in place. A Keogh is a tax-deferred pension account designed for employees of unincorporated businesses or for persons who are self-employed, either full time or part time. They are somewhat more flexible than SEP-IRAs. Up to $35,000 per year in combined contributions by the employer and employee can go into a Keogh. A plan document is required. A Keogh may be ideal for you during the planning stages of your business, but if your start-up incorporates soon, you can establish at the right time a broader retirement plan for yourself and your employees, such as the SEP plan or 401(k) plan, both discussed previously.

Get Good Tax Advice

Because tax laws change frequently, you should make sure you're dealing with the latest provisions. Also, you should definitely seek the advice of a qualified tax advisor. There are numerous factors to consider (e.g., your adjusted gross income, the legal structure of your business entity, the possible conversion of accounts from one type to another, whether you can participate in multiple types of accounts at the same time, and so forth). The right answer will depend upon your particular situation and what you are trying to accomplish.

There are numerous Internet sites that offer you convenient, free access to the latest information and lots of good planning tools. For example, you might check out Quicken at www.quicken.com. However, these sites are not a substitute for you talking with your own trusted tax advisor about your personal needs and the needs of your company.

Section 125 Cafeteria Plan

A *Section 125 cafeteria plan* is a flexible employee benefits plan that allows employees to choose from a menu of specific fringe benefits and pay for these benefits with pretax dollars. Section 125, the section in the Internal Revenue Code that governs these plans, offers advantages to both employees and employers. By paying for the benefits with pretax dollars, employees can reduce their taxes and increase take-home income. They can also customize the plan to meet their particular needs. Employers save some tax dollars and benefit from improved employee morale. A Section 125 plan can cover a number of benefits, including health insurance, life insurance, a dependent care assistance plan, and a 401(k) retirement plan.

Employment Contract

See Ch. 13 for comments on employment contracts for others in your company. This chapter is primarily about you. Since you employ yourself in your new business, you will want to create some form of simple employment contract for yourself. This may sound absurd since it is, after all, your business. But if the business is to grow, you will soon be surrounded by other stakeholders such as investors (shareholders), directors, employees, customers, and suppliers.

These individuals, especially your investors and directors, may assert an intense interest in your business affairs if they do not like how the business is going. Many start-up entrepreneurs are later dismissed from their own companies.

You should consider inserting the following types of clauses in your employment contract.

- Severance pay equal to your salary will continue for several months (say 12 months) after you are terminated (or you are asked to resign) without cause.
- Your health plan coverage (e.g., COBRA benefits), life insurance coverage, and other appropriate fringe benefits will be continued during the severance period, at the company's expense.
- You have the right to resign rather than be fired.
- You will continue vesting in your founders' stock and stock options during your severance period.
- You will be given an extension to the period of time during which you must exercise any outstanding incentive stock options (from the standard one to three months) to three years. (If you take advantage of this extension, your incentive stock options will convert into nonqualified stock options, but that may be preferable to exercising options when stock values are low.)
- If requested by you, outplacement services will be provided for one year after termination or involuntary resignation, or until you start work with another employer.

By the way, most investors will review and, if necessary (from their point of view), renegotiate all employment contracts prior to committing funds, so keep your contract simple and reasonably fair. If your contract is so airtight that you cannot be terminated even for good cause, that's a problem. If they perceive that you are difficult to deal with, that's a problem. Also, they won't want to invest in companies where there is a lot of "clean up" work for them to do.

Emotional Distress Compensation

Fortune 500 companies can have reorganizations, acquisitions, mergers, and recapitalizations that decimate their employee ranks, but start-ups are subject to extermination.

As founder, you can do a lot toward protecting yourself in times of future distress. In the case of bankruptcy of your start-up, the company probably cannot help you very much; however, it is not unheard of for six-figure settlements to go to ousted founders and presidents under bankruptcy proceedings. Sometimes they are called emotional distress payments, with the payments being nontaxable because they are deemed to be personal-injury settlements rather than income.

If your business is flying high, or even not so high, and a future board dismisses you with or without cause, you may feel you deserve some help; you may not get any unless you arranged for it early on. It makes sense to create a written employment contract for yourself that will protect you if you are let go.

If terminated early, you may lose any value in your founders' stock or stock options unless your employment agreement stipulated that your vesting would be extended upon termination (e.g., without cause). If you had only ISOs (which must be exercised within a three-month period), you will lose them regardless of any accelerated vesting schedule if the company is faltering and the stock is worth less than your exercise price. However, if you have nonqualified options and you successfully negotiated to exercise them within the next 3 to 10 years if you are let go without cause, you can go on to a new job or start a new company and possibly cash in later after the new management team turns the company around.

A couple of concepts from larger companies have found their way into some of the employment contracts of start-up companies: golden handcuffs and golden parachutes (discussed in the following sections).

Golden Handcuffs—When and How to Stay

You keep good employees in part by making it financially painful for them to leave. If you arrange it so that when someone leaves early they lose deferred salary, unvested stock options, deferred bonus payments, and the like, you have placed what are known as *golden handcuffs* on that individual. Put handcuffs only on your key employees; avoid them for yourself, or reduce their impact in a reasonable fashion. Be aware, however, that this can be a point of dissension with other sophisticated cofounders and key employees. Also, as discussed elsewhere, your venture investors are almost certainly going to insist that your stock be subject to a vesting schedule.

Golden Parachutes—When and How to Leave

If you are asked to leave your company, or if you agree to do so at some point in the future, it will be to your benefit to have already negotiated the terms of your departure. Insert in your employment contract stipulations regarding your severance and vesting rights. This will give you a cushion—a *golden parachute* to soften your landing.

Severance pay, if you are forced out, should equal at least 3 to 12 months' salary. A lump-sum payment would be to your advantage, but it is more common to pay severance over time just as if it were salary. Vesting of your stock and stock options should continue for some period of time also, certainly during your severance payment period.

Summary

In conclusion, it is obvious that you will need a fair salary and a fair equity position as discussed in earlier chapters. However, it is also important to have needed auxiliary coverage (life insurance, health insurance, asset protection plans, retirement plans, and disability insurance). Construct a fair and simple written employment contract so investors will accept it when providing the funding for your start-up.

Sidebar 18.1 Health Insurance for Small Companies in California— One Approach

PacAdvantage (www.pacadvantage.com) is a nonprofit purchasing pool in California that offers an array of affordable health insurance plans to small businesses in California with 2 to 50 employees. It provides health insurance to more than 11,000 small businesses with about 150,000 members. PacAdvantage was previously known as HIPC (Health Insurance Plan of California).

PacAdvantage was created following the enactment of significant small-business health insurance reforms in California in 1992. These California reforms predated the major federal reforms known as HIPAA, enacted in 1996.

By uniting in PacAdvantage, California's small companies in effect have spread their risks and negotiated better rates from a host of insurers. They now enjoy the same group rates as do large businesses.

Under PacAdvantage, small businesses, together with their employees and dependents, cannot be denied health insurance because of health, age, occupation, or residence. This was a major sea change in the insurance industry and has been very important to small businesses and their employees. Under the practices existing in the insurance industry before the reform legislation, individuals with expensive medical problems and companies with "excessive" medical claims could be passed around the industry like hot potatoes, offered incredibly high insurance rates, or denied coverage.

PacAdvantage offers

- many major health insurance providers to choose from
- an array of plan types for employees to choose from, including HMOs (health maintenance organizations) and PPOs (preferred provider organizations)
- an array of benefits packages to choose from, including health, dental, vision, chiropractic, and acupuncture
- reduced paperwork, including a simplified qualification and enrollment process and one monthly billing statement
- flexible options as to the employer's contribution to the health insurance costs
- competent and responsive customer service

Whatever state you are located in, you may be able to benefit from a similar program. As noted in the text of Ch. 18, the federal law known as HIPAA guarantees access to health coverage for small employers (50 or fewer employees).

DOING IT

Part Five of this book includes a chapter on intellectual property and how to protect it, as well as a chapter on the appropriate legal form for your start-up. This part of *Engineering Your Start-Up* also presents several factors to weigh as you decide whether to leave your current employer and strike out on your own. Sidebar 21.2 describes an exciting experience one of the authors had in launching one start-up. You can learn from the mistakes of others.

Here also is a chance for you to reflect before making the start-up decision. This part offers some final thoughts and briefly reviews the key points of the book to aid you in deciding whether engineering a start-up is the right action for you.

19

Protecting Your Intellectual Property

The best way to have a good idea is to have lots of ideas.

—Linus Pauling

The American legal system provides for many rights and protections for the owners of property. There are various types of property, of course, and the type of property that results from mental labor is called *intellectual property* (IP), which is the subject of this chapter. The main keys to protecting your IP are

- copyrights
- patents
- trade secrets
- trademarks

As you build your technology-based business, you will undoubtedly be creating value in intangible intellectual information. Many entrepreneurs have neglected the area of intellectual property, only to be crushed by their competition. You must understand and take advantage of the laws created for your protection as well as for the protection of others.

Your business may have more valuable intellectual property than you realize. Consider the value of

- new technology you are developing
- perhaps a new way of doing business
- your business plan
- your company name, logo, and website
- product manuals
- advertising programs and materials

Although it makes no sense for you to try to become a legal expert in IP law, a basic overview will help you to protect your company's interests, avoid infringing the rights of others, and work more effectively with your IP attorney. See Sidebar 19.1 for a comparison of the advantages and disadvantages of the four major types of intellectual property protection.

Copyrights

A *copyright* is protection by federal statute giving artists and authors the exclusive right to publish their works and to determine how their work is used. Copyright protection also extends to later versions or editions of the work. You will want your employees to assign to your company (the employer) any copyrights on materials you paid them to produce. Make sure that all employees and independent contractors (i.e., consultants) sign a document before they start working for you, acknowledging their obligation to assign appropriate copyrights and other IP to the company. Your attorney can provide you with a form agreement for this.

Note that a copyright protects only the *form* in which an idea is expressed (i.e., the particular *expression of an idea*), not the *idea* itself. This distinguishes copyrights from patents and trade secrets, which protect the substance of the invention or information, respectively.

For example, by reading this book you are exposed to some original ideas, which now can be freely used by you and anyone else who reads this book. However, if you expressed those ideas in an article or another book in the same form, using the words and phrases that appear here, you would be in violation of the copyright covering this book.

Although copyright protects the expression of an idea, but not the idea, in the real world the line between expression and idea is frequently gray, and thus it may be difficult to predict the outcome of a lawsuit for copyright infringement. If something is copied word for word, that's an easy infringement case. There can also be infringement if the work in question is "substantially similar" to the protected work.

There is a noteworthy exception, known as *fair use*, to the copyright holder's exclusive right to make copies, to make derivative works, and to distribute copies. The fair use exception permits most nonprofit, educational use of the protected work (e.g., for criticism, comment, news reporting, teaching, scholarship, or research).

In sharp contrast to patent protection, it is very easy and inexpensive to obtain copyright protection. In fact, no steps are required to obtain the copyright, since it automatically arises when an *author* (i.e., the creator of the work) creates an *original work* and fixes it in a tangible medium of expression (such as writing it on paper or storing it on a computer disk).

However, it is good practice to always put a copyright notice on the work. This copyright notice should include (1) the word "copyright", or the letter c in a circle— which is ©, (2) followed by the author's name and the year of publication, and (3) the phrase, "All rights reserved." An example is: "© 2003 by John Smith. All rights reserved." The copyright notice puts others on notice of the copyright, thus making it more difficult for an infringer to claim that his use was innocent. In short, the notice can improve the ability of the copyright holder to win damages in an infringement action.

Also, in order to file a lawsuit for copyright infringement in the U.S., the owner of the copyright must have actually registered their work with the U.S. Copyright Office in Washington, D.C. Since the amount and type of damages that may be obtained can be affected by when this registration is made, it is good practice to file your request early. This registration is easy to do and, unlike the patent application process, does not involve any review or approval by the government. You simply file a copy of the work as you register it. Special rules apply to the registration of software copyright, which is also easy to do. You can easily check out the specific forms and procedures at the U.S. Copyright Office website at www.copyright.gov.

Software developers have special concerns. One problem in interpreting copyrights is that the distinction between form (i.e., the "expression" of the idea) and substance (the "idea" itself) can become blurred. In drawings and blueprints, the form becomes the substance, since the form was most important to the creator. Similarly, in works of music, literature, and computer software, form often becomes very important in judging whether someone has stolen the fruits of creative effort. The debates and litigation several years ago as to the ownership rights to the copyrighted look and feel of a particular windows-style graphical user interface (GUI), for example, drive this point home.

For most types of technology and business information, a copyright will not be the best form of protection. You need to protect the substance of your ideas, not just the means or particular form of expressing them. In fact, placing a copyright notice on a document often implies publication to the world, which is inconsistent with trade secret protection (i.e., if you publish something, it is no longer a secret).

Before 1980, software was in a no-man's land in the area of copyrights. The U.S. Copyright Office had accepted copyright registration for software since 1964, but it was not until 1980 that the U.S. copyright law was amended to specifically include software. Where mass marketing of software makes contractual trade secret protection impractical, copyright registration may be the best alternative. Be aware that copyrighting your source code tells the entire world exactly how you wrote a program to perform a function. Copyrights make illegal the kind of outright copying practiced by software pirates. However, just as hardware engineers reverse-engineer semiconductor designs, software developers have become skilled at reverse-engineering software code, thereby writing their own software that performs the same tasks without infringing a copyright. As with patents and trade secrets, it is wise to get expert advice on the use of copyrights.

Because software (unlike hardware) is so easily and cheaply duplicated, the need for IP protection is that much greater. Many attorneys suggest that developers consider protecting their software with both copyright protection and either patent or trade secret protection.

Accordingly, although copyright has traditionally been the most common way to protect software, an important trend in the 1990s and into the 21st century has been a tremendous increase in the number of software patents issued. This reflects a growing belief that patents generally offer greater protection for software than do copyrights.

For individual authors, the term of copyright protection generally extends for the life of the author plus 70 years. For corporate owners of the copyright, the life of the copyright generally is 95 years. (In the U.S., the Sonny Bono Copyright Term Extension Act of 1998 retroactively extended by 20 years the duration of copyright protection to these longer periods of 70 and 95 years.)

Patents

A *patent* (or *patent of invention*) is the grant by the federal government to an inventor of an exclusive right to prevent anyone else from making, using, or selling the patented invention or process during a specified period of time. A patent gives its owner (or the owner's assignee) a legal monopoly during the term of the patent.

Patent infringement is the unauthorized making, use, or sale of an item or process that is patented. It does not matter whether the infringer actually knew of the patent at the time of infringement. Others who knowingly cause or contribute to the infringement may also be guilty of infringement.

The damages in a patent infringement case can be substantial. They may include actual damages, recovery of all profits earned by the infringer with the infringing product, triple damages for intentional infringement, and attorneys' fees.

The U.S. Patent and Trademark Office recognizes three categories of patents, and it is the first category that is of most interest to entrepreneurs.

- *utility patents*—In general, utility patents are for inventions that "do something" (in contrast to *design* patents and *plant* patents). Utility patents may be issued for four general categories of inventions.
  - *machines* (such as a machine for manufacturing integrated circuits)
  - *human-made products* (such as an ink-jet cartridge or a new type of pencil)
  - *compositions of matter* (such as a new chemical)
  - *processing methods* (such as a process for manufacturing razor blades)

Utility patents are the most common type of patent and generally the most important. Also, utility patents frequently cover *improvements* to existing inventions.

- *Design patents*—Design patents can protect new, original *ornamental* (as contrasted with useful) designs of articles or manufactured items (such as the unique shape and appearance of an Apple computer).

- *Plant patents*—Plant patents may apply to certain new varieties of plants. (They are mentioned here only for completeness of discussion and will not be discussed further.)

Utility patents last for 20 years from the date the patent application is filed, and design patents last for 14 years from the date the patent is issued.

As noted in the previous patent discussion, software companies that in the past relied on copyrights for protection now seek patent protection as well. Whereas a copyright covers only the code or instructions for a drop-down menu, for example, a patent may protect the concept of a drop-down menu itself.

An invention is not patentable unless it meets at least the following three criteria.

- *Usefulness*—The invention must be useful, which implies utility. This is generally interpreted to mean that the invention works, not that it is commercially useful. This requirement of usefulness is typically not a problem since profit-seeking companies are unlikely to pursue a patent for something that is useless. Design patents may be obtained for new, original, ornamental designs.

- *Novelty*—The invention must be novel. An invention is not novel if it was previously patented, used or known by others, or described in a written publication.

- *Nonobviousness*—The invention must also be nonobvious, meaning that it is so distinct from existing practice that it is not obvious to a person skilled in the relevant field. The U.S. Patent and Trademark Office will refuse your patent claims if it thinks the differences between your invention and prior art are obvious.

Business information and general know-how are not patentable and are best protected as trade secrets.

Another important issue regarding patents is timing. Delay in filing an application may cause the invention to be unpatentable. In the U.S., a patent application must be filed within one year of the first public use or offer for sale of the invention. Your patent application will be denied if your invention was already disclosed to the public more than one year before the date the patent application was filed. This very real limitation is called the *statutory bar*. Even the limited testing of your product by a few customers may cause a problem if not handled properly.

It is important to note that virtually no other country has this one-year grace period. Thus your patent applications in other counties may be denied if your invention has been disclosed before the *filing date* of your application. The safest approach, therefore, is to file before any sale or public disclosure of your invention. Since the laws and rules regarding these issues are complex (e.g., see the next paragraph), as are patent laws in general, you'll need the help of expert patent counsel—and sooner, rather than later.

Europe has a regional patent system that is run by the European Patent Office (EPO) (www.european-patent-office.org). A patent issued by the EPO is enforceable in most European countries, and the EPO thus represents an economical way, with one application, to get patent protection in several significant countries. Also, there are various treaties relating to patents and other forms of IP, including the Paris Convention, and most countries (including, of special note, the EPO countries, Japan, and the U.S.) are bound by these treaties. Under the Paris Convention, an applicant within a member country who files a timely patent application in one member country can file additional applications in other member countries within one year—and the later applications will receive the benefit of having the priority date of the first application.

Among the complex patent issues that may arise, requiring the attention of patent counsel, are

- deciding which patent applications should be filed
- the strategy as to when, and where in the world, patent applications should be filed
- conflicting patent claims as to a particular invention, and the handling of any patent disputes

It is easy to see why the issue of patents is so important to many companies. Just consider the range of possible outcomes.

- At the best, most wonderful end of the spectrum, the company pursues and obtains a *roadblock patent* that is so central and fundamental that all future inventors in the particular technical area need to use it.
- At the worst end of the spectrum, the company finds itself cut out of its target market because it slept on its rights and failed to file patent applications or otherwise protect its IP.

Here are a few pointers regarding patents and the protection of your IP.

- Keep detailed records, dated and signed (by both the inventor and a witness), of the process of creating the invention. Each employee and independent contractor should be issued an engineering workbook in which entries are made daily. These books should always remain the property of the company.
- Select your patent attorney with care. (See Sidebar 19.2, Intellectual Property Strategy for Entrepreneurs.)
- Each employee and independent contractor that may be involved, directly or indirectly, in the creation of any invention must sign, up front, an appropriate agreement transferring rights to the invention to your company. (Sometimes the company gets title and the employee gets a nonexclusive, royalty-free license.)
- Do not assume that something is not patentable merely because it seems pretty "obvious" to you. Entrepreneurs frequently make the mistake of underestimating what is patentable. Millions of patents have been issued, and the vast majority of them are in the "dry and boring" category, as opposed to something that stands out as "creative and insightful." Although patent attorneys charge high hourly rates, it won't take much time for your attorney to periodically review what you have been developing and to help determine whether a patent

application should be filed. (This review is usually a lot less expensive than is preparing and prosecuting a patent application.)

- Many patents do not cover new "stand-alone" inventions, but rather cover *improvements* to existing inventions. Such an improvement can be to an invention you previously made or to an invention made by any third party anywhere in the world.

- Since you won't have unlimited resources to devote to pursuing patents, you should try to focus on those technical areas and inventions that are closest to your core business.

- You should ask your attorney whether it makes sense in your particular situation to file a *provisional* patent application—which is similar to a utility patent application except that it does not have to contain the patent claims. Such a provisional application is not reviewed by the patent examiner, and it serves in effect as a placeholder for up to one year, giving you that much time to file a regular utility patent application (which later application will have a priority going back to the filing date of the earlier provisional application, provided the appropriate details of the invention have been disclosed in the earlier application). You may save some money doing it this way, at least in the short run, and you can still have the advantage of being able to claim "provisional patent application filed" on the product in question.

- Patents are sometimes used defensively in the event of an IP dispute. Faced with a competitor's claim of patent infringement, a company with a patent position may be able to assert that the competitor is infringing one or more of the company's patents. The resolution of such of a dispute is thus likely to be less costly and may involve a cross-licensing agreement.

- An intelligent IP protection program and a strong portfolio of patents are likely to be favorably viewed by third parties, including prospective venture investors and customers. Even the "Patent Pending" label on a product may assist your marketing and sales efforts.

The process of obtaining a patent consumes both time and money. The first step is the preparation and filing of a patent application, which takes careful thought and attention to detail if done correctly. The application is complex and requires a detailed description of the invention. Diagrams of the invention are typically included. The *patent claims* must be set forth, and this is done in a technical and legalistic style. To really understand and appreciate what this involves, you should read a few patent applications, if you haven't already done so. They are easy to find on the Internet. One good place to start is www.uspto.gov. (In the U.S., many patent applications are confidential until patent issuance, at which time they become part of the public record, and many others are published 18 months from the priority date.)

The patent applicant typically searches the *prior art* before preparing and filing the patent application. Prior art includes anything, whether patented or not, that is in the public domain and may relate to your patent claims. One reason for searching for the prior art is that there is no point wasting time and money filing a patent application if the invention is already patented or in the public domain. Also, the prior art frequently helps the patent attorney to draft the patent claims to get around the prior art. The application must include all prior art of which the applicant is aware, and it is thus usually best to use professional patent search firms to search for it. There can be a lot of frustration and wasted effort if you miss some relevant prior art and it is later discovered by the patent examiner (who does perform an independent search of the prior art) or a third party that seeks to contest your patent's validity. The intentional withholding of relevant prior art may be considered fraud by the U.S. Patent and Trademark Office.

After the patent application is filed with the U.S. Patent and Trademark Office, a patent examiner will review the application to determine whether a patent should be issued. This *patent examination* process (also called the patent *prosecution*) does not begin immediately and may take two years or more. Typically, there are communications back and forth between the patent examiner and the applicant during this process, and frequently the claims are modified or deleted before a patent issues.

The filing fees for a patent application are not insignificant, although they typically are dwarfed by the fees of your patent counsel. In 2001, the basic filing fee for a utility patent application was set at $370 for a "small entity" (fewer than 500 employees) and $740 for large companies. Also, there are other fees, including patent issuance fees ($640 for a qualifying small entity and $1280 for a large company) and patent maintenance fees that are due at 3.5 years, 7.5 years, and 11.5 years after issuance.

You can get lots of good free information about patents from the U.S. Department of Commerce's Patent and Trademark Office or the U.S. Superintendent of Documents. A good place to start is *Patents, Inventions: An Information Aid for Inventors and General Information Concerning Patents*, at www.uspto.gov/main/howdoi.htm.

Trade Secrets

Trade secret law in the U.S. is primarily a matter of state law (not federal law), and thus it varies somewhat from state to state. However, the broad principles of trade secret law tend to be quite similar.

A *trade secret* is generally defined to be

- any formula, plan, pattern, machine, mechanism, tool, compilation, technique, process, know-how, and so on, used in a business that gives the business a competitive advantage;

- that is not generally known by the company's competitors, and cannot be easily discovered by them through lawful means; and

- is subject to reasonable efforts by the company to maintain as secret.

All three of the above elements must be met, or trade secret protection will be lost.

Your attorney can help you establish a trade secret protection program. This can be done at a rather small cost, since many of the elements are similar from company to company. Your company's policies regarding trade secrets should be set forth in a written plan. The plan should give some guidance as to what constitutes a trade secret and how trade secrets are to be handled. Such a plan typically defines categories of information that should be treated confidentially (including a catch-all category for all other valuable secret information not known outside the company) and how the information should be marked (i.e., as "Confidential," or similar words). However, it is important that you not simply mark everything "Confidential." If you do so, a court may determine that you are not entitled to trade secret protection on anything (including your most valuable information) because you didn't view the concept of confidentiality seriously.

There is a line to draw here. You want your program to be comprehensive, but you don't want it so detailed that your employees and contractors will not understand it or be willing to implement it. The steps and precautions taken at a start-up to protect trade secrets will not be of the same magnitude as those taken by a Fortune 500 company. A typical trade secret protection program will include elements such as education and training for employees and contractors regarding the program; appropriate confidentiality agreements with all employees and contractors; both pre-employment and exit interviews; and internal and external security measures (such as passwords on computers, need-to-know considerations, communications with persons outside the company, physical security of business locations, destruction of confidential records, employees and contractors working away from the office, and so forth).

The bottom line is that you must take reasonably prudent steps to protect your trade secrets. Consider this: Why should a court give greater respect and protection to your company's trade secrets than the company itself gives?

In a legal proceeding to protect a trade secret, the claimant must be quite specific in defining the trade secret. Courts have ruled that trade secrets may consist of things such as the Coca-Cola™ formula, customer lists, marketing plans, cost and pricing data, and employee benefit information.

A trade secret (unlike a patent or copyright) need not be unique to the owner—it may be independently known to a few parties. In fact, over time, a trade secret may become a commonly known industry practice, at which time trade secret status will be lost.

There is no particular time limit on how long a trade secret may last. It lasts as long as the trade secret is kept confidential and still has value. Presumably, the soft drink company holding the secret formula for Coca Cola will try to keep the formula secret forever.

An idea does not need to be patentable to receive trade secret protection. Also, it is difficult to protect an invention by both patent and trade secret, since the information in a patent becomes public once the patent issues.

Trademarks

A *trademark* is any symbol, such as a word, combination of words, number, picture, sound or design, that is used by a company to identify its own products and distinguish them from products made or sold by others. A key purpose of trademarks is to avoid the confusion in the marketplace that could result if different manufacturers or vendors used the same trademark (or confusingly similar marks) to identify their products. Trademarks thus are intended to protect both consumers and trademark owners.

The *generic name* for an item, such as *automobile* or *computer*, cannot be used as a valid trademark. It is noteworthy that some words started out as good trademarks by the companies that created them, but then lost their legal status as trademarks when they became generically used by consumers to name the products. Examples are cellophane and aspirin. As a result, some companies, like Xerox, spend a lot of money on advertising campaigns to let consumers know that Xerox should not be used generically to mean "copier," but rather that Xerox is one brand of copier.

You may also encounter two other terms: *service mark* and *trade name*. A service mark is quite similar to a trademark except that it identifies a service rather than a product. The laws that govern service marks are almost identical to those that apply to trademarks. A trade name, however, is quite different from a trademark. A trade name is the official, legal name of a business. Sometimes, however, one word can be used by a company in both ways—such as the company Apple Computer, Inc. also using the word Apple to identify its computers.

Most entrepreneurs not only name their own companies but also select their own trademarks. Certain advertising and marketing firms offer excellent professional services regarding trademarks, but they may be too expensive for you. In any case, there are several factors to consider when selecting trademarks, and you may wish to run your plans by your attorney.

- To obtain the strongest form of trademark, you should pick one that is quite unique and distinctive. *Inherently distinctive* is a term frequently used to describe such strong marks. Made-up marks, such as "Kodak," are among the strongest. On the other hand, marks that are merely descriptive of the product, such as "Fast Truck," are not inherently distinctive, are considered weak marks, and thus typically are not subject to trademark protection.

- It is possible for a trademark that cannot initially be protected (because it is merely descriptive) to later become subject to protection if it acquires *secondary meaning* in the marketplace. The term *secondary meaning* means that many people over time have learned to associate the mark with a particular company. Perhaps the best high-tech example of this is the trademark "Windows." Although initially just descriptive, the term Windows acquired secondary meaning over time as many people began to associate it with Microsoft's operating system for personal computers. (At least, that is Microsoft's argument.) In spite of having its first trademark application rejected in 1993, Microsoft was eventually able in 1995 to register Windows as its trademark, with the obvious intention of preventing other companies from using it.

Note: The official registration of Windows was not the end of the story, since other parties have the right to contest the validity of a registration. In 2002 a federal court ruled that Windows is a generic term and thus Microsoft does not have the exclusive right to use it. The ruling was in a lawsuit brought by Microsoft to stop a company building a GNU/Linux-based operating system from using the terms LindowsOS (for its operating system) and Lindows.com (for its company name). Stay tuned for more appeals and legal challenges.

- A trademark search is necessary to determine that no one has already obtained the rights to the proposed trademark or to any trademark that is confusingly similar to it. The search should extend at least to those geographical areas in which you intend to do business or sell your product. There are state and federal computer databases of trademarks that can be used in this process. Also, trademark searches can be conducted in foreign countries. Trademark searches are frequently done by legal assistants.

- It may make sense to officially register your trademark on the Principal Register of the U.S. Patent and Trademark Office (PTO). After you file your trademark application, a PTO trademark examiner will conduct a search to determine if the proposed trademark is sufficiently distinctive to warrant trademark protection. This PTO process can sometimes drag on, with perhaps additional filings, and legal help may be advisable. A federal trademark registration lasts for 10 years, but it can be renewed an unlimited number of times. It is also possible to file an application for a state registration.

- Under the common law of the various states, a seller can obtain certain rights merely by using a trademark in commerce. It is therefore not necessary to register your trademarks, although doing this offers significant additional protection. A federal trademark registration is certainly advisable for critical trademarks. Among the advantages of a federal registration are the following.

  - the registration creates a presumption that everyone is aware of the trademark (which gets around the argument that any later infringing use was innocent or in good faith, and makes it easier for you to stop someone's infringement and perhaps collect damages in an infringement action)
  - the trademark can be declared incontestable after five years of use
  - the registration is strong evidence of ownership of the trademark, should someone contest it

- Trademarks can also be registered in other countries. They must be registered in each country where some form of trademark protection is sought. The registration of trademarks in other countries can be expensive.

- Unlike a patent or copyright, a trademark can last forever, provided it is not abandoned and the owner takes adequate steps along the way to protect it. There may be a presumption of abandonment if the trademark is not used for two years.

Sidebar 19.1 Advantages and Disadvantages of Different Types of Intellectual Property Protection

	copyright	patent	trade secret	trademark
benefits	Prevents copying of a wide array of artistic and literary expressions, including software; very inexpensive	Very strong protection; provides exclusive right to make, use, and sell an invention; protects the idea itself	Very broad protection for sensitive, competitive information; very inexpensive	Protects marks that customers use to identify business; prevents others from using confusingly similar identifying marks
duration	Life of author plus 70 years; for corporations, 95 years from date of first publication or 100 years from date of creation, whichever is shorter	20 years from date of filing the patent application	So long as the information remains valuable and is kept confidential	So long as the mark is not abandoned and steps are taken to police its use
weaknesses	Protects only the particular way an idea is expressed, not the idea itself; apparent lessening of protection for software; hard to detect copying in digital age	High standards of patentability; often expensive and time-consuming to pursue (especially where overseas patents are needed); must disclose invention to public	No protection from accidental disclosure, independent creation by a competitor, or disclosure by someone without a duty to maintain confidentiality	Limited scope; protects corporate image and identity but little else; can be costly if multiple overseas registrations are needed
required steps	None required; however, notice and filing can strengthen rights	Detailed filing with U.S. Patent and Trademark Office that requires search for prior art and hefty fees	Take reasonable steps to protect— generally a trade secret protection program	Only need to use mark in commerce; however, filing with U.S. Patent and Trademark Office is usually desirable to gain stronger protections
U.S. rights valid internationally?	Generally, yes	No. Separate patent examinations and filings are required in each country; however, a single filing in the European Patent Office can cover a number of European countries	No. Trade secret laws vary significantly by country, and some countries have no trade secret laws	No. Separate filings are required in foreign jurisdictions, and a mark available in the U.S. may not be available overseas

Used with permission from Constance E. Bagley and Craig E. Dauchy, "The Entrepreneur's Guide to Business Law," copyright © 1998, by West Educational Publishing Company.

Sidebar 19.2 Intellectual Property Strategy for Entrepreneurs

The following advice is provided by Edward Radlo, a patent attorney and partner in the prominent Silicon Valley law firm of Fenwick & West.

Intellectual property (IP) consists mainly of patents, trademarks, copyrights, trade secrets, and, in the semiconductor industry, mask work protection. The strongest form of IP protection is obtained with patents. Compared with a copyright, a patent protects the underlying idea and not just the expression of the idea. Furthermore, a patent protects against an infringer regardless of whether the infringer copied the patented idea or came up with the invention on his own.

In October 1982, the patent system in the U.S. was dramatically strengthened by the creation of the Court of Appeals for the Federal Circuit (CAFC), a new court having judges with technical backgrounds and trained in patent law. The CAFC is at the same level within the federal judiciary as a Circuit Court of Appeals (i.e., one level below the United States Supreme Court). Prior to 1982, the federal courts upheld the validity of patents in less than 50% of litigated cases. Since 1982, the CAFC has been upholding the validity of contested patents at about the 80% level. As a result, industry has significantly stepped up the filing of patent applications.

In the 1990s, two major trends in patent law were

- the acceptance of software patents
- the acceptance of patents on methods of doing business

In view of these trends, venture capitalists and other investors now look very carefully at a new company's patent position in determining whether to invest and, if so, at what valuation. Therefore, it behooves the entrepreneur to try to nail down significant patent protection for the crown jewels of a company's technology at a relatively early stage.

First of all, the crown jewels must be identified. Something that is tremendously innovative may not qualify if there is no prospect of a significant market for the innovation in the foreseeable future. Similarly, a new product that is expected to sell well may be difficult to patent if it is in a field in which others have previously staked out strong patent positions. In order for the entrepreneur to get the most value for his dollar, the best candidates for patenting are those inventions that are

- technically very innovative, and
- in emerging strong markets

These inventions should be protected in those countries where there is expected to be significant manufacturing, sales, and/or use.

As for cost, good patent attorneys are not inexpensive. The entrepreneur may be tempted to save money by shopping around for patent practitioners with relatively low hourly rates, and he may attempt to place harsh time or cost restraints upon his patent attorney. This is not a good strategy, because the quality of patent practitioners varies greatly and the degree of protection is related to the level of effort expended on preparing the patent application and in prosecuting it to issuance.

I have seen examples where *a difference of one word in a patent claim has meant the difference of millions of dollars* to the patentee once the patent has been litigated.

The best strategy for the entrepreneur is to choose a patent attorney carefully, performing due diligence on the prospective attorney by asking a lot of questions regarding that attorney's background, experience, and track record. Once the attorney has been selected, the entrepreneur should trust the attorney as a partner and not attempt to micromanage the attorney's time within the attorney's realm of expertise.

Trademarks can also be a very powerful means of intellectual property protection for a young company, and can generally be obtained at less cost than patents. One wonders, for example, whether Apple Computer would have made the great impact upon the nascent personal computer industry in the 1980s if it didn't have the warm and fuzzy trademarks of "Apple" and "Macintosh" luring technologically naïve users into the fold.

With trade secrets, it is important to identify them and to treat them as secrets from the outset. This doesn't require much effort on the part of the entrepreneur, but it has to be done at very early stages in order to be most effective.

Much copyright protection can be automatically obtained with virtually no effort. For minimal effort, copyright notices can be affixed to important creations such as software and written documents. For a little more effort, copyrights can be registered with the U.S. Copyright Office in order to ensure that the copyright owner will be able to collect statutory damages in case of infringement.

Used with permission from Fenwick & West LLP.

20

The Legal Form of Your Start-Up

Form follows function.

—Louis Henri Sullivan

When formally establishing your business, you can choose from a variety of legal entities, and you need to make a wise choice. The one that is most appropriate for you depends upon your particular situation, including some consideration of what you intend to accomplish with your start-up in the years ahead. Who will be the owners, now and in the future? Is the business expected to run losses for quite some time, or will it become profitable in a short period of time? How will you raise needed investment capital for the business? What exit strategy for the company do you contemplate? Perhaps a public offering?

This chapter provides an overview of the main choices. In deciding what's best, you need to work closely with a competent attorney who specializes in business formation. It is important that you properly establish your start-up and operate it in accordance with applicable laws, including the state laws under which it is created. If you don't, the consequences can be severe. For example, if you incorporate your business, you may lose the corporate shield of limited liability if you don't follow certain corporate formalities. Your experienced business attorney can guide you through the process.

A business can be established in one of four main forms.

- Corporation
    - C Corporation (or General Corporation)
    - S Corporation
    - Close Corporation
    - Nonstock Corporation
- Partnership
    - General Partnership
    - Limited Partnership
- Limited Liability Company (LLC)
- Sole Proprietorship

Each of these forms is discussed in the sections that follow.

Corporation

C Corporation (or General Corporation)

Most product-related, high-growth engineering businesses will need to be incorporated, if for no other reason than to establish an efficient mechanism for the ownership and distribution of assets and profits over time as the business grows. A *C corporation*, which is also known as a *general corporation*, is the most common type of corporation for this purpose. (The "C" comes from a subchapter of the Internal Revenue Code, Subchapter C, that sets forth the tax characteristics of corporations in general, and it's the chapter that applies after other types of legal forms have been considered and rejected.) A corporation is perhaps best thought of as a fictitious being or artificial entity independent of the owners or investors. This artificial entity may conduct a business or businesses in its own name much in the way that a real person can. Business is done, assets are acquired, contracts are entered into, and liabilities are incurred, all in the name of the corporation rather than in the name of any individual. Ownership in a corporation is represented by shares of stock that are held by shareholders or stockholders.

A central advantage of a corporation is that it provides its owners (the shareholders) with protection against personal liability for the debts and obligations of the corporation. However, it is important that the corporation be operated properly to maintain this protection. Under the doctrine of *piercing the corporate veil*, if shareholders have blurred the distinction between themselves and the corporation, they should not be permitted to seek protection behind the corporate veil. If the corporate veil is successfully pierced, individual shareholders (in addition to the corporation) may be held liable. To help minimize this risk, it is important to maintain corporate separateness by following corporate formalities and legal requirements, including

- properly issuing stock
- maintaining proper corporate records, including minutes of meetings of directors and shareholders

- keeping separate bank accounts for the corporation and not commingling corporate and personal assets
- making sure the corporation is adequately capitalized

If shareholders have used the corporation to further criminal activity, fraud, or the like, a court may ignore the corporate entity and hold the shareholders personally liable for the obligations of the corporation.

Most professional venture investors (venture capital firms and many corporations) will expect the start-up to be a C corporation and not one of the other types of entities discussed here. A C corporation can have an unlimited number of shareholders, and it's usually the appropriate form for companies planning to sell stock publicly at some point to a large number of investors.

The vast majority of venture funds raise at least some of their money from limited partners that are tax-exempt entities (pension funds, profit-sharing funds, charitable organizations, and the like). Because of tax considerations, these tax-exempt limited partners require that the venture capital fund not invest in any business that is organized as a tax pass-through entity (e.g., a general or limited partnership, a limited liability company, or an S corporation). This is why venture capitalists invest almost exclusively in C corporations.

S Corporation

An *S corporation* is not incorporated as an "S" corporation. Rather, a C corporation simply becomes an S corporation when its shareholders make an election with the Internal Revenue Service that allows the corporation's income and losses to be ignored at the corporate level and passed through to the shareholders. (The "S" comes from the fact that the election is made under Subchapter S of the U.S. Internal Revenue Code.) In order for an S election to be valid, the corporation must meet certain guidelines, which include the following.

- There can be no more than 75 shareholders in an S corporation.
- All of the shareholders must be citizens or permanent residents of the U.S.
- Certain entities, including partnerships, corporations, and trusts, cannot be shareholders.
- The S corporation may issue only one class of stock.
- Not all general corporations are eligible for S status. For example, banks and insurance companies are excluded.

In effect, these restrictions mean that venture capital firms and corporate investors will not invest in S corporations. Of particular note is the requirement that an S corporation have only one class of stock. Venture capital investments are typically structured with two classes of stock, common and preferred, for several reasons, a key one of which is to get around potential tax issues facing founders and employees when they receive so-called *cheap stock*.

It should be noted that an S corporation may be changed into a C corporation through the intentional or unintentional violation of one of the S restrictions listed previously. For example, if the number of shareholders increases to more than 75, then the S corporation automatically becomes a C corporation. Of course, it's better to manage such things with a plan and not by mistake or oversight. The latter would not impress an investor. It may make sense in certain situations to start the business as an S corporation (which, for example, would allow expected losses in the early years to be passed through to the shareholders) and then transform it into a C corporation later.

Close Corporation

Several states have enacted statutes permitting a form of entity called a *close corporation*, with the intention of simplifying the requirements placed on regular corporations. However, in practice, this option is rarely used, and this discussion is included primarily for general background, since you may hear about this form of entity.

A close corporation is a corporation that is owned by a limited number of shareholders (typically from one up to 30 or 35, depending on the state) who generally are active in the business of the corporation. Various restrictions apply. For example, a close corporation typically must first offer shares of stock to its existing shareholders before offering to sell them to others, and there can be no public sale of stock. A close corporation is not recognized in all states. In addition, the law that applies to close corporations is not well developed.

These facts, plus the fact that most attorneys are not familiar with close corporations, tend to make the required legal work more difficult and expensive. It is likely that your attorney will not even consider it an option for your venture.

Nonstock Corporation

A *nonstock corporation* will not be a viable choice for your high-growth, high-tech company. This discussion is included simply for general background information.

A nonstock corporation is an appropriate form for companies dedicated to not-for-profit purposes, including charitable, religious, literary, educational, scientific, or public safety purposes. Nonstock companies may also be used for homeowner associations, political organizations, trade associations, community activities, and the like. Voting members elect a board of directors, which runs the corporation. Bylaws define the qualifications for membership and so forth. As implied in the name, a nonstock corporation has no stockholders. Many of these corporations apply for nonprofit, tax-exempt status under Section 501(c)(3) of the Internal Revenue Code.

Partnership

A partnership is a business conducted by two or more people. A partnership can be either a *general partnership* or a *limited partnership*.

General Partnership

Each partner in a general partnership is a *general partner*, and as such has unlimited liability for the debts and liabilities of the partnership. Each partner can act for the others. Liability issues are therefore of central importance. At a minimum, the general partners should all know one another and have great confidence in each other. Care in selecting the general partners is critical.

A partnership is the simplest form of organization involving more than one person. It is formed by agreement of the partners, who share the right to manage and the right to participate in the profits. Although the partnership agreement does not even have to be in writing, for many reasons it is generally best to have an appropriate partnership agreement prepared and signed. This agreement will cover numerous important subjects, such as the split of profits and losses among the partners, the term of the partnership, salaries, responsibilities and duties of the partners, and what happens if a partner withdraws or dies. The laws governing partnerships permit great flexibility in how partnerships are designed and run. As a result, partnership agreements vary greatly and are more expensive to put in place.

A partnership may be viewed as a separate legal entity for some purposes. For example, it can hold title to property, and it can sue and be sued as an entity. On the other hand, if a partner dies or withdraws from the partnership, the entity dissolves (unlike a corporation, which has a life of its own and survives unaffected by the death of a shareholder)—although the partnership agreement may provide a way for the partnership business to be carried on. For example, it may provide for the election of a new general partner or the continuation of the business by the remaining partners.

Some service-related engineering consultancies could be operated as partnerships (where there is less need for capital), and a simple formula could determine how profits would be divided. The typical start-up entrepreneur who is interested in high-growth, however, will be trying to build value in the equity of an incorporated (and usually product-related) business. That equity should be shared in order to motivate the key players and attract needed investment.

Limited Partnership

A *limited partnership* has at least one *general partner* and at least one *limited partner*. The general partners in a limited partnership each have the same broad powers and liability of general partners in a general partnership. On the other hand, the liability of the limited partners is limited to the amount of capital they have invested in the limited partnership. However, limited partners run the risk of being treated like general partners if they get involved in the control of the limited partnership. Only the general partners may exercise control.

Many business activities that traditionally were conducted by limited partnerships (e.g., real estate investments) are now handled more and more by limited liability companies which, as discussed in the next section, have become very popular.

Limited Liability Company (LLC)

The roots of the *limited liability company* (LLC) in the U.S. go back to 1977 when Wyoming became the first state to pass legislation permitting this form of business

organization. However, its popularity really didn't take off until the IRS, in a 1988 ruling, clarified the tax treatment of an LLC in Wyoming. The central issue raised was
whether the LLC would be taxed as a corporation or a partnership, and the IRS determined that it would be treated as a partnership for tax purposes. This meant that an
LLC's taxable profits and losses could pass through to the individual owners of the
LLC, without the LLC also being taxed as a separate entity. Since one level of taxation
is better than two, LLCs became more attractive and their popularity increased quickly in the 1990s and into this millennium.

An LLC is best viewed as a hybrid between a partnership and a corporation that
enjoys some distinct advantages of each. First, it has the pass-through income tax
advantages of a partnership (*single taxation*, not *double taxation*) while avoiding many
of the drawbacks associated with forming an S corporation (which is also taxed as a
partnership). For example, S corporations cannot have corporate shareholders, but
LLCs can. Also, LLCs can typically have any number of members, while S corporations are limited to 75. Second, an LLC provides its members with protection against
personal liability that is similar to the protection offered by a corporation. The LLC's
owners (referred to as *members*) are not personally liable for the debts and other obligations of the LLC as such, although each member is responsible for his own acts and
omissions relating to the LLC (just as each officer and director of a corporation is
liable for his or her own acts and omissions).

Given the limited liability protection of the LLC, many businesses seeking pass-
through tax advantages find it more beneficial to organize as an LLC than as a partnership (whether general or limited). Although the S corporation and the LLC both
offer limited liability, the S corporation is frequently less beneficial, due to some of its
limitations: only one class of stock; a limit of 75 shareholders; and limitations as to
who can be shareholders (no foreigners and not all types of entities). Many professional
services businesses, such as law firms and engineering firms, are now set up as LLCs.

An LLC is run in accordance with its *operating agreement*. Because this agreement
typically needs to be specially crafted to fit the particular situation, the legal costs tend
to be higher. Also, it is difficult to take an LLC public and, in any case, investors simply don't understand the LLC as well as they understand the C corporation.

An LLC can convert to a corporation at any time by incorporating. Therefore, some
start-ups might find it attractive to start as an LLC (especially if they wanted early substantial losses to flow through to their investors) and then incorporate later (say, for
example, when they planned to pursue more traditional venture capital funding). A
biotech company with corporate investors could fit this situation.

Sole Proprietorship

In a sole proprietorship, the entire business is owned by one person. That person
owns all of the business' assets and is personally liable for all of its obligations. He or
she has complete managerial control. *Sole proprietorship* literally means one owner, and
the business has no legal existence separate from its owner. Most businesses are sole

proprietorships, mainly because most businesses are one-person affairs and a sole proprietorship is the easiest way for them to do business. No separate tax returns are filed for the business; rather, all expenses and income appear on the individual's tax returns. A sole proprietorship typically is not required to have an *employee identification number* (EIN) from the IRS unless it has employees.

How does a person start a sole proprietorship? Nothing could be simpler—the person can just start running the business in his own name, without setting up any special legal entity. (If he wishes to run the company under a name other than his own, he needs to file a *fictitious business name statement*, which is easy to do.) In theory at least, a sole proprietorship could be the largest business in the world, but there are numerous reasons why a separate legal entity would be used in that case.

A start-up could begin as a sole proprietorship and then later be set up as a corporation or other business entity when the time is ripe. In any case, this book assumes that your high-growth start-up venture will very early on be established as a separate legal entity, most likely as a C corporation, for the reasons stated previously in this chapter.

Miscellaneous Legal and Business Matters

Your attorney should provide you with a standard checklist of miscellaneous legal and business items for you to review and act upon as appropriate. Corporate *good housekeeping* is important. Take the time to do things right from the beginning, and you will save time and money in the long run.

Your legal checklist will include items such as

- tax matters (income tax reporting, collecting sales taxes, etc.)
- employee matters (tax withholding, etc.)
- registration as a foreign (i.e., out-of-state) entity in other states
- insurance (general liability, fire and casualty, workers' compensation, etc.)
- company name (selection and protection)
- fictitious business name statements
- trademarks
- business licensing (state, county, and local)

Depending on the particular item, the legal requirements may vary significantly among the states, counties, and local jurisdictions. It is thus beyond the scope of this book to get into the details. Appendix A.2 identifies some good sources of information for these matters. However, it is important that you coordinate closely with your attorney, since it is easy to stumble and the cost of a mistake or oversight can be high.

Work with a First-Class Lawyer

It is very tempting to incorporate your business yourself. While this is quite easy and fun to do, and while there are dozens of books and websites that will lead you through every step of the procedure in your state, you should incorporate with the aid of a good lawyer. Lots of businesses offer incorporation services for a hundred dollars or so, but do not be tempted to use them. If you are serious about creating a high-growth start-up, you will need a good lawyer working with you over the next few years, and you will need expert advice from day one. If you go to a good lawyer with your incorporation papers in hand and ask him or her to represent you, it is likely to cost you more in legal fees than if you had asked him or her to handle everything from the beginning. This is true for a number of reasons: (1) you may have prepared the wrong forms or even classified your company as the wrong type of business entity, (2) the attorney will have to take extra time to review unfamiliar forms, and (3) it's least expensive to have your attorney provide a set of standard legal forms and documents with which he or she is already familiar and which all play together. Although using a first-class lawyer can consume a lot of money very quickly, it will be worth it in the long run if you plan to grow a successful company and take it to an IPO.

21

Making the Start-Up Decision

Do not follow where the path may lead. Go instead where there is no path and leave a trail.

—Entrepreneur's creed

How Committed Are You?

More and more frequently, start-up entrepreneurs are forced to provide some of their own seed funds before attracting venture capital in today's investment climate. If you were fortunate enough to have been able to acquire a house, drawing on your own personal reserves probably means obtaining a loan (probably a second mortgage) against your house, or at least using it as collateral for an equity line of credit. If you are not careful, losing your house is a very real possibility if your business fails. When corporations go bankrupt, most creditors are limited to attaching the assets of the corporation (assuming you have properly run the corporation in accordance with applicable law and thus have not given the creditors any basis for "piercing the corporate veil" and going after you personally). However, if you personally guarantee a business loan and secure it with your house, then you and your house are fair play for your secured creditors. If you loaned your company funds obtained from a loan on your house, on the other hand, or if you purchased preferred stock, you might be in a little better position. Chapter 16 discusses sophisticated ways to best risk your own personal capital (e.g., investment through the provision of real property); it is wise to use these techniques if you decide to mortgage your house.

Leaving a Current Employer

With rare exception, it is best not to give your employer notice or let it know anything about your plans to create a start-up until everything is planned to your satisfaction and you have sufficient funds to see yourself through the concept development stage. (One exception is if you are counting on using technology owned by your employer or you otherwise need to negotiate something with your employer. In this case you will probably need to contact your employer earlier, before you have gone too far down a path only to find yourself blocked, and before you raise any money from outside investors.) See Sidebar 21.1, Summary of Permissible Activities While Still Employed by Another.

Obligations to Your Employer

In any case, it is important that you understand your obligations to your employer and not do anything during employment, or after your employment terminates, that will violate any of these obligations. There are several things to consider, including

- any and all agreements you have with your employer, such as
  - a nondisclosure agreement (which typically prohibits any improper or unauthorized use or disclosure of the employer's trade secrets, confidential information, etc., whether during employment or after employment ends)
  - an assignment of all intellectual property to the employer
  - a *covenant not to compete*
  - an *antipiracy clause* (which prevents you from soliciting or hiring coworkers, typically for a stated period of time after your employment ends)
  - a *no-moonlighting* provision preventing you from engaging in any other business (whether after hours or not, and whether or not it relates to your job with your employer)
- whether, above and beyond any agreements you have signed, there are other obligations generally imposed by law (such as an employee's duty of loyalty, discussed later in this chapter, and an obligation not to misappropriate trade secrets) that may restrict what you wish to do
- the nature of your position with your employer—whether, on one hand, you are an officer, director, manager, or skilled professional (such as a software engineer) who is held to higher standards or, on the other hand, you are an unskilled employee
- whether your planned business activities will compete with your employer's business

- whether your start-up constitutes a *corporate opportunity* that you must first offer your employer before you can pursue it. (These offers are frequently rejected, although you cannot rely on receiving a timely response). Does the opportunity fall within your employer's line of business? Presenting the opportunity to your employer, with the disclosure of all significant facts, helps create a *safe harbor*.
- whether you intend to hire any employees of your employer

The importance of the second point on the list needs to be stressed—namely, that certain obligations and restrictions may be imposed generally by law, even if the employee has no signed agreement with the employer. In particular, the misappropriation (i.e., theft, or improper use or disclosure) of trade secrets is unlawful in all states, whether or not the employee has signed an agreement covering the subject. (Trade secrets are discussed in Ch. 19 and, notwithstanding the foregoing comment, it is strongly recommended that you have appropriate nondisclosure disagreements signed by your start-up's employees and contractors.)

See Sidebar 21.2 for an interesting account of one of Mike Baird's start-ups, including corporate opportunity and related issues.

Obligations of Different Types of Employees

Just as an employer has certain duties toward its employees, all employees have a duty to work in good faith on behalf of the employer and not to do anything that is adverse to the best interests of the employer. The duties of *unskilled workers* usually apply to the actual hours they are on the job; what they do after hours is their own business (except to the extent they harm the employer's interests or there is a contractual restriction, such as a covenant not to compete). Those individuals held to higher standards (often called *key employees* and *skilled employees*) have a *duty of loyalty* to the employer, whether or not there is a written employment contract. (It is sometimes unclear whether a particular employee is a key employee or a skilled employee. In general, key employees include managers, along with officers and directors of the company, and skilled employees for a high-tech start-up include such positions as software and hardware engineers, as well as sales and marketing professionals.) This duty of loyalty usually includes not seizing a *corporate opportunity* (discussed in the previous section) and not operating a competing business while still employed. While employed with the employer, they may make plans to set up a competing business, but they cannot actually operate such a business or solicit employees of the employer.

Whether Your Start-Up Competes with Your Employer

As noted previously, whether your new business will compete with your employer is one key factor in determining what you can and cannot do while still employed with your employer and thereafter. In either case there are restrictions, but the restrictions are greater in the case of a competing business. (In either case, carefully review all items listed previously in the section entitled Obligations to Your Employer.)

If your start-up will not compete with your employer, then in general you are free to set up and operate the business, provided that

- this does not violate any agreement you have with your employer (e.g., a no-moonlighting provision)
- this does not interfere with your job responsibilities to your employer, and
- you conduct all your activities after hours and not use any resources of your employer (such as telephone, computers, and facilities) in connection with your start-up. Unless you have specific work hours, it may be unclear what "after hours" means.

In general, this is true whether or not you are considered a key employee.

However, if your new start-up will compete with your employer, you are much more restricted as to what you can and cannot do. While still employed with the employer, key employees and skilled employees cannot *operate* a competing business. Also, they cannot do anything (such as planning the start-up, etc.) that interferes with carrying out their job responsibilities to their employer.

Assuming you are a key employee or skilled employee who is prohibited from operating a competing business while still employed by your employer, the following are some suggestions of things that you can pursue to prepare for business without actually operating the business while still employed.

- Lease office space and rent furniture.
- Reserve phone numbers and URLs.
- Print business cards and letterhead.
- Work on a business plan.
- Retain and work with your attorney.

You should not, however,

- Order materials.
- Pre-sell customers.
- Hire employees.
- Develop a product prototype (that may then belong to your employer).

To emphasize again, do not prepare your business plan at work or use your employer's resources (computer, copy machine, fax, secretary, telephone, etc.).

Since your new competing venture is unlikely to have any revenue for a period of time, you may be tempted to continue working with your employer after you have started operating your new competing venture. This is definitely not a good idea—don't do it.

The covenant not to compete and hiring coworkers from your employer are discussed in the following two sections.

Covenant Not to Compete

As for competing with your employer after the termination of employment, a *covenant not to compete* (also called a *noncompete clause*) is among the restricting agreements you need to look for as you consider your obligations to your employer. Perhaps you or other participants in your start-up have signed such a covenant with your employer.

These noncompete agreements are subject to state law, which can vary somewhat depending on how the particular state has balanced the respective interests of employers and employees. State law includes both statutes passed by the legislature and law created in written decisions by the judiciary (called *common law*). In general, a covenant not to compete must meet certain requirements in order to be legal and enforceable by a court. These requirements are

- *Limited scope*—The covenant not to compete cannot be too broad in terms of time (duration), geographical area, or activities covered. Courts decide these disputes on a case-by-case basis. Perhaps a one-year restriction makes sense in one case, and a longer duration is permitted in another. Perhaps a 100-mile radius restriction is geographically too broad because the employer does not currently do business in the whole area. What happens if a court concludes that a covenant not to compete is just too broad? It can either throw out the whole clause or it can rewrite and narrow the clause to make it enforceable. This latter process is called *blue-lining*. The typical well-drafted covenant will include a blue-lining clause stating that, in the event the covenant is determined to be too broad, the court should, in effect, rewrite the clause and interpret it to the maximum extent permitted under applicable law.

- *Protection of legitimate interests*—The covenant not to compete must protect clear legitimate interests of the employer, not simply restrict competition. Such legitimate interests may include things such as customer lists, long-term customer relationships, product designs, and other trade secrets or confidential information.

- *Existence of ancillary agreement*—Because of certain public interests (more on this in the next paragraph), the covenant not to compete must be part of some other lawful agreement between the parties, such as an employment contract or an agreement to sell a business. A covenant not to compete simply standing by itself will usually not be enforced. In many states it is considered a *per se* violation (meaning a violation *by itself* or *taken alone*).

- *A balancing of public interests*—When deciding cases involving covenants not to compete, courts look at the various interests of the public that are involved. On one hand, there's a public interest in healthy competition and having individuals free to practice their trades, use their skills, work wherever they want, and even establish their own businesses. On the other hand, employers have an interest in being protected from unethical or shady business practices, such as a former employee exploiting trade secrets or other valuable assets of the employer. (A key underlying belief is that laws that protect intellectual property create an incentive for individuals and companies to spend resources on inventing things and developing better products, and that this protective approach better serves the public interest than would a system that would allow anyone to freely use another's intellectual property.) This balancing process is also reflected to some extent in each of the other restrictions discussed previously.

As noted previously, the law regarding covenants not to compete varies from state to state and is created by both the legislative branch (in legislation) and the judicial branch (in its decisions). Several states have enacted legislation as to the enforceability of covenants not to compete, but it is beyond the scope of this book to present the details. As an example, however, it's noted that California is one of the states with a statute that broadly prohibits the enforceability of these covenants, subject to narrowly defined exceptions (one of which is in connection with the purchase and sale of the goodwill of a business).

Hiring Employees of Your Employer

Take extreme care in hiring other employees of your employer. There are several issues to consider here. You must make certain that anyone you hire does not violate any agreement by which he or she may be restricted (e.g., a covenant not to compete, a nondisclosure agreement, or an employment contract). For example, if the coworker you want to hire is under an employment contract to work for the employer for a certain length of time, it is possible that you could face a claim for *intentional interference with contract*. Whether or not the coworker is restricted by a written contract, you must in addition make certain that the coworker does not bring any trade secrets or other property of the employer to your new venture. Legal claims for theft or misappropriation of trade secrets are all too common and are generally very difficult and expensive to defend. In addition, key employees are further limited when it comes to solicitation of coworkers. Specifically, there may be a claim for *breach of fiduciary duty*, or possibly even fraud, if a key employer induces an employee to leave for a competing venture. This may be the case even if the departing employee has no employment contract.

Hiring employees from your employer while you are still employed may also get you in a lot of trouble. James Pooley, Esq., of Milbank, Tweed, Hadley & McCloy LLP, suggests,

> If approached by members of your present staff, simply thank them for their interest and explain that you cannot respond to their request until you have departed. Then note the solicitation in your records for later reference and follow-up.

One goal here is to avoid a claim by the employer that you are soliciting the employer's employees. When you announce that you are leaving and people ask what you are going to do, you can let them know you are planning a start-up and give them your telephone number. They can contact you later if interested and, if done this way, you are in a much better position to assert that you are not soliciting them.

The Risks and Costs of Litigation

Although it may surprise you, your current employer may frown upon your leaving to create your start-up. After all, anyone with the qualities of a start-up entrepreneur is likely to be a highly valued employee in most larger companies. Also, it seems that you have created a great opportunity, and you may leave behind some envious people. You might very well be accused of everything from theft of company property to denying your employer a business opportunity. Be very careful to do all reasonable legal and ethical things expected of you. Make sure you leave behind or return everything your employer owns or makes claims to, no matter how tempting they might be to take home or photocopy.

In reviewing and meeting your obligations to your employer, don't underestimate either the probability or cost of litigation if you act improperly. It's possible that the costs of litigation alone could kill your new venture. Don't get cavalier about your responsibilities to your employer (such as by misappropriating trade secrets) because you think or hear that "it's not a big deal" or "everyone does it," and that employers often don't do anything about it. Well, not everyone does it. Also, sometimes the employer chooses not to act simply because the start-up is not seen as a serious threat. However, if the start-up does well, the odds of litigation increase because the start-up is a more attractive target.

Any litigation or threatened litigation by your employer can cause bad publicity and have numerous other negative impacts on your fragile start-up. For example, if you are about to close a critical capital investment in your start-up by professional investors, the actual or threatened litigation is probably going to either kill the deal or greatly delay it. In addition, there are various legal remedies your employer could seek—including a claim for substantial damages and a request for an injunction to prevent your use or disclosure of the employer's trade secrets or your employment of "pirated" employees.

As a practical matter, the risks of litigation are much higher when your start-up is planning to do something that competes with or relates to your employer's business or planned business. Also, the risks are typically greater if several employees leave to join the venture, as opposed to one person striking out on his own. You should definitely expect litigation if your employer believes you are misappropriating trade secrets or anything else of value.

By being prudent, proactive, and ethical in planning your business, you can eliminate or at least greatly reduce the possibility of litigation.

Additional Suggestions on Leaving Your Employer

Here are a few additional suggestions for you to consider when leaving your current employer to launch your start-up.

- Make sure you transfer important information and knowledge of technology to the employer when you leave. Depending on your situation, you may decide to offer to consult with them if they need you in the future.

- Return all property of the employer, including information you may have at home. If you have any company information on a home computer, delete all the company files from your hard drives.

- It's a good idea to involve your attorney early in the process, as you plan your start-up and decide when and how you'll leave your employer. A key goal is to do things right and avoid litigation.

- Keep a separate personal calendar and notebook (that you paid for) for documenting activities at your many start-up meetings.

- Be completely honest if you have an exit interview, but do not offer any more information than you are asked for. You are not obligated to respond in great detail to open-ended questions or requests like, "tell me everything you did in preparing for your new business." A suitable response might be, "Can you make your question more specific so that I can give you a meaningful response?"

One of your key goals should be to leave your employer on good terms. Be professional. Take the high road. David Bowen, publisher of *Software Success*, notes,

> You may want to go back to work for your old company, so make sure that you abide by the spirit of your agreements and commitments as well as the letter. If there is any way to leave on good terms, I advise you to do it. Your karma will follow you.

Although Bowen gave this advice several years ago (shortly before his untimely death), it was based on good old-fashioned honesty and fair dealing, and it is especially appropriate today.

As you leave your employer, don't lie about your plans. Departing employees who lie (by saying, for example, that they are planning to start a totally noncompeting business such as a bowling alley) are likely to cause the employer to be angry and suspicious when the truth becomes known. It's human nature to assume the worst when someone lies to you. The "innocent lie" (there's no such thing in this situation) may cause your former employer to assume the worst and hit you with a lawsuit claiming theft of trade secrets and other wrongs.

Of course, there are many other reasons why you should leave on good terms, including your integrity and reputation (valuable assets, which you need to jealously guard), the possibility of doing business with your employer in the future, the need for good references, the need for solid positive feedback when someone (e.g., a prospective investor) does due diligence on you, and the possibility that you may someday wish to work for your employer again.

Your Employer as a Strategic Partner or Investor

It may make strategic sense for you to ask your employer to invest money or perhaps other assets in your start-up. Especially if your new business relates in some way to the business of your employer, you may gain numerous advantages by aligning your interests this way. Perhaps your employer will license to your start-up some technology that can help your development efforts. Perhaps the employer can be a good customer or distributor for your products. In general, this alignment of interests promotes good-will and causes the employer to naturally want to assist you in many unexpected ways.

Stay Fit

Staying physically and emotionally fit during the creation of your start-up is critical to your success. It is strongly advised that you start an exercise regimen that you can maintain in the hectic days ahead. Many entrepreneurs get up early to jog or work out on an exercise machine at home. Joining a health club can be a good way to ensure getting regular exercise, and it is also an excellent way to meet people. It is vital that you take care of yourself during this time of stress and hard work. It is not an option; it is a requirement. This applies to each key member of your venture.

What if Your Start-Up Fails?

Your friends may tell you, "If you attempt to start your own business and you are a competent professional, you cannot lose anything except a little time." They reason that if your start-up fails, you will only have to get a new job, and it may even pay more than the one you left. Meanwhile, you have gained valuable experience you could not have acquired in any other way. Unless you are close to retirement age or in poor health, or have gambled and lost your savings and home in the start-up effort, this reasoning is hard to argue with.

It is worth thinking ahead about the necessity of finding new work if your start-up fails. Actually, you probably should be equally concerned with finding a new job should your current Fortune 500 company have major layoffs or otherwise unexpect-edly fail you. If you are unemployed, it may take you from 12 to 52 weeks to find new work. One old rule of thumb is to figure that you will be searching for work one month for every $10,000 of salary you expect to make. Of course, employment mar-kets are quite volatile, and your particular search will depend upon the market for your particular type of position at the time you are seeking it, coupled with the atti-tude, energy, and luck you bring to the effort. Many employers will value the experi-ence and skills you acquired at your start-up.

Your decision whether to launch your start-up should be based, in part, on satis-fying answers to these questions.

- Are you comfortable with the personal financial risk your start-up entails?
- Can you cleanly sever your current obligations with your employer, avoiding the possibility of a lawsuit as you launch your venture?
- Will you exploit the power of patents, trademarks, copyrights, and trade secrets to protect your new venture's intellectual property?
- Despite your determination for success, will you adequately maintain your health to endure the start-up, and are you prepared for the possibility of failure?
- Do you have buy-in from your family? Does your spouse or significant other understand the risks and opportunities involved and support your decision?

Sidebar 21.1 Summary of Permissible Activities While Still Employed by Another

type of employee	type of venture	
	noncompeting venture	competing venture
key employee, skilled employee	Can prepare for and operate the venture so long as it does not interfere with responsibilities and fiduciary duty. If subject to a no-moonlighting clause, the employee cannot operate it.	Can prepare for the venture so long as it does not interfere with responsibilities and fiduciary duty. Cannot operate it.
unskilled employee	Can prepare for and operate the venture so long as it does not interfere with responsibilities. If subject to a no-moonlighting clause, the employee cannot operate it.	Can prepare for the venture so long as it does not interfere with responsibilities. If under covenant not to compete or a no-moonlighting clause, the employee cannot operate it.

Used with permission from Constance E. Bagley and Craig E. Dauchy, "The Entrepreneur's Guide to Business Law," copyright © 1998, by West Educational Publishing Company.

Sidebar 21.2 Digital Vision Inc., and Contrex, Inc.: Schlumberger Ltd.'s Buyout of One of Mike Baird's Start-Ups

In the early 1980s at Schlumberger's Fairchild Laboratory for Artificial Intelligence Research (FLAIR) in Palo Alto, CA, my team of research computer scientists and I built a successful prototype of a revolutionary new instrument for the automatic optical inspection of microscopic patterns on semiconductor wafers. It was one of the most exciting projects going on inside Fairchild at the time. This invention promised to vastly improve yields in semiconductor manufacturing, which could translate into savings of hundreds of millions of dollars for anyone having access to it.

To be useful, however, this prototype had to be engineered into a complete product. It would take a lot of money to develop, since the machine itself was estimated to sell for $1 million. Fairchild, the renowned semiconductor company from which so many other Silicon Valley semiconductor companies had their origin, was then owned by the giant French oil company Schlumberger Ltd. Schlumberger's culture had little tolerance for entrepreneurship. Furthermore, its Fairchild subsidiary, while a potential customer for purchasing such a machine, was not in the business of developing complex and costly instrumentation. My initial plea for Schlumberger-Fairchild to exploit my invention went unheard.

Thus, the idea for a new company was born in my mind. I would call it Digital Vision, Inc. (DVI), since it used a revolutionary new technology that allowed computers to acquire digital images of objects and visually interpret them to discover killer submicron defects. I knew that I wanted to engineer my start-up, but I did not know exactly how to proceed. Knowing that I needed a top management team to pull this off, I first approached Dick Abraham, a semiretired and highly respected ex-senior vice president of Fairchild. Dick was quickly drawn into the scheme, and he brought along Ron Hayes, the president of Delvotec (a semiconductor instrumentation company) and an astute investor in many start-ups funded by the Hillman family via the Hillman Company venture capital fund. Ron conveyed the business idea to his Hillman connections, and venture capital funding seemed imminent as soon as we put together a suitable business plan.

Dick would be the chairman of the board, Ron would be the marketing vice president, and I would be the president. At my suggestion, we also agreed that I would drop down to the engineering vice president role if needed, either to raise additional funding or to facilitate our planned rapid growth. Recognizing up front my potential limitations to lead this company and accepting the possible need for more experienced management was very important. Bill Gates, the founder of Microsoft, willingly brought in a president to help him out when he needed it, and I was not about to try anything different. We charged forward full speed after that.

Dick, Ron, and I quickly went to work writing our business plan. In order not to use my employer's resources, I spent $2500 to buy a personal computer and printer along with word processing and spreadsheet software. My new credit card spending limit was not up to the task, so when I went to pick up the computer I had to come up with cash instead. Over the next few months I spent eight hours at work and then another six to eight hours every night working on the plan, with help from Dick and Ron. The little dot matrix printer I bought went through hundreds of pages of paper and a new ribbon almost every night as revised versions of the business plan spooled out just before I went to bed.

The three of us collaborated closely with two others who were working at Fairchild. Dr. John Dralla was a semiconductor fabrication manager with a PhD in physics who knew the process well, and he was to head our sales efforts. Peter Fiekowsky was a brilliant young computer programmer who had helped to build the prototype and would help turn it into a real product. Ron introduced us to Mario Rosati, the famous Silicon Valley lawyer, who helped us plan our course of action.

Everyone was excited! The business plan was finally complete. We had a revolutionary product idea already prototyped and tested on real products, an obviously willing and ready market, a pretty good management team, and potential venture capital funds already lined up. In our first meeting at Wilson, Sonsini, Goodrich & Rosati, it was determined that everything was a "go" except for one possible hitch. Counsel wanted Fairchild's blessing before funding our start-up because it was clear that Fairchild had a potential claim on our invention (having funded development of the prototype). The question in our minds was whether Fairchild would let us run with it or demand a big piece of the action. We were not prepared for what happened.

We agreed that I would present the DVI business plan to the Schlumberger-Fairchild management with an open-ended offer for them to invest in the company the way they saw best. They could put up cash and own a good percentage of the business, they could license the technology to us, they could take future royalties, or they could write their own ticket. It seemed to us a more than reasonable and fair proposition for both sides.

What happened surprised us. Fairchild management was furious, accusing the DVI team of denying Fairchild a business opportunity. A call to Mario Rosati by Tony Ley, the top manager at the Fairchild Research Center, promised a lawsuit if anyone put another penny into the newly incorporated Digital Vision. Rosati replied that the last thing he wanted was a lawsuit, and Fairchild could keep its business opportunity.

We ended up having to set aside our entrepreneurial visions for DVI. I was asked to return to Fairchild for three months to rewrite the DVI plan for Schlumberger. Having no real option and a very large mortgage payment to make, and with a wife, two kids, and a dog (none of whom earned a second income for the family), I agreed. The DVI founding team dissolved. Three months turned to six, and the revised "EYESEE" (for Integrated Circuit) business plan was submitted to Schlumberger's top management. Schlumberger's worldwide operating management conducted extensive due diligence. Finally, they made me an offer to fund the plan with $2 million. Ten engineers were to be assigned to develop the product. The product would be designed in secret in a building at Fairchild's Automatic Test Equipment (ATE) Division in San Jose, CA.

I complained that the San Jose location was not very convenient for me and that I would need to do market research and expose the world outside Fairchild to our ideas if we were to build the best product. Also, I would need a motivated management team to build a business as we built the product. I personally would need motivation—if not outright equity ownership in the venture (we had proposed phantom stock options), at least a substantial salary increase. In reply, it was explained to me that I was an employee and I would be rewarded as all managers were: after the achievement of a success. Take it or leave it.

One day later I resigned to pursue backup plan B. Raul Brauner was an entrepreneur in Billerica, MA, who had earlier founded Contrex, Inc., to develop WaferVision™, which also would inspect semiconductor wafers optically. During the previous six months, Raul and I had grown quite close as he saw my invention as a key to growing his company. His repeated attempts to recruit me as an engineering vice president finally succeeded when Schlumberger's offer left me cold. We engaged our lawyers to draw up a resignation letter that would get me cleanly out of Fairchild and into working for Contrex. We agreed, for example, that I would not do any substantive engineering on a related product for six months. To prove our good intentions, I opened a West Coast Applications Development office in Santa Clara, CA, where I would work only on Contrex's existing product for the next six months. I had one salesman and I prepared to hire an applications programmer.

Fairchild was dismayed and asked me to attend four exit interviews. At each interview I was told that I had better keep my promise not to use Fairchild trade secrets. Although my contract with Contrex stipulated that they would pay for any legal fight, we hoped there would not be one. We stuck closely to our agreement, and I ended up commuting to Billerica, spending more time in motels around Boston's Route 128 than I did at home during the following six months.

Six months later, Contrex, Inc., with 65 employees and zero sales, found itself in a severe cash crunch. Because interest by East Coast venture capital sources dwindled, we headed to the West Coast. In the San Francisco Bay Area, we talked to a dozen venture capitalists, three of whom expressed keen interest. However, each also advised us to find a corporate partner if we wished to be funded by them, so we talked to General Signal, Intel, and a few others. Again there was strong interest but no deal; at least not in the time we had left.

Then it hit me. Why not try Schlumberger? I called them, and a day later I found myself in the office of Dr. Marty Tenenbaum, the director of the Artificial Intelligence Laboratory, and my former boss. He had encouraged my entrepreneurial efforts in the past and saw great value in the EYESEE proposal, which was now nearing its end. After Marty complimented me on my boldness, I asked him to take the Contrex business plan upstairs to see if Schlumberger management still had an interest in the semiconductor optical inspection business.

Despite concern at Schlumberger about risk-taking, many saw a road to fame through investing a few million dollars in a highly leveraged start-up like Contrex, which essentially duplicated what DVI and EYESEE proposed to do a little while back. After a few months of due diligence, Schlumberger acquired a reported 51% interest in Contrex, Inc., for about $5 million. The original venture capitalists added a few million more, which equaled our accumulated debt. We paid all our creditors, and the company had a fresh start. While all this negotiation was going on, Mike Kaufman of Oak Investment Partners, our original venture capital investor, brought in a gunslinger to clean house. After the work force had been trimmed down from 65 to about 24 and Raul Brauner had been demoted, I was offered the key engineering position of vice president for product design if I moved to Billerica. While this was an interesting proposition, I nevertheless declined due to overriding personal considerations in California at that time.

Schlumberger now owned the business opportunity they had earlier denied the entrepreneurial Digital Vision team and that was denied to them in their own backyard with my rejection of their offer to fund the EYESEE plan. It was too late, though. Their opportunity was lost because the entrepreneurial spirit had diminished, and Contrex faded away less than one year later.

—Mike Baird (1992)

From the perspective of many years later, what are some of the lessons learned from this early career experience?

- *Learning from mistakes (both your own and those of others)*—There's no regret in having tried and failed. The lessons learned were of immense value, and they helped shape my career. It would have been a much bigger mistake for me to have stayed at Fairchild, continuing in my safe job, and not have pursued my entrepreneurial dream. No one executes perfectly. Of course, it's less expensive to learn from the mistakes of others.
- *Skin in the game*—We should have gotten more commitment, including some cash, from our Fairchild executive and the other senior members of our start-up's team. They had the financial wherewithal and the reward potential, but no real risk in the deal.
- *Getting blinded by greed and the status of others*—The business experience, connections, and particular Fairchild backgrounds of these gentlemen (which is what attracted me to them) should have warned them (and

thus me) that Fairchild's interest in the intellectual property of this deal was potentially fatal. In that sense, greed and the incredible pace of Silicon Valley and the venture capital community blinded all of us.

- *Resolve/avoid IP issues up front*—In hindsight, there was a clear conflict with Fairchild's business interests that could have been, and should have been, avoided. Had the senior members of our team put in some money, at least one of us could have quit his job, and I believe we could have developed better technology independently of Fairchild.

- *Becoming a target*—Rather, we proceeded down the path we were on, put ourselves in Fairchild's crosshairs, and they eagerly pulled the trigger. Early on, we should have reflected more on our strategy and potential issues.

- *Catch-22*—Trying to negotiate an entrepreneurial deal with a big employer frequently feels like a no-win situation. Top management sometimes gets irrationally upset with "traitorous" employees and, if and when you get to negotiations, you may feel like you're on a long, forced march in a bureaucratic swamp.

22

Some Final Comments

Nothing in the world can take the place of persistence. Talent will not; nothing is more common than unsuccessful men with talent. Genius will not; unrewarded genius is almost a proverb. Education will not; the world is full of educational derelicts. Persistence and determination alone are omnipotent.

—Calvin Coolidge

Starting your own company is going to be the most exciting and may be the most rewarding endeavor you will ever undertake. If you decide to engineer your own start-up, your life will be richer and fuller than you would have ever imagined. Each of your days will be more fully lived, and you will experience the intense sensations that go along with struggle and achievement.

Not everyone needs, wants, or can take such an intense lifestyle. Start-up entrepreneurs are often adrenaline freaks, driving in the fast lane. As the boss in the movie *Curly Sue* said to his aggressive female associate, "If you drive 190 miles an hour, you're going to run into something." Start-up entrepreneurs thrive on metaphorical speed and do crash into things. Will you crash and burn? Will you stay in control? What is your comfortable cruising speed?

By this time, you probably know what you want to do: you want to start your own team-driven, high-growth, technology-based business. If you decide to launch your start-up, review the following summary of the most important points presented in this book.

- Build a strong management team of individuals whom you would enjoy working with, and who can help you attract funds and grow a healthy, successful business.

- Create a strong board of directors and an informal board of advisors that will provide your business with the experience and funding sources necessary for you to survive and prosper.

- Identify a growing market opportunity to which you can apply your engineering technology to develop a product for which there are known customers.

- Make sure you have a distinct and preferably unfair competitive advantage.

- Plan your business well in advance, and put your plan into writing.

- Make sure that high growth is one of your business objectives. Thoroughly understand why high growth is important to your success.

- Raise enough money to get started, and do not run out of money.

- Attain profitability and positive cash flow as early as possible.

- Do not produce a product that requires missionary sales.

- Make sure your business model is market- and customer-driven and technology-fueled.

- Enjoy the process of building your new business, but try to balance your work and private life. "Like your work but love your spouse" is an applicable saying. However, prepare to be consumed by your new business, and plan to devote a significant part of your life and most of your energy to making your start-up successful.

- Use stock and stock option grants to motivate and reward those who will help make your business a success.

- Set realistic, meaningful milestones for yourself and your team, and hold yourselves to them in order to avoid being trapped in the land of the "living dead." If your plan is simply not working, get a new plan, or sell or kill the company.

- Never compromise your integrity.

- Beyond all else, persist and persevere until you win the start-up game, recognizing that many very successful entrepreneurs are not successful in their first attempt.

This book has encouraged you to approach your start-up with extreme diligence in thinking things out and conducting extensive market research before attempting to launch your business. You are not expected to do everything suggested in this book, but you should focus on those areas that are unfamiliar to you where you stand to gain (or lose) a lot if you (do not) investigate first. Now, step into the fast lane and get on with what could be the most exciting event of your life!

We have had the pleasure of corresponding with dozens of our readers and striking up many valued relationships in the process. We would be pleased to hear from you as well. As a courtesy, we will do our best, as time allows, to comment on your business plan summary or bounce around a wild idea. The preferred means of communication is email.

Best success in your venture!

James A. Swanson
878 Hoffman Terrace
Los Altos, CA 94024
jswanson@alum.mit.edu
www.firstonline.com

Michael L. Baird
2756 Indigo Circle
Morro Bay, CA 93442
mike@mikebaird.com
www.mikebaird.com

Appendix A.1:
Some Colorful Definitions

Definitions

Some of the terms on this list are humorous, blunt terms used by venture capitalists as shorthand to describe what's going on in their world. Some terms, perhaps casually used years ago by someone, just caught on and survived the test of time. Venture capitalists typically are not trying to be mean when using such shorthand, but it may sound that way to an outsider. Stress creates humor.

Angel or *Angel Investor*—a rich individual who invests in start-up companies. Typically angels invest in "seed" rounds before venture capitalists invest. They may or may not have useful experience and connections for your start-up.

Annex Funds—additional funds raised by a venture capitalist for an already existing fund when more money than anticipated is needed to shore up existing companies in the fund's portfolio of companies. A venture capitalist usually reserves one-third or more of a fund for later investments in these companies, but if the reserve proves to be inadequate, additional "annex funds" may be needed. In general, venture capitalists don't cross-invest their funds (i.e., a portfolio company will receive money from only one of the funds managed by a particular venture capitalist).

Blue Sky Laws—the securities laws of the various 50 states (but not federal securities law). The origin of this colorful term is a 1917 U.S. Supreme Court case in which the court commented that state securities laws were intended to protect investors from transactions that had no more substance than so many feet of blue sky.

Bootstrapping—making your company a success without external venture financing. You pull yourself up, to success, by your own bootstraps. Bootstrapping may be your chosen strategy, but more often it's dictated by the unavailability of venture financing.

Burnout Financing—venture capital jargon for severely diluting the existing investors in a company, that is, burning them out of the opportunity.

Burn Rate—the net amount of cash (typically, your investors' money) that your company is spending ("burning") each month to carry on its business. Although the burn rate could be measured on a quarterly or annual basis, it is typically assumed to be a monthly measure. Thus, if someone says, "My burn rate is $25,000," he most likely means $25,000 per month. Your burn rate is zero at the break-even point, when monthly revenues equal monthly expenses, both counted on a cash basis.

Carried Interest (also known as the *carry* or the *profit split*)—the percentage of profits (perhaps 20–25%) that the general partners (i.e., the venture capitalists) of a venture fund receive out of the total profits realized by the fund. The limited partners (who provide all or most of the money for the fund) receive the rest. The term comes from the practice, in the early days of venture financing, of the general partners putting up nothing but receiving a split of the profits—thus the limited partners were said to have "carried the interest" of the general partners.

Clawback—the repayment by the general partners in a venture fund of any profit split distribution ("carried interest") they previously received, if the fund at the end of its life goes into the red.

Cram Down—a type of "down round," but with more forcefulness and style. The company and earlier investors (the "crammees") accept very severe financing terms, typically because that's the only way the company can survive. Sometimes the terms are crammed down their throats without their consent. When economic times are tough, many struggling start-ups are not even able to attract cram-down investors. In a cram down, the new investors (the "crammers") usually get control of the company. In addition to a greatly lowered price per share (which of course causes lots of dilution) and other tough provisions, the cram down usually involves a painful liquidation preference—that is, in the event of a liquidation of the company, the new investors get double or triple, or even more, times their money back before any earlier investor receives a penny.

Death Spiral Convertible (also known as a *toxic spiral*, *toxic convert*, or *reset security*)—a financial instrument (preferred stock or bond) that pays interest, can be exchanged for common stock, and comes with a catch—namely, that new additional shares will be issued to the investor if the underlying stock falls below one or more trigger points, called "resets." The company gets the cash it desperately needs, and the investor, in effect, gets a guaranty that its share of the company (the underlying stock) will not go below a certain dollar value. It's called a death spiral because the issuance of additional shares causes the other outstanding shares to be less valuable, which can cause the stock price to drop further, which in turn requires more shares to be issued to the investor, and so on. The company desperately hopes that its stock price will go up and that everything will work out. If it doesn't, the company's demise is likely to be accelerated.

Double-Dip—slang for participating preferred stock. In the event of liquidation of the company (including a sale), the preferred shareholders not only get paid the amount of their preference, but they also share pro rata in any proceeds remaining after the preference is paid.

Down Round—a financing round in which the valuation (typically the price per share) for the financing round is below the valuation for the previous round.

Elevator Pitch—a very concise and compelling description of the company and investment opportunity—something that the entrepreneur can tell a prospective venture investor in the short duration of an elevator ride, perhaps 25 seconds.

Hibernation Mode—the operating mode adopted by a start-up (typically one that is having difficulty getting funded) whereby it cuts its expenses to virtually zero (or it cuts its burn rate to virtually zero) as it continues to pursue funding, or as it waits for the venture funding climate to improve.

Inside Round—a financing round in which current investors provide all the funds in the round, with no new investors involved.

Kennel (or *kennel club*)—a collection of several poorly performing companies (i.e., dogs) in a venture capitalist's portfolio of companies.

LBO (*Leveraged Buyout*)—the takeover or acquisition of a company (public or private) using borrowed money. Usually, the assets of the acquired company serve as security for the loan, and the intent is to repay the loan out of the cash flow of the acquired company.

Living Dead—companies that neither succeed nor fail but seem to hang around forever in a depressing section of purgatory. Many give credit for this phrase to Franklin "Pitch" Johnson, a veteran venture capitalist at Asset Management Company in Silicon Valley, who used the term many years ago after watching the horror movie, "Night of the Living Dead."

Mercenary—an individual who starts a company for the sole purpose of getting rich. Venture investors typically don't like this type of entrepreneur. They prefer to invest in "real entrepreneurs" or "revolutionaries," who are people who want to create valuable businesses and make the world better.

Moving the Goal Posts—a series of changing objectives for your start-up that are suggested or recommended by prospective investors. After hearing your pitch they tell you some specific things you should do, with the implication that you'll get funding if you achieve these goals. You then do these things, return to the investors with high hopes of funding, and discover they have new goals for you to achieve. They may have no intention of investing, but rather are only trying to be positive and helpful.

Orphans—venture-backed companies that must fend for themselves because their venture investors are unwilling or unable to participate in the next financing round.

Pay-to-play—a provision, more common in later-stage venture deals, that encourages investors to participate in any following rounds of funding. Typically, the investors agree that their preferred stock will automatically convert to common stock if they do not participate in the following funding. Another variation is that the investors agree that their preferred stock will convert to a new series of preferred with all the same rights as what they had, except that it has no antidilution protection.

PIPE—a private investment in a public entity. Some larger, later-stage venture capitalist firms invest in companies that are already public. Although relatively rare, these investments are more attractive when public markets are depressed and the investors see an opportunity for a strong return in a company that needs their help and generally looks like the type of private company that they invest in—except that the company has gone public too early. The investors buy the shares below market value and usually agree to a lock-up period in which they cannot sell the stock. They actively try to help the company and may take a board seat. Typically, a public company that does a PIPE is not doing well and is having trouble raising money in the public markets.

Red Herring—a preliminary prospectus, which is the first document released to prospective investors by an underwriter of a new stock issue. It's called a red herring because part of the cover page is printed in red ink.

Reverse IPO—under one variation, the acquisition by a still-private company that is in a hot market and doing well (but may be short of cash) of a troubled public company that is sitting on lots of cash. The acquiring company gets the cash it needs and becomes a public company without the cost and hassle of an IPO. Also, it doesn't have to retain the employees of the acquired company.

Runway—the amount of time a start-up can survive on its cash hoard. If the start-up's burn rate is $50,000 (i.e., per month) and it has $200,000 in the bank, then it is looking at four months of runway. The term is loosely taken from aviation—entrepreneurs work hard to get their ventures (aircraft) to take off and soar. Frequently, the term is used in a negative or rationalizing sense, such as, "We had a great product and a great team, but we just ran out of runway and had to shut down." That sounds a lot cooler than saying, "We ran out of money," or perhaps, "We really had a stupid business plan and a weak team, and nobody would buy our rotten product, so we ran out of cash."

Silicon Valley Haircut—the practice of firing a CEO or team of entrepreneurs. The barbers (i.e., the investors) give the haircut by starting the cut at the throat. "Off with his head," the Queen said. Also, the term sometimes refers to financial terms that are very severe, resulting in extreme dilution.

SWOT—an analysis of your company's strengths, weaknesses, opportunities, and threats. A SWOT is typically viewed as a "business school" tool to improve decision making.

Tranche—roughly means "a slice," in French. In investment circles, it means investing money in stages rather than in one lump sum. For example, rather than investing $5 million in one payment that is expected to meet the cash flow needs for 18 or 24 months, venture investors may divide the total into 3 or 4 payments, with each payment tied to specific milestones. This approach is sometimes called a "round within a round." Whether tranches are used depends mainly on what the investors want and how they view the world. Most entrepreneurs would prefer to take the money all at once. When venture financing is tighter, tranche investing becomes more common. Some investors believe that the milestones help entrepreneur teams to focus and execute better, and others believe that too many short-term goals can be counterproductive and divisive.

Turnaround Financing—financing provided to a company at a time of operational or financial difficulty with the intention of improving the company's performance.

Vulture Capitalist—considered a synonym for "venture capitalist" by disgruntled entrepreneurs (who sometimes have no one to blame but themselves).

Washout Financing—a type of very severe financing that may be imposed when the company is screwed up and major surgery is needed. The board and the investors essentially throw out the old valuations and start afresh with a very low valuation. The investors in this round usually then control the company, and old management is out the door. No one invests in a start-up wanting this to happen. Most washouts die, or are sold for less than the total amount invested.

Zombies—same as "Living Dead" above.

A Foreign Language Test

See if you can translate into English the following *venturespeak* example, which is from Scott Herhold of the *San Jose Mercury News* ("Venture Capital Industry Spawns Own Lingo," May 3, 1998).

In Venturespeak:

> Picture the dilemma: You're a VC sitting on the board of a wounded duck, a surprise because the elevator pitch was so good months ago. You have to decide whether your CEO is a boat anchor who can't scale up. You could bring in a good athlete, but there's always the chance he could hit the windshield. Because you're worried that your VC partners have short arms, you're wondering whether to wake the giant. In any case, you're out of bandwidth: You're thinking about putting a ribbon on it and moving into sell mode.

Here's an English Translation:

> You're a venture capitalist sitting on the board of an ailing company, a surprise because it sounded so promising when the entrepreneur first talked to you. You have to decide whether the CEO is hindering the company's growth and cannot run a bigger operation. You could bring in a talented executive from another field, but there's always a chance that he or she could fail. Because you're worried that your VC partners won't participate in a second round of funding, you're wondering whether to talk to Microsoft. In any case, you're exhausted. You're thinking about firing the engineers and selling the company.

.

Appendix A.2:
Resources Available to
Start-Up Entrepreneurs

Entrepreneur and Mentoring Organizations

Young Entrepreneurs' Organization (YEO)

www.yeo.org

This is a volunteer group of business professionals under 40 years of age who are the owners, founders, or controlling shareholders of companies with annual sales of one million U.S. dollars or more. They have chapters throughout the world and offer an array of educational and networking opportunities. World Entrepreneurs Organization is a part of YEO and is for "graduates" of YEO who turn 40, as well as other entrepreneurs who meet the membership guidelines.

Young President's Organization (YPO)

www.ypo.org

This organization connects several thousand corporate presidents and CEOs under the age of 50 for peer relationships, mutual help, education, and idea sharing on business, professional, and personal issues. Individuals must meet certain qualitative and quantitative criteria for admission. Prospective members must exhibit leadership qualities and a high degree of integrity in personal business affairs. Your start-up will initially be too small for YPO, but it could help you greatly after your start-up has achieved some success. Also, the local chapter of YPO would be happy to talk with you and point you to other networking resources in your area.

The MIT Enterprise Forum

http://web.mit.edu/entforum/www/

This organization has more than 20 chapters worldwide, each offering unique programs and networking opportunities for entrepreneurs. Location and current contacts are listed here. They provide numerous links to many excellent resources about business plans.

The IndUS Entrepreneurs (TiE)

www.tie.org

TiE is a global not-for-profit network of entrepreneurs and professionals dedicated to the advancement of entrepreneurship. The name reflects the Indus or South Asian origin of the individuals who chartered the organization. Accordingly, its members are mainly entrepreneurs with roots or interest in India, Pakistan, Bangladesh, Sri Lanka, and Nepal, but the organization is open to all. It has dozens of chapters around the world. There are countless organizations for entrepreneurs throughout the world, and this one is included as a good example.

San Jose Software Business Cluster (SBC)

www.sjsbc.org

This "cluster" offers office space and much more to several start-ups at any one point in time at the SBC's location in Silicon Valley. It boasts a very low failure rate and also that over $400 million in venture capital has been raised by their participating companies. This is an example of many similar organizations that offer space, services, and coaching to entrepreneurs in a cluster or physical incubator model, coupled with the opportunity to rub elbows with other entrepreneurs.

Silicon Valley Association of Startup Entrepreneurs (SVASE)

www.svase.org

This organization, founded in 1995, helps entrepreneurs in Silicon Valley and elsewhere. It shares valuable information and resources with its members, including investor contacts and a network of service providers. It also promotes cooperation with other entrepreneurial organizations and sponsors many excellent meetings with good programs and networking opportunities. Similar organizations may be available wherever you are located.

Organizations for Women

The Women in Technology Foundation

www.witi.org

This outstanding organization for women has dozens of regional chapters worldwide. It offers a lot of value, including a worldwide network of contacts, conferences, publications, education, innovative resources, and support—as well as general inspiration—for women entrepreneurs and early-stage ventures. In recent years it has expanded its constituency from women in technology to women who generally view technology as central to their businesses and careers.

The Forum for Women Entrepreneurs (FWE)

www.fwe.org

Founded in 1993, this organization is for entrepreneurial women in high-growth technology and life science companies. It has several regional offices, and its headquarters is in the San Francisco Bay Area. Join this group and you'll have wonderful opportunities to meet other women who are interested in growing high-technology companies and expanding entrepreneurial opportunities for women.

Professional Services Organizations

Many of the top accounting, consulting, and law firms offer excellent, free publications on obtaining venture capital, securing financing, writing business plans, growing a business, performing business valuations, doing business overseas, going public, and so forth. By simply using the Internet, and perhaps making a few phone calls, you will have more quality reference materials than you will ever need. Some good places to start are as follows.

Accounting Firms

Mergers and reorganizations have characterized the accounting profession. Over a period of years, the "Big 8" accounting firms became the "Big 5." Then, thanks to Enron and other accounting fiascos, Arthur Andersen did a dot-gone and the "Big 5" in effect became the "Big 4," at least for a while. (College basketball fans may prefer to call them the "Final Four.") More important, the services offered by these large firms expanded and changed so much that the label "Big 5" or "Big 4" in reference to accounting firms carries little meaning and, if we had our way, would no longer be used. In many accounting firms there have been disputes between the traditional accounting side of the business (audit, tax, and so forth) and the consulting side. For example, Arthur Andersen and Andersen Consulting engaged in lengthy, acrimonious arbitration that resulted in a complete divorce, with Andersen Consulting changing its name to Accenture in 2001. What a stroke of genius, or luck, for the consulting side!

All of the Big 4 firms have spent enormous sums to train their employees in new technologies and pursue various e-commerce initiatives. They did so in order to capitalize on their inside-track positions as auditors for virtually all of the world's largest corporations. For many years, their consulting business grew much faster than did their traditional accounting services. The SEC has been worried about auditor independence and conflict of interest when the outside auditor also performs lucrative consulting services for the clients they audit or holds substantial equity positions in their clients, which is sometimes the case. Due to industry and political pressure, the SEC had apparently given up on new rules that would have prohibited accounting firms from performing various consulting services. Then Enron imploded, and reform became popular.

Here is some helpful information about the Big 4.

Deloitte & Touche (www.us.deloitte.com) or Deloitte Touche Tohmatsu
www.deloitte.com
Deloitte, a good resource for timely information, maintains a library of publications, surveys, guides, and directories. Like the other Big 4, it has a global practice and probably has helpful information for you in your particular country or countries of interest.

Ernst & Young

www.ey.com

You can check out the Entrepreneurial Services section of the Ernst & Young website. They offer Entrepreneur of the Year awards in numerous countries. In 2000 they sold their information technologies consulting business to Cap Gemini for about $11 billion.

KPMG International

www.kpmg.com

Like the other big accounting firms, KPMG offers lots of valuable free information, as well as links to its offices in countries throughout the world, on its website.

PricewaterhouseCoopers LLP

www.pwcglobal.com

PwC, Venture Economics, and the National Venture Capital Association collaborate in the quarterly survey of U.S. venture capital activity. They track venture capital investments in emerging private companies. See their website at www.pwcmoneytree.com.

Accounting firms, of course, are in business to work with companies, including small companies. Should you decide that you want to work with one of the Big 4 firms above or another large firm, don't assume that the firm will choose to work with you. Typically, they look closely at a start-up venture and its prospects before deciding to enter into a business relationship. They look for a good fit and a situation where they think they have a strong chance of adding substantial value, in addition to getting paid. Some of the large firms have a methodology for reviewing company, somewhat similar to that used by a professional investor. They look at the business plan, market opportunity, competition, management, investors, and so forth. So, if at some point you wish to explore this option, do your homework first and get prepared.

Large Consulting Firms

As mentioned previously, several of the largest consulting firms grew out of the Big 5 accounting firms. These include

Accenture

www.accenture.com

As noted above, they split from Arthur Andersen.

Deloitte Consulting

www.deloitteconsulting.com

Cap Gemini Ernst & Young

www.cgey.com

KPMG Consulting, Inc.

www.kpmgconsulting.com

PwC Consulting

www.pwcconsulting.com

PwC Consulting was the global management consulting and information technology services businesses of the individual member firms of the PricewaterhouseCoopers network of firms. PwC Consulting was acquired by IBM in 2002 and is now part of the IBM Global Services business.

Law Firms

Most large law firms with a broad business and intellectual property practice offer on their websites an array of free articles, guides, and other resources for the first-time entrepreneur. Also, it is essential that you have a qualified, practical, experienced attorney represent your new venture, and you should hire one sooner rather than later.

The Small Business Administration

U.S. Small Business Administration (SBA)

www.sba.org

Many entrepreneurs seeking help overlook the SBA, perhaps because it's a governmental entity. However, the SBA does have several major programs to help entrepreneurs and small business owners, plus lots of other services, including numerous publications and online courses. The SBA also offers various financing options for small businesses. The usual financing structure is that the SBA provides a loan guaranty, with the loan made directly to the small business by a bank or other private lender. (In general, the SBA can guaranty up to $750,000 or 75% of the total loan, whichever is less.) Two of the other SBA programs are discussed in the following paragraphs.

The Service Corps of Retired Executives (SCORE)

www.score.org

SCORE, a nonprofit organization, provides small business training and counseling under a grant from the SBA. A quick visit to SCORE's website will give you the latest on their offerings, and perhaps you'll decide to sign up for its newsletter or other services, such as email counseling. SCORE has more than 11,000 volunteer business counselors, who are successful, retired (sometimes still active) businessmen and businesswomen. Counseling is available face-to-face or via email. SCORE services are free, confidential, and available to all U.S. citizens. With hundreds of chapters, SCORE has locations in every state.

Small Business Development Centers (SBDC)

The SBA administers the SBDC Program, which is a cooperate effort (involving the private sector, universities, and federal, state, and local government) to provide management and technical assistance to start-ups and small business owners. There's typically one central SBDC location in each state, coupled with a network of more than 1000 service centers located across the country (many in universities and colleges).

SBDC assistance is usually free and is tailored to the needs of the local community and individual clients. It can help small businesses apply for Small Business Innovation and Research (SBIR) grants from federal agencies, and it makes special efforts to reach and help certain groups such as minorities and women. You can easily locate the SBDC location nearest you by visiting the SBA website.

Venture Financing

National Venture Capital Association

www.nvca.org

This organization serves and represents the interests of the venture capital and private equity industries. Useful research and other information is available on its website.

European Private Equity and Venture Capital Association (EVCA)

www.evca.com

EVCA's mission is to promote globally and to facilitate the development of the European private equity and venture capital industry. It's a good source of information on the European market. It offers some free information, including a newsletter and a directory of its members.

A List of Venture Capital Directories

See Ch. 11 ("Funding Issues") for a listing and description of several venture capital directories, including ordering information.

Garage Technology Ventures

www.garage.com

Guy Kawasaki (entrepreneur, author, and former Apple evangelist) is one of the founders of this venture capital investment bank that helps their client high-technology companies raise money from venture capital firms, angels, and corporate investors. It runs various conferences and a well-regarded "boot camp for start-ups," and its website also contains some good resources for entrepreneurs.

Venture Economics (Thompson Financial)

www.ventureeconomics.com

This is an excellent source for accurate and timely information regarding investment, exit, and performance activity in the private equity industry. Most of the information is available only to its member firms, but you may want to check it out anyway. Also, you may be able to get the information you need through a member.

vfinance.com

www.vfinance.com

Among the numerous resources on this site is a directory of venture capital firms.

VentureWire

www.venturewire.com

This leading daily news and information service for the venture capital community has a variety of publications and products, including a free newsletter that identifies companies that just received venture funding.

The Band of Angels

www.bandangels.com

The Band of Angels, based in Silicon Valley in California, is a group of about 150 wealthy, high-tech executives and entrepreneurs who provide capital and advice to start-ups. Like many angel groups, the Band of Angels doesn't publish its membership list. Nevertheless, a start-up must be referred through an individual member. Three companies present at each monthly meeting, and there is a thorough due diligence process that determines which companies will be selected to present. The Band of Angels and the Gathering of Angels are good examples of the numerous angel groups found in the U.S. and throughout the world. You can easily identify the angel groups that are active in your area.

Gathering of Angels

www.gatheringofangels.com

The Gathering of Angels started in 1996 in New Mexico with the mission of providing venture funding to promising entrepreneurs in that state. It expanded greatly and now meets in numerous locations around the U.S. It has a process for screening business plans and issuing invitations to present at one of the monthly meetings. Typically, four start-ups are invited to present at each gathering. Applications can be submitted online.

InvestorGuide.com

www.investorguide.com

This site offers a list of angel investors, as well as a list of incubators. Lots of other resources are provided, including free daily and weekly newsletters.

Human Resources and Equity Compensation

Advanced-HR, Inc.

www.advanced-hr.com

This organization publishes pay and stock compensation for VC-backed pre-IPO start-ups. It helps these companies determine how to compensate their employees with cash and stock options by allowing them access to data about similar high-tech companies.

HireRight.com

www.hireright.com

This company, in Irvine, CA, provides Internet-based background screening and pre-employment services (drug screening, skills testing, background checks, etc.).

The Association of Executive Search Consultants (AESC)

www.aesc.org

This professional organization represents recruiters working on a retainer basis, not a contingency basis. Although this site naturally will have a certain bias because it reflects the viewpoint of the professionals it represents, it does contain a lot of valuable information about the search process.

WorkIndex

www.workindex.com

This site is run by Cornell University's School of Industrial Labor Relations. It offers an excellent index for a broad array of human resources information on the web, plus a good search engine to help you.

AssistU

www.assistu.com

This company can partner you with a Virtual Assistant, a trained administrative professional who can perform a variety of support functions for your business, from routine tasks to special projects. You pay by the hour. With the right Virtual Assistant you may avoid hiring an on-site employee and providing office space and equipment.

myStockOptions.com

www.mystockoptions.com

This site contains everything you will ever want to know about stock options—focused articles, tools to help you manage your stock options, and hundreds of FAQs.

MyOptionValue.com

www.myoptionvalue.com

Ditto. There's an annual subscription fee for access to certain parts of the site.

MyBenefitSource

www.mybenefitsource.com

MyBenefitSource (MBS) is an H&R Block Company that provides payroll and benefits administration services to tens of thousands of small and mid-sized companies (with the number of employees ranging from two to a few thousand).

Foundation for Enterprise Development

www.fed.org

The mission of this nonprofit organization is to promote employee ownership and participation, both in the U.S. and worldwide. It offers a wide variety of resources, assistance, and links. Its founder, Dr. J. Robert Beyster, is the CEO and founder of Science Applications International Corporation (SAIC), a 30+ year-old company that has been greatly admired by many over the years. SAIC, with over 30,000 employees, is a $6 billion high-technology firm and one of the nation's largest and most successful employee-owned companies.

National Center for Employee Ownership (NCEO)

www.nceo.org

This private, nonprofit membership and research organization is a great source of information on employee stock ownership plans (ESOPs), employee stock option plans, and related topics. It helps promote an employee ownership culture and holds dozens of workshops and conferences each year. It has been recognized as "the single best source of information on employee ownership anywhere in the world" (*Inc.* magazine, August 2000).

Other Good Resources

Internet Directories

There are several excellent web directories that are valuable sources of information for you and your start-up. These directories organize the web by topic and make it easy for you to drill down to the information you seek. For example, at Google (www.google.com) you can drill down under "Business" to find a rich array of resources regarding venture capital, intellectual property issues, entrepreneurial associations near you, and so forth. Yahoo.com is also a popular directory.

Inc.com

www.inc.com

The home of *Inc.* magazine, this website offers lots of great resources, and you may want to get on their mailing list. The research part of this site (www.inc.com/research/) has good "lists of lists" showing many helpful websites (e.g., sites for researching your competition and your industry and sites identifying venture capital firms). It has a great listing, "Directory of Angel Investor Networks," that gets you to a description of each angel group, with its location, contact, average investment range, and so on.

BusinessWeek

www.businessweek.com

This weekly magazine offers daily briefings and much more, although much of the content is available only to subscribers.

nolo

www.nolo.com

Many consider this company to be the guru of legal self-help. Although it is geared mainly for the average consumer, you should check it out, since it offers a very wide range of legal information. It definitely is not a substitute for you having an experienced business attorney to represent your new company, but it can help educate you and make your interactions with your attorney more effective and probably less expensive. Nolo Press is the largest publisher of legal self-help books, including books that are state specific. For example, you could perhaps benefit from one of their books specific to your state that describes the nuts and bolts of setting up and operating a business, including good housekeeping requirements (sales taxes, employee disability insurance payments, withholding, county forms to be filed, and so forth).

Startupfailures.com
www.startupfailures.com

This site bills itself as "the place for bouncing back." It is a resource and support site for entrepreneurs on the start-up roller coaster.

F_ _ _edCompany
www.f_ _ _edcompany.com

If you want the latest dirt on troubled companies, this is the place for you. The name says it all.

A Film

Whether or not you've lived inside a start-up, it will be worth your time to watch "Start-up.com," a cinema verité about GovWorks.com, whose cofounder left the comforts of Goldman Sachs to pursue his dream. The company raised $60 million before failing. The film is not intended to show you how to do, or not do, a start-up, but it would nevertheless be valuable for a class on entrepreneurship. The cofounders continued their entrepreneurial ways after the fall of GovWorks.com—they started a consulting firm focused on helping troubled start-ups and other technology companies (www.recognitiongroup.com).

References and Recommended Reading

Adams, Rob. *A Good Hard Kick in the Ass: Basic Training for Entrepreneurs*. Crown Business. 2002.

Bagley, Constance E., and Craig E. Dauchy. *The Entrepreneur's Guide to Business Law*. West Educational Publishing. 1998.

Bartlett, Joseph W. *Fundamentals of Venture Capital*. Madison Books. 1999.

Baty, Gordon B. *Entrepreneurship for the Nineties*. Prentice-Hall. 1990.

Baty, Gordon B., and Michael S. Blake. *Entrepreneurship—Back to Basics*. Beard Group. 2002.

Bell, C. Gordon, and John E. McNamara. *High-Tech Ventures: The Guide for Entrepreneurial Success*. Addison-Wesley. 1991.

Blanchard, Kenneth, and Spencer Johnson. *The One Minute Manager*. Berkley Books. 1983.

Bolles, Richard Nelson. *What Color Is Your Parachute? A Practical Manual for Job-Hunters & Career-Changers*. Ten Speed Press. 2001.

Brandt, Steven C. *Entrepreneuring: The Ten Commandments for Building a Growth Company*. Archipelago Publications. 1997.

Christensen, Clayton M. *The Innovator's Dilemma*. HarperBusiness. 2000.

Collins, Jim. *Good to Great: Why Some Companies Make the Leap... and Others Don't*. HarperCollins. 2001.

Collins, Jim, and Jerry Porras. *Built to Last: Successful Habits of Visionary Companies*. HarperBusiness. 1997.

Davidow, William H. *Marketing High Technology: An Insider's View*. Macmillian, The Free Press. 1986.

Drucker, Peter F. *Innovation and Entrepreneurship: Practice and Principles*. Harper & Row. 1985.

Farkas, Maria, and Nicole Tempest. *Meg Whitman at eBay, Inc. (A)*. HBS case No. 9-401-024. Harvard Business School Publishing. 2001.

Fisher, Roger, and William Ury. *Getting to Yes: Negotiating Agreement Without Giving In*. Penguin Books. 1991.

Gosden, Freeman F., Jr. *Direct Marketing Success: What Works and Why*. John Wiley & Sons. 1989.

Grove, Andrew S. *High Output Management*. Vintage Books. 1995.

Hawken, Paul. *Growing a Business*. Fireside. 1988.

Hill, Brian E., and Dee Power. *Attracting Capital from Angels: How Their Money—And Their Experience—Can Help You Build a Successful Company*. John Wiley & Sons. 2002.

————. *Inside Secrets to Venture Capital*. John Wiley & Sons. 2001.

Humphrey, Watts S. *Managing the Software Process*. Addison-Wesley. 1990.

Jenkins, Michael D. *Starting and Operating a Business in the U.S.: National Edition*. Running R Media. 1999.

Karrass, Gary. *Negotiate to Close: How to Make More Successful Deals*. Simon & Schuster. 1987.

Kawasaki, Guy. *Selling the Dream: How to Promote Your Product, Company, or Ideas—and Make a Difference Using Everyday Evangelism*. HarperBusiness. 1991.

Kawasaki, Guy, and Michele Moreno. *Rules for Revolutionaries: The Capitalist Manifesto for Creating and Marketing New Products and Services*. HarperBusiness. 2000.

Kurtzig, Sandra L., and Tom Parker. *CEO: Building a $400 Million Company from the Ground Up*. Harvard Business School Press. 1994.

Lasser Institute, J. K. *How to Run a Small Business*. 7th ed. McGraw-Hill. 1994.

Lucht, John. *Rites of Passage at $100,000 to $1 Million+: Your Insider's Lifetime Guide to Executive Job-Changing and Faster Career Progress in the 21st Century*. Viceroy Press. 2000.

————. *Insights for the Journey*. Viceroy Press. 2001.

Mackay, Harvey. *Beware the Naked Man Who Offers You His Shirt*. Ballantine Books. 1996.

MacVicar, Duncan, and Darwin Throne. *Managing High-Tech Start-Ups*. Butterworth-Heinemann. 1992.

McQuown, Judith H. *Inc. Yourself: How to Profit by Setting up Your Own Corporation*. 10th ed. Career Press. 2002.

Moore, Geoffrey A. *Inside the Tornado: Marketing Strategies from Silicon Valley's Cutting Edge*. HarperBusiness. 1995.

Moore, Geoffrey A., and Regis McKenna. *Crossing the Chasm: Marketing and Selling High-Tech Products to Mainstream Customers*. HarperBusiness. 1999.

Nesheim, John. *High Tech Start-Up: The Complete Handbook for Creating Successful New High Tech Companies*. Simon & Schuster. 2000.

O'Donnell, Michael. *Writing Business Plans That Get Results*. McGraw-Hill Trade. 1991.

Pastore, Robert. *Stock Options: An Authoritative Guide to Incentive and Nonqualified Stock Options*. PCM Capital Publishing. 2000.

Pink, Daniel H. *Free Agent Nation: How America's New Independent Workers Are Transforming the Way We Live*. Warner Business Books. 2001.

Pratt, Stanley E. *Pratt's Guide to Venture Capital Sources*, 26th ed. Venture Economics. 2002.

Pressman, David. *Patent It Yourself*. 9th ed. Nolo Press. 2002.

Rich, Stanley R., and David E. Gumpert. *Business Plans that Win $$$: Lessons from the MIT Enterprise Forum*. Harper & Row. 1987.

Roberts, Edward B. *Entrepreneurs in High Technology: Lessons from MIT and Beyond*. Oxford University Press. 1991.

Robinson, Robert J., and Mark Van Osnabrugge. *Angel Investing: Matching Start-Up Funds with Start-Up Companies—A Guide for Entrepreneurs, Individual Investors, and Venture Capitalists*. Jossey-Bass. 2000.

Sheth, Jagdish, and Rajendra Sisodia. *The Rule of Three: Surviving and Thriving in Competitive Markets*. Macmillan, The Free Press. 2002.

Sindell, Kathleen. *Loyalty Marketing for the Internet Age: How to Identify, Attract, Serve, and Retain Customers in an E-Commerce Environment*. Dearborn Trade. 2000.

Smilor, Ray. *Daring Visionaries: How Entrepreneurs Build Companies, Inspire Allegiance, and Create Wealth*. Adams Media Corporation. 2001.

Stalk, George Jr., and Thomas M. Hout. *Competing Against Time: How Time-Based Competition Is Reshaping Global Markets*. Macmillan, The Free Press. 1990.

Tarrant, John. *Perks and Parachutes: Negotiating Your Best Possible Employment Deal, from Salary and Bonus to Benefits and Protection*. Times Books. 1997.

Yoffie, David B., and Mary Kwak. *Judo Strategy: Turning Your Competitors' Strength to Your Advantage*. Harvard Business School Press. 2001.

Index

as risk taker, 55, 105, 121
as source of capital, 192
as source of product ideas, 117
benefits to, 39
buying cycle, 123
career limiting move, 105
-driven, 40
early adopter, 105
empathy for, 105
fear that vendor will go out of business, 105
focus on, 21, 105
Fortune 500, 55
identify specific, 123
importance of, 43
knowing, 104
listening to, 106
questions for, 104
safety in "buying from IBM," 105
service, 103, 119
target, 103
technologist's curse, 105
technology versus benefits, 117
validation, 57
value proposition, 105

D

Dauchy, Craig, 378, 398
Davidow, William H., 31, 52, 116
Davidson, Gordy, 334
Deal killer, 19
    weak management team, 81
Death spiral convertible, 410
Defensible market segment, 52
Deferred compensation, 269
Dell Computer Corporation, 21, 112
Dell, Michael, 21
Deloitte and Touche, 417
Deloitte Consulting, 418
Deloitte Touche Tohmatsu, 417
Demand registration rights, term sheet, 242
Digital Vision, Inc., 399
Dilution, 219–220, 247, 289
    caused by stock option pool, an example, 252
    number one business issue, 247
Directors, board of (see Board of directors)
Disability insurance, 357
Discounted
    cash flow, 165
    present value, 45
Discount rate, 165
Discrimination, Civil Rights Act of 1964, 95
Disk drive market, 44
Dispute resolution provision, 210
Disruptive technology, 123
Distribution channel, 103, 125
Diversification, to reduce risks, 57
Dividend, cash dividend is rare, 284

Divorce, 31
Doerr, John, 97
Dot-com
    bubble, 189, 197, 270, 286, 311, 312, 329
    bubble, tougher investment terms after, 260–261
    craze, 186, 200, 216
    euphoria, 3, 4
Double
    -dip, 411
    -dipping liquidation preference, 227
    taxation, 386
    -trigger vesting, 242
Down
    period, financing, 4
    round, 300, 411
    round, term sheet, 232
Drag-along rights, term sheet, 241
Dralla, John, 400
Draper Fisher Jurvetson, 25
Dress for success, 203
Drucker, Peter F., 39
Due diligence, 77, 83, 107, 151, 177, 198, 217, 218, 219
    backup file, 170
Duty
    of care, board of directors, 93
    of loyalty, 390, 391, 398
    of loyalty, board of directors, 93

E

Early
    adopter, 105
    -development financing, 59–62
    -stage financing, 59–62
Earnings per share, 160
Eastman Kodak Company, 53, 376
EBay, Inc., case study, 80
EBITDA, 186
EDGAR, 155
Efficiency ratio, 69
Effland, Janet G., 91
EIR (see Entrepreneurs in residence program)
Elder, Bill, 173
Elements of success (see Success, elements of)
Elevator pitch, 411
Emotional distress compensation, 362
Employee
    identification number (EIN), 387
    importance of signed agreement, 95
    obligations of different types, 391, 398
    stock ownership plan (ESOP), 326
    stock purchase plan (ESPP), 325–326
    tips on finding right, 275
Employee benefits, 351, 269–271
    outsourcing, 353–354

balance sheet, 155, 156, 157, 158
cash flow statement, 155, 156, 161, 162
historical, 156
income statement, 155, 158, 159, 160
pro forma, 157, 185–186
Financing, 77–78, 143, 187
acquisition, 59–62
addiction, 64
angel, 62
bootstrapping, 409
bridge, 61, 219
burnout, 410
buyout, 59–62
cheap start-ups, 188
corporate investor, 199–200
cramdown, 410
customers and suppliers, 192
down period, 4
down round, 411
early-development, 59–62
early-stage, 59–62
exit strategy, 64
expansion, 59–62, 190
family and friends, 62
first-stage, 59–62, 190
hibernation mode, 411
inside round, 411
IPO, 59–62
later-stage, 59–62
mezzanine, 61
milestone, 191
milestone, term sheet, 221–223
prospects, 25
punitive, 225
rounds, 60, 62
SCOR, 195–196
second-stage, 61
seed, 59–62
seed, how much needed, 188–190
sources, 191
stages, 59–62
terminology, 59
turnaround, 413
venture capitalist, 196–199
venture capitalist versus corporate, 213
washout, 300, 413
First
Chicago method, 337–338
-stage financing, 59–62, 190
First Chicago Corporation, 337
Fitness, 397
Fixed costs, 163, 164
Flipping, stock option, 304, 310
Food and Drug Administration, 211, 212
Forbes, 117
Ford, Henry, 56
Foreign (out-of-state) corporation, 387

Form S-1, 242
Form S-3, 242, 243
Form SB-2, 242
Fortis Corporation, 311
Forum for Women Entrepreneurs (FWE), 416
Foundation for Enterprise Development, 298, 422
Founder
career path, 19
employment contract, 361–362
fringe benefit issues, 351
nonengineer, 21
roles and responsibilities, 15
types, 21
value of several, 139
warning signs, 21
Founders' round, 62
Founders' stock, 284, 287, 289
value, 26
Founding team, 139
Four Ps plus an S, 109
Franchises, 116
Franklin, Burke, 175
Fringe benefits (*see* Employee benefits)
Frivolous title, 19
Fuji, 53
Full ratchet (*see* Ratchet)
Fully participating liquidation preference, 225, 255
Functional specification document, 126, 128, 132
Fundamental method of valuation, 338
Funding (*see* Financing)
Future value (FV), 165

G

GAAP (*see* Generally accepted accounting principles)
Garage Technology Ventures, xxiii, 420
Gates, Bill, 30, 286, 399
vacations, 28
Gathering of Angels, 421
Genentech, Inc., 296
General
corporation (*see* C corporation), 382
partner, 384
partnership, 382, 383, 384–385
partner, venture capitalist, 196
General Electric Company, 52
General Motors Corporation, 53
Generally accepted accounting principles (GAAP), 185–186
Genus, Inc., 144, 173
Gleba, David, 332
Global competition, 43, 54
Global Crossing, 186
GNU/Linux operating system, 377

SIMPLE 401(k) plan, 359
Sisodia, Rajendra, 54
Skilled employee, obligations to employer, 391, 398
Skin in the game, 402
Skorina, Charles A., 85
Skunk works, 132
Small
  business, definition, 10
  business, vacation statistics, 28–29
  corporate offering registration (SCOR), 195–196
Small Business Administration (SBA), 419
Small Business Development Centers (SBDC), 419
Small Business Innovation and Research (SBIR), 420
Smith, Richard A., 278
Software
  antivirus, 134
  copyright, 369
  patent, 371, 379
  reverse engineering, 370
Sole proprietorship, 382, 386–387
Solvency analysis, 67
Sonny Bono Copyright Term Extension Act of 1998, 370
Sources
  and application of funds statement, 161
  and uses of funds statement, 161
Specialist company, 54, 124
Speed, no substitute for strategy, 57
Spencer Stuart, 274
Spouse, 31, 270, 397, 406
Staged financing, 222
Stages, financing, 59–62
Stanford University, 80
  Business School, 20
Start-up
  allocation of effort, 33
  definition, 12
  failure, 397
  financing terminology, 59–62
  issues to consider, 9
  leaving your employer, 140
  legal form, 381–388
  not a young public company, 60
  opportunities, 5
  outcome statistics, 27
  reasons to start, 7
  scenario, 140
  success, key points, 406
"Start-up.com," a film, 424
Startupfailures.com, 424
Statement
  by Domestic Stock Corporation, 16
  of condition, 157

of financial position, 157
of profit and loss, 158
of requirements document, 126, 127, 132
Statistics
  bankruptcy, 26
  initial public offering, 26
  success and failure, 25
Statutory option, 275
Steady-state stage, 138, 139
Steffins, Sara, 101
Stock, 275, 281–302
  acquiring, 289
  and stock option grant, rule of thumb on number of shares, 306, 307
  and stock options, summary table, 283
  appreciation right (SAR), 324–325
  as part of total package, 308
  board of directors, compensation, 91–92
  cash dividend, 284
  change in ownership interest over time, 284, 285
  cheap, 284, 287, 289
  common and preferred, 286
  common versus preferred, pricing rule of thumb, 286, 287
  consideration for grant, 291
  dividend, 232
  founders', 289
  fully diluted calculation, 289
  in exchange for intellectual property, 322
  in exchange for real property, 322
  issued, 288
  number of shares to grant, 284
  preferred (see Term sheet, preferred stock)
  purchase plan, 321
  repurchase right, 290
  right of first refusal, 292
  risk-reward scale, 282
  Section 83(b) election, 293, 295
  shareholders agreement, 292
  shares, authorized, 288
  shares, outstanding, 288
  split, types, 231–232
  sweat equity, 281
  taking some of the gain, 321
  transfer, securities law, 292
  transferable, 294
  unrelated purchase, 320
  versus stock option, 284, 303
  vesting, 290, 294
  warrants, 323
  when to grant, 296
Stock option, 275, 303–318
  administrative details, 312
  alternative minimum tax (AMT) – ISO trap, 310, 315–316

About the Authors

James A. Swanson has more than 25 years of extensive business experience in Silicon Valley in California. Coauthors Baird and Swanson are founders of Los Altos Incubator, a virtual incubator (firstonline.com) where aspiring entrepreneurs seek expert advice. Swanson has been a founder or CEO of several start-up companies and also of a public company, Ramtek Corporation, where he was elected CEO to lead a difficult turnaround. He has also served as chief financial officer, general counsel, and vice president of sales, as needed. For two years, he served in the U.S. Peace Corps as an irrigation engineer in Morocco, and over the years he has been active in many community services. He and his wife have two sons and live in Silicon Valley. He holds an SB degree from the Massachusetts Institute of Technology (MIT) and MBA and JD degrees from Stanford University.

Michael L. Baird has 30 years of high-tech, hands-on executive engineering and marketing management experience. He was recently a vice president of engineering for Ask Jeeves' ask.com—one of the most successful IPOs in history and a top-five search site on the Internet today. Baird was the chief technology officer for Snap-on Incorporated, a $2 billion Fortune 500 company, and served as the vice president of marketing and engineering in several venture capital-funded start-ups. He has a PhD in information and computer science from Georgia Tech, an undergraduate degree in industrial engineering, and an MBA. More about Mike Baird can be found at mikebaird.com.